Surveying
Public Opinion

SONDRA MILLER
RUBENSTEIN

HOFSTRA UNIVERSITY

Wadsworth Publishing Company
I T P™ An International Thomson Publishing Company

Belmont • Albany • Bonn • Boston • Cincinnati • Detroit • London • Madrid • Melbourne
Mexico City • New York • Paris • San Francisco • Singapore • Tokyo • Toronto • Washington

This book is dedicated to all victims of hate, indifference, and manipulated public opinion, past and present, including those in my own family who were but a tiny part of the six million Jewish and the five million non-Jewish victims—including gays, Christians, Gypsies, political dissidents, people with disabilities, and others—murdered by the Nazis, their supporters, and the silence of public opinion.

Communications Editor: Todd R. Armstrong
Editorial Assistant: Joshua King
Production Editor: Karen Garrison
Designer: Andrew Ogus
Print Buyer: Barbara Britton
Permissions Editor: Robert Kauser

Copy Editor: Jennifer Gordon
Compositors: Brandon Carson,
　　　　　　　　Margarite Reynolds
Cover: Ross Carron Design
Signing Representative: Gerry Levine
Printer: Malloy Lithographing, Inc.

For more information, contact:
Wadsworth Publishing Company
10 Davis Drive
Belmont, California 94002

International Thomson Publishing
Berkshire House 168-173
High Holborn
London, WC1V 7AA
England

Thomas Nelson Australia
102 Dodds Street
South Melbourne 3205
Victoria, Australia

Nelson Canada
1120 Birchmount Road
Scarborough, Ontario
Canada M1K 5G4

International Thomson Publishing GmbH
Königwinterer Strasse 418
53227 Bonn
Germany

International Thomson Publishing Asia
221 Henderson Road #05-10
Singapore 0315

International Thomson Publishing – Japan
Hirakawacho Kyowa Building, 3F
2-2-1 Hirakawacho-cho
Chiyoda-ku, 102 Tokyo, Japan

1 2 3 4 5 6 7 8 9 10—99 98 97 96 95

Library of Congress Cataloging-in-Publication Data
Rubenstein, Sondra Miller.
　　Surveying public opinion / Sondra Miller Rubenstein.
　　　　p.　cm.
　　Includes bibliographical references and index.
　　ISBN 0-534-17856-1
　　1. Public opinion polls. 2. Social surveys. I. Title.
HM261.R73 1994
303.3'8—dc20　　　　　　　　　　94–16428

Preface

ON FEAR, HATE, HISTORY, HOPE, AND PUBLIC OPINION

Fear and hope were the primary motivating forces behind this book. A teacher for many years, I have come to realize that far too many students are passive recipients of information. They prefer to get just what they need or want to know—and their opinions—the easy way, from audiovisual media, rather than from diverse print sources or discussion and analysis. What frightens me is the vulnerability to exploitation that this creates.

I see a cancerous spread of hate over campuses across the country, along with the increasing fragmentation and disunity of our entire society. I worry about the increased number of historical revisionists, the growth of intolerance, and the unabashed ignorance on which hate-filled opinions are based and unashamedly repeated.

Others also have been observing that college students (the ones who do not care about reading history's documented truths and the pursuit of knowledge on their own) are ready recipients for "feel-good" and "feel-superior" messages. The merchants of hate do not care about thinking citizens with informed opinions; they want to *use* students—and all the public—to suit their own political agenda. As a case in point, consider the words of Bradley R. Smith, of the Committee for Open Debate on the Holocaust, speaking in Long Beach, California, in August 1991: "I want to go to students. They are superficial. They are empty vessels to be filled."

Although Smith is peddling lies, he feels he can sell his wares because students are uninformed. Still, as John Milton wrote so long ago, when truth and falsehood grapple, "Who ever knew truth put to the worse, in a free and open encounter?" And that is the responsibility of education—to enable the truth to be heard. Thus my hope in writing this book is that at least those who read it will not be "empty vessels" susceptible to the likes of such masters of deceit as Mr. Smith.

ACKNOWLEDGMENTS

One day Gerry Levine, the Wadsworth regional representative, stopped by my office at Hofstra to discuss the company's latest books that could be of use in the courses I teach. Gerry, a smart and friendly fellow, also took the time to ask if I had any ideas for a new text. In fact, I had just started thinking about the difficulty I had had in finding a text for the new undergraduate course I had developed on surveying public opinion. I sketched my ideas for him and he told me to put together a proposal and to send it along to Wadsworth. It was that simple.

But then began the hard part, and here is where an invaluable support system of members of the "attentive public," consisting of family, friends, professional colleagues, and Wadsworth staff, helped to make it happen. Within Wadsworth, beginning with Gerry through Joshua King, Todd Armstrong, Karen Garrison, and the talented copy editor Jennifer Gordon, I found the smartest, "coolest" professionals who seemed to have unlimited patience and wisdom to dispense. I sincerely thank them and all the others at Wadsworth whose efforts brought this book to fruition.

Through Wadsworth, I benefited from the wise comments of several reviewers, including Roy Atwood, University of Idaho; James Berstein, Indiana University; Sharon Dunwoody, University of Wisconsin, Madison; Donald Granberg, University of Missouri; William Griswold; Patrick A. Pierce, Saint Mary's College; James L. Rogers, University of North Texas; Chris Salmon, Michigan State University; David Sodofsky, California State University, Hayward; Mary Trapp, California State University, Hayward; Charles Whitney, University of California, Santa Barbara; and John W. Windhauser, Louisiana State University. I thank them and assure them that they were all very helpful in the development of this text. Their comments forced me to sort out some of my conflicting opinions and feelings about a myriad of issues.

Naomi Hirsch, my friend of many years, was invaluable to me not only because of her friendship, but also because of her skill as a proofreader and sounding board. Her patience and willingness to read and reread material seemed endless. I appreciate her efforts.

As for family, I have a strange immediate family. We all read the newspapers, listen to political discussion programs, and are always exchanging ideas about the best advice to give political figures on everything from Bosnia to the role of the president's wife. My husband Murray, son Eric, and daughters Leeanne and Paula all write and have always been ready to critique whatever I have shown them. I thank them for their love, support, and professional contributions to this text.

Contents

I   WHAT'S IT ALL ABOUT?

1   INTRODUCING THE STUDY OF OPINION RESEARCH   3

About This Book   4

Is There a Distinction Between Surveys and Polls?   7

What Is Public Opinion?   8

One Opinion of Public Opinion   11

The Media, Polling, and Public Opinion   14

Some Narrow Areas of Agreement   16

Before There Was Public Opinion   17

Emerging Public Opinion   19

Characteristics of Public Opinion   23

Researching Public Opinion	32
Chapter Review	45

2   THE HISTORY OF SURVEYS   **49**

New Land, New Thinking	51
The Earliest Polls	52
The First Straws	53
Growing Interest in Survey Research	55
The Worst Straws	63
Wartime Research	69
Introducing President Dewey	72
Chapter Review	79

3   POLLING GETS MORE PROFESSIONAL AND WORLDLY   **85**

Polling Abroad	86
The First International Conference of Gallup Institutes	92
The First *Time*/Roper International Poll	94
Opinion Researchers Look Eastward	100
Learning from the Polling Flop in Nicaragua	103
Chapter Review	105

4   THE DIVERSE FIELD OF OPINION RESEARCH   **109**

Opinion Research Goes to Market	111
The Woes of Nielsen	112
The Arbitron Way	119

The Hite Reports   126

Chapter Review   136

5   SURVEYS AND MORE SURVEYS   139

Let's Go to Court   140

Surveying the Elite and Other Special Groups   149

The NORC Studies   151

The Census, Mother of Many Surveys   154

Chapter Review   158

II   CONDUCTING YOUR SURVEY

6   FINDING THE *n*TH PERSON   163

Understanding the Theory   165

Determining Whether to Run for Office   168

Finding the *n*th House (or Person)   173

Why LP's Pollster Rejected Non-Probability Sampling   177

Evaluating the Sample Process   179

Sources of Sampling Data   183

Chapter Review   185

7   WORDING THE QUESTIONNAIRE   189

The Importance of Knowing How to Ask   190

Question Reliability, Validity, Structuring, and Scaling   192

Measuring Attitudes   200

Bad Questions   213

Filter Questions and Skip Instructions   218

The Words and the Order   220

The Self-Administered Questionnaire   223

Chapter Review   225

8 THE INTERVIEWER   231

Responding to the Challenge   233

The Interviewer's Role and Problems   234

Understanding Interviewer Effects   240

Interviewer-Related Bias   249

Monitoring, Verifying, and Validating   258

Chapter Review   261

9 THE RESPONDENT   265

Knowledge Structures   267

The Don't-Know Phenomenon   271

Do Respondents Ever Lie?   276

Saying No: Respondent Refusal   279

The Older Respondent   282

Gender and Sensitive Questions   285

Chapter Review   287

10 GETTING AND USING THE RESULTS   293

The Data Reduction Process   295

The Significant Role of Statistics   296

To Report or Not to Report   308

The Media and Opinion Polls   320

Chapter Review   326

III THE UBIQUITOUS POLLSTERS

11 MARKETING PRODUCTS AND PRESIDENTS   333

The History of Focus Group Interviews   335

Marketing Political Candidates   342

Clustering and Segmentation Theory   349

Relying on Typical Town, U.S.A.   357

Questionable Marketing Studies   359

Chapter Review   360

12 POLLS, NEWS MAKING, POLICY MAKING, AND DEMOCRACY   365

Polls as News   366

Using the Polls to Set a Winning Political Agenda   378

The Leadership Debate   382

Pluralism Versus Hyperpluralism   385

Final Words   388

Chapter Review   388

13 NEW TECHNOLOGIES, NEW CONCERNS   393

The Next Generation   394

Regulating Survey Abuse   406

Improving Opinion of Opinion Polls   417

The Ubiquitous Researchers and Closing Words   421

Chapter Review   423

APPENDIX I   **A1**
Introducing Basic Descriptive Statistics

APPENDIX II   **A5**
Survey Research as a Profession

APPENDIX III   **A13**
NORC's Permanent Community Sample

GLOSSARY   **A15**

INDEX   **A23**

LIST OF BOXES

1.1 Definitions   12

1.2 Words from Lord Bryce, an Admirer   23

1.3 Gender Gap?   25

1.4 The 20-Percent Solution   30

1.5 Recent Political Scandals and Crises   35

1.6 The People's Choice   37

2.1 On Surveys and Statistics   57

2.2 Percentage Points   59

2.3 The Clustering System   61

2.4 Gallup Did It   66

2.5 The Beginning of Wartime Radio Research   69

2.6 Something Is Rotten ...   75

3.1 The Dodd Radio Poll 88

3.2 An Unofficial Wartime Poll in Italy 89

3.3 The Saipan Study 90

3.4 Rank of Marketing Research Companies 102

4.1 Nielsen's People Meter 113

4.2 The Median Versus the Mean 121

4.3 Arbitron's Strata 122

4.4 On the Diaries 123

5.1 Jury Selection Matters in Controversial Trials 146

6.1 Segments of Tables of Random Numbers 174

7.1 The Spiral of Silence 210

7.2 The Measurement Process Reviewed 212

8.1 A Typology of Probes 238

9.1 Cognitive Structures by Other Names 272

10.1 Questions Reporters Should Ask 312

12.1 How Jacob Javits Used a Poll the First Time
He Ran for Office 368

12.2 Self-Fulfilling Prophecy 372

12.3 Our Latter-Day Oracles? 380

13.1 Automated Dialing 400

THE PROFESSIONAL VOICES

1. Computer Content Analysis by David P. Fan 32

2. *The Hite Reports on Women and Love* by Shere Hite 126

3. Comments on Hite's *Women and Love* by Eleanor Singer 132

4. Taking Leave of Our Census by Murray Rubenstein 155

5.   Slam! by Lawrence J. Cohen   244

6.   Public Opinion on Fictitious Issues: The Fear
     of Appearing Ignorant by George Franklin Bishop   269

7.   The Survey Researcher as Translator
     by Alicia S. Schoua-Glusberg   316

8.   Focus Interviews with People Who Are
     Deaf and Hard-of-Hearing by Nancy Kaplan   336

9.   An Interview with Lewis M. Gediman
     by Laurie Riederman   341

10. Segmentation Research and Theories
     of Media Audiences by Cecilie Gaziano   352

11. Do Polls Really Measure Public Opinion?
     by Susan Herbst   372

12. The Non-Responder Conspiracy by David P. Farbman   415

13. 1992: Were There Too Many Polls? by Paula Stern   420

GLOBAL VIEWS

1.   AGB Versus A. C. Nielsen   124

2.   Carrying Out a Water Consumption Survey
     in Ghana by Manuel Olin   251

3.   Don't-Know Responses in Soviet Survey
     Research by James L. Gibson   273

4.   Extrapolating Relationships Between Fear,
     Hatred, and National Identity from an Attitude
     Survey by Ofra Mayseless and Reuven Gal   300

5.   Psychographics in Russia: Seeking the "Cossacks,"
     the "Kuptsi," and Other Consumer Clusters   349

PART I

What's It All About?

1

Introducing the Study of Opinion Research

Think about—

What is meant by the word *theory*?

Can we make a distinction between public opinion polling and survey research?

What do *you* mean when you talk about public opinion?

When, how, and why did public opinion emerge as a force to be considered?

What are the characteristics or qualities of public opinion?

What is meant by the attentive public, and why are some of us attentive while others are not?

What role do you think public opinion should play in the decisions of our government?

ABOUT THIS BOOK

This book is meant to demystify public opinion polls and, to whatever extent possible, to demystify the concept of public opinion. It is intended to be an introductory text. My aim is to provide an overview of the subject by presenting different aspects of a complex field that seeks to describe, explain, predict, and represent the views of the public on important issues.

In many respects, the book's organization and its writing style are my reaction to personal experiences both as a student and as a professor. As a student, I always wondered why so many social science textbooks needed professional deciphering. I particularly resented the use of pompous language in discussions on *theories* or *paradigms*, words that seemed to guarantee droopy eyelids among my contemporaries. In defense against the perceived verbal onslaught, I developed the habit of reading with a pencil and jotting down my own interpretive notes and comments in the margins of my books. I soon realized that I could often write one or two sentences conveying the sense of a long (and often boring) paragraph.

By the time I was a graduate student, I had a growing suspicion (a developing theory) that there may have been a hidden agenda that explained the unnecessary complexity of certain textbooks. In cynical moments, I even believed that professors who used such books did so to justify their own existence, their *raison d'être*. Now, as a professor of both communication theory and political science, I think I have a better understanding of why academic writing is sometimes so thick. Academics, I now believe, are more concerned with precision than with ease of reading, especially when they are writing for other academics or experts in their field. However, given that my audience may well consist mostly of novices, I will try to convey the information as clearly as possible.

I believe that theories and paradigms are nothing to fear. They are useful ways of arranging one's thoughts, explaining something, creating a framework for analysis, providing a vocabulary to enable a discussion of ideas, and forming a basis on which some sort of prediction could be made. When we say, "I think such and such because..." we are often expressing a sort of theory to explain our interpretation of something and to justify why we think such and such has happened and is likely to happen again. It is important to understand that, particularly in the social sciences, there is no one theory that is perfect—that can explain anything completely and to everyone's agreement and that is capable of 100 percent accuracy in predicting a future phenomenon. In his dialogue with Bill Moyers on the PBS series "The Power of Myth," Joseph Campbell commented that "no matter what system of thought you have, it can't possibly include boundless life, and when you think everything is just that way... it all blows [away]...."

This book presents different theories about the hows and whys of public opinion formation, polling, the role of the media, and the effects of survey research. It is likely that many professionals and respected scholars will argue the greater validity of one theory over another, and there may even be general agreement as to which theory is best. I have attempted to identify those theories and methods that are generally acceptable, while occasionally including a controversial and interesting alternative approach. In the belief that you are intelligent enough to recognize a theory when presented in the text as part of a scholar's perception, conclusions, or analysis, I have not always flagged the passage by stating, "This is a theory." And although this field of study does require knowledge of a special vocabulary (a professional jargon), I have tried to explain these words without setting off a yawn that launches one into a deep sleep.

At the start of each chapter, you will find Think About questions. I do not expect you to be able to identify the various items or to answer the questions. Rather, I use Think Abouts to clearly state the chapter's learning objectives at the beginning so that you will focus on them and learn. These survey lists are meant to flag those items (mostly concrete and of practical significance) in the chapter that I believe are important. Each Think About is a sort of subliminal plant, meant to start you thinking about those particular items. The review at the end of the chapter enables you to test yourself, to see how well you have understood and can explain what you have learned.

The message of this book is, Yes, you can! While survey research is a complicated process, no one need be frightened or intimidated by it. At various points throughout the text I ask "What do you think?" just as though you were sitting in my class and I wanted to encourage you to share your thoughts on the subject. I do this because I believe in the intelligence of my students and because I respect their opinions. My goal, as explained earlier, is to demystify this subject and to acquaint you with the nuts and bolts of the field. The latter aim explains why most of the material in the Think About lists deals with fact-based items. This is, I hope, a user-friendly book, meant to instill personal confidence—confidence in the validity of your own opinions.

This is not a statistics textbook, nor is it meant to be a self-contained definitive study of the subject. I simply want to make you aware of the essential role played by statistics in poll taking and to realize early on that without statistics—or a hired statistician—you won't get very far as a survey researcher. Remember, however, that although statistical data can provide evidence to support or reject a particular hypothesis, it cannot be said to prove anything, and it can be manipulated. Also, no matter how scientific or systematic the research method may be, there is always room for human error or for intentional decisions about what is or isn't reported. You will learn about the pitfalls, criticisms, and ethical questions raised by the use and abuse of polling data, and I hope you will find it interesting enough to consider pursuing advanced studies in the field. I believe this book can play a positive role in contributing to your understanding of the ways opinion surveys are used in various fields, including business, politics, journalism, and law. Clearly, you don't have to be able to design and implement an opinion survey to become a **critical reader*** of the work of pollsters, one who can evaluate and criticize their findings when you read them.

After discussing whether or not there is a distinction between public opinion polling and survey research, I try to define public opinion—not an easy task. This is followed by an overview of the attitudes toward and theories about public opinion, its evolution, qualities, and characteristics. In Chapters 2 and 3 we examine some early polling efforts here and abroad so that we may learn from the mistakes of others. The goal of the first three

---

*When an important term is introduced, it will appear in boldface type with an explanation of its meaning. These terms are also listed in the Glossary at the end of the book.

chapters is to give you the definitional and historical basis for understanding the concepts of public opinion and the process of polling.

Chapter 4 examines some case studies from the diverse field of opinion research. Chapter 5 discusses various uses for opinion research, including promoting surveys as legal evidence and applying teen attitude and behavioral studies for marketing and policy-making purposes.

Part II focuses on theoretical and practical issues relating to methodology and includes chapters on sampling, questionnaire design, interviewer- and respondent-related concerns, and analysis and interpretation of survey results. It is meant as an introduction to a complex (but not daunting) process and not as a definitive course of instruction. That is why I want to emphasize that Part II is not intended to make a little Gallup out of you. However, I definitely aim to enhance your ability to question and evaluate polling reports disseminated by the media.

In Part III, we move to effects studies, and we focus on the use of opinion research for marketing products and for government and political decision making. We will also examine certain related legal and ethical issues. In the final chapter, our attention turns to new technologies and to their theoretical and practical challenges to our privacy.

IS THERE A DISTINCTION BETWEEN
SURVEYS AND POLLS?

There are many different types of surveys that cover a broad range of topics including people's attitudes, opinions, personal habits and characteristics, behavior, knowledge, and choices. Public opinion polling is a type of survey research. While not all survey research is public opinion research, much of it is related. Personal interpretations, opinions, and decisions (made consciously or subconsciously) determine much—from our attitudes to how we behave, what we choose to wear, eat, learn, and remember, which television programs we watch (see Chapter 4), or which political candidates we decide to support.

While I personally see a public opinion poll as a type of survey and think it is splitting hairs to attempt to make a distinction between a poll and a survey, Catherine Marsh chooses to do so based on the *functions* each is expected to perform and not on any technical or methodological grounds.[1] She states: "A survey is performed to better understand something. The claim for an opinion poll is that it can be part of a process of democracy." I disagree, believing that a poll can also be taken to "better understand something," and a survey can also be part of a process of democracy. Nevertheless, in Table 1.1 I present Marsh's analysis, with some of the distinguishing characteristics of surveys and polls. Although I think the distinctions she has made are debatable, they are interesting, and I believe you should have the opportunity to decide for yourself whether or not the distinctions made are relevant.

What do you think about these distinctions? For instance, it is often assumed that if survey results are ignored, nothing much happens, but if polling results are ignored, some politician will pay the price at the polling booth. I do not necessarily agree with that view; I think that a well-publicized survey can also move people to action. What do you think? Whatever the survey or poll's subject, its function is to collect relevant information for some ultimate goal. This is done by asking carefully crafted questions of individuals deemed representative of the larger population. This effort to gather the desired information is based on proven methods of sample selection. These methods are governed by mathematical laws of probability to assure that everyone in the population to be studied (the **universe**) has an equal likelihood of being included as part of a **representative sample**. Using such methods to select a sample assures replication of the results—no matter how many times the same study is conducted with different representative samples. It also enables us to generalize our findings and conclusions to the general population represented by the sample we selected.

WHAT IS PUBLIC OPINION?

What do you and your friends think about the labeling of controversial rock recordings? What do your parents and their friends think about the same subject? How do people in the recording industry, record shop owners, members of the clergy, people over the age of 50, or between the ages of 30 and 40 view this issue? Do all these groups make up the public or have I mentioned several publics? Is there such a thing as public opinion or should we be speaking of the opinion of the publics that make up a given society—our society, for example?

Many sociopolitical thinkers have attempted to define public opinion. Some have delved deeply (or shall I say stretched), differentiating between the opinions we keep to ourselves (our individual beliefs) and those we share. Is there a difference? As we will see, respondents do not always reveal their true feelings and opinions to interviewers. And some theorists have argued that no opinion can be considered public until it is brought to the attention of those who exercise power to change things, meaning the government. Still others have said opinion becomes public *only when it is measured*. Is that like saying the falling tree makes no sound in the forest if we

Table 1.1 Marsh's Distinctions Between Surveys and Polls

	SURVEYS	POLLS
The Respondents	Treated as informants. Their information is considered important enough to warrant the survey costs.	Treated as citizens. They are *empowered* (meaning they can vote and each vote counts) and supposedly can change things.
	Reason for the interview: Selected on the basis of their knowledge and experience in a particular area, they are considered the most effective source for the data required.	*Reason for the interview:* Interviewers are told to stress the importance of everyone's views being recorded in order to provide a fair picture of what the people think.
The Responses	Treated as data.	Treated as likely votes.
	Theoretical task: To determine whether or not there are attitude clusters and belief structures that might then be used to suggest policy changes. For example, consider whether the responses to a survey on performance lag in colleges could be seen as reinforcing the belief that our universities can be no stronger than our schools and that "public education, despite … years of reform, is still producing inadequately prepared students."[1]	*Theoretical task:* Because the aim is to generalize about what the majority thinks, crossing the 50-percent line is important. There is an expectation (unrealistic?) that the government will take notice and act to fulfill the people's decree.
Inconsistency Between Attitude and Subsequent Behavior	The survey researcher accepts that verbal methods "may be used to get at what people think, or at least what they think they think, but not at what they actually express in social situations."[2] In other words, the inconsistency is taken into account and is considered interesting in its own right.	Inconsistency is glossed over. The presumption is that what the citizen-respondent says and does is in harmony. For example, pollsters generally assume that the respondent will vote on election day according to the opinion expressed in the interview. However, people can change their minds between the time the poll was taken and election day.

Continued

Table 1.1 Marsh's Distinctions Between Surveys and Polls, continued

	SURVEYS	POLLS
Policy Consequences	Not determined by the nature of the inquiry. For example, surveys taken by the Labor Department, the Census Bureau, and other agencies indicated that "less than half the wage gap between men and women could be explained by differences in education or work experience." The most important conclusion is the one drawn by the Older Women's League: Work-force segregation has confined most working women to lower-paying "women's professions."[3] We would hope that the consequences of the survey will include a congressional hearing leading to more stringent enforcement of age and sex discrimination claims by the Equal Employment Opportunity Commission.[4]	The assumption (valid or not) is that government is listening to the people and will respond to their will. For example, a July 1990 poll indicated that only 23 percent of New Jerseyans thought Governor James Florio was doing a good job. The rest (except for the 9 percent Don't Knows), were angered by his proposed $2.8 billion tax increase.[5] In 1993, The Republican candidate, Christine Todd Whitman, defeated Florio. The hated tax increase was her major issue, and Florio was forced to pay the price for disregarding the people's will.
The Audience	The survey audience is usually a community of either social scientists or policymakers. These are people with specific needs and interests in learning the views of the targeted respondents.	The public is typically as interested in hearing the results as are the politicians who are the subject of the poll.

1. Lee A. Daniels, "Performance Lag Found in Colleges," *The New York Times,* Nov. 6, 1989, p. A18.

2. J. Galtung, *Theory and Methods of Social Research* (London: Allen & Unwin, 1979), p. 112.

3. These include secretaries, sales clerks, waitresses, nurses, teachers, and librarians. See Tamar Lewin, "Older Women Face Bias in Workplace," *The New York Times,* May 11, 1991.

4. Lewin.

5. "As Voters Rebel, Florio Reassigns His Top Adviser," *The New York Times,* Aug. 23, 1990, pp. B1, B6.

are not there to hear it? As you can see, there are many individual opinions, and it's not easy to reach agreement on a universally acceptable definition of public opinion—that is, unless you start with the premise that individuals make up an ignorant, amorphous mass waiting to be shaped and told what to think. In that case, you'll have lots of company (see Box 1.1).

ONE OPINION OF PUBLIC OPINION

I long ago accepted the notion that there is no perfect theory, especially when dealing with the social sciences. I try to keep an open mind by weighing the **opinions** (defined here as thoughts, beliefs, attitudes, and ideas) of others, trying to understand conflicting interpretations, and eventually attempting to reach some conclusion or definition that seems right for me. I also try to remember that no one opinion (my own included) will ever gain universal acceptance.

I have always had a problem defining the term *public opinion* because the word *public* adds a degree of ambiguity that is confusing. In the early stages of preparing this text, I even hesitated to give my own opinion of public opinion—what it was and how it was formed. I preferred you to think for yourself and to decide on your own definition. However, some of my colleagues felt that if I did not give my own definition, you might not be sure of what I meant (even if all I meant was for you to decide for yourself). So the following is my personal multipart definition.

1. *Public opinion   The representatively sampled, measured, analyzed, and published results of a scientific survey.* Without getting into which public or the quality of the opinion expressed (how well informed are the individuals?), my simple definition is that public opinion is the opinion of the public. I reserve the term for the *sum of individual opinions*—regardless of how well informed, logical, or attentive the individuals may be—that can be generalized to the larger population with some degree of confidence. If you were to use this term, I would want to know how you gathered your data, how large your sample was, how the individual participants (respondents) were selected, the specific questions you asked, and much more.

   However, to encourage you to give thought to other definitions, I have included in various chapters material from researchers who suggest a broader definition, for example Susan Herbst and Theodore Lowi, discussed in Chapter 12. I have also devoted space to certain non-polling activities, such as focus groups, that are used to determine what people think about particular issues.

BOX 1.1   Definitions

Choose your description or definition—if thinking negatively appeals to you:

First century A.D.   Roman historian Titus Livy: "The opinions of the masses are always fickle."[1]

1820   British statesman Sir Robert Peel: "…that great compound of folly, weakness, prejudice, wrong feeling, right feeling, obstinacy, and newspaper paragraphs…is called public opinion."[2]

1923   American author Mark Twain: "In our late canvass half of the nation passionately believed that in silver lay salvation, the other half as passionately believed that that way lay destruction. Do you believe that a tenth part of the people, on either side, had any rational excuse for having an opinion about the matter at all?…Half of our people passionately believe in high tariff, the other half believe otherwise. Does this mean study and examination, or only feeling?…We all do no end of feeling and we mistake it for

thinking. And out of it we get an aggregation which we consider a boon. Its name is Public Opinion. It is held in reverence. It settles everything. Some think it the Voice of God."[3]

1924   Future German dictator Adolf Hitler: "What we mean by 'public opinion' depends only to the smallest extent on the individual's own experiences or knowledge, and largely on an image, frequently created by a penetrating and persistent sort of so-called 'enlightenment.'"[4]

1925   American journalist Walter Lippmann: "We must assume that a public is intermittent, that it discerns only gross distinctions, is slow to be aroused and quickly diverted; that, since it acts by aligning itself, it personalizes whatever it considers, and is interested only when events have been melodramatized as a conflict…. Thus, we strip public opinion of any implied duty to deal with the substance of a problem, to make technical decisions, to attempt justice or

---

2. *The public's opinion   The opinions of a particular group, one public out of many.* For example, a reporter stops several individuals on a busy street in the financial district of a major city to ask whether they think the president is doing a good job on the economic issues confronting the country. Since I do not see this as a scientific sample, I would conclude that perhaps the opinions expressed on that particular street, at that particular time of day, are representative of the thinking of that particular public. The same is true of those telephone polls that use a 900 area code and the mail–in magazine or newspaper polls. Because of the built–in bias of the self-selection process of these polls, I would hesitate to generalize the opinions

impose a moral precept.... Public opinion in this theory, is a reserve of force brought into action during a crisis in public affairs."[5]

1933 Historian Wilhelm Bauer spoke of opinion voiced in public as either "static," being tradition/custom-based, or "dynamic," "being predominantly rational in character, [it] is built upon the cultivated arts of persuasion and systematic publicity and draw[ing] upon definite historical events or contemporary happenings as the material for its propaganda and agitation."[6]

1969 And then there was Vice President Spiro Agnew, who (using Bill Safire's lines[7]) spoke of the "nattering nabobs of negativism" of the press, blaming them for their "querulous criticism" and for abusing their "vast power." These remarks seemed to cast doubt on the public's intelligence, implying that the people were incapable of differentiating between what Agnew viewed as mediated reality and his own version of reality.

You no doubt realize that in more recent times others have made similar implied criticisms and derogatory remarks about the public's ability to understand the issues of the day, but why belabor the point?

1. Livy, *History of Rome.*
2. As cited in Bernard Hennessy, *Public Opinion,* 4th ed. (Monterey, CA: Brooks/Cole, 1981), p. 3.
3. Charles Neider, ed., *The Complete Essays of Mark Twain* (Garden City, NY: Doubleday, 1963), p. 587.
4. Adolf Hitler, *Mein Kampf* (My Struggle), translated, annotated, and republished in the U.S. (New York: Reynal & Hitchcock; Boston: Houghton Mifflin, 1941), p. 108.
5. Walter Lippmann, *The Phantom Public* (New York: Harcourt, Brace, 1925), pp. 65, 67, 69.
6. Wilhelm Bauer, "Public Opinion," in *Encyclopedia of the Social Sciences* (New York: Macmillan, 1933), pp. 669–674.
7. William Safire, "Bush's Gamble," *The New York Times Sunday Magazine,* Oct. 19, 1992, p. 31.

reported from any street, telephone call-in, or magazine or newspaper mail-in poll. I simply do not believe that these opinions are representative of the larger population.

3. *The publics' opinion   The thinking of different publics or subgroups, as determined by sex, age, occupation, income, race, religion, and so forth, included in the sample being polled.* Depending on the size of the subgroup sampled, it may be possible to generalize from it to the population from which it was drawn (for example, all college-educated white females between the ages of 35 and 45; those individuals earning between $30,000 and $40,000 a year). Here, I would ask you questions about the subgroups used in your sample.

4. *Individual, personal opinion   Private (un-measured) opinion, which should not be generalized.* When a television reporter stops three people on a street to ask them what they think about Hillary Rodham Clinton's role in making health care policy, the responses should be seen as merely the personal opinions of those three people rather than as survey data.

Something interesting to consider is that the Don't-Know category may well act as a catchall, making indistinguishable the opinions of

- those who genuinely do not know anything about the issue and are willing to admit it
- those who truly have not formed an opinion
- those who do not want to state their opinion

The result is that the Don't-Know category can be seen as representing the unmeasurable individual, personal opinions of those respondents.

This multipart definition of public opinion will not please everyone, but perhaps it will encourage a debate, as well as prompt you to form your own opinion.

THE MEDIA, POLLING, AND PUBLIC OPINION

Critics of the media, such as Robert M. Entman, have long asked about "how the media affect what people think—and think they think."[2] Entman himself argues that the interdependency of the media, **elites*** (business, political, and so on), and audiences affects media messages, and these messages "significantly influence what the public and the elites think, by affecting what they perceive and think about." Objectivity, which requires depersonalization and balance (for the sake of neutrality),[†] is nearly impossible to obtain, despite the efforts of journalists. According to Entman,

---

*I use the term *elites* in a political sense, to refer to those in positions of power and influence, such as elected and appointed political figures, business and corporate leaders, those who represent powerful interest groups, and those within the moneyed class whose wealth has brought them (or should I say bought them) influence, particularly in the areas of interest to them.

†In the case of *depersonalization*, reporters are expected to omit their own ideological evaluation of events, persons, groups, or ideas. To achieve *balance*, reporters are expected to seek out legitimate spokespersons and to provide the conflicting sides in any significant controversy with nearly equivalent attention.

Journalists follow the work rules that objectivity lays down, but they cannot realize the aims of objectivity. The objectivity creed contains yet simultaneously camouflages codes and conventions that journalists use in making their news choices. These selections do impart a slant to the news and influence politics.[3]

When you consider not only the depressing findings of various surveys, but the federal report published in September 1993 that some 50 percent of the adult population in the United States is illiterate (or barely literate), it is easy to understand the following comment from Entman:

> Just because on most matters Americans have so little knowledge and such weakly anchored beliefs, the news reports they do notice can significantly shape their attitudes. Not only do the majority of Americans lack detailed, expert knowledge and strong opinions, sometimes they have no old attitudes to defend. Many of the most significant political contests are played out over emerging issues or leaders; audiences have no set attitudes toward them. That clears the path for media influence.[4]

As for public opinion polls, once polling results are published by the media, they may (a) not only influence what the audience is thinking about (often referred to as setting the agenda), but (b) also affect a reporter's perception of a politician and the reporter's news judgment regarding that person. Regarding the former, when a politician's popularity is on the rise, you will usually hear talk of the bandwagon effect—people joining up, becoming supporters, wanting to be on the winning side. The bandwagon effect is controversial. It has been disputed by researchers whose findings indicate that the only ones who join up already have a predisposition toward the candidate; and it has been supported by other researchers, such as Kurt Lang and Gladys Engel Lang, who have found that the bandwagon effect is likely to be greater when an issue is new than when it confronts a long-standing belief.[5]

Regarding the impact of polls on journalistic perception and news judgment, Entman discusses the evaluation biases that affect news slant. He explains that when journalists perceive a president or other political figure as being unpopular, a "relatively negative news slant tends to arise." It appears that the reporter's watchdog commitment (also called the surveillance function) encourages the reporter not only to convey the public's sentiment of disapproval but to provide evidence of the reasons for the public's coolness. Likewise, "when they perceive a president [or other politician] as popular, journalists become more hesitant to convey damaging information."[6]

Of course, polls are not the only basis for a journalist's assessment of a politician's standing with the public. Reporters interact with other political figures and elite sources, such as the leaders and officials of various interest groups, businesses, and agencies, who convey their own sense of the individual's standing. Elite criticism as expressed to journalists tends to be muted when a president is seen as wielding power in a skillful manner and is popular. On the other hand, journalists usually have no difficulty finding willing critics once the elites conclude there has been presidential slippage, for whatever reason. More will be said on this subject in Chapter 12.

SOME NARROW AREAS OF AGREEMENT

Despite all the controversy regarding polls and their impact, in the world of commercial pollsters—where income is derived from measuring and interpreting public opinion data—there seems to be at least implicit agreement on the following points:

1. The opinions being collected and measured are those of individuals who have *verbalized* their thoughts, feelings, and attitudes on a subject or situation considered generally known and important enough to warrant the efforts of those involved.
2. The *aggregate opinions* reflect the divisions and alignments within the greater society toward a given issue.
3. Such data are considered to have *monetary worth* by those who undertake the effort because they have determined that there is a marketplace for the information.
4. Decision makers in a variety of fields use public opinion information *to design and implement a strategy* for their programs (for instance, getting elected or reelected, gaining support for or against proposed legislation, marketing a product or an idea or a person).

While commercial pollsters seem to agree on what they are measuring, many sociopolitical thinkers disagree on the value of public opinion. Walter Lippmann argued in *Public Opinion* (1922) and in *The Phantom Public* (1925) that Mr. and Mrs. Average American were too busy earning a living and taking care of the family to be sufficiently knowledgeable to understand the complex public issues of the day. This is putting it a bit more kindly than Lippmann actually did when he wrote:

> The individual man does not have opinions on all public affairs. He does not know how to direct public affairs. He does not know

what is happening, why it is happening, what ought to happen. I cannot imagine how he could know, and there is not the least reason for thinking, as mystical democrats have thought, that the compounding of individual ignorances in masses of people can produce a continuous directing force in public affairs.[7]

Abraham Lincoln once said he wanted "to get done what the people want, and the question [was] to find that out exactly." Lincoln was not just acknowledging the difficulty of the task. Unlike Walter Lippmann (a twentieth-century journalist), the Civil War president was placing a high value on public opinion and on the importance of finding out what the American people desired. Lincoln was, of course, assuming that the people were informed enough to understand and to know what was best for them and for our country. There has been an enduring discussion about whether our citizens are sufficiently attentive to develop an informed public opinion that could be of value in participating in the governance of the people.

BEFORE THERE WAS PUBLIC OPINION

We can trace concern with public opinion back to the fourth century B.C., to the days of Plato, the Greek philosopher. His beloved teacher Socrates vocally opposed his government's involvement in a war with neighboring Sparta. Socrates was accused and tried for corrupting the minds of Athenian youth by raising questions about the reasons for Athens' going to war against Sparta. Sitting in judgment, his fellow Athenians left him with little choice—either he ended his own life or he could remove himself from Athens to live out his life in exile. As explained in Plato's *Crito*, Socrates rejected exile and a life outside his country, its laws, and the Athenian public. Hannah Arendt, among others, saw Socrates' decision to end his life as consistent with the Greek sentiment that exile—life outside the public—was unthinkable. (Note that the public—and Athenian democracy—excluded women, slaves, and resident aliens.) Thereafter, Plato held public opinion in such low esteem that he viewed the citizenry as rabble. He therefore advocated a ruling class of philosopher-kings (see Plato's *Republic*)—rulers who would feed the masses stories, keep them distracted with circuses (TV?), and generally pay them little heed.

Plato's student Aristotle also feared popular sovereignty, but took a different approach. In *Critique of Plato's Republic*, Aristotle spoke of a society of two classes—the rich and the poor. Yet he argued for an educated, active citizenry that would evolve into a stabilizing middle class. The collective wisdom of this middle class, Aristotle said, should not be ignored. Among the contributions of Greek culture to Roman society were oratory, the theater, a pamphlet-type literature, and methods of publicity. The publication *Acta Diurna,*★ initiated by Caesar in 59 B.C., reported the activities of the Senate and Assembly and was influential in molding public opinion. Marcus Aurelius was among those Romans who believed that individual men could form their own opinions. In *Meditations*, he described the Stoic philosophy, explaining how our opinions, thoughts, and beliefs shape our lives.

However, centuries of turmoil followed. The Germanic tribes, the Arabs, and the Magyars swept over Europe. The masses, kept in ignorance, were easy to intimidate and to dominate. There appeared to be a return to Plato's belief in the irrationalism of the rabble and in the unworthiness of their opinions. During this period, people fled the population centers, seeking shelter in the hinterlands. Thus cities declined as political, economic, and intellectual centers. The city of Rome, for example, went from a population of about 1 million in the first century A.D. to less than 500,000 by the fourth century and to approximately 17,000 in the census of 1377.[8] Throughout Europe, an estimated 25 million people died in Europe's Black Death (bubonic plague) between 1347 and 1351.

Through all this turmoil, it was the institution of the Church that most represented stability. It retained its favored economic and cultural position by controlling vast landholdings and by maintaining a monopoly of learning and technical knowledge. Kept in ignorance, the masses adhered to Church doctrine. Their opinions, if they had any, were ignored by the Church and those in power.

However, with Johannes Gutenberg's invention of the movable type printing press around 1450, things began to change. Literacy spread slowly; with literacy came the acquisition of information. More and more people began to think for themselves. Martin Luther's economically motivated *Treatises* of 1520 and 1523 were meant to encourage the German princes to rebel against the Church. However, Luther (a soon-to-be authoritarian in his own right) emphasized that God had ordained government. The masses, he said, must obey their rulers, whether they be just or unjust. The world, according to Luther, was too wicked. It did not "deserve to have many wise and pious princes."[9] The ideal citizen was characterized by blind obedience; individual thinking was dangerous. What about public opinion? According to Niccolo Machiavelli's *The Prince* (1513), *if* it existed, rulers

---

★The Roman *Acta Diurna* ("day's actions") is often referred to as the first newspaper. It was a daily handwritten document that reported government decisions on laws and hangings, births and deaths, the games and other forms of entertainment, and so on. It was posted in various public places next to the *Acta Senatus*, the formal Senate report.

could influence, mold, and control it. And Benedict (Baruch) Spinoza (1632–1677) warned in his *Ethics* (Part IV):

> He whose honour depends on the opinion of the mob must day by day strive with the greatest anxiety, act and scheme in order to retain his reputation. For the mob is varied and inconstant, and therefore if a reputation is not carefully preserved it dies quickly.

Clearly, the European rulers during that period were only concerned with controlling and manipulating public opinion, not with honoring it.

EMERGING PUBLIC OPINION

With the Age of Enlightenment came a greater emphasis on man as an individual, capable of rational thought. This new belief gave rise to the concept of the general will, which we might recognize as our sort of public opinion. John Locke, a seventeenth-century British philosopher, saw man as rational, willing to form a social contract to create an organized society and government in order to protect himself and his property. (Locke does not seem to consider women in his writings.) In his *Two Treatises of Government* (1690), Locke speaks of the public good and explains that the people have "reserved to themselves the choice of their representatives." The consent of the governed is also discussed by Charles-Louis de Montesquieu in *The Spirit of the Laws*, where he expresses his faith in the ability of the people to choose "those whom they are to entrust with part of their authority."

Just as Aristotle had recognized different subgroups within the public— such as the rich, the poor, and an evolving middle class—so, too, did Jean-Jacques Rousseau when he spoke of the influence of such groups on the general will. Around the time Rousseau was writing in *The Social Contract* in 1762 that "man is born free, and everywhere he is in chains," sweeping changes were under way in England, the first country to experience the impact of the technological and industrial revolutions then in process.

The farm and landed estate were soon replaced by the factory as the key unit of production and wealth. Towns and cities expanded rapidly in the last years of the eighteenth century and the early years of the nineteenth century. With improved living and health conditions, the rate of population growth accelerated. Gradually, a dominant new social class of merchants, financiers, manufacturers, and professionals came into existence, replacing the old landed aristocracy in the social hierarchy.

For example, Manchester underwent a rapid transformation from a market town to the center of England's expanding cotton industry. The city's inhabitants were forced to determine for themselves (as are the people today in the former Soviet Union and its satellites) the ways and means of handling the new social, economic, and political challenges confronting them. A number of principles and opinions developed from the experiences of dealing with these often conflicting elements. By 1820, there emerged an economic philosophy, a program known as the Manchester School. In *The Development of Public Opinion in Manchester, 1780–1820*, Leon Soutierre Marshall provides an excellent case study of the evolving power of public opinion in an industrializing capitalist society.

For there to be *informed* public opinion, there must be access to information. Jeremy Bentham referred to a "tribunal of public opinion" to suggest legislative reform and to prevent misrule. Bentham (1748–1832), founder of philosophical radicalism and utilitarian philosophy, was a prolific writer and was one of the first to stress the importance of public education. He felt that an informed people would make informed decisions and that government actions must not be kept secret. (Imagine his horror over Watergate, the Iran–Contra affair, Iraqgate, or the savings and loan fiasco.) According to Bentham and the following generations of Benthamites (such as James Mill and his son John Stuart Mill), the rule of passion must be replaced by the judgment, morality, and common sense of an educated people.

Demophobia or Fear of Crowds

Toward the end of the nineteenth century, a number of Italian, British, and French sociologists and psychologists became interested in the behavior and power of crowds. They viewed the urban masses as purposeful as they hurried to and from their daily activities. To Scipio Sighele in Italy, Gabriel Tarde, Gustave LeBon, Auguste Comte in France, and Wilfred Trotter in England it seemed that—after centuries of striving for recognition of their individuality—people had somehow become aggregates. Were they now masses on the march, exhibiting herding characteristics and inferior judgment? Had we lost our individual identities? And if we had, was public opinion nothing more than the product of mass hysteria?

Sighele focused on the nature of group decisions, regarding a crowd as a single, compact organism that was "more disposed to evil actions than the individual." One example he used to illustrate the process of imitation, collective suggestion, and the spread of irrational behavior was that of an English lord who jumped into the volcano Mt. Vesuvius and was then followed by many Englishmen.[10] Still, Sighele believed that public opinion somehow differed from the collective thinking of an emotional mob, and he wrote that there were even different publics with different interests. Unfortunately, these publics sometimes become crowds that then engage in irrational acts. Interestingly, Sighele believed that publics in the nineteenth century were more diversified, less defined, than in previous periods of history. He claimed the power of journalism (and its production of accessible information) was a contributory factor in the development of thinking individuals.

His contemporary, Gabriel Tarde, is considered one of the earliest significant investigators of public opinion. Tarde based his work on applied social psychology and took note of the traditional differences in values, belief structure, and thinking between the elites and the masses. He wrote that democratic periods, however, were characterized by reduced distance (and therefore reduced distinction) between the socioeconomic classes.[11] Democracy, along with social and economic opportunity, allowed an *outward imitation* of the upper class by the lower class. (Think about cheap copies of designer clothes; stylish, low-priced cars; and the paperback libraries we accumulate today.) Tarde notes that in contrast to his modern era (around 1900) there were only crowds in the Middle Ages, with the transition to publics occurring once the printing press made possible the dissemination of information. As a result of the advent and impact of "true journalism" (as opposed to the controlled flow of information), we see an evolving public as a small elite during the French Revolution.

Tarde provides us with an understanding of the role of the press in the formation of publics and with a useful qualitative distinction between publics (consisting of informed people) and crowds (consisting of rabble). He states that publics are characterized by rationally based opinion; crowds, on the other hand, are characterized by emotional, irrational, sentimental responses. However, on the down side, opinion is seen as transient (here today, gone tomorrow) when contrasted with tradition (considered as enduring behavior). According to Tarde, *opinion* often forms to oppose traditions that no longer seem acceptable. Consider, for example, the worthy use of public opinion to fight certain long-held (traditional) prejudices.

Tarde also differentiates between the press and journals. The former is more market-oriented, concerned with attracting masses of readers and advertisers. It is therefore a less stable basis for public opinion. As an example of the press in the late nineteenth century, consider America's period of yellow journalism. For contemporary examples of the press, consider some of today's tabloid-style newspapers and the infotainment programs of the electronic media.* All of these are dependent on advertisers and readers or

---

*Most of the content of local news programs—violent crimes, scandals affecting elites in the community, unsubstantiated accusations of official malfeasance, and banter between the usual male and female co-anchors—and some news magazine programs such as "A Current Affair," "Lifestyles of the Rich and Famous," and "America's Most Wanted" fall into this category of sensational-style journalism.

viewers. However, Tarde, thinking mostly about European journals, explained that they were the traditional organ (the voice) of political parties. As such, they tended to be a more consistent, durable, stable basis for public opinion. Organized groups, he said, attempt to introduce and communicate their ideas through their journals. Somewhere along the way, the mass media (the daily press) may become interested and choose to popularize ideas initiated by the journals. In this way, according to Tarde, publics (groups that have informed opinions) are formed. Thus, for Tarde as for Sighele, mass media are seen as providing a necessary (albeit less traditional or stable) source of information in a process that generates publics.

On the other hand, the French social psychologist Gustave LeBon denigrated the importance and significance of communicated thought. He wrote about the power of propaganda, saying that it was based on "prestige, affirmation, repetition, and contagion."[12] According to LeBon, even the most intelligent cannot escape the *contagion of the collective mind*. Unlike Tarde, LeBon did not differentiate between public opinion and traditional judgments. In fact, he felt that public opinion included the weight and power of tradition, as well as new ideas and fads.

Auguste Comte took a less negative position on the progress and intelligence of humankind in *Positive Philosophy* (1830–1852):

> It is only through the more and more marked influence of the reason over the general conduct of man and of society, that the gradual march of our race has attained that regularity and persevering continuity which distinguish it so radically from the desultory and barren expansion of even the highest animal orders, which share, and with enhanced strength, the appetites, the passions, and even the primary sentiments of man.

Lord James Bryce noted in his treatise of 1888, "The Nature of Public Opinion," that there was "little solidity and substance … in the political or social beliefs of nineteen persons out of every twenty." When these beliefs are examined, according to Bryce,

> … they resolve themselves into two or three prejudices and aversions, two or three prepossessions for a particular party or section of a party, two or three phrases or catch-words suggesting or embodying arguments which the man who repeats them has not analyzed.[13]

Although Bryce tempers these statements with some thoughts on the role of education (see Box 1.2), such extreme thinking was common in class-conscious Great Britain in the nineteenth century.

BOX 1.2   Words from Lord Bryce, an Admirer

James Bryce, a British jurist and ambassador to the United States, expressed his hope for "government by public opinion" when he wrote:

> In some countries the mass of the voters are not only markedly inferior in education to the few who lead, but also diffident, more disposed to look up to their betters. In others the difference of intellectual level between those who busy themselves with politics and the average voter is far smaller. Perhaps the leader is not so well instructed a man…perhaps the average voter is better instructed and more self-confident. Where both of these phenomena coincide, so that the difference of level is inconsiderable, public opinion will evidently be a different thing from what it is in countries where, though the Constitution has become democratic, the habits of the nations are still aristocratic. This is the difference between America and the countries of Western Europe.

SOURCE: *The American Commonwealth*, Vol. II (New York: Macmillan, 1916), pp. 251–266.

Britain's Wilfred Trotter, in *Instincts of the Herd in Peace and War* (1916), claimed that our gregarious nature and our vulnerability to suggestion lead us to join and to follow the herd. Our opinions are not really ours—individually attained—but are, rather, those of the herd. That line of reasoning is extremely disturbing to those of us who have faith in the ability of individuals to form their own opinions. Our concern, though, is that opinion be formed rationally, on the basis of diverse sources of information.

CHARACTERISTICS OF PUBLIC OPINION

V. O. Key, Jr., is one of many twentieth-century theorists who examined the nature of public opinion. His theory of the distribution, properties, and formation of opinions is considered a valuable contribution to our understanding of this subject.[14] Key analyzed the *distribution* (how widely a particular opinion is held and who holds it) and the direction of opinion—including the degree of *consensus* (agreement and support), *conflict* (disagreement and opposition), or *concentration* (how pervasive the opinion is).

When an issue is of interest only to certain groups or to small segments of our population, the opinion is said to be concentrated in, or restricted to, those who hold it. Analysis of the distribution of an opinion tells us who holds the opinion—which groups (based on socioeconomic class, ethnicity, religion, age, sex, and so forth)—and where they are located (the geographic distribution—the cities, the farms, the Midwest, the South, and so on). This is important for policymakers to know so that they can be responsive to the needs of the people; that is (from a self-serving and pragmatic point of view), if they want to be elected and reelected.

Key also considers the importance of the "interrelations of opinion." This refers to the combinations of opinions we hold on various issues, at various times. Pollsters can create a profile of a group of respondents (the people being interviewed for the poll) by cross-tabulating the answers to various questions, enabling us, for example, to learn that there is—or isn't— a gender gap (see Box 1.3).

Although there have always been problems with categorizing and labeling people in an attempt to predict their voting patterns, the complexity of life in today's society has made the effort more challenging. With the blurring of traditional liberal and conservative positions,[15] it has become more and more difficult to create an accurate profile, to accurately pigeonhole people. At first glance, this blurring might be viewed positively as a sign of building consensus in our society (if the divisions left–right, liberal–conservative are weakening, consensus ought to be growing). But that is not necessarily the case. For example, many liberals have themselves challenged traditional liberal support for sex education in the schools, quotas, affirmative action programs, free trade, and foreign aid; and many conservatives now question some of the '80s values based on materialism, consumption, acquisition. This does not mean that there will necessarily be a consensus on how to resolve the problems we have or on who should bear the burden of sacrifice.

Despite the blurring in some areas and the remaining significant differences of opinion in others, we might ask whether or not there is a **dominant social paradigm (DSP)**,[16] some dominant belief structure, within the country that is based on free-marketplace and old Yankee values (however you care to define them). After all, isn't there a consensus on the really important issues? Or are we now in a transitional period in which the old paradigm, the old social framework, is being reevaluated and a new paradigm has not yet gained acceptance? Do the old liberal–conservative designations make any sense in our rapidly changing society? Do most of us still believe in unregulated industrial activity, in economic growth over environmental preservation, in an unlimited supply of natural resources? Do we believe that, without our changing our behavior, science and technology will resolve the social and environmental problems afflicting our country and improve the quality of our lives? So many questions have been raised to

BOX 1.3   Gender Gap?

When Dianne Feinstein won the Democratic nomination for governor of California (51 to 42%) in June 1990, her victory in the primary raised questions for experts who had anticipated a gender gap, a difference in the level of support she would receive from men and women. When the exit polls revealed no real gender gap, Kathleen Frankovic, in charge of polling for CBS News, studied them further and made an interesting discovery:

> [T]he relatively small differences in the support Feinstein got from men and from women paled in comparison with the differences in her support among three groups of women: those who said they had made up their minds early, those who decided in the last two weeks before the June 5 primary and those who decided in the last three days.[1]

Frankovic found that the *earlier* the women decided to vote for Feinstein, the more likely they were to support and actively campaign for her. While her support among male voters continued more or less at the same level, those women who decided in the last three days of the primary campaign voted more heavily for Attorney General John K. Van De Kamp, Feinstein's opponent. The profile of the early deciders (more than two weeks) shows that these women are politically motivated and active, anxious to see another woman succeed, pro-choice (supporting legalized abortion). The late deciders (last three days) tended to be older and viewed themselves as more liberal than Feinstein, who campaigned for capital punishment.

Her slogan, "Tough but caring," attracted male voters impressed by the strength of her early support; but her tough stance may have worked against her with older women, who tended to perceive Feinstein as challenging the traditional role they had accepted for themselves.

Polls completed a few days before the November general election gave conflicting (and confusing) indications as to whether Feinstein would benefit from the women's vote. According to the California Poll, Senator Pete Wilson, Feinstein's Republican opponent, had a 6-point lead among women (46 to 40%) and a 12-point lead among men (48 to 36%). *The Los Angeles Times* Poll showed Feinstein 6 points ahead among women, but 9 points behind among men.[2] Was there or wasn't there a gender gap?

The final count showed Senator Pete Wilson won with 49 percent of the vote, compared to Feinstein's 46 percent. Robert Reinhold of *The New York Times* reported on an exit poll by Voter Research and Surveys indicating that "while Ms. Feinstein did have an advantage among women of about 16 points, that was overcome by other factors," such as crime, drugs, and a faltering state economy.[3] Also, Wilson's 16-point lead among men was sufficient to offset the Feinstein lead among women. So, does a 16-point difference qualify as a gender gap? Yes…

Continued

BOX 1.3   Continued

but, at least in this case, the gap was not the significant determinant in the decision-making process.

In general it is a mistake to pigeonhole any group of voters based on a single demographic factor (such as gender) because this ignores the individual voter's belief structure, which includes a multiplicity of interests. However, the gender issue became very important to many women after the Clarence Thomas–Anita Hill sexual harassment hearings (of October 1991), which followed Thomas' hearings before the Senate Judiciary Committee and preceded the Senate vote approving his appointment as a Justice to the United States Supreme Court. In reaction to the way Anita Hill was treated by the "Committee of Males" (as some women called it), 1992 was dubbed the Year of the Woman. In November 1992, California sent two women to the United States Senate. Dianne Feinstein won the special election to fill the remaining two years of Pete Wilson's Senate term. She trounced Senator John Seymour (appointed to succeed Wilson), winning 55 percent of the vote to his 38 percent, with

three other candidates sharing the remaining 7 percent of the vote.[4] In a somewhat tighter race (48 to 43%, also with five candidates), Representative Barbara Boxer defeated her Republican opposition, winning a full six-year term to succeed Alan Cranston in the United States Senate. Although many see these victories as feminist triumphs, others see them as President Clinton's coattails at work.[5] Clinton won 47 percent of the popular vote in California, compared to Bush's 32 percent.[6]

---

1. Michael Oreskes, "Washington Talk: Unmasking the Fallacy of the 'Women's Vote,'" *The New York Times,* June 19, 1990.
2. Robert Reinhold, "Recent Polls Look Bleak for Feinstein," *The New York Times,* Nov. 4, 1990.
3. Voter Research and Surveys is a national consortium of various news organizations.
4. Adam Clymer, "The New Congress," *The New York Times,* Nov. 5, 1992, p. B6.
5. Adam Clymer, "On Clinton's Coattails, Democrats Overcome Anti-Incumbent Anger," *The New York Times,* Nov. 4, 1992, p. B1.
6. "The 1992 Elections—State By State," *The New York Times,* Nov. 5, 1992, p. B13.

---

challenge the old DSP that a **new environmental paradigm (NEP)** appears to be slowly emerging, supported by people on both the left and the right of the political spectrum. Various studies since the first Earth Day in 1970 have shown that there is growing support for environmentalism, despite our deep concern with economic issues. On election day 1992, results from an exit poll in California reported that 50 percent of the voters saw themselves as environmentalists and that more than 6 out of 10 of them voted for Bill Clinton. However, a nationwide exit poll reported that the environment was seen as an important issue by only 1 in 20 voters; two-thirds of the exit poll respondents cited the economy as the major issue.[17]

Besides the new environmental paradigm, several other belief systems have emerged both here and abroad to compete in the marketplace of ideas and opinions. The disintegration of communism has meant the near dismantling of one belief structure, and the rise of religious fundamentalism around the world has challenged another—the movement toward secularism.★ In the United States a good deal of attention has been given to the economic concept of comparable worth. This is the idea that dissimilar jobs in our society should be considered equally important and worthy. During the late 1980s, low-paid municipal office workers (mostly women) across America argued that their worth was comparable to that of other employees (mostly men) in the areas of maintenance, fire fighting, and police work. There was also a rash of campus strikes when skilled but low-paid secretaries and clerks (again, mostly women) demanded that their work be considered of comparable worth to those better-paid and male-dominated tasks performed on campus by security guards, maintenance workers, and gardeners. In addition to the belief in economic equality, another somewhat related belief system seems to be gaining in strength: There is a growing backlash against affirmative action programs and quota systems designed to encourage equal opportunity and to right racial (and gender-related) inequities of the past.

This ongoing, evolutionary change in our belief and value structure is challenging public opinion researchers who are attempting to create profiles of voters or consumers. Thus it is an exciting time to be monitoring the ideological changes taking place and to be studying what Key called the *properties of public opinion*. These include:

Intensity   Key's first property of public opinion involves how strongly or deeply you feel about something. We may have opinions on many issues, but feel very strongly about only a few. For example, some people are vehemently opposed to abortion—while others are vehemently pro-choice—no matter what the circumstances are.

Stability Versus Fluidity (Instability)   Key's second property concerns hopping on the bandwagon or changing your opinion. Some opinions, based on long-held sociopolitical values or religious beliefs, are stable and

---

★Also consider the much-criticized takeover of the Republican party by the religious right, as demonstrated by both the party platform and the rhetoric heard during the Republican National Convention in August 1992.

very slow or unlikely to change. As Key states, such opinions "possess high viscosity." On the other hand, some opinions are so fluid that they can literally change overnight. (Remember Tarde's characterization of opinion as transient?) For example, with the Japanese attack on Pearl Harbor on December 7, 1941, pro-isolationism (noninvolvement) gave way to war fever literally within hours. A more recent example occurred in the fall of 1990 during the military buildup against Iraq's Saddam Hussein, whose army had invaded and occupied Kuwait the previous August. While Congress debated and apprehension grew among certain segments of the population (those who did not appreciate President Bush's surge in popularity), the polls showed that more and more Americans viewed the Iraqi leader as the new Hitler on the international stage and that they supported Bush's decision to send in the troops. Within days of the announcement to send troops, more and more Americans set aside their fears of another Vietnam and hopped on the president's bandwagon.

Latency Versus Salience   For Key, latency and salience characterize opposite qualities in regard to how our opinions are formed. These properties define how passively or actively you hold an opinion. We hold some opinions so passively, unbeknownst even to ourselves, that it takes a peculiar set of circumstances to bring the opinions to our own attention. Consider: "I couldn't believe it. I didn't know they were such bigots until that happened. I guess they *really* felt that way all along." Thus something can occur that will disturb us, activating our latent opinions on subjects about which we had not previously, and consciously, thought.

For example, consider George Bush's 30-second campaign ad on the Massachusetts "revolving-door" criminal justice system and its predecessor, the controversial Willie Horton ad. These commercials were used by Republicans during Bush's 1988 presidential campaign against Massachusetts Governor Michael Dukakis. The former ad was paid for by the Bush campaign. The Willie Horton commercial was sponsored by a group that was technically independent from the Bush campaign, a conservative PAC (political action committee). The Horton ad ran only a few times before it was withdrawn as a result of the Bush campaign's official request. It had focused on Horton, a convicted criminal who committed another brutal crime while on a weekend furlough from prison. Some claimed that the ad gained notoriety primarily from repeated airings on network TV news stories about negative campaigning, and that Bush was not initially aware of the content of the ad. This opinion might be considered an instance of revisionism.

Although the other ad, the "revolving-door" commercial, did not use Horton's image or name, it was used in combination with campaign events and other free media appearances in which the candidate (Bush) and his handlers associated Horton with the furlough program. Willie Horton, a black man, thereafter became a symbol of everything wrong with the American legal system in general and with the Massachusetts system in particular. By pushing the right buttons, this commercial may well have triggered latent bigotry in many voters, awakening and legitimizing an already existing fear and prejudice (see Box 1.4). Most people were unaware that prison systems throughout the country, including Bush's "home" state of Texas and many other states, have similar programs and that some prisoners—white as well as black—in those systems had also abused the furlough privilege, which was originally designed to ease the transition from prison to civilian life and to relieve prison overcrowding.

A salient opinion, on the other hand, is readily discernible because it is based on an issue that is perceived as significant that is capturing a good deal of public attention. For example, what is the major front-page headline in today's newspaper or what is the lead story on the broadcast news? Does it deal with election politics, the economic situation, some dastardly local crime, or an event abroad? It is not enough for a subject to be merely topical—that is, to occupy time and space in the media. It is the issue's perceived relevance and importance to the individual that creates a salient opinion. That is why, in the 1992 presidential campaign, most Americans were focused on the country's economic situation rather than on the character issue pushed by the Republican party.

Some argue that the media affect not only the *properties* of public opinion but also its *formation*. Do the news media, through their choices of what to report (their gatekeeper function), lead public opinion (see David Fan's essay on content analysis, The Professional Voice 1)? Or do the actual facts about the political events reported in the media influence people? In the latter case, the media are seen as an objective mirror of society, merely reflecting political events. Consider the following example from the 1992 election campaign: In the last weeks of the campaign, Special Prosecutor Lawrence Walsh, charged with investigating the Iran–Contra scandal,★ raised new questions about George Bush's role in the unauthorized sale of arms to Iran. Walsh went public with information obtained as a result of his examination of former Defense Secretary Caspar Weinberger's private papers and notes, indicating Bush had firsthand knowledge of the arms sales.

★This dealt with the discovery in 1986 of the unauthorized fundraising for the Contras, the rebels seeking the overthrow of the communist-supported Sandinista government in Nicaragua, headed by Daniel Ortega. Ronald Reagan's White House aide, Colonel Oliver North, organized the effort to raise the funds and to transfer them to the Contras. In this complex maze of dealings, without congressional knowledge and approval, arms were being sold illegally to Iran, and the funds from those sales were then transferred to the Contras.

BOX 1.4   The 20-Percent Solution

As a result of a racially charged campaign, George Bush won only 9 percent of the black vote in 1988. His campaign was damaging to southern Republican incumbents in their reelection bids to Congress. Soon after Bush took office, many Republicans began to express concern over the 1990 congressional election, recalling that nearly monolithic black support for southern Democrats had also helped defeat Republican incumbents in the 1986 House and Senate elections.

Therefore, almost immediately after the 1988 election, Bush set out to court blacks under what has been called the 20-percent solution.[1] Lee Atwater, then chairman of the Republican National Committee, and other Republican strategists determined that it was not necessary to attempt to win black support en masse, but if they could cut into that support, say by 20 percent, Republican candidates could win. To implement the strategy, Bush named a number of blacks to prominent jobs (best example: General Colin Powell, chairman of the Joint Chiefs of Staff). And, when South Africa's Nelson Mandela visited the United States in June 1990, Bush welcomed him to the White House with a far greater show of attention than is normally accorded to a non–head of state.

Polls taken soon after showed that 56 percent of blacks approved of the president's performance in office. At the time, it appeared that the wooing was successful and, to many observers of the American political scene, this illustrated an effective manipulation of public opinion.

However, by way of illustrating the fluidity of public opinion, Bush's approval rating among blacks again fell after his veto in mid-October of the controversial Civil Rights Act of 1990. This act would have allowed religious minorities and women to collect damages if they were able to prove intentional discrimination. The president argued that the bill would have resulted in quota systems being imposed by employers seeking to prevent lawsuits.

Despite the dip in President Bush's popularity among blacks, according to *The New York Times*/CBS News Poll, Republican candidates for House seats won 22 percent of black votes in the November 1990 election. The table opposite illustrates the degree of success that the GOP had in eroding black support for the Democratic party after the first congressional election under President Reagan.

Was the 20-percent solution working to elect Republican candidates? Even with an extensive state-by-state analysis, it would be difficult to say with certainty because of the complexity of the issues and structure of voting coalitions. However, we might consider the following three examples from the 1990 campaigns:[2]

1. Massachusetts: Blacks made up 2 percent of the voters, and 42 percent of them supported the victorious Republican gubernatorial candidate William F. Weld.

Black Support for Republican Candidates for the House of Representatives

		1990	1988*	1986	1984*	1982
All Blacks		22%	15%	14%	8%	11%
Age:	18–29	15	16	19	6	9
	30–44	19	14	16	7	12
	45–59	32	13	9	10	9
	60+	26	18	10	13	15
Area:	East	22	10	13	7	10
	Midwest	27	14	16	5	13
	South	22	18	7	8	7
	West	16	15	17	16	—

*These were presidential election years, with Ronald Reagan being reelected in 1984 and George Bush defeating Michael Dukakis in 1988.

SOURCE: The table is based on exit poll data drawn from *The New York Times/ CBS News Poll,* published in *The New York Times,* Nov. 8, 1990, p. B7.

2. North Carolina: Blacks made up 19 percent of the electorate and cast only 7 percent of their votes for Republican senator Jesse Helms, who still won reelection.
3. Illinois: Blacks made up 16 percent of the electorate, and they cast 21 percent of their votes for Republican gubernatorial candidate James Edgar, who won.

Perhaps in a continuing effort to implement the 20 percent solution following the late Supreme Court Justice Thurgood Marshall's retirement in 1991, President Bush nominated Clarence Thomas, another black, to serve as Marshall's replacement. In the bruising hearings that followed the publication of sexual harassment allegations by Professor Anita Hill in October 1991, the Republicans emphasized Thomas' claim that the committee's airing of the charges represented a high-tech lynching. Judging from the polls at the time, a large percentage of the American people agreed.[3] But, did the 20-percent solution work in the 1992 presidential election? What do you think?[4]

1. Michael Duffy, "The 20% Solution," *Time,* July 2, 1990, p. 20.
2. Data for the three examples can be found in "The 1990 Elections," *The New York Times,* Nov. 8, 1990, pp. 8–9.
3. However, as Donald Granberg of the University of Missouri, Columbia, noted, "[I]t is also true that one year later the figures reversed. That is, shortly after the hearings, the ratio of Thomas believers to Hill believers was about 2:1; a year later it was reversed to 1:2." Granberg added, "I haven't heard a convincing explanation of why this shift in public opinion occurred."
4. See "Portrait of the Electorate," *The New York Times,* Nov. 5, 1992, p. B9. The data were provided by Voter Research and Surveys, collected at 300 polling places around the country, where 15,490 voters completed questionnaires. Blacks made up 8 percent of the sample; 82 percent voted for Clinton, 11 percent for Bush, and 7 percent for Perot.

What role did media coverage of this event play in Bush's defeat? Did he lose the election (a) because the media chose to headline the Walsh findings implicating Bush in illegal activities (thereby destroying his trust/character strategy against Bill Clinton) and to ignore positive news on the economy, or (b) because there was nothing positive to report on the economy and Walsh's timing in going after Weinberger and his findings made the news irresistible, or (c) for other reasons not mentioned here? In the first instance, the media, in their gatekeeper role, are seen as powerful agents shaping public opinion. In the second case, the media are not power brokers; rather, they are mirroring real-world political events. In the third instance, the media may or may not even have played a noteworthy role. The truth is probably somewhere between the two extremes: media as power brokers and media as mere reflectors of events.[18]

RESEARCHING PUBLIC OPINION

Using a computer-designed method of content analysis, David Fan, a professor at the University of Minnesota, conducted a study that suggests that "the press does indeed mold opinion in a predictable manner." Fan's content analysis is both an attempt to understand the impact of the media on public opinion and an example of another research tool (other than polling) used to discern the formation of public opinion.

The Professional Voice 1
Computer Content Analysis
David P. Fan

Since the early 1980s, progressively more newspapers, wire services, and magazines from around the world have entered electronic databases. As a result, it is possible to use a personal computer to dial a database by modem and retrieve the texts of news articles verbatim. With ready access to news stories in machine-readable form, it is feasible to perform computer content analysis of the retrieved text,[1] to relate press coverage with public opinion polls, and then to show that the public responds predictably to mass media messages.

One example involves the presidential race of 1988 with George Bush and Michael Dukakis as the principal contenders.[2] We retrieved 2,603 stories, at random, from over 11,000 that appeared in the Associated Press mentioning one or both candidates. We used the new method of *successive filtrations* to analyze the text. The analyst enters into the computer a customized dictionary and set of word-relationship rules. The computer implements these instructions and makes decisions for individual paragraphs, the unit of analysis used. The analyst then compares the desired decision based on a human reading with those made by machine. If needed, changes are made in the dictionary and in the rules until the results are satisfactory (defined typically as 70–80% agreement between human and machine judgments).

For the Bush–Dukakis race, we first performed a *filtration* step in which the computer was instructed to discard all paragraphs except those mentioning one candidate or the other. Then, the remaining paragraphs were read, and a new dictionary and set of rules were constructed to score for the extent to which individual paragraphs were either favorable or unfavorable to either Bush or Dukakis. Each paragraph was given a score of 1.0 and paragraphs supporting more than one position were given fractional scores. At the end of the scoring, each AP story had a date and a number of paragraphs for each of the four positions of *favorable* and *unfavorable* and for *Bush* and *Dukakis*. Some stories were irrelevant and had zero scores for all positions.

After they were calculated by computer, the scores were entered to calculate an expected opinion time trend. The computation began on September 20, 1987, with the results of the first poll comparing Bush and Dukakis to each other and no other candidates. The model states that, after this time, press information favorable to Bush and unfavorable to Dukakis should persuade some fraction of the Dukakis supporters to prefer Bush. Simultaneously, there could be cross-movement in the other direction due to the opposite types of information.

Therefore, the computer calculated opinion every 24 hours beginning with the September 20 poll value, with new media information pushing people from each group into the opposing camp. The result was a time trend with points spaced at 24-hour intervals. When this time trend computed from AP stories was overlaid on 120 opinion poll results for the year before the election, the average error was 2.7 percent, very close to the uncertainties in the polls themselves.

During the computation period, there were important opinion shifts. Bush was far ahead of Dukakis before the Iowa caucuses. Then the two candidates approached parity during the primary. After Senator Robert Dole withdrew as the other main Republican contestant, favorable news about Bush diminished to low levels while Dukakis coverage remained high due to the interest in the Jesse Jackson candidacy. During this period, Dukakis surged into the lead. After the two party conventions in July and August 1988, Bush consistently received more favorable press, resulting in his maintenance of a steady lead over Dukakis until election day. This study and others suggest that the press—especially the news portion, which far outweighs editorial information—

does indeed mold opinion in a predictable manner.

David P. Fan is in the Department of Genetic and Cell Biology at the University of Minnesota.

1. David P. Fan, *Predictions of Public Opinion from the Mass Media: Computer Content Analysis and Mathematical Modeling* (Westport, CT: Greenwood Press, 1988).

2. David P. Fan and A. R. Tims, "The Impact of News Media on Public Opinion: American Presidential Election 1987–1988," *International Journal of Public Opinion Research* (1989), 1, pp. 151–163.

An earlier example of a computer-generated content analysis study was conducted in 1968 by G. Cleveland Wilhoit and Kenneth S. Sherrill, using a computer for content analysis of wire service copy. The computer, rapidly coming into its own in the field of statistics, was programmed to recognize the names of United States senators in order to determine the degree of their visibility.[19]

Content analysis provides information on the frequency of occurrence of particular items. In one phase of his effort to study the typical stands of certain newspapers (that is, liberal versus conservative) and the newspaper medium's impact on public opinion, researcher Robert Entman used the 1974 Michigan Content Analysis Study, consisting of nearly 18,000 front-page news and editorial-page items from 92 newspapers throughout the United States.[20] In still another phase of his research, Entman concentrated on the coverage of two particular scandals (Billygate and the Donovan indictment) and two crises (the aborted Iran hostage rescue mission and the Beirut bomb attack) involving President Carter and President Reagan (see Box 1.5). He examined the Vanderbilt Television News Archives Indexes to study network (ABC, CBS, NBC) placement of these news reports, the number of stories during the period following the breaking of the news, the total number of minutes allotted for coverage of each story, and the total number of days each story was covered by all three networks. To analyze the perception of presidential linkage and personal connection to the crises, Entman examined two issues each of *Time* and *Newsweek* published after the aborted rescue mission and after the bombing of the Marine barracks. While Carter was directly linked to a policy failure, Reagan was not.

BOX 1.5   Recent Political Scandals and Crises

Billygate, in 1980, involved President Carter's brother Billy's acting as a representative of the Libyan government without registering as a foreign agent, as is required by law. A second scandal, in 1984, involved President Reagan's Secretary of Labor Raymond Donovan, who was indicted for his alleged involvement in a fraud conspiracy that involved a reputed member of organized crime. In 1987, Donovan was cleared of all charges. Public opinion researcher Entman, arguing that there is no way reporters—in 1984—could have known that the secretary of labor was ultimately going to be cleared, was attempting to understand why the Donovan scandal attracted so little media attention (enduring only a few days), while the Billygate scandal lingered in the news for many weeks. For the interesting details of Entman's methodology and findings, see his Chapter 3, "Straight Talk on Slanted News: 'Bias' and Accountability in Reporting Carter and Reagan."

Entman also studied political crises. The first crisis occurred on Carter's watch, in April 1980. It was the failed attempt to rescue the Americans held hostage in Iran. Nine servicemen died in the Iranian desert as a result of accidents during the aborted mission, and Carter was heavily and personally criticized by the press. A second crisis occurred in October 1983, during Reagan's first term as president. A suicide bomb attack against our Marine barracks in Beirut killed 265. (Entman puts the number killed at 241, but see Michael Emery, "The Grenada Story that No One Wanted," in the *Enterprise,* a suburban Los Angeles daily newspaper, Nov. 4, 1984.) Reagan was not blamed or personally criticized by the press, although an incident the previous spring should have been seen as a warning to beef up security around American personnel (a car bomb explosion near the U.S. embassy in Beirut had killed 17 Americans and 43 others).

SOURCE: Robert Entman, *Democracy Without Citizens: Media and the Decay of American Politics* (New York: Oxford University Press, 1989).

Perhaps this was partly due to the fact that two days after the Beirut bombing American forces invaded the small Caribbean island of Grenada, leaving both the media and the public duly distracted. (The reasons given by the Reagan administration for the operation were ostensibly to liberate the island from a growing communist influence—evidenced by the increased presence of Cuban workers building a lengthy landing strip, far beyond the needs of a small resort—and to rescue American medical students caught up in the Soviet–Cuban attempt to control the island, portrayed as "in our backyard.") Entman, analyzing the results of relevant public opinion surveys in the light of his findings, attributes Carter's subsequent slippage and Reagan's enhanced standing in the polls to media biases that shaped the news slant for these stories.[21]

Questions usually arise as to the validity and reliability of attempting a link between the results of any content analysis study and its effect on public opinion. Pollsters will tell you that unless the researcher actually samples public opinion, the argument supporting a linkage remains one of logic and conjecture and not of statistics.[22] This is probably why Entman attempted both to carefully document his content analysis research and to compare his findings with those of legitimate polls. His goal went beyond collecting data on public opinion. He was more interested in the forces that shaped it.

Besides content analysis, various techniques (including, among others, small-group studies, depth interviews, and nonprobability studies) have been tried by researchers. These methodologies have proven useful when the aim of the researcher was to describe existing behavior. However, researchers interested in the formation and assessment of public opinion have found that they could not generalize legitimately from the individual or small group to the larger population because those chosen to participate had not been selected on a random basis and could not be relied upon to be representative of the entire population. Thus, despite a variety of other research methods, those who regularly study public opinion have found that polling through the use of a random probability sample is the most cost effective.

Influencing Public Opinion

One of the best-known older studies on the formation of public opinion and the power of the press to shape it was undertaken early in 1940 in Erie County, Ohio. Researchers Paul Lazarsfeld, Bernard Berelson, and Hazel Gaudet studied media impact during that year's presidential election campaign (see Box 1.6). The *People's Choice* studies in the 1940s led to the two-step theory of opinion formation and to Bernard Berelson's conclusion that "the less informed people are on an issue, the more susceptible they are to opinion conversion through the influence of the communication media.[23] Todd Gitlin's study about the impact on public opinion of television coverage of the Vietnam War and the antiwar movement during the late 1960s–early 1970s raised a good deal of consciousness and questions about the importance of this medium in opinion formation.[24] Some social scientists now argue that with the advent of television and its enormous impact on the political environment, the Erie County study has been reduced to

---

BOX 1.6   The People's Choice

In 1940, while television was only in an experimental stage, Paul Lazarsfeld, Bernard Berelson, and Hazel Gaudet undertook a study of opinion formation in Erie County, Ohio.[1] Erie was deemed a typical American community because it had voted as the nation had in every previous presidential election since the turn of the century. Many stimulus-response studies (such as the Pavlovian conditioning of animal behavior) had been conducted in the past. What was new in the Erie study was that the research was tied to an election campaign. Today there are many more influences (stimuli) on public opinion. Yet what remains relevant to us in this complex media environment is the way in which the individual's latent predispositions were activated.

Pre-TV stimulus material was print and radio coverage. The research design called for a panel study that consisted of a random sample of 600 residents. They were interviewed privately, in their homes, each month for several months so that the researchers could study the effects of the stimulus material, as follows:

1. *Obvious effects*   Researchers considered obvious effects to be participation in the campaign by seeking information on the candidates and the issues; formulating opinions and decisions on how to vote; and actually voting on election day.

2. *Less obvious effects*   The researchers found that a process of crystallization of opinion occurred among those respondents with latent predisposition to vote for a particular candidate. In other words, at some point during the campaign their opinions formed and they were activated, motivated to vote. It was also learned that respondents who were early decision makers (reminding us of the Feinstein poll discussed earlier) unwittingly reinforced their decisions by continuously selecting partisan material from the media. Social category memberships, such as socioeconomic status, residence, education, age, and sex, were key variables that determined interests and whether or not early or late decisions were made.

3. *Unanticipated effects*   Informal social relations and primary group ties played a far greater role in the formation of public opinion than did the media. Respondents more frequently mentioned political discussions among friends and acquaintances than exposure to print and radio when they were asked to report on any sort of campaign-related communications.

When the researchers became aware of this factor of interpersonal communication as an opinion-forming variable, they were about halfway through their study. In the remaining interviews, they learned that there was actually a two-step process: Many respondents obtained most of their campaign information

Continued

BOX 1.6   Continued

Figure 1.1

from others who had gotten it first-hand from the media.

Called *the two-step flow* (Figure 1.1), this pretelevision, opinion-formation theory can be described as follows: The mass media (then meaning radio and the print media) collect/interpret/disseminate information. Then opinion leaders act as conduits for the media-generated information; they filter out undesirable data, select what to pass on, supply their own interpretations, use their personal influence, and activate individuals to examine the issues and to vote. Individuals, with less exposure to the media, depend on others for their information. If their source of information appears informed and trustworthy (and there is more or less a congruence of values), the source is perceived as and becomes an opinion leader.[2]

If we consider this two-step theory of indirect mass media influence to now encompass television, cable, computers, electronic mail, and other new technologies, does the theory remain relevant to explain how public opinion is formed? Have these technologies, with their multiplicity of channels to disseminate information, taken over the role of the opinion leaders by directly reaching individuals? Or, consistent with the theory, have the opinion leaders

retained their traditional role of information processors, and has that role actually been enhanced?

I would argue that with the increase in audience fragmentation and with the decrease in the amount of newspaper and other reading individuals do, the opinion leaders have become increasingly important conduits. They have the difficult task of accessing information from diverse sources, analyzing the bits and pieces, formulating cogent arguments, and conveying their opinions. For me and for many others, the two-step theory still seems clearly relevant when we talk about interpersonal communication, between the opinion leader and the individual. However, there remains the nagging question of what happens when an opinion leader appears on a popular television program. Who gets credit for influencing your opinion—the television medium, the network or station that carried the program, the program's producer (gatekeeper), the sponsor for supporting the program, the guest personality, or you for not changing the channel?

So what do you think? Is the two-step theory merely a historical footnote as some claim? When you consider the massive technological changes since the theory's publica-

---

BOX 1.6   Continued

tion, how would you design a more relevant, up-to-date flowchart to describe the formation of public opinion?[3]

---

1. Paul F. Lazarsfeld, Bernard Berelson, and Hazel Gaudet, *The People's Choice* (New York: Duell, Sloan & Pearce, 1944).
2. Also see Bernard Berelson, "Communications and Public Opinions," in *Mass Communications,* Wilbur Schramm, ed.

(Urbana: University of Illinois Press, 1949); Berelson et al., *Voting* (Chicago: University of Chicago Press, 1954); Elihu Katz, "The Two-Step Flow of Communication: An Up-to-Date Report on an Hypothesis," *Public Opinion Quarterly* (Spring 1957), pp. 61–78.
3. For a reformulation of this theory, see J. Robinson, "Interpersonal Influence in Election Campaigns: Two-Step Flow Hypotheses," *Public Opinion Quarterly* (1976), Vol. 40, pp. 315–25.

---

an interesting historical footnote left over from a pretelevision era when opinion researchers were merely concerned about the degree of influence attributable to radio and the print media.

Many theorists, building on the work of Lazarsfeld, Berelson, and others, began to focus on the *attentive public,* the group that consists of the opinion leaders. In 1950, after the takeover of eastern Europe by the Soviet Union and early in the era known as the Cold War, Gabriel A. Almond[25] studied foreign-affairs awareness levels in the United States. He created a four-category hierarchy:

1. Elected/appointed leaders and policymakers
2. Policy and opinion elites
3. The attentive public
4. The general public

According to Almond's theory of the attentive public, it appears to be educated, with a good income, and interested in and knowledgeable about foreign policy. On the political relevance of the attentive public, V. O. Key wrote:

> Obviously the highly attentive public, as they monitor the actions
> of government and let their judgments be known, play a critical
> role in assuring a degree of responsiveness of government to non-
> governmental opinion.[26]

In other words, consistent with Tarde's explanation, publics that have informed opinions become attentive publics, able to have an impact on government decision making. In the decades since Almond wrote about the attentive public, the omnipresent electronic media have played a powerful role in the diffusion of information. Today, this is so true that, other than those on the lowest rungs of the socioeconomic ladder, *one remains uninformed mostly by choice*—consciously or subconsciously. That is, people may decide *not* to read newspaper articles covering the goings-on in Washington or elsewhere, or to watch the news or discussion programs on television. Instead they may watch a sitcom, rent a video, or read the sports pages. It is also true, I believe, that even people who are reasonably well-off economically may feel powerless to affect the course of events, and this perception may cause them to pursue other, more satisfying interests. The point is that they set aside the choice of being an attentive citizen.

Besides the media and the opinion leaders/attentive public, there are other institutions that contribute to the formation and the relevance of public opinion.

The Family   One such institution is the family, including its socioeconomic, political, and religious values and affiliations. Karl Marx, writing during the mid-nineteenth century about the era of industrialization, discussed a society in which there was an absence of upward social and economic mobility for the uneducated working class. Simply put, the members of the proletariat (the propertyless, powerless masses) were going no place. He also wrote about *economic determinism* as a major factor in the formation of our beliefs and values. He argued that our economic perspective begins at home. If we were born into a poor or low-income home where unemployment has been a recurring or continuing experience and where there is scant opportunity for upward mobility, we would presumably be more sympathetic to those politicians who advocate federal training and work programs. By the same token, the theory holds that those born into affluence, the bourgeoisie—those who own the means of production—have little tolerance for the homeless, the poor, the unemployed. They are exploiters of the working class and, unless forced to undertake and to contribute to social reforms, they will do nothing, except try to ensure their own continued prosperity.

For example, in the film *Roger and Me*, Michael Moore interviews four well-to-do women who are playing golf at their country club. They are asked their opinion about the loss of approximately 30,000 jobs, the result of General Motors President Roger Smith's decision to close auto plants in Flint, Michigan. The GM plan was to build new plants in Mexico and elsewhere in Third World countries, where non-union workers would accept extremely low salaries (under a dollar an hour). Although we know nothing of their origins, the women's appearance of affluence and indifference may lead us to conclude that they have little or no experience with poverty. Completely indifferent to the human suffering caused by loss of work, foreclosures, evictions, and so on, the women's response is, "There are lots of other opportunities if people really want to work."

Some argue that the theory of economic determinism is flawed when applied to a society that provides real opportunities for advancement and upward mobility. There are, of course, many examples of individuals who have managed to achieve financial success *despite* their economically deprived upbringing; some of them will retain memories of their years of deprivation and contribute time and money to help those who are less fortunate. There are also many examples of individuals who have escaped poverty, achieved financial independence and social acceptance, and become conservative and resentful of being taxed to pay for government-funded programs for the disadvantaged. A case in point is the conservatism of Justice Clarence Thomas, mentioned earlier. Thomas is typical of those who espouse the philosophy: "I did it by myself, by dint of hard work; you can too if you really want to." And there are those children of wealth and privilege who assume the philosophy of *noblesse oblige*, behaving generously toward others of lower socioeconomic status.

While many of us are influenced by our parents' political values, at some point our interests may diverge. We may then decide to align ourselves with an opposing political ideology. During the late 1980s there was a popular television series called "Family Ties" in which the character Alex clearly rejected the values of his parents, two flower children who matured in the 1960s and were part of the peace movement. Alex, a conservative Republican, was majoring in business and economics, admired the ideology of then President Ronald Reagan, and rejected his parents' support for all liberal causes: pro-choice, assistance to the homeless, daycare for children of working mothers, a national health program, and so on. For those of us who know a real-life Alex and the ideological differences between such a person and his or her parents, it is important to understand the many forces that shape one's frame of reference.★

Among those outside influences that have shaped our value systems and opinions, Michael Parenti argues, are the films and television programs that

---

★Recalling the flap in the spring of 1992, when Vice President Dan Quayle denounced "Murphy Brown" (Candice Bergen's TV character) for having a child out of wedlock and for appearing to legitimize what he saw as the decline of family values in the United States, I realize some may say that it is a poor practice to use a television show as an example. Perhaps, then, you might think about whether your own friends and acquaintances have accepted their parents' value systems.

propagated "images and ideologies ... supportive of imperialism, phobic anticommunism, capitalism, racism, sexism, militarism, authoritarian violence, vigilantism, and anti-working-class attitudes." He cites the following economic-based values among those we can and do acquire from our media:[27]

- Individual effort is preferable to collective action.

- Free enterprise is the best economic system in the world.

- Private monetary gain is a central and worthy objective of life.

- Affluent professionals are more interesting than blue-collar or ordinary service workers.

- All Americans are equal, but some (the underprivileged) must prove themselves worthy of equality.

- The ills of society are caused by individual malefactors and not by anything in the socioeconomic system.

- U.S. military force is directed only toward laudable goals, although individuals in the military may sometimes abuse their power.

As for opinions based on religious teachings in the home, here too there are many intervening variables. For example, some people's opposition to abortion may be predetermined by their religious convictions; for others, who also consider themselves religious, their right-to-choice stance may be the result of exposure to and tolerance of different value systems. Although the latter group may experience cognitive dissonance (the uncomfortable feeling of holding apparently conflicting beliefs), they have come to accept different behavior patterns from others. In certain instances, outside influences—such as friends, school, professional colleagues, or various life experiences—may lead some to convert to another religion and others to become more or less religious than their parents. You may have met individuals from extremely religious homes who have rejected their parents' teachings and chosen to lead secular lives, and you may know others from nonreligious homes who pursue a lifestyle dominated by newly inspired religious beliefs. Thus, as we mature and confront different experiences, we may carry with us the same beliefs our parents held or we may radically diverge from our parents' views.

Religious Institutions   While the establishment clause of the First Amendment forbids an institutionalized state religion, it does not prohibit religious institutions from attempting to exercise their influence through legitimate means. Religious groups do organize for political purposes, lobby politicians, and use their resources to influence public opinion. Witness Cardinal John O'Connor's spring 1990 speech threatening pro-choice advocates with excommunication. The New York cardinal also ordered an expensive anti-abortion advertising campaign. During the 1992 presidential campaign, conservative Republicans tried to make abortion an issue. The result was that many moderate Republicans who were pro-choice defected to the Democratic party. Have these attempts changed people's minds on the abortion issue? What do you think?

Consider, too, the example of New York's late Rabbi Menachem Schneerson, spiritual leader of a small sect of orthodox Jews in the United States and in Israel. Dissatisfied with a particular proposal by the Israeli government in the late 1980s, the rabbi (from his home in New York) told his followers in Israel to withdraw their support for the Israeli government. Critics said that when the rabbi "blinked" in America, the proposed fragile coalition government in Israel disintegrated. Because of the multiparty system in Israel, a tiny party—representing barely 2 percent of the population—can make the difference in determining which party can put together a coalition and thereby control the government. Although his following is small in Israel and minute in the United States, Schneerson was and is an opinion leader for those who adher to his beliefs.

That prominent religious leaders are recognized as opinion leaders cannot be denied. Among the deeply committed, their word may well be the most important determinant. Consider the power of Iran's late Ayatollah Khomeini, whose condemnation and call for assassination of British author Salman Rushdie★ has not been retracted, despite the author's pathetic attempt to recant and the death of Khomeini. The point is that although for some people religion is merely one variable to be considered in the formation of public opinion, for others it is the guiding principle for their personal beliefs.

The Educational System   This includes schools, teachers, books selected, programs, guidance, and so on. Here, too, we can acknowledge the role played by the educational system in our socialization and in the formation of many of our opinions. At least in part, we acquire our societal norms

---

★See Salman Rushdie's *The Satanic Verses* (New York: Viking Penguin, 1989). Rushdie was condemned to die because his book was considered an insult to Islam. Four years after the publication of his book, he was still in hiding, surfacing briefly for some interviews and a speech denouncing censorship. From time to time Rushdie has appealed to world leaders to use whatever influence they may have to prevail upon the Iranians to rescind the order. On September 18, 1993, the BBC reported that the British and Iranian governments, although anxious to normalize relations, were thus far unable to resolve the issue of the *Fatwa*, Khomeini's death order. In the meantime, Rushdie continues to live in fear.

and values (such as being law-abiding, cooperative, sharing, respectful, tolerant, participating citizens) from our educational experiences. Advocates and supporters of particular positions therefore lobby hard for their beliefs to be included in the curriculum and in other aspects of university life. Think about the ongoing debate on college campuses relating to demands for the institution of courses that are more representative of the American mosaic. The language of the debate includes such terms as *multiculturalism* and *PC*, referring to the political correctness of our speech. PC calls for increased racial and ethnic awareness and sensitivity.

G. B. Trudeau used his Doonesbury cartoon to convey his frustration with those who wish to use the university to further their position in the debate. In one of his cartoon strips, Trudeau shows the black student adviser, Campbell, talking to a white university administrator. The dialogue goes like this:

> Campbell: I just met with the African-American Student Council, Sir...
>
> Administrator: Great. A new separatist demand, right?
>
> Campbell: Well...
>
> Administrator: I don't get it, Campbell. The black students now have separate dorms, fraternities, cafeteria tables, student center, studies program and graduation. After 25 years of intensive progressive action in pursuit of racial justice at this college, we've managed to produce a fully segregated campus. [Sigh...] What a legacy I've created... and to think I marched with Dr. King in Selma... So what is it now?
>
> Campbell: Um... The kids want their own water fountains.[28]

While advocates for further change struggle on, there now appears to be a growing backlash, particularly among those born after the great struggle for civil rights. Lacking a reference point based on knowledge and understanding of what happened—and feeling resentful over affirmative action, multicultural programs, and what Trudeau called separatist demands—those opposed to PC look on it as a curtailment of their freedom to express themselves and as an imposition of censorship. Hence, educators who advocate PC are accused of using their schools and universities as political platforms to influence opinion.

However, while noting the influence of educational institutions, we must again consider the existence of intervening variables. In other words, as we go through life, things happen that may cause us to reevaluate our education, along with the beliefs and values we may have acquired from particular

Table 1.2 Voting Trends

	1960	1964	1968	1972	1976	1980	1984	1988	1992
Percent voter turnout	63	62	61	55	54	53	53	50	55

SOURCE: Adapted from information in Robert Pear's "The Turnout," *The New York Times*, Nov. 5, 1992, p. B4.

teachers or professors. I should also note that there is an enormous body of research that shows that our level of acquired information is linked to our level of education. Key points out, for example, that "on questions of foreign policy the disinclination to express an opinion is especially marked among persons with only grade-school education."[29] It also appears that the more knowledgeable we are, the greater our inclination to express opinions on all sorts of topics. Sadly, too many of us are not as well informed about the issues confronting our country as we should be, and this inattentiveness has manifested itself in nonparticipation in our political system. However, I am hopeful that, as can be seen from Table 1.2, the 1992 voting rate of 55 percent has finally begun to reverse a 30-year decline.

I believe it is important that we not undervalue the power and impact of our opinions and that we not take for granted our right to vote. Whenever we are bombarded with 30-second political spots on television, we should remind ourselves that our opinions and our votes are valuable. If they weren't, why would anyone expend so much effort and expense to influence us? We should also remember that it is a recent phenomenon, and still not universal, that the public's voice or opinion is deemed worthy of consideration by those who govern.

CHAPTER REVIEW

- From ancient times through the Middle Ages, the ruling elites generally paid little heed to public opinion. Since they believed they ruled by divine right, there was little need to consult the masses. Increased literacy and the Age of Enlightenment led to new thinking, a greater sense of awareness, and a sense of the power of ordinary people. Although the industrial revolution unleashed a spirit of individualism and entrepreneurialism, not everyone was sanguine about people's ability to act rationally.

- Toward the end of the nineteenth century, demophobia was characteristic of the thinking of many sociologists and psychologists. Some viewed public opinion as merely the product of mass hysteria, and some differentiated between an informed public and an ignorant aggregate capable of irrational and dangerous acts.

■ Others, such as Auguste Comte, were less negative and saw humankind as capable of attaining reason. While Lord James Bryce, a British jurist and ambassador to the United States, did not generally hold public opinion in high esteem, he did admire the average American voter and our democratic system, which encouraged full citizen participation.

■ Despite the difficulty of defining public opinion, researchers do agree that it is out there and that there is a market for information about it. There is a consensus that opinion, when made public, can be scientifically measured and used to understand and predict certain types of behavior.

■ V. O. Key's descriptive analysis of the characteristics, qualities, and properties of public opinion adds to our understanding. We discussed opinion distribution, intensity, stability and fluidity, latency and salience, and the way in which we form our opinions and our belief systems.

■ It has become increasingly difficult to pigeonhole people because political lines have blurred and what was once the dominant social paradigm is now in transition. A number of new belief systems at home and abroad are in the process of evolving.

■ Although the media play a role in affecting public opinion, we are uncertain as to the impact. We discussed the media as power broker versus the media as a reflector of political events.

■ While *The People's Choice* (1944), by Lazarsfeld, Berelson, and Gaudet, indicated that public opinion leaders had greater influence than the media on public opinion, the subsequent research of Todd Gitlin and others, particularly on the impact of television, disputed this point.

■ Acknowledging that many questions remain, other researchers point to the increased audience fragmentation resulting from the plethora of diverse new technologies. These researchers focus on the enhanced information-processing role of the opinion leader and continue to see the relevance of the two-step theory.

■ David Fan's computerized study also suggests that the news portion of the print media seems to "mold opinion in a predictable manner."

■ Fan's computerized system of content analysis exemplifies another method that can be used to study the impact of newspaper coverage on public opinion. However, despite the existence of this and a variety of other research tools, public opinion researchers have found that polling through the use of a random probability sample is the most cost effective and the most accurate.

- There are many variables that affect our world view, our frame of reference, and that determine whether we evolve into active or passive citizens. Family values, economics, religious and educational institutions all play a role in shaping our opinions.

- The attentive public in a democracy, according to Gabriel Almond, performs important functions. It monitors government actions, expresses opinions, and ensures some degree of government responsiveness. However, in recent years, Americans have been participating less and less in their political system, while complaining more and more about the lack of government responsiveness.

NOTES

1. Catherine Marsh, *The Survey Method: The Contribution of Surveys to Sociological Explanation* (London: Allen & Unwin, 1982), pp. 125–135.

2. Robert M. Entman, *Democracy Without Citizens: Media and the Decay of American Politics* (New York: Oxford University Press, 1989), Chapter 4.

3. Entman, p. 31.

4. Entman, p. 79.

5. Kurt Lang and Gladys Engel Lang, "The Impact of Polls on Public Opinion," *The Annals of the American Academy* (March 1984), pp. 129–142.

6. Entman, pp. 46–47.

7. Walter Lippmann, *The Phantom Public* (New York: Harcourt, Brace, 1925), p. 39.

8. William Ebenstein, *Great Political Thinkers*, 4th ed. (New York: Holt, Rinehart & Winston, 1969), p. 242.

9. Ebenstein, p. 304.

10. Francis Graham Wilson, *A Theory of Public Opinion* (Chicago: Henry Regnery, 1962), pp. 126–127.

11. Gabriel Tarde, *The Laws of Imitation*, E. C. Parsons, trans. (New York: Henry Holt, 1903).

12. Wilson, p. 126.

13. *The American Commonwealth*, Vol. II (New York: Macmillan, 1916 ed.), pp. 251–266.

14. V. O. Key, Jr., *Public Opinion and American Democracy* (New York: Knopf, 1967).

15. Lester W. Milbrath, "The Context of Public Opinion: How Our Belief Systems Can Affect Poll Results," *Annals*, AAPSS, 472 (March 1984), pp. 35–49.

16. Milbrath.

17. Jeffrey Schmalz, "Clinton Carves Wide and Deep Path Through Heart of Reagan Country," *The New York Times*, Nov. 4, 1992, pp. B1, B4. Also see R. W. Apple, Jr., "The Economy's Casualty" on p. A1, reporting on a *New York Times*/CBS News Poll to the effect that three-quarters of the American people disapproved of the way Bush was handling the economy.

18. See Entman's *Democracy Without Citizens* for some interesting discussions on the failure of our press to provide us with the information we need to make intelligent choices and to understand the issues that confront us.

19. G. Cleveland Wilhoit and Kenneth S. Sherrill, "Wire Service Visibility of U.S. Senators," *Journalism Quarterly* (1968), 45, pp. 42–48.

20. Entman, pp. 144–157.

21. Entman identifies the following biases: (1) evaluation biases, dealing with the perceived popularity and power of the individual; (2) production biases, dealing with media requirements for simplicity, personalization, and symbolism; (3) event context, dealing with the timing of the event in relation to other important and concurrent events; and (4) skill in news management on the part of the individual. See pp. 69–70.

22. *Research Methods in Mass Communication*, 2nd ed., Guido H. Stempel III and Bruce H. Westley, eds. (Englewood Cliffs, NJ: Prentice-Hall, 1989), Chapter 7, "Content Analysis," and Chapter 8, ``Statistical Designs for Content Analysis," both by Stempel.

23. Bernard Berelson, "Communications and Public Opinions," in *Mass Communications,* Wilbur Schramm, ed. (Urbana: University of Illinois Press, 1949), p. 502.

24. Todd Gitlin, *The Whole World Is Watching: Mass Media in the Making and Unmaking of the New Left* (Berkeley: University of California Press, 1980). Also see Daniel Hallin's *The Uncensored War: Vietnam and the News Media*, a book by Gitlin's dissertation advisee.

25. Gabriel A. Almond, *The American People and Foreign Policy* (New York: Praeger, 1960 ed.), p. 137.

26. Key, p. 546.

27. Michael Parenti, *Make-Believe Media: The Politics of Entertainment* (New York: St. Martin's Press, 1992), pp. 2–3.

28. Trudeau's syndicated cartoon appeared in the comics section of New Jersey's *Sunday Record*, Sept. 12, 1993. DOONESBURY copyright 1993 G. B. Trudeau. Dist. by Universal Press Syndicate. All rights reserved.

29. Key, p. 333.

2

The History of Surveys

Think about—

Why do we bother to study the history of surveys?

What were the earliest methods used by politicians to predict an election outcome?

When was exit polling introduced?

What was the origin of clustering and what purpose(s) does it serve?

What purposes did the earliest straw polls serve?

Why were straw polls considered unscientific?

What went wrong with the *Literary Digest* sample size of 10 million voters? Wasn't it big enough?

What went wrong with the 1948 polls? (Hint: Why do you think the pollsters kept polling nearly up to the last minute of the 1992 presidential campaign?)

What are the problems with quota sampling?

What is the purpose of a filtering question?

The purpose of this chapter is to introduce some of today's polling terminology, outlined in the Think About questions. I believe that we can learn some valuable lessons by examining the attempts and mistakes of earlier researchers who have tried to describe, explain, predict, and represent public opinion on the important issues of the day. You will find that while many aspects of modern polling techniques are not so modern, we are definitely getting better at polling all the time.

The history of government-initiated surveys for various purposes is centuries old. The gathering of demographic information dates back to biblical times. In the books of Exodus and Samuel, we find mention of census surveys (c. 1500 B.C.) and of public concern with the collection of such data for purposes of levying taxes and raising an army. Genealogical records were also maintained by scribes. In ancient Egypt, China, Greece, and Rome, government envoys were sent to remote provinces to collect crop and population data. For example, the Spring and Autumn Annals in China provided the emperor with such information. And, as part of the Athenian democratic reforms of Solon (c. 590 B.C.), every citizen had to reveal the amount and source of money amassed during the year. Solon's intention was to see that taxes were levied fairly on those who could pay (today this is called progressive taxation).

At the height of Roman power, during the Punic Wars (third century B.C. to the end of the second century A.D.), a census was taken in Rome every five years to discover every citizen's worth. Incidentally, the censor—Cato, for example—was not only in charge of the census, but also of morals. He was empowered to cross off the senatorial list anyone he considered of questionable morals (an early form of McCarthyism!★).

A huge survey of all his lands was ordered by William the Conqueror as a result of the Norman Conquest of 1066. Completed in 1086, it was called the *Domesday Book*. Its primary purpose was to ascertain and record the king's "fiscal rights" (to assess, levy, and collect tax revenue).[1] In this and in all other early surveys, the citizens were passive: They and their worth were being counted merely to benefit the rulers, and no one asked their opinion on anything.

NEW LAND, NEW THINKING

From ancient times through the Middle Ages, little attention was paid to the utility of public opinion. Increased literacy and the Age of Enlightenment, however, led to new thinking, a greater sense of awareness, and a sense of the power of ordinary people. Although Europe's industrial revolution unleashed a new spirit of individualism and entrepreneurialism, not everyone was sanguine about people's ability to act rationally. While Europeans studied and debated the meaning, value, and utility of public opinion, thinking on the subject took a more positive turn in the United States. Despite British colonial rule, which included licensing restraints, taxation of the press (often called "taxes on knowledge"), and various forms of censorship, the colonists recognized the importance of information and several attempts were made to publish unauthorized newspapers.

In September 1690, Benjamin Harris attempted an unlicensed paper—*Publick Occurrences, Both Forreign and Domestick*—and his first issue was his last. In 1723, Benjamin Franklin's older brother James provoked the wrath of the colonial government with his *New England Courant* and was forbidden to

---

★During the Cold War years of the 1950s, Wisconsin Senator Joseph McCarthy cast a huge net in search of individuals and groups suspected of communist affiliation or sympathy. The result of his intensive investigations was that the lives of many innocent people were ruined. People in the media, the theater, the arts, the sciences, politics, in all walks of life were guilty by suspicion, fired from their jobs, blacklisted, and unable to find work.

publish the newspaper "or any other pamphlet or paper of the like nature, except it first be supervised by the secretary of this Province."[2] These and other incidents illustrate the Crown's attempts both in the colonies and at home to control public opinion. I believe they also illustrate the fear of colonial public opinion and of the power of the colonial press to inform and influence it. Samuel Adams clearly understood the power of communication and the need to influence and activate public opinion. He organized Committees of Correspondence, linking the colonies into a network that approximated a press association. By 1772, a communications network was in place from Boston to Savannah. It became an indispensable tool in unifying public opinion against British rule. And, once the Revolution was over and our first form of government under the Articles of Confederation proved a failure, the Founding Fathers used the press to influence public opinion (through publication of the *Federalist Papers*) to accept a constitution that would establish a "more perfect union."

THE EARLIEST POLLS

One of the earliest polls, according to researcher Richard Jensen, was conducted in 1787 when John Hancock won the gubernatorial race in Massachusetts against the incumbent Governor James Bowdoin. A Boston supporter decided to find out why his candidate, Bowdoin, had lost. The post-election poll by an "impartial Observer" showed Bowdoin's strongest support came from "Merchants and traders," "Tradesmen," "Physicians," "Lawyers," and "Independent gentlemen," while Hancock's supporters were mostly "Labourers, servants, and so on," with the "Tradesmen" vote split.

Reacting to this, a Hancock supporter, regretting the "very great error in the arrangement of the votes," announced his own poll three days later, revealing the "authentic breakdown" of the vote. This poll showed Hancock's support coming from four groups, the latter two being broad enough and prestigious enough to include all those who really counted for something: "Merchants, tradesmen, and other worthy members of society" and "friends to the revolution." Bowdoin's base of support, on the other hand, included the worthless and near-worthless in society: "Speculators in public securities," "Stockholders and directors of the Massachusetts Bank," "Usurers," "Persons under British influence," and one person in the category "Wizards."[3]

The Alien and Sedition Laws of 1798, which were intended to silence the dissident press reacting to the policies of the Adams administration, backfired. The result was a greater political awareness on the part of the electorate, which defeated Adams and turned the presidency over to Thomas Jefferson in 1800. For Federalist supporter Fisher Ames of Massachusetts, the Adams defeat signaled the need to reconsider the party's approach: "We must court popular favor, we must study public opinion, and accommodate measures to what it is and still more to what it ought to be, for that last will remain and uphold us."[4] Ames was merely proposing to do what every modern-day politician does: "study public opinion." (And "accommodate measures to what it is" sounds to me like the beginning of the let's-camouflage-our-differences philosophy of today's **spin doctors**—the political pollsters and media consultants hired by contemporary politicians.)

In New England in the early 1800s, canvassing soon became a regular occurrence as candidates tried to identify and list their supporters. These were not opinion surveys as we know them today because they did not question the respondent's attitude toward particular issues. He was merely asked about his voting intentions. (Women, you will recall, were enfranchised—granted voting rights—only in 1920.) Although the framers of the Constitution were well schooled in classical philosophy and believed in a system of participatory democracy, they differed as to just how much participation should be entrusted to the less-educated masses. Witness the lack of female and black suffrage, the electoral college, and the indirect election of senators by the state legislatures, as well as the various state requirements (including property taxes) to vote.

THE FIRST STRAWS

In the presidential campaign of 1800, 11 of the 16 state legislatures selected their electors (members of the electoral college). The remaining five states chose theirs by popular vote. However, in 1824, 18 of the 24 states chose electors by popular vote. This was, therefore, the country's first contested presidential election primarily determined by popular vote. Tom Smith, of the National Opinion Research Center at the University of Chicago, analyzed the origins of election polls and discussed the changes that took place in our political system after the national unity government of President George Washington disintegrated:

> Starting with Jefferson's victory over Adams in 1800, the Virginia
> Dynasty of Jefferson-Madison-Monroe won the next six presidential
> contests. By 1820, the Federalist party had ceased to be a con-
> tending national political power and Monroe [of the Democratic-
> Republican Party] was reelected without Federalist opposition.[5]

Monroe's second term initiated the so-called Era of Good Feeling, a designation that masks the intraparty feuding that ensued. A number of presidential candidates emerged, all running as Democratic-Republicans: General Andrew Jackson (Tennessee), Secretary of State John Quincy Adams (Massachusetts), Speaker of the House Henry Clay (Kentucky), and Secretary of the Treasury William Harris Crawford (Georgia). Around the same time, many people began to criticize the congressional party caucus that had always selected the Democratic-Republican presidential candidate. This process, unintended by the framers of the Constitution,[6] was now seen as undemocratic and elitist.

The existence of all these candidates from the same party—in the absence of an opposing political party and an acceptable nominating process—created a confusing situation. This resulted in the importance of endorsements by various state legislative caucuses, statewide conventions, county-level conventions, ad hoc groups of citizens, political rallies, political leaders, newspapers—all anxious to influence public opinion and to have a say in the nominating process. The summer and fall straw polls of 1824 evolved out of all this activity.

These "proto-straw polls" emerged from counts at various meetings, such as militia musters, grand juries, tax gatherings, Fourth of July celebrations (including the number of toasts made for the various candidates), and from poll books left in taverns and other public places for people to record their preferences.[7] The results, based on unscientific methodology, were published by newspapers, which often updated their running tallies. In addition, various newspapers sent reporters to inquire among the citizens as to their choice for president.

How accurate and honest were these polls? First of all, they bore no relation to the science of statistics or to probability theory because of the biased, haphazard nature and unrepresentativeness of their sample and because they often included people who were not even eligible to vote. Also, it seems that the counts were often rigged and that there were elements of coercion.★ Albert Ray Newsome reported the remarks of a supporter of Treasury Secretary William Harris Crawford:

> In almost every Captain's company the drums were beating and fifes whistling for the hero of New Orleans. The officers would

---

★As a visiting professor in Guayaquil, Ecuador, during the summer of 1992, I noted a similar phenomenon occurring in the presidential campaign then under way. Whenever a rally was arranged by any of the runoff candidates, the attendance was massive. It was explained to me that Ecuador's poor always came in huge numbers to all rallies because of the free refreshments, T-shirts, and entertainment. This deceptive turnout during the campaign tended to confuse those who equated attendance and the crowd's enthusiasm with support.

treat their men, make them drunk, and then raise the war whoop for General Jackson. Then the poor, staggering, drunken, and deluded creatures would sally forth for the place pointed for them to vote. The result was always in favor of Jackson. I have conversed with some of them afterwards who told me they did not intend to vote that way at the proper election, they voted so just to please their officers.[8]

Although Crawford had secured the nomination from the rump congressional caucus (a small group of congressmen, acting on their own in February 1824), it was General Jackson who won a plurality of the popular and electoral votes (99) in the presidential election. Henry Clay, with only 37 electoral votes, was eliminated as a factor. However, since Jackson did not obtain the required electoral college majority, it was left to the House of Representatives to choose from among the top three winners: Jackson, Adams, and Crawford (99, 84, and 41 electoral votes, respectively). The House selected Adams as president, despite the fact that he was the runner-up!

Putting aside the actions of the House in selecting Adams, how well did these straw polls do in predicting the election returns? According to Tom Smith, quite well. He explains:

In North Carolina the straw polls showed Crawford running far behind Jackson, and the anti-Crawford People's slate of electors won handily and cast their votes for Jackson. Similarly, scattered returns from South Carolina showed Jackson in the lead, and he carried that state. Likewise, a few returns from New England showed Adams in the lead, and he swept his home region in the election.[9]

In the 1840s, some newspapers tried to sample the local population in an attempt to predict election outcomes. Although straw polling of sorts continued, this method of prediction would not be taken seriously until the late 1890s.

GROWING INTEREST
IN SURVEY RESEARCH

In 1850, census director J. D. B. DeBow sampled 23 counties, cross-tabulating data on marriage, schooling, and income in order to discern societal patterns. Influenced by Edward Jarvis, an American physician, DeBow introduced standardized interview schedules, a concept then being developed by the London Statistical Society, where professional interviewers were being trained to conduct social surveys. The census of

1850 was not the first time that statistical data had been collected (see Box 2.1) for purposes other than levying taxes and raising an army, as discussed earlier.

Exit and Street Polls

Counting, listmaking, and canvassing of voters were commonplace in the latter half of the nineteenth century. Precinct leaders sounded out their neighbors in order to pass along to party bosses some sense of where their candidates stood.[10] These estimates often differed substantially from the actual votes cast. Claude E. Robinson would later call the difference—between the estimated tally and the actual vote tally—the **plurality error**.[11] In 1880, some 26,000 Civil War veterans were canvassed when Indiana Republican Senator Benjamin Harrison (elected president in 1888) became concerned over reports that they were leaving the party fold. Harrison was relieved to learn that 69 percent had remained loyal to the Republican party.[12]

In 1883, the editor of the *Boston Globe*, General Charles H. Taylor, developed an *exit polling system*, which was basically the same as that which we currently see on television every election night. Taylor sent reporters to selected election precincts.[13] The data they gathered enabled the next day's *Globe* to project the winner in an age when tallying was a long and arduous process. While the *Globe* initiated a new type of straw poll, the typical method for predicting voter preference in the last two decades of the nineteenth century remained political canvassing. Such efforts grew ever larger and more costly. The Democratic effort in 1892, for example, cost $2.5 million—a large sum even today. Pamphlets, personalized letters, advertising, 14,000 field workers and orators[14] were all part of the enormous task of reaching and influencing voters, in a successful bid to return the lackluster Grover Cleveland to the White House after a four-year hiatus.

Cleveland would be blamed for the Panic of 1893 and the depression that followed. Various state bureaus of labor statistics soon began to assess the impact of the economic downturn. In 1894, for example, the Michigan Bureau of Labor Statistics surveyed 5,600 farm laborers, questioning them about their hardships and their attitudes on immigration.[15] Thus the election of 1896 was one of the most acrimonious presidential campaigns in the history of the United States—even taking into account the George Bush–Michael Dukakis race of 1988.

With Ohioan William McKinley running against Nebraskan William Jennings Bryan, it looked to the Chicago press as though the primary battle

BOX 2.1 On Surveys and Statistics

Statistics was the name given to collections of data on matters of state importance. But it was during the age of mercantilism in the seventeenth and eighteenth centuries that merchants, bankers, and traders became interested in the collection of population data for their own purposes.

Then, too, there were those who were merely curious. L. John Martin describes the work of John Graunt, a London dry goods merchant, who undertook the first systematic analysis of birth and death records during the Great Plague of 1665. Graunt compared the data for London and for the rest of the country, noting the city's rapid recovery. William Petty, Graunt's friend, undertook a similar study of the Irish population in 1671–1676.

Sampling and probability theory were first described by a Swiss mathematician, Jacques (Jakob) Bernoulli (1654–1705). In a posthumous work (published in 1713, Basle), Bernoulli stated that a small, randomly selected population sample will prove to be representative (that is, have the same characteristics—in the same percentages) of the entire population from which the sample is drawn. The margin of error, he wrote, was small and calculable.[1] Incidentally, his nephew Daniel (1700–1782), also a professor of mathematics, spent several years teaching in St. Petersburg. Have you heard of the St. Petersburg coin toss game?[2] (Heads or tails, what are the odds?)

Toward the end of the eighteenth century, Sir John Sinclair— a Scottish landowner, member of Parliament, and first president of the Board of Agriculture—polled the Scottish clergy on matters relating to their parishes and congregants. Although he did not *sample* the clergy (attempting to include all the parishes), he is credited with having introduced three innovations to the field of data collection at that time:

1. *Questionnaire* He used a questionnaire with more than 120 questions, sending them to 881 parishes.
2. *Follow-up letters* He sent letters to those who neglected to respond.
3. *Follow-up interview* Those who failed to respond to the follow-up letter received a visit from one of Sinclair's envoys, sent to assist in the completion of the questionnaires.

Although Sinclair did not use a scientific sample, intending instead to survey the entire universe of the Scottish clergy, his idea was clever. He was using as informants the clergy (nongovernment officials), who do in fact interact with a wide cross-section of their community and who have ample opportunity to influence public opinion.

Jeremy Bentham, among others, paid tribute to the statistical quality of the study's 21 volumes, containing information on the natural history, population, and production of the country.[3] Martin notes that Sir John's *Statistical Account of Scotland* (1791–1799) "so impressed parliament that

Continued

BOX 2.1   Continued

it agreed to conduct the first British decennial census in 1801."[4]

After Napoleon was exiled to Elba (May 1814), the four great powers of the Quadruple Alliance (Russia, Austria, Prussia, and Great Britain) convened the Congress of Vienna to discuss the spoils of his empire. Britain's Viscount Castlereagh conceived of the idea of a "Statistical Committee" to ascertain the populations of the conquered territories. Although Talleyrand represented the defeated country and was clearly at a disadvantage, he brilliantly argued for French participation on this committee and thereby turned the Council of Four into the Council of Five. (How different this was from the post–World War I Versailles Treaty and the bad feelings it engendered among Germany's elites, leading to World War II.)

The Statistical Committee, appointed on December 24, 1814, worked rapidly and efficiently, providing complete population statistics on January 19, 1815. The quantitative "enumeration of souls," Talleyrand next argued, "bore no relation to the actual human value of the territories transferred," and "it was a mistake to assume that the inhabitants of the Rhineland were qualitatively equal to a similar number of Galician Poles." But the Prussians retorted, "Souls were souls." And thus, using the data gathered by the Statistical Committee, "purely quantitative standards for the 'transference of souls' became the yardstick which the Congress adopted."[5]

1. See the *International Encyclopedia of Social Sciences, Encyclopaedia Britannica*, and L. John Martin, "Genealogy of Public Opinion Polling," *The Annals of the American Academy* (March 1984), pp. 20–21.
2. Robert P. Abelson and Ariel Levi, "Decision Making and Decision Theory," *The Handbook of Social Psychology*, Vol. I (3rd ed.), Gardner Lindzey and Eliot Aronson, eds. (New York: Random House, 1985), pp. 244–245; also see the *Encyclopaedia Britannica*.
3. D. Caradog Jones, *Social Surveys* (London: Hutchinson's University Library, 1948), Chapter III, pp. 23–33.
4. Martin, pp. 15–16.
5. Harold Nicolson, *The Congress of Vienna, A Study in Allied Unity: 1812–1822* (New York: Viking, 1961), pp. 145–146.

would be fought in the midwestern states. While the *Chicago Tribune* sent reporters to canvass Illinois factory and railroad workers, the *Chicago Record* spent over $60,000 to send postcard ballots to the 328,000 registered Chicago voters and to 1 out of every 8 voters in 12 midwestern states. The attempted random sample of 12 states failed, but the *Record*'s finding that McKinley would take 57.94 percent of the Chicago vote was off by only .04 percentage points (see Box 2.2). The Republican National Committee, building on previous experience, spent $3.5 million[16] to canvass individual voters in an effort to defeat Bryan, the 36–year-old radical firebrand, nominee of the Democratic party. The result was a huge conserva-

---

BOX 2.2 Percentage Points

While social scientists generally deal in percents and not in percentage points, pollsters usually speak about their errors in terms of **percentage points** (meaning the number of points between what they predicted and the actual result). Thus a red light should go on whenever pollsters, using percentage points, talk about the differences between their prediction and the actual election outcome. Critics of polling consider such use of percentage points a way to cover the degree of inaccuracy in the results.

For example, Roper predicted Harry S Truman would get 37.1 percent as opposed to Thomas Dewey's predicted 52.2 percent of the votes in the four-candidate 1948 election. Roper was off by 12 percentage points in his attempt to accurately predict Truman's winning 49.5 percent. However, looked at more carefully, the 12 percentage points actually represented a difference of nearly one-fourth (25%) of Truman's vote (close to 50%).

This use of percentage points (12 points in this case), rather than percent (25% of Truman's total vote) raises an ethical question for the pollster who prefers to appear reasonably accurate. Simply put, *the use of percentage points understates the degree of error for those unschooled in the vagaries of statistics.*

---

tive voter turnout—what V. O. Key dubbed a "critical election"*—that sent McKinley to the White House, entrenching the Republicans until 1912.

By then, newspapers in 37 states were conducting surveys, such as the street-corner polls conducted by the New York *Herald*. Reporters interviewed 30,000 registered voters to ask their preferences in the presidential elections of 1904 and 1908. The *Herald* also formed a syndicate with the *St. Louis Republic*, the *Cincinnati Enquirer*, the *Chicago Record-Herald*, and others to conduct presidential polls in the northern states. In 1912, the *Boston Globe* and the *Los Angeles Times*, cooperating with the *Herald* group, undertook personal canvassing, interviewing people in their homes.[17]

---

*Key defined a critical election as (a) one caused by critical issues such as states' rights, slavery, and the proposed challenge to the sanctity of the Union (1860); economic panic, characterized by bank failures, railroad receiverships, unemployment, strikes, the debate over the gold standard (1896); and the Great Depression (1932); (b) one preceded by heightened awareness and increased political activity; and (c) one that results in a political realignment of the electorate, described by Key as "sharp and durable." See V. O. Key, Jr., *The Responsible Electorate* (Cambridge, MA: Belknap Press of Harvard University Press, 1966).

Booth's Classification System

By the turn of the century various forms of social surveys had become common both here and abroad. Charles Booth, one of the founders of the great Booth Steamship Company, labored for 15 years to create *Life and Labour*, a 17-volume research study (published in 1902) on London's working class and the plight of the aged poor. He devised a 38-section occupational classification system based on the employment characteristics of the heads of families. He also divided families into eight classes based on their apparent status and means as shown below.

Booth's Means Classification

H	Upper middle class
G	Lower middle class
F	Higher class labourers
E	Regular standard earnings

——— the line of poverty ———

D	Small regular earnings
C	Intermittent earnings
B	Casual earnings
A	Lowest class of occasional labourers

On class B, he wrote: "These people, *as a class* are shiftless, hand to mouth, pleasure loving and always poor; to work when they like, and play when they like, is their ideal." In a paper to the Statistical Society, Booth commented that they were "a constant burthen to the State," absorbing the charities of both rich and poor. Although he had no solution, his impressive study led to the British Pensions Act of 1908.[18] While Booth's classification scheme was unidimensional (focusing only on the employment characteristics of the heads of families), it may have inspired the complex, multidimensional (incorporating many variables) modern-day system of *cluster analysis* (see Box 2.3).

Studying the Working Class

When German sociologist Max Weber visited the United States in 1904, he was interested in studying the effects of American capitalism. On returning to Germany, he wrote about the informal surveys he had taken. On the condition of black Americans, Weber wrote: "I have talked to about one hundred white Southerners of all social classes and parties, and the problem of what shall become of these [black] people seems absolutely

BOX 2.3   The Clustering System

In 1974, Jonathan Robbin, a computer scientist, matched zip codes with census data and consumer surveys and used computers to sort our 36,000 zip codes into 40 "lifestyle clusters." His company, Claritas Corporation, based in Virginia, has serviced *Time*, General Motors, and American Express, among others, supplying them with databases of buyer behavior, media patterns, political orientation, and lifestyle habits. PRIZM (Potential Rating Index for Zip Markets), Robbin's computer program, has been widely imitated.

Michael J. Weiss, fascinated by the PRIZM capability, recognized that this was a "new way of looking at the nation—not as fifty states but rather forty neighborhood types." He used a computer to select communities that "mirrored the demographic profile of each neighborhood type," and set off to meet the people who lived in them. As he explains in *The Clustering of America*, the *Zone Improvement Plan* (your zip code) "has come to reveal more about you and your neighbors than any postal clerk ever thought possible." Among the community types he visited were the following:[1]

Claritas Cluster Type[2]	*Major Characteristics*
Blue Blood Estates	Home to 1 in 10 millionaires, the residents can afford whatever they want and they are predominantly conservative (in 1984, 72% were Reagan supporters).
Young Influentials	A yuppie inner-ring suburb, white singles and childless couples living in apartment and condo dwellings, they are called moderates politically (61% supported Reagan).
Gray Power	An upper-middle-class retirement community, politically conservative (73% supported Reagan).
Single City Blues	A downscale, multiunit urban area, racially mixed, which attracted lower-middle-class baby boomers who are politically moderate (50% voted for Vice President Mondale, as opposed to Reagan).
New Beginnings	A middle-class singles community that emerged in a former blue-collar family area, they are moderates politically (64% supported Reagan).
Black Enterprise	An upper-middle-class minority neighborhood populated by affluent blacks who are predominantly liberal (78% voted for Reagan's opponent, Vice President Mondale).
New Melting Pot	An immigrant community, populated by middle-class Asians and Latin Americans (one-third attended college), they are deemed politically moderate (64% voted for Reagan).

Continued

BOX 2.3 Continued

Coalburg & Corntown	A small midwestern town where the economic base is split between farming and light industry and where most residents are high-school-educated, earn under $35,000 a year, and are politically moderate (yet 65% voted for Reagan).
Mines & Mills	A lower-middle-class milltown, predominantly white, high-school-educated, blue-collar workers with a strong moral tradition and politically moderate views (although 75% supported Reagan).

1. See Michael J. Weiss, *The Clustering of America* (New York: Harper & Row, 1988).
2. Based on the Claritas Corporation's target marketing system of 40 clusters.

---

hopeless."[19] His study of the working class in the United States was followed by more comprehensive studies of labor and industrial psychology in Germany. He was active in establishing a sociological society and encouraged collective research enterprises, including the work of Adolf Levenstein, who sent out 8,000 questionnaires to laborers. Between 1907 and 1911, Levenstein collected data on their beliefs, hopes, and attitudes toward work, religion, and politics, even asking them about their drinking habits.[20] Weber reviewed Levenstein's data with him, explaining how to analyze it and encouraging him to publish his findings. Weber also encouraged the study of voluntary associations (including athletic leagues, religious sects, and political parties), and he proposed a methodical study of the press using questionnaires.[21]

At the time Max Weber and other social scientists were increasingly interested in assessing public opinion and the power of the press, earlier mathematical and statistical efforts in sampling and probability theory were coming to their attention through the efforts of the International Statistical Institute. For example, Professor Arthur L. Bowley, a British mathematician and economist, based his 1912 study of working-class conditions in Reading, England, on methodology he had learned while attending Institute conferences in Bern (1895) and Budapest (1901).[22] Constrained by money and time, he did what pollsters do today. He determined the number of interviews he could afford to conduct and then devised a method by which he would sample that number of households. More will be said about Bowley's methodology when we discuss sampling theory in Chapter 6.

In 1912, the United States Department of Agriculture undertook its first statistical surveys in our farming communities, and the *Farm Journal* became the first United States magazine to conduct polls. Concerned about countering the effect of enemy propaganda on public opinion during World War I, President Woodrow Wilson appointed journalist George Creel to head the Committee for Public Information. The Creel Commission, as it became known, undertook a domestic and foreign effort to influence public opinion. The government also employed psychologists to study the public's reaction and to create and administer intelligence and aptitude tests for our recruits. Social scientists were later able to apply their experience studying patterns of behavior and response to questionnaire development and other aspects of opinion research.

THE WORST STRAWS

Did you ever hear of the long-defunct *Pathfinder*, *Farm Journal*, or Rexall Drug Store presidential polls? Neither did I until I researched this text. They were about as scientific as the other straws blowing in the wind.

> Trying to use a straw poll to predict the outcome of an election is a little like tossing a handful of straw into the air to see which way the wind is blowing. If the wind is coming strongly and steadily from one direction, this method may work. But if there's a lull in the wind or a sudden gust from another direction, the straws won't tell you much of anything.[23]

In 1916, *Literary Digest*, a popular weekly magazine in the United States, began its soon-to-be-infamous series of straw polls. Based on a return of over 20,000 *Digest* ballots, the magazine correctly predicted Woodrow Wilson's election victory. It continued to successfully predict the election of Warren G. Harding (1920), Calvin Coolidge (1924), Herbert Hoover (1928), and Franklin D. Roosevelt (1932). How did the *Digest* editors do it? Their theory was simple: Ask a huge number of people how they are going to vote and your prediction will have to be right. Wrong! In fact, as we shall see, this methodology was too simple. Consider the following on how the *Digest* poll developed.

Before the party conventions were held in 1920, 11 million telephone owners received ballots asking for their presidential candidate preference, and then during the fall campaign, postcards were sent to voters in six states. In 1922, 8 million ballots were again sent to telephone owners to query them on their attitudes toward Prohibition. In 1924, using directories of

Table 2.1 *Digest* Ballot Results

PRESIDENTIAL ELECTION YEAR	AVERAGE STATE-PLURALITY ERROR	BALLOTS MAILED	BALLOTS RETURNED	
1916	20%	1 million+	20,000	(~2%)[1]
1920	21	11 million	—[2]	
1924	12	16.5 million	2.5 million (15%)	
1928	12	18 million	2.3 million (13%)	

SOURCE: Claude E. Robinson, *Straw Votes, A Study of Political Prediction* (New York: Columbia University Press; reprinted in 1979 from the 1932 ed.), pp. 72–74.

1. The 2 percent return for 1916 is merely an approximation because we know only that over 1 million ballots were mailed.

2. Information on the number of ballots returned in 1920 was unavailable.

automobile owners and telephone subscribers, they sent 16.5 million ballots throughout the country. Of these, 2.5 million were returned, enabling the correct prediction of the Coolidge victory and of the states the three candidates would win. However, the *Digest* results overstated the actual vote of the Progressive candidate, Robert LaFollette, and erred on the size of the Republican victory.[24] The *Digest* average state-plurality errors are shown in Table 2.1.

In both 1930 and 1932, 20 million ballots were sent to telephone subscribers and automobile owners (the so-called tel-auto population). Approximately 5 million were returned in 1930, and 3 million in 1932. Because Prohibition was the big issue of the day, attitudinal questions on it appeared in both polls.[25] Pollster George Gallup commented that "due to off-setting factors," the *Digest*'s most accurate poll was taken in 1932, with an error factor of 0.9, considered "almost magical accuracy."[26]

In the years following the stock market crash of October 1929, the *Digest* results consistently showed a Republican bias and, except for the 1932 poll, became increasingly inaccurate. Why? In 1932, Claude Robinson analyzed the *Digest* methodology, as well as those of other straw polls.[27] He identified eight possible sources of error worthy of our careful consideration now and each time we read or hear about the results of some write-in or phone-in opinion poll:

1. *Manipulation*   The count of straw ballots may be dishonest. The sponsors of the poll may manipulate the returns to aid a candidate in whom they are interested.

2. *Stuffing the ballot box*   Polling safeguards may be insufficient to prevent duplication in voting by lazy canvassers or by a candidate's enthusiastic friends.

3. *Geographic bias*   A straw poll in a city may neglect a strong Democratic or Republican ward, or a statewide poll may be taken in the cities and fail to include the farm vote.

4. *Class bias*   A straw poll may cover a geographic territory inclusively, but the ballots may be gathered disproportionately from one economic or social class, thus coloring the poll with the political views of this class.

5. *Bias of selection in cooperation*   All classes may be given an opportunity to participate in a poll, but one class may cooperate with the sponsors more than another. As we will soon see, the self-selection bias turned out to be a major problem for the 1936 *Digest* poll.

6. *Bias of participation-nonparticipation*   People may participate in a straw poll, but because of age, citizenship ineligibility, or disinclination, they may fail to vote in the official election.

7. *Adequacy of sample*   The number of straw ballots gathered may be too small to provide a valid (or representative) sample.

8. *Change of sentiment (conviction) over time*   People may honestly vote for candidate Brown in a straw poll, then change their minds and vote for candidate Jones in the official election.★

Specifically, with regard to the *Digest* polls, Robinson wrote that the "tel-auto" population selected by the *Digest* was "more Republican" and less representative of the general voting population. Therefore, "overprediction for this party can be expected from year to year, and the predictive error shown by one poll can be used to correct the bias of the succeeding poll."[28]

Ignoring Robinson's advice, in their prediction of the 1936 presidential election between Democrat Franklin D. Roosevelt and Republican Alfred M. Landon, the *Digest* poll was "off by a mile, plus." The *Literary Digest* issue of October 31, 1936, announced the "Final Returns in the *Digest's* Poll of Ten Million Voters." While 10 million ballots were sent out, there was less than a 25-percent participation rate, with 2,376,523 participants. The poll results were: Landon winning with a projected 55 percent of the vote (1,293,669), Roosevelt losing with 41 percent (972,897), and the third-party candidate receiving 4 percent (83,610). But when the real ballots were counted, President Roosevelt won reelection by a huge margin: 61 percent (27,751,597) to 37 percent (16,679,583).[29]

★We saw examples of such fluidity during the last weeks of the Bush–Clinton campaigns in 1992. The debates, which were held during the early part of October, influenced many undecided voters. However, others did not make up their minds until the final days, and still others may even have decided only when they were about to cast their vote on election day.

BOX 2.4   Gallup Did It

George Gallup received his Ph.D. in applied psychology from Iowa State University. For his doctoral dissertation, he developed techniques to measure newspaper and advertising readership. One of his findings was that most adults, as well as children, read newspaper comics. Advertisers soon learned about the efficacy of using comics as an advertising medium.

In the early 1930s he joined Young and Rubicam, an advertising firm in New York City, as a researcher to determine the types of advertising that most influenced people. He soon became interested in political polling, and in 1932 he conducted his first political survey for his mother-in-law, Ola Babcock Miller. She was then deciding whether she, as a Democrat in a Republican state, could become the first woman and the first Democrat elected secretary of state in Iowa. He conducted a poll using a sampling method he developed and reported that she had a good chance of being part of the predicted nationwide Democratic sweep. He was right; his mother-in-law won.

In the congressional election campaign of 1934, Gallup used "small but carefully selected samples taken in areas that had accurately mirrored the shifts in political opinion in previous elections."[1] His results correctly predicted a Democratic victory, signaling the first time in this century that the party that controlled the White House also gained congressional seats.

---

1. George Gallup, *The Sophisticated Poll Watcher's Guide* (Princeton, NJ: Princeton Opinion Press, 1972), p. 223.

Why was the *Digest* so dead wrong? The debate has endured for over 50 years, and numerous public opinion researchers have expended great amounts of money, time, and energy seeking the answer. (Your library's computer system will no doubt yield many titles of articles and books on the failure of the *Digest* poll.) Among those who were on the scene to give an almost instantaneous analysis were Archibald M. Crossley, Elmo Roper, and George Gallup (see Box 2.4).

In 1935, George Gallup established the American Institute of Public Opinion in Princeton, New Jersey, and released the first of his weekly *Gallup Polls* to sponsoring newspapers. That same year Elmo Roper, of the marketing research firm Roper, Cherrington, and Wood, began the *Fortune Quarterly* poll, marking the beginning of the *Roper Polls*. Archibald M. Crossley, who had been on the research staff of the *Digest*, set up his own *Crossley Survey* and was becoming a recognized scientific pollster. Crossley's polls, based on face-to-face interviews and small, carefully selected samples,

Table 2.2 Election Poll Results in 1936

POLL	SAMPLE SIZE	ROOSEVELT	LANDON
Literary Digest (final)	2.3 million (returned)	41%	55%
Gallup (AIPO)	3,000[1]	54	46
Crossley Survey	3,000[1]	52	28
Roper/*Fortune*	3,000[1]	74/61.7[2]	26
Actual election results	—	61	37

SOURCES: Peverill Squire, "Why the 1936 Literary Digest Poll Failed," *Public Opinion Quarterly* (Spring 1988), pp. 126-127. William Albig, *Public Opinion* (New York: McGraw-Hill, 1939), p. 229; Frank Teer and James D. Spence, *Public Opinion Polls* (London: Hutchinson University Library, 1973), p. 14. The rounded numbers are a compromise.

1. According to Teer and Spence, Squire appears to confirm that Gallup used a 3,000-person sample; no mention is made of the specific sample sizes for the Crossley and Roper polls. However, Albig states that Gallup used a "combination of mailed ballots and interviews with a sample never exceeding 300,000, and usually much less than that." He also claims that the Crossley Survey used about "30,000 interviews," but confirms that Roper/*Fortune* "was based on about 3000 interviews." Michael Wheeler, *Lies, Damn Lies, and Statistics: The Manipulation of Public Opinion in America* (New York: Liveright, 1976), p. 70, states: " ... Gallup worked with no more than 60,000 interviews, a number many called incredibly small." (Even a veteran pollster would be confused by these numbers!)

2. Albig's figure of 74 percent (p. 229) seems way out of line for Roper's poll. However, Wheeler, p. 70, states: "Roper was closest to Roosevelt's actual vote, 60.7 percent; he had predicted 61.7. Gallup was somewhat further off with 53.8."

were published by William Randolph Hearst's King Features Syndicate. These three men—Gallup, Roper, and Crossley—used systematic sampling procedures to predict that President Roosevelt would be reelected. In addition, Gallup, using his methodology to select a 3,000-person sample from the "tel-auto" directories used by the *Digest*, was able to predict the magazine's erroneous polling results prior to its publication. Table 2.2 shows how the various polls called it in 1936.

So what went wrong with the *Digest* poll? Peverill Squire sums it up:

> ... the 1936 *Literary Digest* poll failed to project the correct vote percentages or even the right winner not simply because of its initial sample, but also because of a low response rate combined with a non-response bias. Those who reported receiving straw vote ballots were supportive of the president. But a slight majority of those who claimed to have returned their ballot favored Landon.[30]

Thus there are three components to the answer:

1. *The initial sample* The "tel-auto" population was not representative of the general electorate. By 1936, the Depression hit many who

could no longer afford their telephones and cars. Thus the base of President Roosevelt's support—the unemployed masses, the poor, and even the under-employed—was pretty much excluded from the *Literary Digest* sample. However, Squire argues in his analysis that a post-election Gallup survey (May 19–24, 1937) indicated that within the *Digest* sample there were many "tel-auto" owners who did support Roosevelt but who did not necessarily return their ballots. Don Cahalan also conducted a post-election survey in Cedar Rapids. Between December 13, 1936, and February 15, 1937, Cahalan called every fifteenth person listed in the Cedar Rapids telephone book, for a total of 693 calls. From this random sample, he completed 554 interviews (80% of the selected sample). Of the remainder, 8 percent refused to be interviewed and 12 percent were unreachable—they no longer had phones, had died, had moved, or did not answer after repeated calls. Cahalan found: "A significantly higher proportion of Roosevelt supporters (67%) than Landon supporters (52%) claimed they had *not* received a *Digest* ballot or were not sure—despite the fact that all of them were on the mailing list."[31]

2. *The low response rate*   Squire concluded that if everyone who had received a ballot had returned it, "the results would have, at least, correctly predicted Roosevelt a winner. The projected vote percentages, however (because of the sample bias), would have greatly underestimated the president's margin of victory." Therefore, *"the response rate was an important source of error."*[32]

3. *The non-response bias*   In his Cedar Rapids study, Cahalan found that "the bias in the *return* of questionnaires was much greater than in the sample." Of those in Cedar Rapids who received questionnaires and who supported Roosevelt (251), only 15 percent said they *returned* their ballots. Compare this to the 33 percent of the 282 Landon supporters who returned theirs. "The findings thus indicate that the much stronger bias in return in 1936 interacted with the Republican bias in the sample to cause a fatal error."[33]

By 1938, *Literary Digest* was out of business. The Depression, combined with the disastrous poll and the growing popularity of *Time* (the new Henry Luce–Briton Hadden newsmagazine), finished it off. *Public Opinion Quarterly*, begun in 1937 and edited by Hadley Cantril, Harold Lasswell, E. Pendelton Herring, and O. W. Riegel, was rapidly becoming the forum for the infant field of scientific polling. Crossley, Gallup, and Roper were basking in the new respect and confidence the public felt toward the developing field of public opinion polling.

BOX 2.5 The Beginning of Wartime Radio Research

Almost a half century after Paul Lazarsfeld took Robert K. Merton to a radio studio and provided him with his first focus group experience, Merton described what happened:

> I see a smallish group—a dozen, or were there twenty?—seated in two or three rows. Paul and I take our places as observers at the side of the room as unobtrusively as we can; there is no one-way mirror or anything of that sort. These people are being asked to press a red button on their chairs when anything they hear on the recorded radio program evokes a negative response—irritation, anger, disbelief, boredom—and to press a green button when they have a positive response.... their cumulative responses are being registered on a primitive polygraph consisting of the requisite number of fountain pens connected by sealing wax and string ... to produce cumulative curves of likes and dislikes.[1]

This primitive instrument became known as the Lazarsfeld–Stanton[2] program analyzer. After the group's likes and dislikes were recorded, one of Lazarsfeld's assistants questioned the small audience about their reasons. Merton writes:

> I begin passing notes to Paul about what I take to be great deficiencies in the interviewer's tactics and procedures. He was not focussing sufficiently on specifically indicated reactions, both individual and aggregated. He was inadvertently guiding responses; he was not eliciting spontaneous expressions of earlier responses when segments of the radio program were being played back to the group.

---

1. Robert K. Merton, "The Focussed Interview and Focus Groups," *Public Opinion Quarterly* (1987, Vol. 51), pp. 552–553.
2. Frank Stanton, president of the Columbia Broadcasting System, was also extremely active in the American Statistical Association.

WARTIME RESEARCH

In October 1941, with war on the European continent a reality, the United States Army established the Research Branch of the Morale Division, later called the Information and Education Division. In November, President Franklin D. Roosevelt's Office of Facts and Figures, concerned with American morale, contacted Professor Paul Lazarsfeld at Columbia University in New York City. You will recall from Chapter 1 that Lazarsfeld and his colleagues conducted a study of the media impact on opinion formation in Erie County, Ohio, during the presidential election campaign of 1940. Lazarsfeld, the founding Director of the Office of Radio Research, was asked to test audience responses to radio morale programs (see Box 2.5).

Robert K. Merton, a colleague of Lazarsfeld at Columbia University, also joined the effort, becoming the liaison research person between the group at Columbia and the Army Research Branch. Merton had honed his interviewing skills while working his way through Harvard's graduate program during the Great Depression. In 1932, while working for the Works Progress Administration (the WPA was a federally subsidized program that provided jobs for people in a variety of fields—writers, artists, actors, and so on), he interviewed hoboes and homeless men and women in the Boston area. Now he would interview groups of soldiers in army camps, questioning them about their responses to such morale-boosting films as Frank Capra's *Why We Fight* series and certain army training films.

During the 1940s, Columbia University's Office of Radio Research evolved into the Bureau of Applied Social Research. It is credited with developing a special type of group interview. By 1943, *focussed interviews* (as *focused* was spelled by Merton) were used with individuals as well as with groups. More will be said in Chapter 11 about how the focused interview evolved into today's focus group interviews and how the two differ.

Carl I. Hovland, on leave from Yale, headed the Experimental Section of the Army Research Branch. He and some 30 associates from such fields as anthropology, sociology, social psychology, and political science undertook a large-scale research project to study the nature and effect of communicator credibility, message content, and audience response. Hovland was particularly interested in the determinants of attitude change and its relationship to opinion formation. He designed and directed controlled experiments to test draftee responses to training and morale-building films. For example, in one study he used the following procedure:

1. Questionnaires were first tested on some 200 soldiers.
2. The finalized questionnaires were given to several hundred men undergoing training.
3. The men were then divided into control and experimental groups.
4. The control group was shown a non-war film, while the experimental group saw one of Frank Capra's *Why We Fight* films.
5. Both groups were then given a second questionnaire basically containing the same factual and opinion-oriented questions as the first had. However, the questions had been sufficiently altered and rephrased to limit the possibility that repeated exposure to the questions would account for any changes in the answers to the two questionnaires.

The results (much the same for all films used) showed that while factual knowledge increased and opinions on specific items discussed in the films may have been changed, the films did not cause broad attitudinal changes. As some wise person put it: "Entrenched belief is never altered by the facts." These results became known as the **minimal–** or **limited–effects theory**[34] of media impact on public opinion.* The Lazarsfeld–Merton group was then able to convince Hovland of the necessity of going beyond *quantitative* inquiry to include the *qualitative* research provided by focused interviews.[35]

In addition to a wide variety of government-supported public opinion research projects, many private efforts were undertaken. One example was the polling of experts conducted by the Bureau of Applied Social Research (BASR) at Columbia University and funded by *The American Magazine*. In 1944, BASR contracted with the magazine to publish each month "a popular summary of authentic expert views on some issue of public interest and significance."[36] The titles of the 12 topics covered by these "Polls of Experts" (1945–1946) give us a sense of the changes taking place as the United States moved from war to peacetime considerations:

Effects of Universal Military Training on the Trainees

Value of Intelligence Tests

Means for Improving Negro–White relations

Wartime Food and Nutrition Needs

Post-war Treatment of Japan

Post-war Labor-Management Relations in the United States

Changing Position of White Collar and Professional Workers

Medical Care and Compulsory Health Insurance

The Role of Public Schools in Post-war America

Problems of Unequal Regional Economic Development (South and West versus East)

Policies with Respect to a World Organization (the evolving UN)

Role of Heredity in Accounting for Individuals' Mental Traits

The estimated readership of these polls, based on magazine circulation surveys, was 4 to 6 million.

BASR used a short questionnaire of five or six items, calling for checked responses. Some respondents, though, volunteered answers, comments, and

---

*This, you will recall, is consistent with the findings of the contemporary Erie study that resulted in the two-step theory emphasizing the role of the opinion leader (see Chapter 1). Michael Parenti's book, *Make-Believe Media: The Politics of Entertainment* (New York: St. Martin's Press, 1992), represents a powerful argument to counter the minimal- or limited-effects theory.

qualifications. The responses were then summarized to reflect all opinions expressed, without citing any particular expert. As the first step in creating the mailing list, 5 to 10 recognized authorities were consulted. These advisory experts were asked for their recommendations to create a mailing list of the most-qualified persons. Approximately 100 on the specific topic thereafter received a mailed questionnaire, designed to reflect not their personal opinions but their relevant knowledge. While the response from the general public was good, public opinion researchers criticized:

- *The brief questionnaire*   This was seen as inadequate to elicit meaningful responses. As we will see in Chapter 7, the length, structure, wording, and order of the questionnaire are all of major importance.

- *The experts' objectivity*   The experts were seen as merely presenting their subjective judgments.

- *The objectivity of the presenter*   The writer summarizing the responses was assumed to emphasize or de-emphasize views depending on the writer's subjective judgment. As we will see in Chapter 12, this remains a criticism of newspaper reporting of polling results.

- *Blind acceptance/outright rejection*   Researchers noted the tendency of individuals either to blindly accept the experts' opinions or, where there is disagreement, to reject it outright as a personal statement. They feared the experts could thus be discredited. (This last statement reveals something about American society at that time; namely, its concern with respect for authority figures. The cynical might even call it blind faith.)

- *The sampling methodology*   This was by far the most seriously criticized area. Critics said: "It is impossible to select a true sample of experts; results will simply reflect the arbitrary choice of participating specialists."[37]

As you have seen, the problem of sampling methodology has long troubled pollsters. In 1948, it would prove embarrassing even to the best of the systematic poll takers.

INTRODUCING PRESIDENT DEWEY

Some of us who have been around for a long time still chuckle when we recall the big grin on Harry Truman's face the morning after his election in 1948, as he held up newspapers such as the New York *Daily News*, the *Washington Post*, and the *Chicago Daily Tribune*, proclaiming his defeat.

Table 2.3 Polls and Election Results in 1948

POLL	DEWEY	TRUMAN
Roper	52.2%	37.1%
Gallup	49.5	44.5
Crossley	49.9	44.8
Actual vote	**45.1**	**49.5**

Note: The data omitted are for the other two candidates: Strom Thurmond and Henry Wallace.

"Dewey Defeats Truman," the *Tribune*'s headline announced. In the pre-computer age, reliable results were not available until days after the press rushed to meet their post-election deadlines. Many had put their trust in the polls.* They believed that the pollsters, having successfully predicted the presidential elections in 1940 and 1944 (with average errors of about 2 percentage points), had proven their scientific mettle. But this time, they erred drastically in predicting Truman's defeat (review Box 2.2). They underestimated the president's percentage of the national vote by 4 to 12 percentage points (see Table 2.3).

In the aftermath of this polling debacle, the Social Science Research Council set up the Committee on Analysis of Pre-Election Polls and Forecasts. The committee, a technical group, was to examine available polling and election data in an attempt to learn why the polls had failed and to make recommendations.

The Committee Reports

We have, as winner in the category of famous last words, Elmo Roper, pollster of *Fortune* magazine. Roper enjoyed the public's confidence because of his highly accurate forecasts in 1936, 1940, and 1944, with errors of only 1.5, 0.5, and −0.2 percentage points in favor of the Democratic candidate.[38] The October 1948 issue of *Fortune* proclaimed that Governor Dewey would be elected president in November, "barring a major political miracle," and that the September figures included in the article were so decisive that Roper planned "no further detailed reports of the change of opinion" in

*The following story is still circulating: As they retired on election night, New York's Governor Thomas E. Dewey said to his wife, "Tomorrow night you will sleep with the President of the United States." The next day Mrs. Dewey said, "Tom, am I going to the White House or is Mr. Truman coming here?"

the remaining days of the campaign, "unless some development of out-standing importance occurs." Dewey, the piece concluded, "will pile up a popular majority only slightly less than that accorded Mr. Roosevelt in 1936 when he swept by the boards against Alf Landon."[39] Roper erred, off by 12.4 percentage points.[40]

The runner-up in the famous-last-words category is George Gallup, who had also correctly predicted the previous three presidential elections but who had tended to err consistently on the Republican side. In 1936, 1940, and 1944, Gallup's under-predictions of the Democratic share of the two-party vote were 6.5, 3.0, and 2.3 percentage points.[41] His historic pre-election statement was: "We have never claimed infallibility, but next Tuesday the whole world will be able to see down to the last percentage point how good we are."[42] He under-predicted Truman's vote by 5 percentage points.[43] And, in the I-told-you-so category, words of William Funk, former editor of the *Literary Digest*: "Nothing malicious, mind you, but I get a very good chuckle out of this."[44]

As with the polling disaster of 1936, volumes have been written attempting to explain what went wrong in 1948. The first report was written by the Committee on Analysis of Pre-Election Polls and Forecasts, which consisted of a distinguished group of academicians and professionals schooled in statistics, from such fields as mathematics, psychology, and political science.[45] It identified the following eight major steps that were taken by all pollsters:

1. Design the overall plan for sampling respondents—decide the method for choosing states, cities, communities, streets, houses, individuals—to ensure that the sample is *representative* of the entire population.

2. Design the questionnaire and instructions on interviewing procedure.

3. Select the specific respondents in the field.

4. Interview the respondents.

5. Decide which respondents will actually vote, making sure you are not biasing ("padding") your results by including unregistered individuals or those who do not intend to vote.

6. Decide what to do about those who either will not reveal their preference or who say they are undecided.

7. Process the data, adjusting and correcting for trends and other factors (for example, sample bias and non-response bias).

8. Interpret and present the results and predictions based on available data.

BOX 2.6   Something Is Rotten...

Three of the many ignored signs that something was amiss:

- Leslie Biffle, the secretary of the Senate, posed as a butter and egg salesman and traveled around the country, talking to people, listening to conversations over lunch counters and in bus stations. "Truman's a shoo-in," he said. "What else would you expect an ardent Democrat to say?" said the sophisticates.
- Kansas City's Staley Milling Company sold 20,000 of their feed bags bearing the legend "A vote for the Republicans" or "A vote for the Democrats" and discovered that by September, the Democrats were leading by 54 to 46 percent. But since the scientific polls said otherwise, Staley Milling gave up on its promotional stunt.
- When the Denver *Post* and the Chicago *Sun-Times* surveyed their readers and found that Truman was ahead, the *Post* fooled with the data to give Colorado to Dewey and the *Sun-Times* simply did not publish the results.

SOURCE: Michael Wheeler, *Lies, Damn Lies, and Statistics: The Manipulation of Public Opinion in America* (New York: Liveright, 1976), pp. 73–74.

The committee then summarized their conclusions and made recommendations. First, their conclusions concerning the flawed predictions:[46]

1. *Too close to call*   The election was too close to call, and the pollsters were guilty of having operated under false assumptions and unrealistic expectations. Had Governor Dewey carried Ohio, California, and Illinois, which he lost by less than 1 percent of the vote, he would have won the election. Overestimating their ability to accurately predict the election led the pollsters to ignore the possibility of a close election (see Box 2.6) and the need to measure accurately voter preferences as close to election day as possible in order to determine "whether a flat forecast could be made with confidence."

2. *Neglect of past errors*   Their failure to ascertain late campaign shifts (which led to a close election) was due to a lack of attention to past errors that *tended to underestimate the Democratic vote in presidential elections* while overestimating it in the intervening congressional elections. Although Gallup, Crossley, and Roper were successful in correctly predicting the three previous presidential elections (1936, 1940, 1944), their average errors should have sounded a warning. In the earlier elections, their errors varied from state to state. While the

individual errors were off by an average of only 4 to 5 percentage points in one direction, when all the state results were tallied, the *cumulative errors* skewed the national polling results. There should have been recognition of this cumulative error effect, and the necessary adjustments and refinements should have been made. There was, in short, an absence of careful consideration and analysis of their data.

3. *Complexity of the polling process*   Errors may occur in each of the eight major steps. However, evidence indicates errors in the following steps caused major damage to the forecasting results: (1) sampling—design and implementation, (4) interviewing, (6) dealing with undecided voters, and (7) detecting trends and shifts.

The committee criticized use of *quota sampling* and recommended future use of *probability sampling*. As we will see in Chapter 6 when we turn our full attention to sampling methodology, the probability method randomly selects the individuals to be interviewed. On the other hand, success of the quota method is first dependent on the researchers' setting reasonable quotas (the number of individuals within a given group) to start with and then on the field supervisors' overseeing the interviewers to ensure the strict implementation of the guidelines and procedures established by the researchers. In this instance, the interviewers were left too free—within the guidelines and restrictions for each quota—to select those to be interviewed. The report stated: "It is impossible to separate the error introduced by the quotas set from that arising in the process of selection by interviewers."[47] Too few people with only grade-school education and too many college-educated people were interviewed than proportionally existed in our population. The justification for excluding from the sample a greater number of non-college-educated individuals was that the less educated tended to vote less. While it is true that more non-voters are proportionately found among those with little education, the way to eliminate any non-voters from a sample is not through exclusion based on level of education but through the use of **filtering** (screening) **questions**. A major error therefore occurred as a result of sample bias. Many Truman supporters were excluded from the sample because of the assumed relationship between their lower educational level and a tendency toward non-voting.

Quota sampling tended to *under-sample* both the highest and lowest income groups in the population. As the committee explained, in the "fair-weather" elections of 1936, 1940, and 1944, the successful pollsters had used a number of corrective statistical devices to eliminate, adjust, or offset errors inherent in the quota sampling method. However, adjustments made in the 1948 data (based on past experience) proved to be insufficient. The

impact of two major elements on public opinion had not been given sufficient consideration:

1. The changed circumstances in the country: The war had ended, rent
    control as a device for economic stabilization during the war was
    being dismantled, the government's farm policy was in flux, the
    Cold War had begun, and so on.
2. The four-way race: Harry Truman, Tom Dewey, Strom Thurmond,
    and Henry Wallace.

Quotas based on economic level, age, sex, race, geographic area,
farm/nonfarm residence, education, and so on were assigned to interviewers. Four major economic groups had been created and each was assigned a
quota—a specific number of respondents, supposedly reflective of that
group's proportion of the country's population—according to census figures. The report noted that the groups had originally been based on a
"crude measurement of economic level that may have been badly disturbed
by recent economic changes." Specifically, rent had been used as a quota
variable during the war. The usefulness of this variable—unadjusted—no
longer made sense because in some areas there had been a relaxation of rent
control after the war.

Also, the sampling designs were defective because the quotas for states
were not based on the population of voting age but on the actual vote in
1944. In addition to problems with the grade-school and college-educated
groups, the rural population was not fully represented in the sample, as
there was a tendency for interviewers to choose respondents who were easy
to reach.[48] Once in the field, interviewers—apparently inadequately supervised—had been expected to follow the guidelines and to fill the quotas assigned to each group. Unfortunately, this had not been done in accordance
with the guidelines. (More will be said about this problem in Chapter 6.)
There was, the committee stated, no way to "measure accurately" the components of the error due to the quota sampling method used.

As for the questionnaire, although its design reflected years of polling
experience, it did not provide sufficient information on which to base a
prediction as to whether or not the respondent would actually vote on election day. While Crossley used a filter question to eliminate those unlikely
to vote, the questionnaires generally did not adequately probe undecided
respondents as to which way they were leaning. Pollsters also erred seriously, the report said, in not continuing to poll into the final two weeks of
the campaign, when one voter out of seven made his/her decision. As determined by post-election polls, three out of four of the late deciders said

they had voted for Truman. The report attributed the pollsters' inability to detect such late shifts in public opinion to over-confidence that led them to assume that earlier voting intentions (including indecisiveness) would remain the same.

You will recall Box 1.3, discussing Dianne Feinstein's primary victory in 1990. Although Feinstein won the Democratic nomination to run for governor, the real surprise was that women who decided in the last three days of the campaign tended to vote more heavily for her opponent, Attorney General John Van De Kamp. In the Feinstein case, polling continued to the end of the campaign for the Democratic nomination. However, in another case, Janice Ballou, director of the Center for Public Interest Polling at Rutgers University, stopped polling one week before the general election on November 7, 1990. Her organization's last poll showed United States Senator Bill Bradley with a lead of 26 percentage points and 18 percent undecided. Among those who claimed to be "very interested" in the campaign, Ballou found that the incumbent Democrat led his Republican opponent, Christine Todd Whitman, by only 2 percentage points. Ballou admitted that although this was apparently a hint of things to come, it was something she had not published. Her last poll had also shown that New Jersey Governor Jim Florio's $2.8 billion in tax increases were an issue in the Senate election. Bradley, who had outspent Whitman by 12 to 1, was reelected by barely 3 percentage points (a difference of 55,000 votes). Ballou, interviewed by *New York Times* reporter Wayne King, expressed regret for not having polled during the final week of the campaign: "I want to kick myself." (The moral of the story: Don't assume anything. Keep polling to the end. Learn from the mistakes of others.)[49]

Back to 1948 for more lessons. Various statistical devices could have been used to correct or adjust the 1948 survey results. For example, Gallup increased his accuracy to some extent by adjusting for (1) the bias in his sample of the under-represented grade-school-educated and the over-represented college-educated, and (2) the individual's voting behavior in 1944 as an indication of voting intentions in 1948. The adjustment for the education bias decreased Dewey's expected vote about 2.5 percentage points and increased Truman's by 1.3. Gallup had also analyzed his results on the basis of whether or not a person had voted ("didn't vote, too young, didn't remember") and how the individual had voted ("Roosevelt, Dewey, or other") in 1944. These adjustments reduced Dewey's percentage by 1.2 and raised Truman's by 0.8. Gallup then averaged the results of the two adjustments, reducing Dewey's expected vote by about 1.8 and increasing Truman's by 1.1.[50] This, of course, helped, but was not enough. Gallup was still off by 5 percentage points on the Democratic side.

As for Roper, I need only mention that although he was aware that his sample over-represented the South (giving it 26 percent of the quota, while it cast only 17 percent of the popular vote), he felt that this would offset underestimation of the Democratic vote in the North, a problem in previous elections. However, the unconsidered variable here was Strom Thurmond, the Dixiecrat, who pulled southern Democratic votes from Truman. Roper's over-sampling of the South did cut the Dewey vote by 1.4 percent, but it increased Thurmond's vote by 1.3 and raised Truman's vote by only 0.2 percent.[51] Thus helpful errors in regional quotas offset only a part of the other errors. Although we could further dissect the 1948 polls, enough has been said to give you a sense of the complex nature of the errors that occurred. As for the recommendations, more research in sampling design, questionnaire development, respondent selection, *weighting* (for purposes of statistical correction), and less arrogance were good starting points to improve the accuracy of predictions in future elections.

Perhaps the first law of polling was born with the disaster of 1948: A good prediction is a right prediction, regardless of how close to the actual voting returns the poll comes. Although the percentage errors in predicting the election outcome in 1936 were greater than those of 1948, the pollsters were hailed in the former and criticized in the latter. The polling results of 1948 not only brought the pollsters and their methodology under scrutiny, but raised questions about the way the press wrote about and publicized the polls. Before the election, for example, Gallup's American Institute of Public Opinion was providing four reports a week to 126 newspapers with 20 million readers.[52] In reaction to all the criticism, some newspapers disassociated themselves from political polls, canceling contracts with polling firms. The polling industry, which had previously grossed approximately $25 million a year operating in dozens of states and local communities, saw 1948 as a temporary setback for the role it hoped to play in American politics. Marginal polling organizations ceased to exist, but the major pollsters swallowed hard and held on, expanding the commercial side—the marketing research capability—of their business.

CHAPTER REVIEW

- The Constitution of the United States is more than a description of fundamental laws and procedures of government. Its appended First Amendment—providing for freedom of speech, press, and religion and the rights to petition and assemble—can be seen as testimony to the importance and appreciation of public opinion.

- The gathering of demographic information goes back to biblical times, but concern for surveying public attitudes is a recent phenomenon.

- The earliest straw poll emerged from counts at various public meetings during the election of 1824.

- An early example of sampling occurred in 1850 when census director Debow sampled 23 counties, cross-tabulating data on marriage, schooling, and income in order to discern societal patterns.

- Edward Jarvis, an American physician, encouraged the use of standardized interview schedules in the 1850 U.S. census. Interviewing techniques were then being developed by the London Statistical Society, which trained professional interviewers to conduct social surveys.

- Arthur L. Bowley was a British mathematician and economist who undertook a study of working-class conditions in five towns, using sampling methodology.

- Max Weber, a German sociologist, was among the early twentieth-century social scientists who encouraged survey research.

- In 1935, George Gallup established the American Institute of Public Opinion. Gallup, Archibald M. Crossley, and Elmo Roper were considered to have used systematic sampling procedures in 1936 to correctly predict the election and the failure of the *Literary Digest* poll. The *Digest* poll failed because of bias in the initial sample, the low response rate, and the non-response rate.

- President Franklin D. Roosevelt's Office of Facts and Figures (later the Office of War Information) and the Experimental Section of the Army Research Branch attracted such talented researchers as Paul Lazarsfeld, Robert Merton, and Carl I. Hovland, among many others. During the war years, great strides were made in developing effective survey methodology and interviewing techniques, including the "focussed" interview.

- The problem of sampling design had long troubled pollsters, and in 1948 it proved embarrassing even to the best of the poll takers. Quota sampling was discredited; probability sampling was recommended, as was the use of filtering questions.

- In the aftermath of the 1948 election, one too close to call, the Committee on Analysis of Pre-Election Polls and Forecasts reviewed and criticized not only the flawed polls of that year but the neglect of past errors.

NOTES

1. D. Caradog Jones, *Social Surveys* (London: Hutchinson's University Library, 1948), Chapter I, pp. 15–22.

2. John Hohenberg, *Free Press/Free People: The Best Cause* (New York: Columbia University Press, 1971), p. 34.

3. Richard Jensen, "Democracy by Numbers," *Public Opinion* (Feb./Mar. 1980), p. 53.

4. Jensen, p. 53.

5. Tom W. Smith, "The First Straw? A Study of the Origins of Election Polls," *Public Opinion Quarterly* (Spring 1990), p. 22.

6. Herbert Agar, *The Price of Union* (Boston: Houghton Mifflin, 1950), pp. 199, 213.

7. Smith, pp. 24–27.

8. Smith, pp. 27–28, citing Albert Ray Newsome, *The Presidential Election of 1824 in North Carolina* (Chapel Hill: University of North Carolina Press, 1939), pp. 139–140.

9. Smith.

10. Claude E. Robinson, *Straw Votes, A Study of Political Prediction* (New York: Columbia University Press, reprinted in 1979 from the 1932 ed.); see Chapter I, "The Politician as Predictor."

11. Robinson, p. 6.

12. Jensen, p. 55.

13. George Gallup, *The Sophisticated Poll Watcher's Guide* (Princeton, NJ: Princeton Opinion Press, 1972), p. 221.

14. Jensen, p. 55.

15. Jensen, p. 54.

16. Jensen.

17. Gallup, pp. 221–222.

18. Jones, Chapter IV.

19. H. H. Gerth and C. Wright Mills, *From Max Weber: Essays in Sociology* (London: Oxford University Press, 1946), pp. 16–21.

20. L. John Martin, "Genealogy of Public Opinion Polling," *The Annals of the American Academy* (March 1984), p. 18.

21. Gerth and Mills, p. 21.

22. Martin, pp. 19–20, citing A. L. Bowley, "The Application of Sampling to Economic and Sociological Problems," *Journal of the American Statistical Association* (1936).

23. Ann E. Weiss, *Polls and Surveys, A Look at Public Opinion Research* (New York: Franklin Watts, 1979), p. 10.

24. Robinson, Chapter IV; also see Gallup, p. 222.

25. William Albig, *Public Opinion* (New York: McGraw-Hill, 1939), pp. 227–228; Gallup, p. 222; and Weiss, pp. 17–18.

26. Gallup, pp. 222–223.

27. Robinson, pp. 77–78.

28. Robinson, p. 72.

29. Peverill Squire, "Why the 1936 Literary Digest Poll Failed," *Public Opinion Quarterly* (Spring 1988), pp. 125–133. Also see Don Cahalan's "Comment: The Digest Poll Rides Again!" in *Public Opinion Quarterly* (Spring 1989), pp. 129–133, a response to Squire's article. In 1938, Cahalan had based his M.A. thesis on an analysis of the *Digest*'s polling failure in 1936. Apparently Squire, unaware of Cahalan's research, reached the same conclusions.

30. Squire, pp. 131–132.

31. Cahalan, pp. 130–131.

32. Squire, pp. 129–130.

33. Cahalan, pp. 130–131.

34. See Carl I. Hovland, A. A. Lumsdaine, and F. D. Sheffield, *Experiments on Mass Communications* (Princeton, NJ: Princeton University Press, 1949); Carl I. Hovland, I. L. Janis, and H. H. Kelley, *Communication and Persuasion* (New Haven, CT: Yale University Press, 1953); and Carl I. Hovland and Walter Weiss, "The Influence of Source Credibility on Communication Effectiveness," *Public Opinion Quarterly* (1952), Vol. 15, pp. 635–650; also Daniel Katz et al., eds., *Public Opinion and Propaganda* (New York: Holt, Rinehart & Winston, 1954).

35. Robert K. Merton, "The Focussed Interview and Focus Groups," *Public Opinion Quarterly* (1987), Vol. 51, p. 557.

36. Arthur Kornhauser, "Experience with a Poll of Experts: The Problems and the Possibilities," *Public Opinion Quarterly* (Fall 1948), pp. 399–411.

37. Kornhauser.

38. Frederick F. Stephan and Philip J. McCarthy, *Sampling Opinions, An Analysis of Survey Procedure* (New York: Wiley, 1958), p. 27.

39. Norman M. Bradburn and Seymour Sudman, *Polls & Surveys* (San Francisco: Jossey-Bass, 1988), p. 29. Also see Wheeler, p. 73.

40. Stephan and McCarthy.

41. Norman J. Powell, *Anatomy of Public Opinion* (New York: Prentice-Hall, 1951), p. 115.

42. Michael Wheeler, *Lies, Damn Lies, and Statistics: The Manipulation of Public Opinion in America* (New York: Liveright, 1976), p. 75.

43. Powell; and see Bradburn and Sudman, p. 29.

44. Wheeler, p. 75.

45. The *Report on the Analysis of Pre-Election Polls and Forecasts* was published by the Social Science Research Council in 1949. Cited hereafter as "*Report*," it also appeared in *Public Opinion Quarterly* (Winter 1948–1949), pp. 595–622. Among the committee members were Carl I. Hovland (Yale) and Samuel Stouffer (Harvard), both of whom had been involved in the army research program.

46. *Report*, pp. 600–603.

47. *Report*, p. 608.

48. See the Social Science Research Council's "Report on the Analysis of Pre-Election Polls and Forecasts," *Public Opinion Quarterly* (Winter 1948–1949), p. 612.

49. To help underscore the point that although polls appear to be getting better, they are still not infallible, see Roger Jowell, Barry Hedges, Peter Lynn, Graham Farrant, and Anthony Heath, "Review: The 1992 British Election: The Failure of the Polls," *Public Opinion Quarterly* (Summer 1993), pp. 238–263. This is an analysis of how the British polls erroneously predicted a Labour party victory in 1992.

50. *Report*, pp. 616–617.

51. *Report*, p. 617.

52. Jensen, p. 59.

3

Polling Gets More Professional and Worldly

Think about—

What role did George Gallup play in internationalizing polling?

What is meant by the *universe* of a poll?

What problems were encountered when polling went abroad? How can these problems be avoided?

Why are public opinion researchers flocking to eastern Europe?

What is the connection between opinion research and marketing research?

What are some of the problems pollsters encountered in Nicaragua? What are the lessons to be learned from that polling experience that can be applied in eastern Europe and elsewhere?

When we talk about surveying public opinion, attitudes, behavioral traits, and tastes, we are talking about a money-making enterprise; when we talk about an international effort to gather such information, we are talking about big money. Don't limit yourself to thinking about selling political opinion data to newspapers, magazines, and broadcast media. As we will see in Chapter 11, today's corporations use and want this type of information to create and implement national and international marketing strategies, and they are willing to pay for it. Government agencies (on all levels) and private organizations use such data to shape and adjust their policies and to formulate their decisions. In this chapter, we will first look at the early development of international polling and then examine the spillover of opinion research into the field of marketing research. The sophisticated methods used to discern public opinion are also used to discern public taste for all things marketable—from ideas to products to political candidates.

POLLING ABROAD

Gallup established the British Gallup poll in 1937 and the French poll in 1938. Polls were brought to Australia in 1940 and to Canada in 1941. The Government Social Survey, a British agency, was established in 1941, as part of their war effort. Its work, similar to that of the United States Army

Research Branch, was concerned with monitoring wartime morale and attitudes. During 1943 and 1944, polling organizations were also established in Denmark and in Switzerland. Also in 1944, Joe Belden reported on Mexico's first regular public opinion poll for *Public Opinion Quarterly*. *Tiempo*, a Mexican weekly newsmagazine, became the sponsor of a "regularly-recurring poll, the first candid and realistic attempt originating within the country to measure public opinion."[1]

In the final stages of World War II, as the United States Army began to occupy defeated enemy territory, the government became interested in public opinion in those areas. In March 1944, Stuart C. Dodd, who had previously conducted a pioneer radio poll in Lebanon, Syria, and Palestine in order to test reliability (see Box 3.1), prepared *A Manual of Social Surveying in "Liberated Territories"* for the Psychological Warfare Branch (Allied Force Headquarters). This manual was used to train personnel in all aspects of polling. Some unofficial surveys (see Box 3.2) were also undertaken during this period.

One official survey was taken on Saipan in late 1944 and early 1945, after our troops forcibly ejected the Japanese.[2] Much of the civilian population of Japanese, Koreans, and Chamorros hid in caves in the hills; some took the way of *Seppuku* (suicide). Using Nisei (American citizens, born of immigrant Japanese parents and educated in the United States) interpreters and with considerable effort, a study was undertaken using two groups (one of 100 persons, the second of 500) of identical composition. The sample was designed to approximate a representative selection of the mainland population with regard to four variables: age, sex, occupation, and education.

Understanding the people's emotional strain and reluctance to impart any useful information, the authorities drew up a tentative questionnaire that Nisei interpreters pretested on the smaller sample. Many items were then altered or eliminated. Finally, 31 questions were asked of the larger sample of 500 (see Box 3.3). The study revealed the complexity of Japanese beliefs and thinking and was an early indication of the difficulties the occupation forces would face in helping to restructure an authoritarian system into a democratic one.

It was one of many Japanese surveys. Lieutenant (J.G.) Andie L. Knutson had been an opinion analyst for the American Telephone and Telegraph Company before going to work for the Office of War Information. While serving in the Navy, he prepared economic, political, and social studies. In 1945, he advocated intensive opinion research in Japan "to locate social and political 'blind spots' which must be eradicated before democratic thought is possible."[3] In terms of the developing field of opinion research, these studies provided an opportunity to test a number of ideas and to recognize the problematic nature of polling abroad.

BOX 3.1   The Dodd Radio Poll

In 1944 Stuart Dodd of the Psychological Warfare Branch studied response reliability in mideastern countries. Ten percent of all radio owners in Lebanon, Syria, and Palestine were selected to respond to 100 questions asking basic information about themselves and their listening habits, such as programs, stations, languages, hours, and preferences for the 14 Allied nations broadcasting to their countries. The study's purpose was to determine the reliability of the public response where there were many enemy sympathizers and where no previous opinion studies had ever been conducted.

Researchers wanted to know how consistent people were in their responses. Obviously, the greater the consistency, the greater the reliability. The variables used to measure reliability were different interviewers; different respondents within a family; different intervals between interviews; different sample sizes, ranging from 1 percent of the population to 10 percent; different degrees of acquaintance between interviewer and respondent, varying from total strangers to close friends.

Dodd and his assistants found that while *individual reliability* measured 75 percent (referring to individual consistency in their replies), the measure for group or family reliability was over 99 percent. Dodd reported that "sincerity of response for the group as measured by degree of identity of information given to intimate friends and given to complete strangers under controlled conditions was well over 99%." In other words, although a single family member might not be consistently reliable in his or her responses, others in the family would be. The result was that the unreliability of a single group member was offset by the reliability of the group as a whole.

By ensuring response reliability, researchers were able to provide data that guided the U.S. government as to how radio could best be used for propaganda purposes.

SOURCE: Stuart C. Dodd et al., *A Pioneer Radio Poll in Lebanon, Syria and Palestine* (Palestine: Government Printer, September 1943), originally available from the American Documentation Institution, Washington, DC; A.D.I. Document No. 1817; also discussed in *Public Opinion Quarterly* (Summer 1946), p. 291.

In May 1945, immediately following the liberation of Holland, Jan Stapel, together with W. J. de Jonge, founded the Netherlands Institute of Public Opinion. In 1945, Gallup expanded his operations into West Germany (EMNID—Institut GmbH & Co.), into Finland (Suomen Gallup O/Y), and into Norway (Norsk Gallup Institut A/S). In 1946, DOXA, Instituto Per Le Richerche Statistiche E L'Analisi, the Italian Gallup, was organized. All this activity indicated a growing movement toward world

---

BOX 3.2 An Unofficial Wartime Poll in Italy

An unofficial survey was taken in southern Italy in late 1943 and early 1944. Reports (in the form of letters) on public opinion in the south of Italy were sent to *Public Opinion Quarterly* and provided "an on-the-spot record of public opinion in the making" regarding support for the Allied effort to eliminate Mussolini and Fascist rule of Italy. These reports contained more or less systematic interviews with 100 Italians in the south of Italy. The small sample was broken down (and percentages were rounded to the nearest whole number) as follows:

Percent of Sample	Age Group
28%	under 19 (adolescents)
33	20–29
17	in their 30s
13	in their 40s
8	50+

This was what we now call a **convenience sample** (based on the availability and willingness of people to speak about their political preferences in the middle of a war). I doubt that the sample was selected on the basis of any predesigned quota system. The ratio between rural and urban individuals was 5:3, and between men and women it was 7:3. The unidentified pollster noted the difficulty of interviewing women and those over the age of 50, who were often suspicious and reticent. Also, it was easier to speak with the Italian farmers than with the more sophisticated urban dwellers, who were more cautious. The not-too-surprising results showed that 9 out of 10 interviewed rejected Mussolini and the Fascists "with feeling." (If you *had* supported the Fascist regime freshly ousted by the occupation forces, would you have admitted it?)

SOURCE: "Public Opinion in the South of Italy," by the staff of *Public Opinion Quarterly* (Summer 1944).

---

surveying, and in July 1946, at the conference of North American public opinion agencies, a unanimous vote called for the establishment of a world association of public opinion reporting agencies. Such an international surveying organization ultimately did evolve, known today as the World Association of Public Opinion Research (WAPOR).

When Polls Came to Czechoslovakia

During the Nazi occupation, the only way to get outside information was by listening to foreign broadcasts. Despite Nazi death threats to those caught, many Czechs continued to listen. Among them were two famous Czech authors: Joseph Kopta and Vladislav Vancura. Listening to England's

---

BOX 3.3   The Saipan Study

Major Paul C. Bosse, director of this poll, reported that it was futile to ask questions with abstract words, such as: "Would you like to see a *democratic* form of government in Japan?" The majority had "no concept of democracy," he explained. In the following questions that were asked, note the high percentage of Don't-Know (DK) responses—probably the result of fear:

- Would you like to live under a government in which the people rule?
  Yes—11.8%
  No—58.0%
  Don't Know—30.2%

A related question was:

- Do you believe it would work?
  Yes—7.4%
  No—57.0%
  Don't Know—35.6%

Some of the other findings were:

- Who actually controls the Japanese government?
  Emperor—39.0%
  Cabinet—11.0%
  Military—27.2%
  Don't Know—22.8%

- Do you think the Emperor favors the war?

Emperor favors war—27.6%
Does not favor war—39.6%
Don't Know—32.8%

- Who do you think has the strongest navy in the world?
  United States—14% (70 people)
  Japan—54% (270 people)

  (The remainder either said they did not know or named England or Germany.)

- Who will win the war?
  United States—8.2% (41);
  Japan—52.8% (264);
  Uncertain—39% (195)

SOURCE: Maj. Paul C. Bosse, "Polling Civilian Japanese on Saipan," *Public Opinion Quarterly* (Summer 1945), pp. 176–182.

BBC, they learned about public opinion polling. They were impressed with it as a tool for democratic government and hoped to introduce polling when peace finally came. Vancura was killed by the Nazis, but Kopta survived the German occupation; when the war ended, he became a high official in the Ministry of Information. He was then able to implement his plan to establish a polling organization in Czechoslovakia, despite the limited government resources available. The Czechoslovak Institute of Public Opinion was to operate on the basis of two fundamental principles: (1) Its surveys must be in the public interest, and (2) they must be nonpartisan and devoid of propaganda favoring any particular ideology.

Beginning in December 1945, the institute found that after six years of Nazi oppression and Gestapo methods, the public was suspicious of people asking questions. A publicity drive was launched to educate the public about the work of the institute and to recruit interviewers. Even though radio and press appeals clearly stated that the work was unsalaried, many volunteered, believing they would be helping a free government understand its people. Those selected received three correspondence courses covering interviewing techniques, and after a while the institute was able to pay the volunteers some nominal amount on a quarterly basis. The institute, supported by the Czech government, did not sell its services. The main criterion in the selection of research topics was usefulness of the survey information. Research projects were suggested by government agencies, public organizations, cultural institutions, and newspapers, as well as initiated by the institute itself. The United States embassy also submitted proposals. Among the studies conducted by the institute were:[4]

- attitudes toward welfare institutions (Czech Ministry of Social Welfare)

- working morale (Ministry of Industry)

- habits of reading, going to the movies, theaters, exhibitions (Cultural Department of the State Planning Office)

- attitudes toward the Two-Year Plan and Children's Weeks; the effects of various information campaigns, rumors, and so on (Ministry of Information)

- attitudes toward land reform (Ministry of Agriculture)

- whether consumers use all the food rations they are entitled to buy (Ministry of Food)

- the relationship between infant mortality figures and ignorance and/or superstition (Ministry of Health)

The questionnaire usually consisted of 14 to 16 questions, and surveys were conducted every 2 or 3 weeks. The method used was **quota sampling**, based on a sample size of 1,300. The following **demographic variables** were controlled (meaning that based on the following factors, quotas were set to ensure proportional representation of each group making up the sample): (a) sex; (b) age—three groups: 18–29, 30–49, 50 and over; (c) social classes: workers, white-collar workers of higher and lower grades, farmers, self-employed; (d) community size: up to 1,000, 1,000–2,000, 2,000–10,000, 10,000–100,000; over 100,000; and (e) geographic distribution (consisting of 11 regions).

Interviewing was conducted orally on a one-to-one basis (no witnesses), at home, at work, or on the street. Respondents were guaranteed anonymity. Survey results were published through the institute's own journal and through public news agencies that provided the data to newspapers and radio broadcasters. Because the relationship between the Czech area and Slovakia had not yet been constitutionally defined, the institute's survey work was limited to Bohemia, Moravia, and Silesia.

While the issue of Czech–Slovak relations was under discussion, the communists, backed by the Red Army, destroyed the fragile postwar coalition government, taking control of Czechoslovakia in late February 1948. Thus, by the end of that year, Czechoslovakia disappeared behind what British Prime Minister Winston Churchill called the "iron curtain."

Twenty years later, during the Prague Spring of 1968, free public opinion resurfaced briefly—that is, until the Soviet tanks reinstated order. Twenty-one years after that, toward the end of 1989, communism and its iron curtain disintegrated and the Czech people were finally free. New efforts were immediately initiated to take the pulse of a free people. Such polling efforts have continued despite the country's subsequent nonviolent split into Slovakia and the Czech Republic.

THE FIRST INTERNATIONAL

CONFERENCE OF GALLUP INSTITUTES

On September 17, 1946, George Gallup announced that the Brazilian Institute of Public Opinion (Instituto Brasileiro de Opiniao Publica e Estatica—IBOPE) had become affiliated with his American Institute of Public Opinion (the Gallup Poll).[5] Several months later, in May 1947, the various national Institutes of Public Opinion affiliated with Gallup's American Institute of Public Opinion held a conference in England. This First International Conference of Gallup Institutes included participants from the United States, England, France, Canada, Australia, Finland, Holland, Sweden, Denmark, and Norway (the director of the Brazilian Institute was unable to attend). Representatives from Italy and Czechoslovakia attended as observers.

The stated intentions were to tighten their affiliation and to improve their capacity to conduct international surveys. To accomplish their aims, they formed the International Association of Public Opinion (Gallup) Institutes and created an administrative body, the Central Committee (C.C.). Five C.C. members were selected as follows: one each from the American, British, French, and Australian Institutes, and one representing the group of participating Scandinavian organizations. Their work included:

- collecting information on all opinion research projects
- passing on the qualifications of new applicants for membership in the International Association
- examining the character of the operating heads of proposed new member institutes
- disciplining members, if necessary
- setting standards of research requirements

A three-member Technical Committee (T.C.) was also created to assist the C.C. in its work. The T.C. was to examine the methodology and work of new applicants for membership, including:

- the size, distribution, and adequacy of their polling sample
- their general sampling and cross-sectioning procedures
- the quality, efficiency, and work of their interviewers

With the organizational work completed, the members discussed cooperation in a series of international polls. Each of the member institutes contributed a list of questions for international polling. More than 100 questions were assembled and the members then voted on each question. The top 20 questions were scheduled for international polling at the rate of approximately 1 per month. Gallup Institutes from the larger countries said they would conduct joint polls on several additional questions monthly. The data collected would be shared among the member institutes and published in subscribing newspapers.

Thus it was that the American polling disaster occurred when interest in international polling was reaching new heights. The domestic polling fiasco of late 1948 served as a warning to pollsters abroad, reminding them of the even greater difficulties to be surmounted before any undertaking of international polling could be successful. A report evaluating the international poll taken in the spring of 1948 appeared in *Public Opinion Quarterly* (published after the presidential election). In it, the researchers compared the methodology used in the international poll to that used in the 1948 election forecasts:

> It is regrettable that the methodology needed for accurate appraisal
> of international opinion remains largely to be developed. Despite
> the U. S. election forecasts of 1948, we are probably in the "Bronze
> Age" of development in measuring public opinion within a single
> country. But internationally we are, by any admission, in the
> Paleolithic era of flint chipping.[6]

THE FIRST *TIME*/ROPER
INTERNATIONAL POLL

On January 23, 1948, months before the election misreading, Elmo Roper and *Time* decided to undertake a 10-country poll. Their intention was to complete it within a 12-week period, in time for an upcoming international forum in New Orleans. Although the New Orleans forum was canceled, the results of the poll (unaccompanied by any clear explanation as to sample size or methodology) were published in the magazine's issue of April 12, 1948, interspersed among *Time*'s chatty paragraphs about sidewalk cafes in Paris, children sailing toy boats in a Luxembourg Gardens pond, the "fitfully" shining sun in West Germany, minstrels singing in Naples, and so on. Almost a year later, an analysis appeared in *Public Opinion Quarterly* (Winter 1948–1949, the same issue that dissected the Truman–Dewey polling disaster).

The *Time* international poll proved to be a valuable learning experience because pollsters encountered difficulties that did not usually arise when they conducted opinion studies within their own countries. But why, decades later, does it remain of interest to us? Since the late 1940s, there have been enormous improvements in transportation and communication, making it difficult for most of us to relate to any problems in those areas at that time. With advanced computer and satellite technology, electronic mail and faxing, most of the logistical problems of the past no longer exist. Yet the study remains of interest to us because we are experiencing—within our own country—many demographic and population shifts and changes, as can be seen when one examines the 1990 census data. As a result, researchers in the United States still encounter a number of challenges similar to those that confronted the pollsters who undertook the first international opinion survey in the post–World War II period. As we examine the problem areas described below, it is worth considering their relevance to today's poll takers.

The Universe and Sub-Universes of the Study

The actual *universe* of the *Time* poll (that body of public opinion on which the sample was to be based) was huge. It included the United States, Canada, Mexico, Brazil, Argentina, France, England, Italy, Switzerland, West Germany,* and Sweden. The inaccessibility of certain areas and countries (for example, the French and British zones of Germany, East Berlin, and East Germany as a whole), due to the postwar situation at that time—the recovery of war-torn Europe and the dawning of the Cold War era—made it difficult to describe western European public opinion.

Inaccessibility (circumstances that hinder poll-taking efforts) can still be a problem if the desire is to undertake an international poll. For example, while it is now possible to poll in most of eastern Europe and the former Soviet Union (excluding those areas marred by political turmoil, rebellion, or civil war), there are many other parts of the world where dictators block access to their people. Think about Iraq and Iran, for instance.

In the *Time* study, there were also nonpolitical problems that added to the difficulty of the task: the short time period allotted, harsh winter weather in certain countries, great distances, and a still unrepaired and war-damaged communication system in some parts of Europe. Eric Stern of Roper sailed to Europe to help coordinate the work of the Swiss, French, Swedish, and Italian organizations. As Stern explains, even if the pollsters could gather the necessary data to describe the universe of western European public opinion,

> … new problems of adjustment and weighting would be encoun-
> tered. Units of such different sizes as Switzerland with 4 million
> people and France with 40 million require special sampling designs.
> Within each country, of course, a minimum number of interviews
> are needed to hold the error to bearable limits. It is questionable
> whether weighting on a straight population base would be ad-
> equate. In a … Western European Union, voting strength of the
> various countries would not be in direct proportion to population
> [meaning that each country in the Union gets only one vote
> regardless of its population—as is the case in the United Nations
> General Assembly].[7]

Thus, beyond describing opinion, problems arose as to how to present the data from the different countries. Should opinions from the various countries of different-sized populations be given the same **weight**? (Should the results of a poll in Rhode Island or Wyoming be considered of equal significance with poll results from California or New York?) Should the size of the Swiss sample, drawn from 4 million people, be the same or one-tenth the sample drawn from France, with a population 10

---

*Although the British, French, and Americans had not yet united their West German zones, created after Hitler's defeat, there was a high level of cooperation. The Soviets, on the other hand, were just beginning the process of engulfing East Germany and would refuse to relinquish control, imposing a communist government that remained in power until the Berlin Wall came tumbling down in those memorable November and December days of 1989. The *Time* article included data only for England, France, Sweden, Switzerland, Italy, and the American zone in Germany.

times as large? As we will see in Chapter 6, these questions remain relevant today. However, as you will realize, sample size is not conditional solely on population size, but it must be representative.

The *Time* survey used **stratified samples**, sub-groups of the population based on census data from each country. Right there we can see a problem that still confronts pollsters. Consider the now well-publicized inaccuracies of our own 1990 census which undercounted people (mostly minorities) in many poor, urban areas throughout the United States. (Something to think about: How representative can the sub-groups of a sample be if their percentage is based on a census of questionable accuracy?) Difficulties arose not only in creating the strata or sub-groups, but also in the interpretation of the demographic data, as in the areas of educational attainments, car ownership, community size, and occupational breakdowns. For example, the pollsters soon realized that the *Baccalaureat* in France, the *Matura* in Switzerland, and the high school diploma in the United States all represented different levels of educational achievement, even though each was the admission prerequisite for a university or college education. Then, too, the universe of car owners in the various countries did not yield a homogeneous profile. For example, even today, car ownership is economically easier to attain in the United States than in most other countries. Also, the demographic breakdown of places by population size caused problems: A Swiss town of 5,000 had a significantly higher socioeconomic and cultural standing than a similar-sized community in France or in the United States. Finally, in the United States there was no occupational classification corresponding to Europe's shopkeeper-craftsmen, who were considered a very significant (skilled and highly valued) group.

In Germany gender differences were paramount. The German polling sample was drawn to correspond exactly to the German census figures: 43 percent men and 57 percent women. The names of specific respondents were randomly drawn from lists of ration cardholders, and interviewers were given no discretion in the matter. Since German women were generally reluctant to express opinions, especially on anything relating to politics, it was imperative that interviewers maintained the correct population ratio of men to women. Had this not been the case, many interviewers might have chosen males to avoid the difficulty of dealing with reluctant female respondents,[8] and the results would not then have been representative. An example of the type of question the German respondents faced is: "Are there any countries on this list where people do not have a right to say or write what they believe without fear of punishment?" While 90 percent of the men said yes, only 74 percent of the women gave that answer. Such a large difference of opinion would not have shown up had the integrity (the representativeness) of the sample not been maintained.

Question Wording and Translation Problems

One question written by an American asked: "Do you have a washing machine in your home?" In two out of the three countries where this question was posed, a very small percentage of the respondents answered yes. However, in the third country the number of yes answers was very high. It was soon realized that respondents in the first two countries were thinking about an electric washer, as had the author of the question, while respondents in the third country were thinking of a commonly owned mechanical contraption, a hand-driven agitator that was mounted on a wash-tub. Only with the type of extensive pretesting that is now commonplace could translation and wording problems have been revealed.

To avoid such translation problems, we must consider the reactions evoked by the words used. Today's pollsters recognize that some words cause a reaction based on some objective image that the word calls to mind. People do have their own individual frames of reference. And, pollsters know that still other words trigger an emotional reaction based on (a) the social usage, background, circumstances, or socioeconomic class we generally associate with the item described, or (b) the structure of the word itself (the length, sound, tone).[9] Pollsters learned from the *Time* study that differences in meaning can be discerned only by those who have an intimate knowledge of the *local frame of reference* and a precise understanding of the question's original purpose. One way to avoid translation and wording problems is for the originating agency to include a set of notes explaining in detail each word or phrase used, supplying synonyms and alternative phrasing in order to convey the exact nature and intention of the question.[10] For example:

> *Question*: What style of furniture would you prefer to have in your dwelling: antique or modern?
>
> *Explanatory Note*: We are asking … with what type of furniture a person would like to live … [W]hether people … incline more toward the modern or more toward former days; whether the nostalgic longing for things past prevails over the joys of the present…. [T]hese preferences may show themselves in different ways in the case of a single individual, depending on whether one is speaking of music, furnishings, theater, architecture, or something else, and we chose to ask about the field with which the respondent was most likely to be deeply and frequently involved—the furnishings in his own home—in order to gain some insight into the deeper reactions of the individual…. [T]o learn these preferences, we use the conditional "would you prefer to have," in order to make it clear that we

would like to know the respondent's choice in the event that he should be able to satisfy his desires, without regard to such problems as supply or expense. By "furniture" we mean all furnishings, large and small, which go to make up a house. By "dwelling" we mean the house or apartment where one lives, or where one sleeps or eats. As for the term "antique," we leave it to the individual to determine when furniture may be considered in this category. By the same token, we do not distinguish between genuine and imitation antique furniture.

Perhaps you can relate to this problem if you think about the linguistic and semantic problems you would encounter were you to undertake a study today within the state of California, wherein you would have to interview immigrants from various Asian countries (China, Taiwan, Cambodia, Thailand, Vietnam, Japan and so on), from Mexico, and from Central and South America, in addition to those who have resided in California for many years and those who migrated to the West Coast from other parts of the United States.

Researchers analyzing the translation and wording problems found in the German part of the *Time* poll recommended extensive preliminary consultation. This would reduce the ethnocentrism of any survey formulated in one country but intended to be conducted in several other countries. Such consultation would also result in greater local and international validity and relevance for specific questions. Researchers determined that some of the questions had to be omitted from the German survey because they were inappropriate. For example, a question dealing with a proposed Western European Union read in part: "people could travel freely from one country to another, so that they could work wherever they liked." At that time, Germans were not even permitted to travel from the American to the French zone without an interzonal pass, nor could they get in or out of Berlin, then under Soviet control.★

Timing Problems

Simultaneous interviews are necessary if an accurate comparison of various countries is to be made. Intervening, changing circumstances, such as

---

★In fact, the situation would soon deteriorate. On June 24, 1948, the Soviets blockaded West Berlin. President Truman responded with the famed Berlin airlift, supplying West Berlin with food, fuel, clothing, and raw materials for its industries. The siege lasted until May 2, 1949, impressing the Soviets with the Western commitment and providing the final impetus for the creation of the NATO military alliance. The Cold War was off to a freezing start, according to subsequent opinion polls taken here and abroad.

the fall of the coalition government and communist takeover in Czechoslovakia, affected the respondents' opinions. For example, take the question, "In the present conflict between Russia and the U.S.A., who is winning ground and who is losing ground?" Interviewers found that the French (but not the French-speaking Swiss) tended to take questions literally. Pretesting in France indicated that "ground" was interpreted as "territory," so the phrase was changed to "Who is marking points?" However, while interviewing was under way, the communists took control of Czechoslovakia; thereafter, many respondents (even non-French participants) assumed the reference was to territory. Since Switzerland had an excellent communications system and small distances, the *Time* survey was completed in seven days, before the Czech crisis could significantly affect opinions. On the other hand, French interviewers, contending with far greater distances and a communications system that had not yet recovered from the impact of the war, needed 19 days, and Swedish interviewers, slowed by severe winter weather and with greater distances to cover, needed 22 days. As a result of the delays, comparison of the various national results to this question became useless.[11] Better pacing of the interviews was suggested so that even though it might not be possible to synchronize the start of interviews in the various countries, at least all interviewing would end on the same day.

The Order of Questions

The French survey led to several recommendations: (1) Begin with questions of the most personal interest to the respondent; (2) continue with queries of decreasing importance; (3) when approaching the end, return to the remaining questions of interest; and (4) save the most difficult items for the very end. Ideally, it is possible to create an optimal order for each national group so as to minimize the **refusal rate** (number of turndowns) in each country. (Something to think about when we reach Chapter 7, on the questionnaire.)

In addition to the attitudinal information gathered and presented to the public by Elmo Roper and the six participating overseas research organizations, this study led to a careful analysis of the problems encountered. The lessons learned from both the international exercise and the Truman–Dewey polling disaster helped make the last years of the 1940s one of the most exciting eras for the relatively new field of political opinion polling.

We will now fast-forward to the present era, returning to the past whenever it is relevant to opinion research today.

OPINION RESEARCHERS
LOOK EASTWARD

Warren J. Mitofsky of CBS News commented in April 1989 on the rush of opinion researchers to the Soviet Union. They were going there to cover the first election in 72 years where the outcome was not preordained, since this was the first time there was more than one candidate on the ballot.[12] Western news organizations sent reporters and poll takers to Moscow to interview some 2,300 voters as they left polling places in 29 election districts. Although the ballots were not counted until the following day, exit polling made it possible for American television audiences to learn—just after the polls closed that Sunday night—that Boris Yeltsin had won election to the Congress of People's Deputies.

Mitofsky noted, "No one has yet complained about the canvassing or blamed it for the shockingly low turnout—80 percent, as opposed to the customary 100 percent in a Soviet election." It probably won't be long, he added, before "some alarmists in the Kremlin ... raise the dirty question: Did the reporting of early returns from Moscow discourage some voters from coming out in Minsk?"[13] He is, of course, referring to the controversial exit polling incident that occurred in the United States on election night in 1980. The combined results of pre-election polls, exit polls, and early returns from closed precincts in the East led President Jimmy Carter to concede the election to Ronald Reagan about 8:20 P.M. Eastern Standard Time (EST). However, the voting sites were scheduled to remain open across the country up to another three hours. There were even reported cases of people on their way to vote who, having heard the news over the car radio, turned around and went home, thereby undermining local elections. Mitofsky adds: "Now that we have imparted our exit polling technology to the Soviet Union, the least we can do, in the true spirit of *glasnost*, is export the experts and strategies we have accumulated to cope with the supposed problems."

On November 9, 1989, Vladimir Andreyenkov, the head of the new Gallup Moscow, addressed a New York meeting of the American Association of Public Opinion Researchers (AAPOR). Andreyenkov stressed the newness of public opinion polling in the Soviet Union and the amazing rapidity with which changes were then occurring. He discussed a poll taken with private face-to-face interviews where respondents were first assured of their anonymity and then asked for their opinions on various issues. These data were then compared with another poll, in which television viewers were asked to phone in their opinions on specific questions. Andreyenkov laughingly acknowledged that he and his staff wondered who, having lived under the KGB (secret police), would pick up the telephone to phone in personal opinions. Their expectation was that the results of the telephone poll would be skewed. To their surprise, the results of the telephone poll were nearly identical to those of the in-person poll. One explanation might be that although assured of their anonymity, those interviewed face to face were still not about to state their opinions candidly. In other words, both types of respondents were equally afraid. (Remember the discussion of the Czechs' fear in the post–World War II period?) If that were the case, it would account for the similarity of results from the two sets of respondents. Still, at the end of 1989, it appeared from Gallup's tie-in with a Soviet polling outfit that *glasnost* was indeed viewed as representing openness, reform, and liberalization. Since then, a great many polls have been taken in the former Soviet Union and in eastern Europe in an attempt to understand public reaction to the rapid changes taking place.

The interest of Western pollsters, however, lies not just in discerning political trends. Remember, opinion research is also important in business. Marketing research is, after all, a form of opinion polling. What we choose to buy and why is important and valuable information, as Jonathan Robbin of Claritas realized back in the 1970s.

Long before the Wall came down in November and December 1989, East Germans had a window to the West through West German television, permitting them to become familiar with Western ideas[14] and to develop an appetite for our products. This television exposure has resulted in a greater awareness of Western ideology, lifestyles, and brand-name products among the East Germans than even exists among West Germans because the latter are bombarded with newspaper ads, billboards, and other media. As a result, the message—whether it is political or commercial—tends to get diluted. Because of this previous exposure and because, since reunification, the German government has been attempting to raise their standard of living, East Germans are considered a more promising market than is the rest of eastern Europe. Hence, Nielsen (of television ratings fame) started to concentrate its efforts on East Germany, tracking food, drugs, and durable goods in some 100 large retail stores in East Germany's major cities. The data are combined with information gathered through the use of TV diaries kept by a *panel sample* of 1,000 TV households that shop in these stores.[15] The resulting analysis has formed the basis of marketing strategies.

Although Nielsen continues to rank first (see Box 3.4), it is already facing strong competition internationally as other researchers look eastward. For example, the GfK Group, Germany's largest research company, moved quickly to open offices in Hungary and Poland, beginning research for international clients anxious to tap into these east European markets. GfK

BOX 3.4   Rank of Marketing Research Companies

Top 12 Marketing Research Companies by U.S. Research Revenue

RANK 1990		REVENUE IN MILLIONS 1990	1989	RANK 1989
1.	A. C. Nielsen (Illinois)	$468.6	$426.0	1
2.	Arbitron (New York)	230.6	253.5	2
3.	IMS International (Switzerland)	199.1	181.0	3
4.	Information Resources, Inc. (Chicago)	136.3	113.8	4
5.	Westat (Maryland)	74.8	65.9	5
6.	M/A/R/C (Texas)	56.9	47.9	6
7.	Maritz Marketing Research (Missouri)	53.2	46.1	7
8.	MRB Group (England)	45.8	44.6	8
9.	NFO Research (Connecticut)	45.5	42.0	9
10.	Abt Associates (Massachusetts)	43.4	37.9	11
11.	Gallup Organization (New Jersey)	40.5	37.0	12
12.	Market Facts (Illinois)	40.2	39.0	10

SOURCE: *Advertising Age*, June 10, 1991, "Research Business Report," compiled by Kenneth Wylie and Kathy Welyki. Also see Elena Bowes, "Researchers look eastward: GfK, Nielsen begin to track buying tendencies," *Advertising Age*, June 11, 1990, "Research Business Report."

---

began its study of East German buying patterns in May 1990 by monitoring a sample of 2,000 East German households. During the summer of 1990, the company was considering opening offices in Czechoslovakia and the former Soviet Union.

However, at that point in 1990, not everyone was as sanguine about making money from east European consumers. Some felt that once the excitement died down and Western businesses began to weigh the costs, they would realize that western Europe was much less expensive and easier to market. By 1991, this appeared to be true. The enormous costs of rebuilding East Germany following German reunification were increasingly apparent. A Gallup Poll in early January 1991 reported that 88 percent of the Czechs and Slovaks expected 1991 to be a year of economic difficulty.[16] And they were correct. The economic situation in Poland continued to deteriorate,* Yugoslavia was soon in the midst of a civil war, and the costs of decades of communism throughout eastern Europe made it a less appealing marketplace for the time being.

---

*In September 1993, the Poles voted into office a number of former communists who promised to slow the economic reforms that had led to the closing of inefficient companies and resulted in a disturbing increase in the unemployment rate.

Still, surveys taken prior to the attempted KGB-military coup in August 1991 indicated that most east European and Soviet consumers *were* creeping toward capitalism. One such study, designed to compare the free-market inclinations of Muscovites and New Yorkers, had included the question, "Does a table manufacturer have the right to raise prices if the company can't keep up with private demand?" The results of 391 interviews in Moscow and 361 in New York City were close: "Most of the Soviet and U.S. consumers responded just as Adam Smith would have: 'Yes, the manufacturer should be able to raise prices.'"[17] Since the failed coup, the transition to a free-market economy has been cautious. Even before the second attempted coup (this time against Russia's president Boris Yeltsin) and the subsequent election resulting in the ousting of many reform-minded Russian legislators, market researchers were taking a more sober look at the economic potential of the former Soviet Union and the countries in eastern Europe.

Despite the uncertainty of events in the former communist world, the people's interest in opinion surveys continues to increase, while it appears that in the United States, we are survey-saturated, deluged with polls on many different topics. Yet our scientific methodology has improved to the point where, as we will soon see, survey data continue to gain acceptance as courtroom evidence. In fact, in the United States, where most of us have telephones and published addresses, we not only take for granted the science of survey research, we also take for granted the absence of the fear and intimidation that exist elsewhere and that affect the outcome of polls.

LEARNING FROM THE

POLLING FLOP IN NICARAGUA

When Violeta Chamorro was elected president of Nicaragua in early 1990, pollsters who had predicted her defeat at the hands of incumbent Daniel Ortega wondered where they had gone wrong. What wrong assumptions had they made? Mostly, they had assumed that a poll is a poll is a poll, or, put another way, all polling is alike. They soon found otherwise. Consider the following problems pollsters then had to face in Nicaragua, an impoverished country with a nondemocratic government and one that had been in a state of war for several years:

1. *Sampling problems*   Most Nicaraguans do not have phones; many live in remote, inaccessible villages.
2. *Respondent problems*   Most are illiterate and very poor. They are

frightened and suspicious after years of being caught between the soldiers representing the dictatorship of the Sandinista government and the Contras who, supported by the United States government, brutally opposed President Ortega's rule.

3. *The large number of undecideds*   The pollsters were faced with a large bloc of undecided voters at the same time that Ortega's popularity rating had slipped below 50 percent. Forced conscription of Nicaraguan youth to fight in a long and devastating civil war had taken its toll on the Sandinistas' standing among the people. Few pollsters heeded the warning bells that should have indicated that most "undecided" respondents were avoiding admitting either the intention to vote against Ortega or the intention to abstain.

4. *The problem of selective perception*   Although war-torn Nicaragua's economy was a shambles, Ortega ran a smooth and polished campaign that dazzled the pollsters more than the voters. By contrast, Chamorro's campaign was that of a novice who often appeared to stumble. American reporters and pollsters concentrated on the campaign trappings as opposed to the reality of life in this Central American country.

5. *The intimidation problem*   Two of the few who looked behind the glitter of Ortega's campaign and focused on the reality of Nicaraguan life were Stephen Solarz and Richard Moren. Solarz, then a New York congressman, ignored the pro-Ortega polls with their large number of undecided voters and correctly predicted the Chamorro victory, saying that, considering Nicaragua's plight, there was no way Ortega could win. *Washington Post* analyst Moren focused on the intimidation problem that caused people to conceal their intention to vote against Ortega.[18]

Howard Schuman and Katherine Bischoping were members of a pre-election polling group. They conducted a test poll of 299 interviews in and around the city of Managua, using only one variable: the interviewers' pens,[19] which bore the symbolic colors of the candidates:

- One-third of the interviewers used pens with the red and black Sandinista colors and with *Daniel Presidente* (an Ortega slogan) printed on them.

- One-third used pens with the blue and white colors of the National Opposition Union, bearing the letters *UNO.*

- One-third used neutral-colored pens with no print on them.

Table 3.1 Pre-Election Polling Results in Nicaragua

	PRO-ORTEGA	PRO-CHAMORRO	NUMBER OF INTERVIEWS
Actual votes	41%	55%	–
UNO blue-and-white pens	44	56	48
Ortega red-and-black pens	63	37	57
Neutral pens	60	40	48

Omitting the other parties, secret ballots, and Don't Knows/No Responses, we can summarize the findings for the two main candidates as shown in Table 3.1.

Note the similarity between the actual election results and those obtained when interviewers used UNO pens. Of even greater significance and interest is the similarity between the results obtained when interviewers used Ortega pens and neutral pens. How would you explain this? While qualifying his analysis with the warning that the results of the field location (the Managua area) cannot be "rigorously generalized to the whole country," Schuman explains that the results suggest that respondents may have suspected that "neutral" was not really neutral. He adds: "Possibly the interviewers, mostly young women who described themselves as associated with a university, were thought likely to be sympathetic to Mr. Ortega rather than seen as purely professional."[20] Thus it appears that distrust based on fear and intimidation was a major factor in this polling failure. The Nicaraguans, believing the election process would rid them of Ortega, played the game their own way. Norman Ornstein takes the analysis a bit further, warning that while polls are indispensable and invaluable, "it is time we learned their limits as crystal balls before we rush to repeat, and compound, our mistakes abroad."[21]

CHAPTER REVIEW

- Interest in polling had begun to spread abroad prior to World War II.

- During the war, the United States government used survey research to determine morale, the response to propaganda, and so on.

- The government also used polls toward the end of the war to sample public opinion in occupied countries.

- In January 1948, Roper undertook a 10-country poll. This was the first major international polling effort. The study highlighted a number of challenging problems, including sampling, questionnaire, language, translation, and timing difficulties. The intervening communist takeover of Czechoslovakia also caused major problems because it affected the interpretation of a number of questions.

- While most logistical problems confronting international polling efforts have been resolved, linguistic, semantic, and political problems still abound.

- Much that we have learned from studying early international polling efforts can be applied to today's changing demographic conditions within the United States.

- Although survey researchers have been flocking to eastern Europe and the former Soviet Union on behalf of their clients who are interested in tapping new markets, the slow economic progress and various political upheavals there have had a sobering effect.

- Pollsters encountered a number of disturbing problems during their work in Nicaragua. Intimidation was a major concern.

- Lessons learned from that polling experience can be applied elsewhere in the developing world where similar problems exist. Can you identify those problems?

NOTES

1. Joe Belden, "Mexico's Public Opinion Poll," *Public Opinion Quarterly* (Spring 1944), p. 104.

2. Maj. Paul C. Bosse, "Polling Civilian Japanese on Saipan," *Public Opinion Quarterly* (Summer 1945), pp. 176–182.

3. Lt. (J.G.) Andie L. Knutson, "Japanese Opinion Surveys: The Special Need and the Special Difficulties," *Public Opinion Quarterly* (Fall 1945), pp. 313–319.

4. Cenek Adamec and Ivan Viden, "Polls Come to Czechoslovakia," *Public Opinion Quarterly* (Winter 1947–1948), pp. 548–552.

5. See "Brazilian Gallup Poll," *Public Opinion Quarterly* (Fall 1946).

6. David Wallace and Julian L. Woodward, "Experience in the *Time* International Survey: A Symposium," *Public Opinion Quarterly* (Winter 1948–1949), pp. 709–721.

7. Eric Stern, "The Universe, Translations, and Timing," *Public Opinion Quarterly* (Winter 1948–1949), p. 711.

8. Max Barioux, "Techniques Used in France," *Public Opinion Quarterly* (Winter 1948–1949), p. 719.

9. Barioux.

10. Barioux, pp. 716–717.

11. Stern, pp. 714–715.

12. Warren J. Mitofsky, "The Pollsters Are Coming," *The New York Times*, April 1, 1989, p. 27.

13. Mitofsky.

14. Elena Bowes, "Researchers look eastward: GfK, Nielsen begin to track buying tendencies," *Advertising Age*, June 11, 1990, "Research Business Report."

15. Bowes.

16. See Stephen Engelberg, "Czech Conversion to a Free Market Brings the Expected Pain, and More," *The New York Times*, Jan. 4, 1991, p. A3.

17. *Time*, "Business Notes, Surveys: Creeping Capitalism," July 30, 1990, p. 52. Unfortunately, the *Time* article supplied only the number of completed interviews and not the percentages of those who agreed that the manufacturer should be able to raise prices.

18. Norman Ornstein, "Why Polls Flopped in Nicaragua," *The New York Times*, March 7, 1990, p. 25.

19. For a detailed discussion of this poll, see Katherine Bischoping and Howard Schuman, "Pens and Polls in Nicaragua: An Analysis of the 1990 Preelection Surveys," *American Journal of Political Science*, Vol. 36, No. 2, May 1992, pp. 331–350. For a summary, see Howard Schuman, "3 Different Pens Help Tell the Story," *The New York Times*, March 7, 1990, p. 25.

20. Schuman, p. 25. A fuller explanation appears in the detailed study (p. 346).

21. Ornstein.

4

The Diverse Field of Opinion Research

Think about—

What are some of the opportunities in the opinion
research profession, beyond political polling?

Who are some of the "big guys" in the field of audience measurement?

What is the connection between public opinion polling and
measuring the audience size of radio and television programs?

Is tuning to a particular channel an example of expressing one's
choice or opinion, or is it an example of a restricted-choice situation?
What are the implications of the latter?

What is the problem with Nielsen's People Meters?
Is Nielsen's sample too small?

Do people selected by ratings services as part of their sample really
record in diaries what they listen to on the radio or what they view on
television? How accurate are these diaries?

What is a Parent Sample? How about a Parent Sample Field Location?

What did Arbitron's ScanAmerica offer its clients that was new?
Why did Arbitron leave the TV ratings service arena?

Have you heard about *The Hite Reports on Women and Love*?

If you were assured of confidentiality, would you answer
a questionnaire that asked about your private life?

Political opinion polling is just one aspect of the huge and diverse field of opinion research, which also includes some aspects of marketing research (for instance, surveying consumer preferences), itself a complex area. When we are asked our opinions and preferences (regarding political figures, magazines, automobiles, breakfast cereals, or television programs), that information is useful and that is why we are being asked. In most cases, there is a similarity in the ways in which such information is gathered and analyzed. In this chapter, we will look at some variations on a theme—the theme being opinion research and the first variation being audience measurement.

The rating services would have us believe that whenever we change from one television channel to another, we are expressing an opinion. But are we? Some would argue that we may be participating in a restricted-choice situation. We may not like any of the available choices, but may decide on LOP, the least objectionable program. As Michael Parenti puts it:

> With enough conditioning, consumers will consume even that which does not evoke their great enthusiasm. It is like living in one of the many places in America that specialize in mediocre restaurants: customers settle for the dismal fare that is served them, having access to nothing better.[1]

And we may leave the TV on—even if we don't like any of the offerings—merely because we prefer to hear some human sounds as opposed to silence. Still, one could argue that when we change to another channel, we are expressing a preference for something—anything—other than that which we were viewing; and that is what those who pay others to measure audience size want to know. So long as that TV is on, the theory goes, there is always an opportunity for the advertiser to get the message out. Repetition of the commercial throughout a program (indeed, throughout several programs targeting similar audiences), increased sound volume, a montage of colorful flashing images, catchy tunes, animation, sexual innuendo, and celebrity presence are only a few of the tactics used—all in the belief that if they know where to find you, sooner or later they'll get your attention.

Later in the chapter we will look at another variation of opinion research. *Women and Love* was a controversial study by Shere Hite. It focused on women's opinions and feelings on extremely personal and sensitive issues. Through a point-counterpoint analysis, you will have an opportunity to decide for yourself whether the criticisms of Hite's work were justified. My purpose in this chapter is to introduce the study of methodology—terminology and pitfalls—some of which you have already learned from your reading thus far.

OPINION RESEARCH GOES TO MARKET

Among the hundreds of marketing research firms throughout the country, Elrick and Lavidge was ranked eleventh domestically in 1989 by *Advertising Age*. E&L is a good example of a dynamic nationwide organization that offers a full range of research services to determine the markets most interested in their clients' products, how those products are used, and how well they perform in day-to-day situations, and to determine the degree of customer satisfaction or dissatisfaction. Imagine you are in charge of hiring for the company. Beyond the general office staff and sales specialists, think about the type of personnel E&L needs in each of the following areas, representing various phases in the research process:

1. *Data collection*   Its data collection facilities include: CATI (computer-assisted telephone interviewing) from 6 telephone centers with over 200 positions; shopping mall interviewing at more than 40 permanent locations; qualitative (in-depth) interviewing from over 45 focus group facilities; and face-to-face interviewing in homes, offices, stores, and factories on a nationwide basis. With a staff of

5,000 full-time and over 5,000 part-time personnel, plus a network of 1,100 offices in over 200 cities, E&L is capable of conducting nationwide studies on behalf of its clients.

2. *Data processing*   Its programming personnel and other data processing specialists work with mainframes and microcomputers, customized programming, and statistical packages to report research findings.

3. *Analysis and presentation*   Statisticians analyze and interpret raw numbers, turning the data into useful information on which recommendations are based. It takes a skilled communicator to present complex data in both written and oral reports.

   While E&L is one of the top marketing research outfits in the country, the king of the international survey research field, according to most sources, is the A. C. Nielsen Company, best known for its broadcast ratings service. What follows is an extensive discussion on the type of survey work conducted by Nielsen and two rival companies—Arbitron, another American company that until recently was a Nielsen competitor, and Pergamon AGB, based in Great Britain. I believe this discussion will provide insights regarding the complex area of survey methodology, with a special focus on the sampling techniques used to discern audience size and opinion.

THE WOES OF NIELSEN

Nielsen, ranked first by *Advertising Age*,[2] is probably best known because of its media research operation, begun in 1950. However, the company has been around much longer than that. In 1936, Arthur C. Nielsen, Sr., began measuring radio audiences, using the Audimeter developed by Robert Elder and Louis Woodruff of the Massachusetts Institute of Technology. The company began commercial network radio service in 1942, and in 1949 it issued its first National Nielsen Ratings. One year later, Nielsen's national probability sample of all households, the National Television Index (NTI), began. Recordimeter-controlled diaries were introduced in 1953, followed, in 1958, by the introduction of the Instantaneous Audimeter in New York. By 1960, NTI was reporting ratings based on 1,100 households around the country. The company began to service Japanese and Canadian television in 1961 and 1962, respectively. Responding to changing technologies, Nielsen released its first report on cable television in 1969 and its first study on the VCR in 1980, and began national testing of its **People Meter**, a sophisticated microprocessor, in 1983[3] (see Box 4.1). Nielsen increased its national sample to 1,700 households in 1984 and expanded its People Meter

---

BOX 4.1   Nielsen's People Meter

The People Meter automatically records the channels we watch. Smaller than a cigar box, it is placed on each television set in the household. An accompanying remote control device permits electronic entries from anywhere in the room. Each household member is assigned a *personal viewing button*, which is identified by name on the People Meter. Viewers push their assigned buttons when they are watching (there are "visitor" buttons, too) and a green light goes on. Red and green lights near each button indicate who is or isn't watching.

However, if someone falls asleep in front of the TV, or leaves the room, that information is supposed to be indicated, but that doesn't always happen. (There goes part of the accuracy!)

---

test to 1,000 households nationwide in 1986. One year later, the national People Meter service supplied data from 2,100 households and VCR playback measurement began. By 1988, the People Meter had been installed in 4,000 homes; it is now in 5,000 homes.

Today, Nielsen can provide the following research services (beginning with the most familiar):[4]

1. *Nielsen Television Index*   NTI supplies general daily and weekly estimates of television viewing and of network audiences, as well as national daily ratings of network programming. This group produces the *National Audience Demographics Report*, which estimates audiences by categories based on household demographics:

   - women and men (ages 18–34, 35–54, 55+)
   - teens (female/male, ages 12–17)
   - children (2–5, 6–11)

   Using the collected demographic data in conjunction with estimates and ratings, this Nielsen group is able to provide a wide range of specialized analyses.

2. *Nielsen Station Index*   NSI measures television station audiences for over 200 *local* markets, providing season-to-season reports that include data on viewing times and programs, broken down demographically. Campaign media experts use such Nielsen services to schedule their 30-second political commercials, in the belief that they will "get you where you live"—that is, while you are watching your favorite programs. (Think about how you form a political opinion.)

3. *Nielsen Metered Market Service*   NMMS provides daily and weekly reports on television audiences in major markets: New York, Los Angeles, Chicago, Philadelphia, San Francisco–Oakland, Boston, Washington (DC), Detroit, Dallas–Fort Worth, Houston, Atlanta, Tampa–St. Petersburg, Minneapolis–St. Paul, Seattle–Tacoma, Miami–Ft. Lauderdale, St. Louis, Denver, Phoenix, Sacramento–Stockton, Hartford–New Haven, Indianapolis, Milwaukee, Cincinnati, and Portland (Oregon).

4. *Nielsen Homevideo Index*   NHI measures the cable television and related home video services (cable satellite networks, local cable systems, pay-TV services and program suppliers).

5. *Nielsen Syndication Services*   Syndicators and distributors sell programs to stations on a (a) cash basis, (b) barter basis—stations get free programs in exchange for permitting the distributor to run a number of commercials during the program breaks, (c) cash-plus-barter basis—stations pay something and trade away less commercial time, so that they can also earn some revenue by selling local commercial time. The rating of syndicated programs is therefore an important determinant of the program's value to the local station, which must decide whether (and how) to buy a syndicated program.

Nielsen also sells samples to those interested in conducting their own research for whatever purpose. The *"for sale" samples* are drawn from the Nielsen Total Telephone Frame (TTF), kept reasonably current through updating three times a year. The TTF is first sorted by county within state; exchange coordinates; zip codes (remember the Claritas clusters based on zip code analysis—review Box 2.3); area codes/exchanges (consisting of blocks of 100 numbers); number of listings in each working 100-number block. After sorting, the TTF is used by the Nielsen Station Index and made available for sale to research organizations. The TTF can be broken down in a number of ways, using the following definitions: (a) total United States; (b) telephone exchanges; (c) Standard Metropolitan Statistical Area (SMSA); (d) census regions; (e) states; (f) Nielsen TV Designated Market Areas (DMAs); (g) counties; (h) counties by population density breaks; and (i) zip codes (for which Nielsen charges more). Sample sizes can vary from under 1,000 to 200,000, with costs ranging (in 1990) from $260 to $12,000 (when the TTF samples are supplied on computer tape or disk) and $17,000 (on cards or forms). Nielsen samples are available in 48 hours; faster service is possible, depending upon computer use and at additional cost.[5]

Considered an "impartial umpire" in media research, Nielsen ran into some difficulties beginning in June 1990.[6] Television network viewing in the first six months of 1990, according to the Nielsen ratings, declined as viewers turned off the networks and turned on their VCRs, a nonnetwork channel, or cable television. Nielsen reported, according to John Lippman of the *Los Angeles Times* News Service:

> From January to March [1990], one of the peak ratings period of the year, television viewing of soap operas, game shows, and evening news programs among young men and women fell 10 percent to 14 percent from year-ago levels.

During April and May, viewing picked up a bit. However, Lippman reports that "the networks' newscasts and late-night talk shows still continued to suffer declines of 13 percent and 6 percent, respectively," among the prized target audience of young adults.[7] There is a problem with the way Lippman's article is worded. Consider the following: If the networks' previous share of the audience was 20 percent, a drop of 10 percent would bring their share of the audience to 18 percent, representing a drop of 2 percentage points (see Box 2.2), usually well within the margin of error. Without more information, such as the actual previous ratings, we cannot tell whether these rates of decline are significant.

Still, bear in mind that each national ratings point equals 921,000 households,[8] and that any slippage in the number of viewers between the ages of 18 and 49 translates into diminished advertising revenue. By June 1990, advertising losses for the three major networks were estimated between $150 million and $200 million, with projected losses for the rest of 1990 reaching as high as $400 million. Because the networks had to give advertisers free airtime for their commercials to compensate them when programs failed to reach the guaranteed number of viewers, the Nielsen report was really bad news.[9]

The three major networks—NBC, CBS, and ABC—have since questioned the accuracy of Nielsen's People Meter, which automatically records the channel watched and which was intended to speed the delivery of ratings information by replacing the Nielsen diaries. Actually, Nielsen uses two systems to measure programs: NTI, which measures network, cable, and syndication programming through data collected from today's 5,000 People Meters, and NSI, which measures local TV viewing. The networks, critical of Nielsen, cite the following points relevant to our understanding of opinion research methodology:

Sample Size and Makeup The data collected are considered representative of programs watched in 92.1 million homes (equaling the 98 percent of the total U.S. households that own television sets). According to Nielsen, your chance of being selected as part of their random sample is roughly 1 in 24,000. They select housing units from the Census Bureau data on all housing units in the United States. Surveyors are sent out to locate each sample housing unit in the country—obviously not an easy task. According to Nielsen literature, "surveyors ... have found living quarters in railroad boxcars, in beer trucks, in caves and in trees."[10] Housing units that are occupied and have a television set can be asked to become part of the sample.

Researchers have found that viewing patterns of households in the same block tend to be similar because of neighborhood similarities: (a) television signal reception, (b) presence or absence of cable, (c) household demographics (income, social status, number of children per household, and so on). Therefore, no more than one housing unit per block is selected. Also, to reduce any skew that might occur because of sample fatigue, Nielsen reports that it replaces households that have been in the sample for 24 months, arguing that

> ... reducing the length of time a household can stay in the sample increases the number of different households in the sample across weeks and months, resulting in lower sampling errors. It also decreases the possibility of any substantial demographic differences developing over time between the population as a whole and the Nielsen sample.

However, some Nielsen households, as was the case with the Fischer family in Olney, Maryland, have remained as part of the sample for as long as four years,[11] resulting, no doubt, in the sample fatigue Nielsen had hoped to avoid. The networks, unhappy with the message of decreased viewership, attacked the messenger by raising the old bugaboo about the sample size being too small and nonrepresentative of their audiences.

Yet there appears to be greater justification for their other criticisms regarding Nielsen's methodology, and I cannot help wondering whether the sample isn't inevitably skewed because of **self-selecting bias**. That is, there are certain socioeconomic groups who will and who will not agree to being part of the sample. Todd Allan Yasui reported in the *Washington Post* in 1988 that Nielsen offered "several small benefits" besides hiding the wires that are needed to connect the television sets, the VCR, and video games to meters: Nielsen would pay half of any TV repair bills necessary during the time the family remained part of the sample, and they would give the family $5 per month per television set, plus $25 toward any new set.[12] However, consider the inconvenience of monthly service checks and the loss of privacy—such as when Mr. and Mrs. Fischer received a friendly call telling them to put the television sets back in their children's rooms after they had been removed because the kids had not done their homework. It seems clear that the "small benefits" and the notion that the household "statistically represented about 52,000 other American households" would probably not motivate everyone to participate in the Nielsen sample.

Does the Nielsen sample reflect the correct proportion of the following groups in the United States: college-educated, professionals, owners of small businesses, upper-middle-class and higher-income families? Although these households theoretically have an equal chance of becoming part of the sample, are they equally likely to agree to participate? And, if not, what does that tell us about the impact of Nielsen ratings on the type of television programming offered?

Validation Problems Critics note that the two Nielsen systems have, in the past, been used to validate each other, but they now show ever-widening discrepancies. For example, for the first quarter of 1990, the national system showed a 10-percent decrease in daytime viewing among women 18–49, while the local system showed a decrease of only 6 percent. As a result of the disputed Nielsen ratings, Larry Hoffner, NBC's executive vice president of sales, put NBC's first-quarter losses for 1990 at $40 million.[13]

Human Error/Laziness The networks say people are watching but are forgetting to push the meter's buttons to register the fact. Although claiming that people *are* pushing People Meter buttons, Nielsen acknowledges its efforts to perfect a passive system. The company cites the work of its engineering staff (over 80 people) to develop the **infrared scanning system**, capable of sweeping an area in seven seconds, detecting and recording heat generated by the presence of people. The computer programming of this passive system enables the scanning device to distinguish between humans and other heat sources such as pets, appliances, and lamps.

Changing Lifestyles Network executives have commented on changes in television viewing habits between the 1950s (when the Nielsen system originated) and today: Alan Wurtzel, senior vice president at ABC, explains that in the 1950s there were only a few channels and only one TV set (in the living room), which the family watched together (and the parents controlled) during the evening hours.[14] All of this has changed: There are now a multiplicity of cable channels, two or more television sets in many homes, and a remote control device that enables us to switch from channel to channel in search of TV nirvana.

Nielsen has responded that people watch less network television because they are spending more time viewing cable, satellite programming, pay TV, and VCRs and are also more involved with video games and computers. In fact, the Nielsen engineers have developed ways to measure all those signal sources, including a VCR, and Nielsen claims that its field representatives undergo an intensive 10-week training program, learning how to meter different VCRs, TVs, cable converters, satellite dishes—anything attached to the television set.

Non-Home Viewing and Use of VCRs   The networks complain that the Nielsen system does not measure outside-the-home viewing, such as in bars, dormitories, and offices, nor can it tell when a VCR is playing a prerecorded program.[15] All of that seems true.

As a result of the ratings dispute, during the summer of 1990 NBC decided on a measuring system of its own. The new system used data from two sources: (a) the cumulative national audience data supplied by Nielsen from its People Meters for the previous eight years, with a "calibration" of (b) data from the Nielsen and Arbitron diaries that viewers would fill out either on an occasional-week (Nielsen) or weekly (Arbitron) basis.[16] The obvious problem with diaries, as anyone who has ever kept one knows, is that people do not always remember to write in them on a daily basis. There is always the possibility of people playing catch-up at the end of the week, trying to recall what they watched, not to mention the human tendency to glorify ourselves by claiming to have watched more intellectual fare than we usually do when we want to relax.

The new NBC plan to count its viewers for purposes of setting advertising rates was based on a projection of what ratings would be if an eight-year trend (using 1982 as the base year) were to continue. The year 1982 was chosen because that was the year television viewing leveled off, ending its annual increase. Since then, it has experienced a moderate annual decrease. Assume, for example, that the eight-year trend indicated a 1-percent decline each fall for women viewers aged 18–49. Using the NBC plan, another 1-percent decline in the following fall season would be expected. Thus, if the Nielsen rating during that fall season were to experience a drop in viewing of 3 percentage points for that group, NBC would consider the Nielsen data an aberration but would make a statistical adjustment for the decline.[17] ABC, which had initially decided to use an average drawn from the previous three years, decided to follow the NBC plan, while CBS said it "agreed in principle."[18] Fox Television, emerging as the fourth network, decided to stay with Nielsen, selling its commercial time based on the reported ratings.

In February 1994, Elizabeth Kolbert reported in *The New York Times* that the three major networks were underwriting their own multimillion-dollar research effort to create an alternative ratings system to Nielsen's. The network executives reported that they had hired Statistical Research Inc. (based in Westfield, New Jersey) to develop a "state-of-the-art TV ratings laboratory." In an attempt at damage control, Nielsen president John A. Dimling said that his company was pleased to work with all their customers, "to explore ways to improve the measurement and reporting of television audience behavior."

THE ARBITRON WAY

In October 1993 Lawrence Perlman of the Ceridian Corporation, the owners of Arbitron, announced that, unable to compete with Nielsen, Arbitron was pulling out of the television ratings business. Critics of Nielsen echoed the words of Paul Schulman, president of a media buying company, "Everybody wants Arbitron to challenge Nielsen, but nobody wants to pay for it." Looking to Arbitron's future, Stephen B. Morris, president of Arbitron, said the company was "developing qualitative research into the buying habits of television viewers and radio listeners."[19]

Known as the major company that surveys and measures radio listening in 260 U.S. markets, Arbitron had also competed with Nielsen in the local television ratings game. It had used diaries to measure 212 markets and meters to measure 14 major markets: Atlanta, Boston, Chicago, Cleveland, Dallas–Ft. Worth, Denver, Detroit, Houston, Los Angeles, Miami, New York, Philadelphia, San Francisco, and Washington, DC. The meters had enabled Arbitron to provide overnight ratings information. Overall, the company had sampled 6,325 television households and had tried to compete with Nielsen head-to-head in the network ratings business.

Although Arbitron is rethinking its television ratings efforts, its sampling methodology remains of interest. The company divided the United States into **Areas of Dominant Influence (ADIs)**, each of which had to have at least one commercial, nonsatellite home station. ADIs (also identified as Primary Sampling Units, or PSUs) were updated annually to take into account such changing market conditions as:

- new commercial stations
- existing stations that leave the air
- changes in network affiliation
- changes occurring in parent/satellite station relationships

In drawing a new meter panel sample,[20] Arbitron created a parent sample of 6,000 to 10,000 housing units (varying in size according to the market and over time as a result of changing conditions). The parent sample (PS) was representative of all housing units within the ADI. They then selected the specific housing units from the PS for recruitment into the meter panel and always maintained and controlled the demographic composition of the installed meter panel sample, which they updated on a regular basis.

In the first phase of creating the PS, Arbitron used a custom-designed Metromail **sampling frame**.* Using the statistical techniques (and taking into account the area's population density, region within the ADI, county within the region, zip code, presence or absence of cable, ethnic composition, *median* family income (see Box 4.2), average household size, and median education of persons age 25 and older), Arbitron randomly drew a selection of parent sample field locations with geographically defined boundaries, indicating starting and ending points.

Professional field **enumerators** were sent out to list all housing units in each selected field location (including those with/without TV, phones, listed/unlisted telephone numbers, and occupied/vacant housing units). Thus all households in the field location had an equal chance of being part of the PS (even though they might not have been part of the initial Metromail sampling frame). Field enumerators visited each household in the PS and administered a questionnaire to obtain household demographic data and information relating to television, cable, and VCR use.

In the second phase, Arbitron drew information from the questionnaires to delineate 25 to 50 major demographic **strata** (groupings) that were mutually exclusive and exhaustive (see Box 4.3). The third and fourth phases, dealing with maintaining the integrity of the sample and updating it as attrition and other changes occurred, were necessary to ensure accurate representation. A turnover of sampling locations occurred on a gradual basis. As the original parent sample field locations were subdivided into three areas, each area was replaced over time by newly constituted PS field locations. Over a five-year period, an entirely new sample was drawn.

As for the Arbitron television diary system, Arbitron selected a completely new sample of households for each week of a diary survey (see Box

---

*Metromail Advertising is an independent company that provided Arbitron with the information it needed for its sampling frame. This frame was created from two annually updated elements: (1) *Metromail's Detailed Record File* of all listed-telephone households, with limited coverage of unlisted- and nontelephone households; and (2) *Metromail's Address Coding Guide File* of street names and street address ranges (for example; One Maple Street to 333 Maple Street), as originally coded by U.S. Census Tract, Block Group, and Enumeration District numbers, and by postal zip and other geographic codes.

BOX 4.2   The Median Versus the Mean

The **median**, as distinguished from the average or the **mean**, refers to the *midpoint*, where there is an equal number of items above and below. In the example that follows, I list the incomes of 22 people. The reason for not using the average (or mean) when we speak of income or education is that it can skew the results, giving a misleading impression. Why? Take, for example, the average (mean) of the following incomes:

$100,000
100,000
90,000
75,500
70,000
61,000
61,000
52,500
50,000
32,000
30,300
25,000
23,750
18,000
17,500
17,000
15,000
15,000
15,000
12,000
12,000
10,000

If you add this column and divide by 22 (the number of individual incomes listed), you will find that the mean (or average) is $40,909.

However, if you examine the column (arranged with the highest incomes on top), you will find that the median (the number that indicates the midpoint) is $27,650. The median, in this case, falls between $25,000 and $30,300. Note that there are an equal number of incomes above the median and below it.

The mean and the median are two different ways of summarizing the data. However, the mean is affected by extreme scores (high incomes in this case), while the median is not.

4.4). Here, too, respondents were randomly selected within each market area. The selected households kept weekly diaries (Wednesday through Tuesday) for each television set in the home. As is the case with Arbitron radio diaries, those for television viewing provided space for each family member (and visitors) to record their age, gender, and the programs they watched, with program entries being made every 15 minutes. This enabled

---

BOX 4.3   Arbitron's Strata

As is generally the case in opinion research sampling, the strata were based on combinations of categories. Arbitron used the following demographic variables:

- status of the housing unit (whether it is occupied or vacant)
- presence or absence of a television set
- region of the country
- size of the household
- race
- age of household head
- presence or absence of cable TV
- number of TV sets (one versus two or more)

Then housing units of the parent sample that had been placed in the 25 to 50 groups were further stratified. The sub-groupings (*substrata*) from which the ultimate random sample would be drawn were achieved when the housing units were sorted according to the following additional characteristics:

- presence or absence of children in the home.
- level of education of the head of the household
- county
- location within the parent sampling field location
- specific address and housing unit within the field sampling location

---

Arbitron to calculate an average quarter-hour audience. Demographic information, recorded at the back of the pocket-sized diary, included data on the following variables:

- location of the household
- family size
- the diarykeeper's race/ethnicity
- whether there are working women in the household
- how many hours a week the different family members work
- whether they have cable (which channels)
- whether they have pay television (which services)

When the diaries were returned to Arbitron, those from households with more than a single television set were edited to eliminate duplication. For example, if two diaries showed the same program being watched on two different TV sets in a given household, Arbitron edited the diaries to indicate one entry. Some experts questioned Arbitron's diary-checking process,

---

BOX 4.4   On the Diaries

Question 1: Do those who participate and take the time to fill in and return the diaries behave differently from those who (a) refuse to participate, or (b) participate but fail to complete or return the diaries?

Question 2: Without the People Meter to record what is actually being viewed, will Mr. and Mrs. Average Joe American, writing a diary, record that they watched some PBS public affairs program, rather than "Roseanne"?

Clue: Arbitron acknowledged these problem areas and others.[1] In addition to its test run of People Meters in Denver and elsewhere, the company experimented with Scan

America, SAMI, a tracking service. SAMI matched supermarket purchases with TV viewing habits.[2] Do you see any problem with that? After all, isn't the whole purpose of finding out what we watch to enable advertisers and political media consultants to place their messages on the most popular programs, where we will see and be influenced by them?

1. *Arbitron Rating/Television*, "Description of Methodology" (January 1989), pp. 54–55.
2. Arbitron began ScanAmerica locally in 1987 and nationally in 1991. Although CBS backed it, other networks and large advertisers gave it little support. As a result, Arbitron ended ScanAmerica in 1992.

---

referring to it as a hit-and-miss operation, and saying that the validity of the survey was in doubt.

Then followed the process of data reduction, with the handwritten information being coded and typed in so that it could be computer-processed. The data were tabulated and collated into ratings books that were mailed to subscribing organizations. Arbitron, as is the case with Nielsen, reported that of the diaries sent out, they were able to use approximately 50–55 percent.

The Research Business Gets Tougher

While Nielsen temporarily suffered both network criticisms and Arbitron's initial competition, the late British media mogul Robert Maxwell was eyeing the possibility of his market research company, Pergamon AGB, challenging Nielsen for the American market (see Global View 1). Yet the outlook was far from bleak for Nielsen, which was already tracking the buying tendencies of East Germans.

Global View 1 AGB Versus A. C. Nielsen

Score: 8,591   Nielsen People Meters worldwide
          8,530   AGB People Meters worldwide[1]

In 1990, the A. C. Nielsen Company, already operating in Melbourne, Australia, successfully challenged Robert Maxwell's Pergamon AGB in four other Australian cities. Nielsen executives said that those five markets made up about 95 percent of Australia's television viewers. Despite the Australian losses, AGB claimed to have installed People Meters in Ireland, the Netherlands, Belgium, Spain, Italy, Greece, Portugal, Turkey, Hong Kong, Thailand, the Philippines, New Zealand, and France. "We have more ... installed and in more countries than anyone," an AGB executive said.[2]

Nielsen also challenged AGB in Great Britain, where it tried to win the huge ratings contract administered by the Broadcasters' Audience Research Board, jointly owned and controlled by the British Broadcasting Corporation (a government body) and the Independent Television Association (consisting of Britain's 16 commercial TV broadcasters). Nielsen lost that round when the board made its decision to split the annual $10.9 million contract between AGB and Research Services Millward Browne (RS). The actual division of the money was not made public.

The seven-year contract began on August 1, 1991, and called for RS to select the 4,435 sample households (up from about 3,000 under the previous contract) that would receive the People Meters. AGB would install the meters, collect/process the data, and distribute the results. The board announced that the makeup of the new viewer panel would be disproportionate, with younger and wealthier viewers given increased representation, since these are the viewers advertisers most want to reach.

Although AGB has used People Meters since December 1984, and was generally credited with operating an "extremely good service,"[3] the television and advertising industries had two major criticisms: (1) The meters in use did not provide the gender and age of any viewers visiting sample households; and (2) they could not tell when a VCR was playing back a previously recorded program.

Gareth Morgan of the Independent Television Association explained that some 62 percent of British homes had at least one VCR.[4] AGB intended to introduce a new People Meter, capable of electronically imprinting a videotape as it was being recorded by a

VCR. When the tape was played back, the meter would then be able to recognize its electronic footprint.

The next AGB–Nielsen battle was fought on American soil. AGB rated the 1987–1988 television season in the United States. At that time, only CBS was willing to buy the service, leaving AGB with losses estimated at $70 million. However, now that the three major networks seem unhappy with Nielsen, AGB[5] might just get another chance to dethrone Nielsen.[6]

1. Steven Prokesch, "AGB Losing Its TV–Ratings Monopoly in Britain," *The New York Times*, July 2, 1990, Business section, p. 6. These are Nielsen figures; Pergamon AGB declined to give any figures.

2. Prokesch.

3. Prokesch, according to Alec Kenny, media director of Saatchi & Saatchi Advertising.

4. Prokesch.

5. AGB was sold by Maxwell in 1991. His apparent suicide in the fall of that year was followed by an intensive investigation, revealing how debt-ridden he was.

6. The potential for a conflict of interest exists when a network pays someone to gather and report information that may displease it. In that situation, there would be an obvious business incentive for the research organization to avoid reporting information that could send the client looking for another researcher.

Other Uses for Survey Data

The Nielsen and Arbitron efforts to describe, explain, predict, and represent our media consumption habits are only two examples of the commercial uses of survey research. There are many other types of research undertaken to understand people, their needs, wants, and fantasies. As we will see in later chapters, in addition to the court's use of survey research, a good deal of survey work takes place predominantly in academic settings, and some of it has policy-making implications. Some years ago, for example, sociologist James Coleman's studies of ethnic diversity in school districts led to court-ordered busing to integrate our public schools throughout the country. And a number of contemporary social scientists are studying the links between the ownership of firearms and the rate of death due to accident and improper use. Also, the Centers for Disease Control and other government agencies have been exploring the sexual practices and attitudes of the American people to learn how to control the spread of AIDS.

Another interesting example of a survey with policy implications is the one sponsored by the National Science Foundation every decade since the 1960s. Called the National Survey of College Graduates, it is conducted by the Census Bureau, taking advantage of their expertise with surveys. The results of the survey of college graduates are used by government, businesses, and universities to help match the graduates to jobs in various fields. This study and the others mentioned previously are just a few examples of the ways in which researchers have been enlisted to gather the data that will form the basis of policy-making decisions. In subsequent chapters we will examine the use of data collection for marketing and political purposes. Before moving on, I would like you to consider the following point-counterpoint discussion of a different type of survey research, one that has come under great criticism from a substantial number of individuals in the profession of data collection.

THE HITE REPORTS

In this final section of the chapter, we will consider another variation of public opinion research, a study that asks for our opinions and feelings on extremely personal and sensitive issues. On reading the Hite study, I thought of my own ambivalence toward answering a long questionnaire that delves into private matters and wondered who would want to respond. Many researchers have raised questions about Shere Hite's methodology, but among those familiar with her work, many agree that she made a valuable contribution to the general debate about the concerns, problems, and roles of women in a changing society. Of equal importance, Hite's work stimulated discussion among professional opinion researchers about the perceived weaknesses in her chosen methodology. And perhaps of even greater importance, the debate—and Hite's subsequent relocation to Europe—raised concerns about a researcher's desire and attempt to explore new methods. Hite discusses her work in The Professional Voice 2. Eleanor Singer's point-counterpoint analysis and critique follows in The Professional Voice 3.

The Professional Voice 2
The Hite Reports on Women and Love
Shere Hite

I faced unique challenges in devising the methodology for The Hite Reports, *which comprise a three- volume study of over 15,000 women and men in the United States, 1972–1987. The Hite* Reports on Women and Love *is basically a study of emotions and inner belief systems. There is an ongoing and abstruse discussion in the field of methodology (a subsection of psychology and sociology, which is not a specialty of every sociologist or psychologist) as to how best to study emotions and attitudes.[1] Should they be quantified at all? The questions, "How do you love the person in your current relationship?" and "What kind of love is it?" are difficult to answer and analyze, not to mention build into statistical findings. Thus, the methodology for* The Hite Reports *was carefully designed to use a new combination of elements that would bring out complex data yet retain first-person narratives, women's voices, that are related to women's state of consciousness now, 20 years after the women's movement and at the end of the twentieth century.*

QUESTIONNAIRE DESIGN

Many believe that multiple-choice questionnaires represent the height of scientific objectivity in that they can be quantified easily and need no interpretation. However, this is fallacious reasoning since, as Max Weber pointed out 100 years ago, all researchers have a point of view, a way of reflecting the cultural milieu in which they were brought up, and these assumptions are subtly filtered into the categories and questions chosen. A strong case can be made that multiple-choice questionnaires (especially those asking about attitudes and emotions) only project onto respondents the researcher's assumptions.

In other words, simple multiple-choice questionnaires could not be used for this study because they would have implied preconceived categories of responses and, in a sense, told respondents what the allowable or normal answers would be. Multiple-choice questions would have closed down dialogue with the participants when the aim was the opposite—to stimulate dialogue between those participating and, later, between readers and participants. Although much easier to work with, such a questionnaire would have subtly signaled the participant that the research categories were equated with reality or allowable reality, whereas my intention was to permit women's own voices to emerge. Specifically, my intention was to elicit in women's own words their deepest reflections on the nature of love and to listen to them during a historic period of questioning our own inner assumptions about society and the nature of relationships/personal life.

In addition to the use of an essay questionnaire, it was crucial to the integrity of the study to assure anonymity so that women could say anything they wanted, in their own words, without fear of being judged or seen as foolish, picking the wrong man, and so on. Thus, I chose a written questionnaire format, rather than face-to-face interviews, with respondents specifically asked not to sign their names, although other demographic data were taken.

The necessity for anonymity also dictated the methods of

questionnaire distribution: It was not possible to do a probability or random sample because then anonymity would not have been possible. Only by soliciting replies through church, university, and other groups, letting members decide on an individual basis whether or not to respond, could they be assured of total privacy.

DISTRIBUTION OF QUESTIONNAIRES AND COMPOSITION OF SAMPLE

While women in this study include a vast cross-section of American women from different socioeconomic groups and classes, are they representative of American women? All in all, 100,000 questionnaires were distributed; 4,500 were returned. This is almost twice as high as the standard rate of return for this kind of distribution.

The confusion in some public commentary about the adequacy of this percentage can be explained: There are two basic kinds of questionnaire distribution. In one, the respondents are not anonymous; their names and addresses are known to those taking the survey, and typically they have been picked because they are representative of the larger society. In this type of sample, a probability or random sample, the return rate must be 70 percent or more in order to include enough of the spectrum chosen in advance to remain representative.

However, in another type of distribution, such as that used here, where it is important that respondents have complete anonymity, people cannot be picked. Rather, questionnaires must be offered through various types of groups and at locations across the country, and responses allowed to be returned until the demographic composition begins to approach the general demographics of the population at large. Then, as is usually done in a random sample, the small missing statistical groups can be patched in.

Almost no major research using essay questions today is done via random sampling methods, since the return rates tend to be low (and, as mentioned, in a random sample, almost all of those chosen must reply to validate the sample). Most survey research now tries to match its samples demographically to the general population in other ways; for example, by weighting responses to conform to the population profile. This is why so many sociologists who are not specialists in methodology speak of the necessity of a return rate of at least 70 percent. They are not familiar with the type of study done here or the methodology necessitated by a need for anonymous distribution. (Indeed, few studies require the anonymity that is essential to *The Hite Reports*.) Also, many people do not recognize that *Women and Love* is basically a psychological study done with an exceptionally large database—a cross, in fact, between sociology and psychology.

Why didn't *The Hite Reports* use small samples the way most psychological studies do? Certainly Freud never attempted a large sample, nor do most psychologists working in research today. (Freud used a handful of upper-class Viennese women on which to base his theories of female psychology. Typically, articles in psychology journals are based on samples of graduate students or other groups of less than 50 people.) Perhaps some in psychology still assume that their samples need not try to approximate the larger population, since they believe (as did Freud) that the behavior they are studying is biologically based. However, if one believes that a large component is created by the social environment and social pressures, then the largest possible spectrum of opinion must be looked at and debated—and other historical philosophical positions considered as well—in order to critique a society's definitions of standard male and female psychology. In addition, "what is" must also be measured against "what might be," insofar as possible. In any case, sufficient effort was put into the various forms of distribution so that the final statistical breakdown of those participating according to age, occupation, religion, and other

variables known for the U.S. population at large closely resembles that of the U.S. female population.

ANALYSIS OF REPLIES

Analyzing data from essay-type questionnaires is a complex endeavor; compilation and categorization of such answers is quite labor-intensive. However, the resultant data are rich: It is precisely the possibility of reaching deeper levels of introspection that makes the use of an essay questionnaire so important here, as opposed to multiple choice.

Analysis of data in *The Hite Reports* involved an intricate process of first placing the answers of each respondent (who received an identification number) on charts. I then began the process of locating patterns and categories in the answers and prepared statistical figures by totaling the number of women in each category. Following that, I selected representative quotes.

Any attempt at condensation or computerization at an early stage of the analysis would have defeated the purposes of the study: to find the more subtle meanings lying beneath the easily quantifiable parts of the replies, and to keep intact individual voices so that participants can communicate directly with readers. After all the replies were charted and the process of identifying categories completed, with representative quotes selected, statistical computation was possible.

To replicate this study, the same procedure must be followed. One cannot, as in the ABC/*Washington Post* Poll, simply turn the final statistical results into questions, provide these questions with multiple-choice answers, and then ask them (over the telephone) of people who are not at all anonymous, and claim to have replicated a study.*

PRESENTATION OF FINDINGS

Most basic to the methodology of these reports is separation of findings from analysis and interpretation. This is done by choice of research design, questions, and method of analysis, and, in particular, by the style of presentation of findings. I planned the presentation of data to serve more than an informative function. Rather than simply giving readers statistics plus my analysis of data, my aim was to create an inner dialogue within the reader, as s/he mentally converses with those quoted. Therefore, large parts of text comprise first-person statements from those participating. My statements further debate how these may fit into categories of social ideology.

*Editor's Note: Hite is referring to the attempt by an ABC/*Washington Post* Poll to repeat some of her questions in a national poll, using a representative sample. The marginal percentages in that poll were very different from those reported by Hite.

Unique to this study, my viewpoint as the researcher is separated from the data gathered. A reader can find participants with whom s/he agrees and disagrees and may also choose to accept or reject my theoretical conclusions—because the reader is given access to the original data, that is, the voices of the women responding. This is virtually unheard of in research; usually one must simply accept what the investigator says. Freud's women were never allowed to speak for themselves. In fact, as sociologist Jessie Bernard has pointed out, where else can you find a sample of 4,500 women speaking in their own voices?

In addition to first-person statements and the researcher's theoretical perspective, 170 tables giving a breakdown of the major findings are presented. Rarely has so much information been given about the way in which a study was done, and almost never have the actual data received been shown.

Science or Philosophy?

While as many scholars have praised the research methods as have criticized them, are arguments over methodology really the point? This is an interdisciplinary study, one that tries not only to show what is, but also to illuminate a debate that is raging within many women and many relationships over values and the family, the definition of the self.

As Professor John L. Sullivan, a specialist in methodology, explains, the debate over representativeness really misses the point: Yes, *The Hite Reports* are good research. Yes, they are scholarly, but more important.

The great value of Hite's work is to show how people are thinking, to let people talk without rigid *a priori* categories, and to make all this accessible to the reader. Hite has many different purposes than simply stating population generalizations based on a probability sample. Therefore questions of sampling are not necessarily the central question to discuss about her work. Rather, it is a matter of discovering the diversity of behaviors and points of view....

Her purpose is clear: to let her respondents speak for themselves. What purpose would it have served to do a random sample, given the aims of Hite's work? None, except for generalizing from percentages. But Hite has not generalized in a nonscholarly way. Many of the natural sciences worry a lot less about random samples, because their work is to test hypotheses. And most of the work in the social sciences is not based on random samples either; in fact, many if not most of the articles in psychology journals are based on data from college students, and then generalized.

Interestingly, they are not criticized in the same way Hite has been.

And so, while debates over methodology have their merit and their place, in the case of *The Hite Reports* to argue over numbers is to miss the forest for the trees: What this study is really about, what women are really doing here, is carrying on a massive debate about female psychology and the ideology of our times, choices for the future and the values of life we want to continue. Are we forever and always the mothers and nurturers of society? Should we give up our age-old interest in emotions and in a special kind of intimacy and supportive relationships? Become more like many men, join the "male world?" Or can we join that world only at our own and society's peril? Yet another possibility: Can we join that world, and still, as Martin Luther King remarked in a somewhat similar context, by retaining our values, thereby change that world? Can a less competitive value system ever fully share in power?

It is probably for these debates that the *Reports* are attacked, and not for the methodology. Whatever the advantages and disadvantages of the methodology I have chosen (and the research design has been cited as "revolutionary," "ground-breaking," and "a great contribution to research" by many scholars[2]), I believe that only through these means could

I have elicited from women such deep and private testimonies, enabling us all to debate and reevaluate our definitions of love and the self in this important historic period of massive social and ideological change.

Shere Hite, Ph.D., is a professional researcher. She now lives in France and Germany and frequently visits London, where *The Hite Report on the Family*, her fourth major study, is about to be published.

1. Dr. Gloria Bowles, University of California, Berkeley, has discussed the new trend in social science research in *On the Uses of Hermeneutics for Feminist Scholarship* (*hermeneutics* is the science of interpretation and explanation):

> Feminist scholarship has not only stood critical in a "negative" sense of traditional conceptual assumptions, but has made the positive move of putting forth alternative epistemologies which use experience, intuition and evaluation (both of women as individuals and of women as a "class") as modes of knowing....
>
> Throughout male recorded history, men have been the "takers," while women have assumed (or have been forced to assume) the role of "caretak-

ers." Women live in a world where little is impersonal and much is personal, where little is fixed or certain and much is ambiguous and volatile, and where little is value-free and much requires an evaluative response.

Traditional thought claims to be able to leap out of the hermeneutical/interpretive circle and to speak of so-called "value-free," "disinterested," "objective," and "ethically neutral" knowledge.... Feminist thought, precisely because it acknowledges and asserts its "prejudices," must, from the hermeneutical perspective, be judged as one of the only available theoretical postures which holds good claim to intellectual integrity and sophistication.

2. Among such scholars are: Mary Steichen Calderone, M.D., Founder, Sex Education and Information Council of the U.S.; Robert M. Emerson, Professor of Sociology, UCLA; John L. Sullivan, Professor of Political Science, University of Minnesota, and editor of the authoritative textbook on methodology, *Quantitative Applications in the Social Sciences* (Sage University Papers series); Richard Halgin, Professor of Psychology, Amherst; Gladys Engel Lang, Professor of Communications and Political Science, University of Washington; Professors Nancy Tuana, University of Texas, Frank Sommers, University of Toronto, and Jesse Lemisch, SUNY, Buffalo.

The Professional Voice 3
Comments on Hite's *Women and Love*
Eleanor Singer

Surveys can be used for many purposes. They can be used to find out which brand of soap people prefer, and why; which candidates voters like, and why; what kinds of potential jurors are most sympathetic to a defendant's cause. They can also be used by social scientists to study social phenomena: for example, the causes of racism, or changing attitudes toward sex roles, love, and marriage.

When surveys are used for practical ends, the most direct test of how good they are is in their results. Does Brand X, preferred by most people in the survey, get the major market share? Does the candidate preferred in the polls win the election? Is the defendant acquitted who picks the kinds of jurors suggested by the survey? If the survey passes this test, its methods are rarely questioned. Only if it fails—as happened, for example, in 1936 and again in 1948—are they examined in detail.

But when a survey is used in the service of social science, we often cannot test its goodness so directly. Then, in order to satisfy ourselves that its conclusions are valid, we have to scrutinize its methods, applying to them the same criteria used to evaluate any other scientific method. From that perspective, the debate over Hite's methods is neither abstruse nor beside the point, but goes directly to the heart of the matter: Namely, can we believe her findings? The answer, very simply, is that we cannot.

Here, I will briefly talk about three elements of her research that lead me to this conclusion: *sampling, questionnaire design,* and *analysis.* For a more detailed discussion of these and related issues, the reader is referred to Tom W. Smith's excellent "Sex Counts: A Methodological Critique of Hite's *Women and Love*."[1]

SAMPLING

Hite is not simply interested in describing the attitudes and behaviors of the 4,500 women who responded to her survey. She wants to generalize her findings to the population of women in the United States. For that, she needs a representative sample.

The best way of assuring representativeness is to draw a probability sample—of telephone numbers or addresses—and to interview everyone selected. This ideal is never achieved, though the best surveys, such as the Current Population Survey of the U.S. Census Bureau, achieve response rates well over 90 percent. Hite's "sample" is at furthest remove from this ideal. Questionnaires were distributed to a variety of organizations—church groups, political organizations, women's groups—with a request to pass them on to their members. Of 100,000 questionnaires distributed in this way, some 4,500 were returned—a response rate of 4.5 percent. Although direct-mail sales campaigns are well satisfied with a return of 2 percent, the standards of response rates to a survey are very different.

Low response rates are important because they indicate that the women who return the questionnaires are highly self-selected, and probably differ in important ways from those who do not. In particular, as Smith notes, responses usually come disproportionately from those most concerned about an issue, making it likely that the "small minority of women who responded would be heavily drawn from those who were dissatisfied with their personal relationships with men."[2]

Hite insists that her method of distributing questionnaires was necessary in order to assure respondents' anonymity. But in most surveys done today, neither the interviewer nor the survey organization knows the name of the respondent: What is known is a telephone number, chosen at random from a series of randomly created numbers, or an address chosen at random from a listing of dwelling units. Surveys on highly sensitive topics (drug use, sexual behavior, criminal acts) have been done successfully using samples drawn in this way.★ Because the researcher can follow up non-respondents and try to persuade them to take part in the survey, the bias due to self-selection can be reduced, if not entirely eliminated.

QUESTIONNAIRE DESIGN

Hite argues that only open-ended questions can succeed in gathering unbiased data from respondents, since the categories used by researchers in framing closed-ended

---

★*Editor's note*: Some might argue that it is not that clear what the standard of success might be. While many such surveys have been done, we do not know with certainty that they have always been successful.

questions subtly cue respondents about what the acceptable answers are.

Although such cueing undoubtedly takes place,[3] Hite's own questionnaire is not exactly neutral. For example,

> What is the most important part of this relationship, the reason you want it? Is it love, passion, sexual intimacy, economics, daily companionship, or the long-term value of a family relationship? Other? (Q. 27)

> Is this relationship important to you? How important? The center of your life? An important addition to your relationship with yourself and/or your work? Or merely peripheral—pleasant, but lacking somehow? What would make you leave it? (Q. 44)

Hite's questionnaire consists of 127 open-ended questions, many with numerous subquestions and follow-ups, as in the above illustrations. The task of completing such a questionnaire, especially *in writing*,[4] seems insurmountable, and indeed Hite told her respondents, "it is not necessary to answer every question[!] ... feel free to skip around and answer only those sections or questions you choose." Thus, to self-selection among respondents is added self-selection among questions, with similar possibilities for biasing the conclusions drawn.

ANALYSIS
OF RESPONSES

Hite purports to be interested in reaching "deeper levels of intro-spection," but her analysis is replete with simple marginal frequencies: For example, 87 percent of women feel "they are not really 'seen' by the men they are with," 56 percent are being "undermined or sabotaged psychologically." Such marginal frequencies are the most susceptible of all survey measures to distortions caused by sampling and question wording, but Hite shows no awareness of this. Furthermore, readers are never told the base for these percentages—that is, how many women actually answered the question being analyzed. Since respondents were encouraged to skip around and selectively answer questions, this concern is not a trivial one.

But it is not only the numerical base for percentages that is lacking. Much, perhaps most, of the time, it is impossible to match the descriptive statement in the text with any of the questions asked in the questionnaire. For example, what does it mean for a woman to say she is not really "seen" by the man she is with, and from which questions was it coded?

Unbiased coding of responses to open-ended questions is one of the most demanding tasks faced by a researcher. Hite provides no documentation for how she accomplished this, beyond saying that the responses to each question were examined for patterns, and that the "categories more or less formed themselves." As someone who has repeatedly worked with coding open-ended materials, I know that categories usually do not form themselves, and that reliability of coding—that is, agreement by two or more coders on how to assign responses to categories—is very difficult to achieve. Such disagreements are a source of error, and how responses are classified may also be a serious source of bias. Hite shows no awareness of these dangers, nor does she seem to have taken any precautions against them, such as specifying coding rules, training coders, or checking for reliability. Thus, rather than being separated from the data, as Hite contends, the viewpoint of the researcher is likely to dominate its interpretation and the way it is presented.

IMPLICATIONS

Hite's research reaches a wide popular audience that may be tempted to take her findings at face value. And her work is not alone in claiming scientific legitimacy but largely escaping scrutiny by social scientists until after it has been widely disseminated. Thus it raises difficult issues of how truth is to be sorted from fiction in the marketplace of ideas. I would argue that, contrary to Hite's contention, what's needed is more emphasis on the methods used in a piece of research, not less. Her point of view appears to gain legitimacy from the weight of the 4,500 women for whom she claims to speak. The reader has a right to know how accurately portrayed and how representative those views really are.

Eleanor Singer is a Senior Research Scholar at the Center for the Social Sciences, School of International Affairs, at Columbia University.

1. In Charles F. Turner, Heather G. Miller, and Lincoln E. Moses, *AIDS: Sexual Behavior and Intravenous Drug Use* (Washington, DC: National Academy of Sciences Press, 1989), pp. 537–547.

2. Turner, et al., p. 540. Although Hite claims that the characteristics of her respondents closely match those of American women in general, Smith's analysis conclusively discredits her evidence: "[I]n a number of cases, Hite does not appear to have collected the information that she [claims to have] matched with the census; in other cases, the matches, although possible, would have been extremely difficult; and in still other instances, either numbers fail to add up or definitions do not fit the data" (p. 543).

3. See, for example, the work of cognitive psychologist Norbert Schwarz.

4. This method of questioning also calls into question the representativeness of the sample. Considerable sophistication is needed even to understand the questions, much less to answer them in writing.

In a telephone conversation with Shere Hite in August 1991, I learned that she had moved to London. Although her work had been a huge commercial success in the United States, she felt that her American critics had been extremely harsh and that she had been virtually hounded out of the States. She said she had found it increasingly difficult to have her work published here. In February 1994, Victoria McKee reported in *The New York Times* that Hite was living in France and Germany and that her *Report on the Family* was about to be published in Britain and the Netherlands. McKee also noted Hite's feeling that her work had been trivialized and trashed in the States. Hite's experience made me wonder if history has reversed itself, with the British now being more accepting than Americans of individuality and freedom of speech.

CHAPTER REVIEW

- This chapter began to examine other forms of opinion research besides political opinion polling. The major focus in the chapter was on three case studies: Nielsen ratings, Arbitron ratings, and the *Hite Reports*. These studies were meant to illustrate some possible uses of surveys, as well as the complexity of commercial research and the problems of polling.

- The research firm of Elrick and Lavidge, ranked eleventh domestically in 1989 by *Advertising Age*, uses CATI (computer-assisted telephone interviewing) in their data collection facilities.

- Qualitative interviews can be conducted either on a one-on-one basis or in a focus group session.

- Marketing research is often concerned with quantitative studies, utilizing face-to-face interviews (in a home or at a central location, such as a shopping mall), telephone interviews, or mail surveys.

- In 1987 the Nielsen national People Meter service supplied data from 2,100 households, and the meters are now installed in 5,000 homes. The company's VCR playback measurement service is an acknowledgment of the changing viewing habits of media consumers.

- Nielsen lost credibility with its network clients as viewing habits changed and people turned on their VCRs or a cable station instead of a network channel. NBC and the other networks, suffering millions of dollars of lost advertising revenue, searched for other options to discern the public's taste in programs and to measure audience size.

- Nielsen also sells samples to those interested in conducting their own research. Its "for-sale" sample business services political media consultants, among others.

- Arbitron, ranked second by *Advertising Age*, is known as the major company that surveys/measures radio listening in 260 U.S. markets. But what happened when Arbitron competed with Nielsen in the TV ratings area?

- AGB hopes to compete with Nielsen by using its new People Meter, capable of electronically imprinting a videotape as it is being recorded by a VCR. When the tape is played back, the meter will then be able to recognize its electronic footprint. What is the advantage of that?

- In the point-counterpoint discussion of Shere Hite's methodology, we looked at issues relating to her questionnaire design, the way in which her questionnaire was distributed, the composition of the sample she selected, and the ways in which the replies were analyzed, collated, and reported.

- While Hite saw her study as creating "a new interactive framework," a dialogue between the respondent and the researcher, Eleanor Singer saw the project and its methodology as extremely flawed. What is your opinion?

NOTES

1. Michael Parenti, *Make-Believe Media: The Politics of Entertainment* (New York: St. Martin's Press, 1992), p. 207.

2. See *Advertising Age*, June 10, 1991, "Research Business Report," compiled by Kenneth Wylie and Kathy Welyki.

3. Nielsen Media Research, *The System for Success* (1988), pp. 8–11.

4. Nielsen, *1990 Report on Television.*

5. Nielsen, *Do you need a reliable sample for some upcoming research?*

6. See Kenneth Wylie, "Nielsen, Arbitron lead the pack—But robust growth of previous years evaporates," part of the "Research Business Report" in *Advertising Age,* June 11, 1990.

7. John Lippman (for the *Los Angeles Times* News Service), "Nielsen Taking the Heat for Sharp Drop in Ratings," *The Record*, June 29, 1990, p. 32.

8. Ray Eldon Hiebert et al., *Mass Media VI* (New York: Longman, 1991), pp. 22–23.

9. Lippman.

10. Nielsen, *The System*, p. 5.

11. Todd Allan Yasui, "Confessions of a Nielsen Family: What Happened When the 'TV People' Came to Stay," for *The Washington Post,* reprinted in Pennsylvania's *Reading Eagle*, Jan. 31 1988, Arts & Entertainment section, pp. 1, 3.

12. Yasui.

13. Bill Carter, "NBC Alters Its Count of Viewers," *The New York Times*, June 13, 1990, Business Section, pp. 1, 9.

14. Nielsen, *The System*, p. 5.

15. Steven Prokesch, "AGB Losing its TV-Ratings Monopoly in Britain," *The New York Times*, July 2, 1990, Business section, p. 6.

16. Bill Carter, "NBC Weighs a Change on Viewer Count," *The New York Times*, June 2, 1990, Business section, pp. 1, 37.

17. Carter, "NBC Alters Its Count of Viewers."

18. Bill Carter, "ABC to Use NBC Plan on Ratings," *The New York Times*, June 15, 1990, Business section, pp. 1, 17.

19. Joshua Mills, "Arbitron Decides to Pull Out of the TV Ratings Business," *The New York Times*, Oct. 19, 1993, Business section, pp. 1, 30.

20. *Arbitron Rating/Television*, "Description of Methodology" (January 1989), pp. 41–43.

5

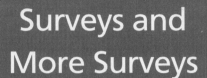

Surveys and More Surveys

Think about—

What was the justification used by the courts to keep surveys from being admitted as legal evidence?

On what basis have the courts only recently accepted survey research as evidence to establish scientific and legal truths?

Besides political polling, market research, and opinion research for legal purposes, what are some of the other uses for opinion and attitude studies?

Why is there a large market for the Gallup youth studies, covering everything you ever wanted to know about teen attitudes and behavior?

Why is a glance at a sample list of NORC studies during the past five decades much like reading a historical recap of that period?

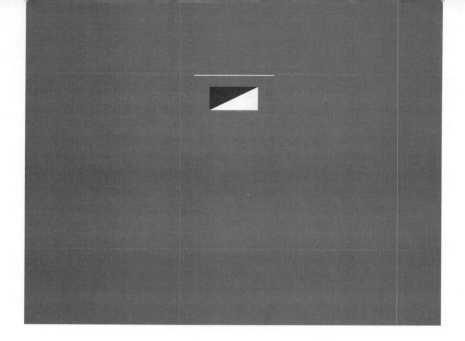

surveys were not always admissible as evidence in court because they were considered hearsay testimony. However, since their acceptance, they have been used in legal matters for the following purposes: (1) to protect trademarks, (2) to prevent deceptive advertising, (3) to assist the attorney in deciding whether to petition the court for a new trial site, (4) to assist the attorney in the jury selection process, and (5) as evidence in obscenity and pornography cases.

LET'S GO TO COURT

If you were asked in a survey, which of the following would you say is the original and which is the copycat:

- The Metropolitan Opera Association or the Metropolitan Symphony Orchestra?
- The Elgin Clock Company or the Elgin National Watch Company?
- The Polarad Electronics Corp. or the Polaroid Corp.?
- Holiday Rambler or Rambler?[1]

Surveys of sorts were taken in each of these trademark cases, in which it was necessary to prove public perception that the copycat had infringed on the rights of the original company. The copycat had confused and deceived the public, causing financial loss and/or damage to reputation and prestige. The basic question, the court stated in *Mushroom Makers, Inc. v. R. G. Barry Corp.* is "whether there is any likelihood that an appreciable number of ordinarily prudent purchasers are likely to be misled, or indeed simply confused, as to the source of the goods in question."[2]

One of the most interesting trademark cases in which survey research was used to prove damage was the case that established *the Polaroid formula*.[3] Although not all aspects of the formula can effectively be part of a survey, researchers hired by attorneys in trademark cases have generally tried to provide data on the following criteria established by the court to assess the likelihood of consumer confusion:

- *Strength of the trademark* How vigilant has the owner been to guard against the word or phrase becoming generic, part of the everyday language that associates it with a variety of sources? Trademark protection once covered *cellophane* and *escalator,* but not now.[4] The Murphy name, when linked to the type of bed that folds into a wall compartment or closet, was recently ruled to be an adjective rather than a trademark. Thus anyone can now use the name *Murphy* to describe such a bed without fear of being sued for trademark infringement.

  One way owners of trademarks show vigilance is by sending a letter of protest to those in the media who fail to capitalize the first letter of the protected word. The court also considers how long the trademark has been used and the size of the advertising budget.

- *Degree of similarity* Is *Polarad Electronics Corp.* too much like *Polaroid Corp.* to avoid confusion? In the Murphy bed case, while the court said that the word *Murphy* could be used as an adjective, it warned that the words *The Original* could not be used before the words *Murphy bed*.

- *Proximity of the products* Will the products be sold in the same market regions of the country?

- *Channels of distribution* What is the likelihood that they will use the same sales channels? Are they targeting the same socioeconomic class of customers?

- *Degree of actual confusion* What percentage of the people surveyed actually confused the two products? Would you confuse Kentucky Fried Chicken with Kennedy Fried Chicken (assuming they were both sold in your neighborhood, through the same sales channels, and similarly priced)?

  It is left to the presiding judge to determine what is meant by "substantial" confusion, and most have ruled that a confusion rate of

15 percent or more of those surveyed constitutes substantial confusion, with rates of under 5 percent designated as insubstantial, and 5–15 percent considered debatable (to be considered along with other variables).[5]

- *Defendant's good faith*   Did the defendant intend to capitalize on a known brand, or was he or she acting in good faith when choosing the trademark? (Was the fellow's name actually Kennedy, or did he intend to benefit from the Kentucky Fried Chicken reputation?)

- *Product quality*   Are the products similar in quality and appearance, or is one much more expensively made and different in appearance? (Does Kennedy Fried Chicken look like Kentucky Fried Chicken?)

- *Buyer sophistication*   How much care is exercised by customers buying such products? Do they generally pay attention, comparing prices and quality, or do they buy without regard to the differences between the products?

Various federal agencies, such as the Food and Drug Administration (FDA), created in 1906, and the Federal Trade Commission (FTC), created in 1914, have encouraged the use of surveys to prove their cases. The FTC, charged with policing unfair business practices, has used surveys in cases of deceptive advertising. State agencies, too, have used surveys. For example, in a case under New York banking law in the 1950s, an opinion survey was taken to determine consumer understanding of the terms *savings, thrift, compound interest*, and *special interest*.[6]

However, these surveys were not always welcomed by the court. In fact, it was not that long ago that survey data were excluded as evidence from court proceedings on the ground that they were **hearsay**, testimony that could not be subjected to cross-examination.

Hearsay Versus Legal Evidence

In 1953, Lester Waterbury, vice president and general counsel of General Foods Corporation, discussed the following three methods then available to attorneys to prove consumer opinion in trademark cases and the problems attorneys encountered in gaining the court's acceptance of opinion surveys as admissible evidence:[7]

1. *Judicial notice*   This is an assumption that the judge knows something that therefore need not be proven. Usually, this concept of official knowledge applies only to such things as statutory law, rules of the court, and so on. In practice, however, judicial notice can extend further, as it did in *Metropolitan Opera* when the judge wrote:

So well known is the plaintiff that I have no hesitation in taking judicial notice of the fact that the Metropolitan Opera or the Metropolitan Orchestra or the Met Orchestra are all normal ways of referring to the plaintiff and that the use of the words "Metropolitan Orchestra," whether coupled with the words "Symphony" or "Opera," is misleading when used by any group in New York not connected with the plaintiff.[8]

As Waterbury explains, although the Met won, the "weak reed" of judicial notice cannot always be trusted; "something stouter is needed to establish consumer facts."[9]

2. *Expert witnesses*   These are usually recognized authorities on the subject matter of the case being heard. Expert witnesses are not called on to testify as to specific facts in a case; rather, they are asked related, hypothetical questions. They are then cross-examined by the opposing attorney. In *Elgin Watch* the judge used the rules on expert witnesses to reject a survey that had been presented to the court. The director of the opinion survey was mistakenly treated as delivering an expert opinion while he was merely relating what certain consumers had said in response to certain questions. The judge considered the survey director's testimony to be hearsay and rejected it.

3. *Public witnesses*   In *Elgin* the judge was willing to treat the survey results as a collection of testimony, and he advised the plaintiff that the way to establish consumer opinion was to bring the respondents to court as public witnesses who could be subjected to cross-examination. He said:

> Of course, to call one such witness would be insufficient, as no court would place much, if any reliance upon the evidence of one such witness. But then how many such witnesses ought the plaintiff to call? It may be stated that he ought to be prepared with from 20 to 30.... [However,] the plaintiff must not take them all from one locality, but from different parts of the country, and in particular he ought to have some from the locality where the defendant's trade is carried on.

The problems with the public witness method are that it can be expensive and cumbersome, as well as deceptive and futile. If witnesses are not selected randomly and impartially, they may lose their credibility under cross-examination. Also, survey organizations function on the basis of confidentiality, insisting on protecting the anonymity of their respondents. Without the guarantee of anonymity, the underpinning of survey research would be lost.

Not only did the courts until rather recently emphasize their preference for anecdotal accounts—which can be subjected to the test of cross-examination—over survey data; they also viewed statistics as having limited value. In a mid-1980s case involving Sears, Roebuck and Company, the court ruled:

> More important than any statistical evidence … is the testimony of Sears' witnesses.… Each … had substantial personal knowledge of the checklist system at Sears. The court found them … highly credible witnesses and was persuaded by their testimony.… The witnesses' uncontradicted testimony helps "bring to life" Sears' statistical evidence.
>
> … [The Equal Employment Opportunity Commission] presented no credible witnesses with personal knowledge of Sears who could contradict the testimony of Sears' witnesses, or give any life to EEOC's inadequate statistical data and analyses.[10]

Over the years it became clear that for survey data to be admissible as evidence, it had to overcome two major obstacles: the hearsay barrier and the adversarial nature of our legal system, which is based on opposing testimony. Thus survey results are now presented to the court as data revealing a defined population's state of mind at a specific time, and all those who engaged in the various steps of design, implementation, and analysis—professionals as well as interviewers—can be subjected to cross-examination. Eugene Sylvester summarized the issue:

> *Are* the results of modern questionnaire consumer polls, when used in unfair trade cases, validly subject to ban under the hearsay rule? It is beyond dispute that whether you have the head of the research firm or his interviewers testifying, they must in effect state that a given number of persons were asked a specified list of questions and that they responded by saying so-and-so. Those replies were given out of court, by persons not under oath and who are not available for cross-examination (frequently being completely anonymous). But whether the traditional safeguards restricting judicial proof ought to be rigidly applicable to such evidence is arguable. *The unusual nature of the facts to be found require an indication of the status of public opinion.* [Emphasis added.] This may involve consumers of a product nationally distributed or it may merely involve a much more localized consumer body. In either circumstance, it is impossible to procure the sworn testimony of all or an appreciable portion of such interested consumers on which to base a generalization as to the presence or absence of confusion, or the likelihood thereof.[11]

To Change a Venue, to Select a Jury

Think about how you would answer the question: If a woman dies during an abortion performed by a doctor, should the doctor be charged with the crime of manslaughter?[12] This question refers to a case in which William Homas, a Boston attorney, used a poll to determine whether a change of venue (place of trial) would substantially improve his client's chances of getting a sympathetic jury. The survey convinced Homas not to file a change of venue motion. However, he used the survey results to persuade the court to allow more extensive *voir dire* (examination of prospective witnesses) than is usually permitted because he was able to show that 14 percent of the respondents said they would vote to convict regardless of the judge's instructions.

Besides using survey data for advisement purposes to determine whether or not a change of venue motion should be filed, attorneys have commissioned surveys to obtain data useful in the jury selection process (see Box 5.1). For example, in 1971–1972, during the period of demonstrations against U.S. involvement in Vietnam, the defense team of the Harrisburg Seven, which included the Reverend Philip Berrigan, hired sociologists Jay Schulman and Richard Christie to create a profile of sympathetic jurors. The result, a hung jury with 10 out of 12 voting for acquittal, seems to indicate a successful strategy. Schulman and Christie subsequently used their survey research techniques to become jury selection specialists. They worked for the defense teams in some of the trials connected to the Attica prison riot of September 1971; the trial of the Indian leaders involved in the 68-day confrontation between armed Oglala Sioux Indian insurgents and federal agents at Wounded Knee, South Dakota (1973); and the trial of Joann Little, the controversial black activist. In August 1975, after Little's jury of six whites and six blacks deliberated for 78 minutes, she was acquitted of a second degree murder charge in the death of her North Carolina jailer, whom she had accused of attempted rape. Her attorney Jerry Paul unabashedly proclaimed that Little's acquittal had been "bought" and he listed the elements: the best counsel (modesty was not one of his qualities), thorough investigators, the funds to fly in expert witnesses, and an extensive jury selection process.[13]

When President Richard Nixon's cabinet members, former Attorney General John Mitchell and former Secretary of Commerce Maurice Stans, were tried in New York (1974–1975),★ their lawyers also commissioned a

---

★John Mitchell was found guilty of conspiracy, obstruction of justice, and three counts of perjury in the Watergate case. In early 1975, he was sentenced to 2½ to 8 years in prison. In March 1975, Maurice Stans was acquitted of perjury, conspiracy, and obstruction of justice. See *The Washington Post* or *The New York Times* for the day-to-day coverage.

BOX 5.1   Jury Selection Matters in Controversial Trials

The outcome of some trials can be determined by the jury selection. For example, the Reverend Philip Berrigan (whose brother, the Reverend Daniel Berrigan, was paroled after serving a short sentence for destroying draft board files) and other defendants were charged with conspiring to kidnap President Nixon's advisor, Secretary of State and National Security Advisor Henry Kissinger, and with conspiring to blow up the heating tunnels under the Capitol building. The jury consisted of nine women (one of whom was black) and three men (two of whom were black). The result was a hung jury, indicating that the jury selection process worked for the defense.

Jury selection also played a role in the Attica prison trials. On September 10, 1971, more than 1,000 inmates, mostly black and Puerto Rican, seized 32 guards as hostages and took over Cellblock D. The inmates set fires, broke windows, shredded fire hoses, issued a list of demands, and killed two of the hostages. Under orders from Governor Nelson Rockefeller, guards stormed the cellblock after four days. Thirty-seven men were killed, including 9 hostages and 28 inmates. After an extensive investi-gation, some 40 trials (involving 60 prisoners) were conducted during 1973–1975. See *The New York Times* for coverage pertaining to the incident, the investigation, the jury selection process, and the trial itself.

Finally, the jury selection process prompted dismissal of charges in the Wounded Knee trial. After one juror became ill and the government refused to allow the remaining jurors to decide the case, federal judge Fred Nichol dismissed the charges against Russell Means and Dennis Banks, the defendants in the Wounded Knee trial. Judge Nichol charged the U.S. Justice Department, federal prosecutors, and the FBI with misconduct on the grounds that, by refusing to allow the 11-member jury to continue, they showed they were more interested in convicting Indians than in justice. See *The Washington Post* or *The New York Times* coverage of this controversial incident. By the way, as a result of Wounded Knee, Marlon Brando symbolically protested U.S. government action by turning down an Oscar. That in turn led to many polls asking whether Brando acted in good taste when he politicized the Academy Awards presentation.

---

poll to aid them in selecting jurors. In reaction, a letter to *The New York Times* argued that the defense tactic of hiring a market research organization to determine a profile of a juror who would be sympathetic to the defense "makes further mockery of the legal system." The writer called the practice unethical "but probably legal."[14] Thus it was that the polling tactic originated by the political left gained acceptance by the political right.

The practice of using survey data in the jury selection process in criminal trials has raised some questions about whether it should be permitted, on the grounds that it creates an inherent inequity.* Clearly, such data have proved their value to those who have been able to afford the additional expense, and it is equally clear that not all defendants can afford such an undertaking. So there is an inequity between defendants not unlike that which existed before legal aid was made available to indigent defendants. Then, too, there is concern about the way in which the practice may work to undermine the objectivity of the jury system. While recognizing the difficulty of enforcing a ban, some extremely knowledgeable individuals have expressed concern for this use of polls to stack a jury. Two distinguished survey researchers have even suggested that "judges be allowed to play a greater role in jury selection, perhaps by selecting half or a majority of the jurors. If surveys are to have any role in jury selection, they should be available to both sides and to the judge."[15]

While I recognize the danger of using surveys to impanel a jury, I also see this proposal as negating the intended basis of our judicial system: a jury of one's peers. The judge is meant to be an umpire who rules on points of law, already empowered to remove from the jury box those who give the appearance of bias. Allowing the judge an even stronger role in jury composition through the selection of "half or a majority of the jurors" blurs and therefore compromises his or her role as overseer of the trial. No longer the impartial embodiment of the law awaiting the trial's outcome, the judge who chooses part or most of the jury might have predetermined the outcome of the trial. This would deny, or at the very least undermine, a defendant's right to a fair trial judged by peers.

Yes, in an ideal situation, if the defense in a criminal case uses polling data, the prosecution should have access to it, as is the case with evidence and witnesses who are cross-examined. Barring that, the solution lies not with further empowering the judge but with increased vigilance on the part of the prosecuting attorney (representing the state's interests) in criminal cases and the opposing attorneys in civil cases.

Is It Obscene or Not?

The Commission on Obscenity and Pornography, established in 1967 by President Lyndon Baines Johnson, spent $2 million and two years studying the "puzzle of pornography." A number of surveys were undertaken to determine the effects of pornography on persons who consume it. In one

---

*You may recall the controversy in 1991 over the use of a survey—commissioned by the successful defense team—to create a profile of sympathetic jurors in the rape trial of William Kennedy Smith.

much-criticized study, people were asked if they had experienced a moral breakdown or had gone "sex crazy" from having viewed sexually explicit material. Another study targeted patients in selected mental hospitals, asking a sample of those who had committed sex crimes about the influence of pornography on their behavior. One of the most quoted surveys produced two interesting and conflicting pieces of data: (1) 60 percent of those sampled said adults should be free to decide for themselves what to read or view, and (2) 73 percent said that sex scenes in films that merely titillate should be censored. In their conclusions, 12 of the 17 commission members reported no link between viewing pornography and antisocial behavior. They therefore recommended to the succeeding Nixon administration that laws restricting adult consumption of such materials be repealed. President Nixon rejected the commission's findings,[16] saying, "Centuries of civilization and ten minutes of common sense tell us otherwise.... American morality is not to be trifled with." It would seem that Nixon understood better than the commission where public opinion really stood on the issue of legislating morality: Harris and Gallup polls in 1969 (some months before the commission's findings were published in 1970) indicated that approximately 80 percent wanted stricter laws to combat the perceived threat from obscenity and pornography.

Since 1973–1974, when the Supreme Court struggled through a series of cases attempting to define and reshape the legal test for obscenity/pornography, survey data have been used from time to time as evidence in such cases. At that time, *Miller v. California* (1973)★ became the central case in a group of decisions. Speaking for the majority in a 5–4 ruling, Chief Justice Warren Burger stated:

> The basic guidelines for the trier of fact must be: (a) whether "the average person, applying contemporary community standards," would find that the work, taken as a whole, appeals to the prurient interest ... (b) whether the work depicts or describes, in a patently offensive way, sexual conduct specifically defined by the applicable state law; and (c) whether the work, taken as a whole, lacks serious literary, artistic, political, or scientific value.

How do we know the standards of our community? Some defense attorneys have introduced polling data on local attitudes as evidence that the ma-

---

★Marvin Miller was charged with violating the California Penal Code. He had sent unsolicited, sexually explicit advertising brochures to a Newport Beach restaurant, and the recipient complained to the police. *Miller v. California*, 413 U.S. 15 (1973). In Chief Justice Burger's ruling, point (c) is usually referred to as the LAPS test (literary, artistic, political, scientific).

terial in question has not exceeded the community's tolerance level, and from time to time, Gallup, Harris, and others have taken polls on specific obscenity controversies. For example, a Gallup/*Newsweek* telephone poll of 605 adults taken June 20–21, 1990 (before the Iraqi invasion of Kuwait distracted their attention) showed that although many were offended by a Robert Mapplethorpe exhibit of controversial photographs (depicting homosexual acts) and by the lyrics of 2 Live Crew (particularly in the group's "As Nasty As They Wanna Be" album), they still believed in freedom of choice.[17] (The Mapplethorpe exhibit also unleashed a controversy involving federal funding of arts projects. The Gallup Poll indicated that 63 percent of the respondents were willing to let "experts" judge the merit of the art project, while 30 percent wanted more official control if federal funds were involved.)

The poll indicated that 75 percent believed it was more important for adults to have the right to determine for themselves what to see, read, or listen to than for there to be laws to ban material considered offensive to some segments of the community. Depending upon the way we choose to state the findings, a Florida poll could be interpreted as indicating substantial support or even *growing* support for such a ban: 38 percent for a ban to 53 percent against. (I hesitate to use the word *growing* because it implies time-series data, while we may be using data only from a single survey.) *Newsweek*'s David Gates, however, chose a positive interpretation of the data, saying that "Floridians opposed banning 2 Live Crew, 53 to 38 percent."[18] What is your opinion for or against a ban?

SURVEYING THE ELITE AND OTHER SPECIAL GROUPS

As we have seen, some researchers specialize in politics, others in advertising and market research, and still others in legal matters. Another area that has attracted their attention is surveying special groups. Pollsters have discovered there is a market for the information derived from interviewing business leaders, members of Congress, high-level bureaucrats, lawyers, doctors, and others who may be perceived as opinion leaders. For this task, such organizations as Harris and Yankelovich have trained a staff of executive interviewers, usually college-educated men and women, many of whom are former business executives.

To analyze the impact of the October 1987 stock market crash on future investment strategies and to gather data useful to those involved in designing and marketing mutual funds, Response Analysis Corporation (RAC), located in Princeton, New Jersey, conducted a nationwide study. It was sponsored by 10 financial services companies and involved 203 telephone interviews with stockbrokers, insurance agents, banks, and financial planners, as well as face-to-face interviews with 761 investors and prospective investors. As part of its study, RAC also included content analysis of print advertising.

Pollsters who have specialized in economic forecasting have asked people about their present financial situation (including their salary, employment, and conditions in their locality) and their expectations (likelihood of a raise, intentions to make a major purchase such as a new car or a home, whether or not they would apply for bank loans, and so on). In the mid-1970s, Albert Sindlinger used such data to create a consumer confidence index. His subscribers paid several thousand dollars annually for access to his weekly reports, which enabled them to make informed decisions regarding investment, expansion, or retrenchment strategies.

For approximately a hundred dollars, you can purchase *The Gallup Study on America's Youth: 1977–1988*, which tracks and analyzes over 200 trends relating to teen attitudes and behavior. There is, as you can imagine, a large marketplace for such data. The following is a partial list of the topics covered by this massive Gallup survey:

self, family, and parents   satisfaction with personal life; arguments with parents; strictness; topics teens want to discuss

marriage, divorce, children, sex   dating, sex education; marriage intentions; family planning; attitude toward divorce

education   rating of public schools and teachers; violence in schools; extracurricular activities; cheating; promotion and graduation requirements

college   selection criteria; college tests; opinion of importance of college; how education will be financed

careers   post–secondary school plans; expected career; career path; earning forecasts

media   time spent with media; television and movie viewing; radio listening; periodical readership

sports and recreation   favorite spectator sports; sports attendance and participation; exercising

music   sources and preferred forms; interest in music videos; the individual's practice of recording, purchasing, and copying

heroes and role models   most admired men and women; favorite movie stars, and so on

values, religion, ethics   school prayer; belief in supernatural; importance of religious beliefs; Bible reading; confidence in organized religion and values considered important *political opinions*   confidence in the United States; interest in politics; presidential approval ratings and party preference; attitudes toward minority candidates

causes and issues   charitable activities; opinion of mixed marriages and of women's job opportunities; causes teens are serving or would like to serve

foreign affairs   influence of prospect of nuclear war; peace efforts by United States and former Soviet Union; opinion of U.N.; most important issues

business   federal regulations; opinion of profit motive; ethics; career interests

substance abuse   drinking and driving; marijuana experimentation; tobacco use; drug screening; impact of alcohol on family; substance abuse at school; prohibiting tobacco sales

Other topics include allowances and part-time work, national service and attitudes toward a draft, shopping and shoplifting, food and eating out, favorite snacks and vegetables, crime and violence, electronics and computers. *Question:* To whom and why would such data be useful? *Answer:* To those in business, marketing, sales, education, social work, government, and youth organizations, as well as researchers in various fields.

THE NORC STUDIES

Over the years the National Opinion Research Center (NORC), affiliated with the University of Chicago, has conducted numerous large-scale comparative community studies.[19] A glance at a partial list of their research projects is much like reading a quick history of the past five decades and the problems confronting Americans during those years.

During the 1940s, NORC undertook a number of wartime studies for the Office of War Information Surveys Division. Labor problems, absenteeism, morale, and attitudes toward the progress of the war were examined, as were inflation, price controls, shortages, and rationing. The role of women in the war effort and media coverage of the war news and its impact were also studied. Other NORC surveys during the 1940s examined the following areas:

pre- and post-election, 1944

atomic energy and the bomb

socialized medicine

radio listening

Palestine, Zionism

race relations

drinking behavior and alcoholism

knowledge of cancer

Contract research undertaken during the 1950s included a number of foreign affairs studies for the State Department, as well as studies that examined the effects of television on sports attendance. Some of the other topics studied under contract during this period were:

philanthropic giving

anti-Semitism

behavior in disasters

aircraft noise

communism, conformity, and civil liberties

the academic mind

dental health and practices

Among the other NORC surveys during the 1950s were those that focused on mental illness, examining people's knowledge and attitudes; life on skid row; the health of the elderly; hospitalization in Massachusetts; and interest and opinions relating to phonevision. In an effort to ensure the quality of its work, NORC also analyzed interviewer effects in survey research.

Contract research undertaken during the 1960s seemed to signal our society's growing concern with the quality of life in the United States. Among their topics of research were:

the people look at television

popular tastes in music

aircraft noise and sonic booms

the "Hidden Blind"

occupation and childrearing

the health of Spanish-American war veterans

ethics and honesty in the United States

the Job Corps

the Nisei

first-graders in Woodlawn, Chicago

problems of widowhood

neighborhood health centers in 11 areas

civil defense and fallout shelters

Other NORC surveys during the 1960s focused on the desegregation of public schools and the integration of neighborhoods in the United States. The Catholic priesthood was studied, as were crime victims, the electric power blackout in New York, and the impact of the Kennedy assassination.

NORC contract research during the 1970s examined smoking behavior among health professionals, drug use and postwar adjustment among Vietnam vets, health of New York's Harlem adolescents, and Boston desegregation. Sexual beliefs, attitudes, and practices and high school students' use of drugs were also studied. NORC surveys during the 1970s included:

the general social survey

public school desegregation

study of American values

study of American journalists

the use of sensitive questions in survey research

ethnic drinking

farmers in the Dakotas

farm decisions on production and marketing

During the 1980s, NORC projects[20] focused, to a great extent, on issues relating to women and children, education, and labor. Among these were:

the Education Longitudinal Studies Program: High School and Beyond (includes followup of the National Longitudinal Studies of the classes of 1972, 1980, 1986, 1988)

excellence in schools

study of MBA students

expanding opportunities for minorities in medicine

the National Longitudinal Studies of Labor Force Behavior/Youth Cohort (sampling 12,000 youths, including oversamples of blacks, Hispanics, and the economically disadvantaged)

male–female differences in job mobility

life cycle fertility and female labor force experience

empirical analysis of the timing and spacing of births

survey of absent parents

the state of the child

teenage pregnancy and public policy

follow-up survey of problem drinking among women

smoking among Hispanics

study of black political participation

While much of NORC's work deals with behavioral studies, opinion and attitudinal elements are almost always present. Despite similarity in methodology (for example, in the procedures used to determine the size and composition of the sample), certain statistical procedures commonly used in behavioral research are not always used in opinion polling. In either case, today's sophisticated computers and statistical programs have greatly aided the social scientist's work.

THE CENSUS, MOTHER
OF MANY SURVEYS

Because many references will be made throughout this text to the much-used and much-abused decennial federal census, it is worth pausing to consider the controversy that surrounds the one taken in 1990. Reacting to James Gleick's *The Census: Why We Can't Count,*[21] Congressman Thomas Sawyer, chairman of the Subcommittee on Census and Population, wrote:

> The Census Bureau has … carried out the census it planned.
> However, the size, diversity and mobility of our society have
> rendered time-honored census methods imprecise, at best. We
> still employ counting techniques pioneered 200 years ago, when
> Secretary of State Thomas Jefferson sent out 600 marshals on
> horseback.[22]

Well, our enumerators are no longer sent out on horseback, but they might just as well have been, considering the experiences of Murray Rubenstein, a freelance writer who decided to see what census taking was all about (see The Professional Voice 4). In August 1991, congressional auditors estimated that census takers had made up to 25.7 million errors in 1990.

According to the General Accounting Office, "millions of Americans were counted twice, listed as living in the wrong place, counted when they shouldn't have been, or not counted at all." After extensive "corrective" efforts, the Census Bureau admitted that it had "overlooked about 5.3 million people in the nation, or about 2.1 percent of the population."[23]

The Professional Voice 4
Taking Leave of Our Census
Murray Rubenstein

No one knows how accurate—or inaccurate—the 1990 census is. In theory, it should have been very accurate; and it might very well have been if almost everyone had bothered to respond by mail. The sad fact is that only slightly over 63 percent of the forms distributed were ever returned. An army of enumerators—consisting of some 350,000 people—was then hired by the government to visit the housing units of those who hadn't replied. The name for this first sweep was "Non-response Follow-up." The stated goal was to count 100 percent of the population. What optimism!

There were many factors that contributed to the 1990 census being far less accurate than the one carried out in 1980. First, more people mailed in their census forms in 1980. This parallels a drop in voter turnout over the years. Perhaps people just don't want to get involved. Perhaps it's the yuppie ("me first") generation. Perhaps there are other reasons for the poorer response.[1]

In some cases, enumerators were threatened with bodily harm by people who just didn't want to participate in the census. Some thought that the information requested wasn't any of the government's business. Perhaps some citizens just didn't trust their government or thought that the information furnished might be used against them.

There are amusing sidelights connected with this. In one case a young enumerator visited the home of an elderly couple. He sat down at the kitchen table with the head of the household and had begun receiving answers to the questionnaire data when the man's wife entered the room. She glanced at the 17-year-old high school student who was a part-time enumerator, and, pointing to the youth, screamed to her husband, "Don't tell him anything. He's a Russian spy!" The woman then began throwing cookies at the startled young man, who beat a hasty retreat. This housing unit, needless to say, wasn't enumerated. It was labeled a "non-response."

Other reasons exist for inaccuracies that have crept into the results. A particular street had four different names over its rather short length (some two blocks). Name changes occurred in midblock, although the house numbers were an unbroken series for the entire length of the thoroughfare. The first census map of that zone called the entire street by just one name. Misdelivery forms, deletion forms, and additions were promptly completed. The system called for a misdelivery form to indicate that the address was incorrect; the deletion form then deleted the incorrect address; and, finally, an addition was supposed to list the correct location of the housing unit. This cumbersome system might have worked if enumerators were highly trained. As often as not, the system broke down. In this case, supervisors ultimately deleted the entire street and none of the people were counted. We can only guess how frequently this happened throughout the United States.

Another major source of errors occurred in apartment houses where the housing units were listed in the register used by enumerators as "Housing Unit #1, #2, #3," and so on. Usually this didn't correspond with actual apartment numbers, so all of the assigned numbers had to be deleted and correct apartment numbers assigned. Does all of this confuse you? It also confused many enumerators.

Twenty percent of all questionnaires were long forms, which asked, in addition to the usual demographic questions, for information such as household income, occupation, a breakdown of utility costs, and so forth. Long and short forms were preassigned with ID numbers for apartments "#1," "#2," and so on, which, as previously mentioned, usually did not correspond to the actual numbering system in the apartment buildings (for instance, 2A or 4C). When matching questionnaires to housing units, there were some enumerators who went out of sequence and assigned the onerous long forms to empty apartments even if this meant ignoring directions and skipping numbers. For example, apartment 1A (short form) would be matched to ID #1; apartment 1B (short form) would be matched to ID #2; empty apartment 1C would be matched to ID #12 (long form) to save the enumerator the task of preparing a multipage questionnaire. Once the sequence was broken, short of going back to each and every apartment, there was no way of telling which apartments had been enumerated. This was so because questionnaires carried addresses but no names. Some conscientious field supervisors caught on to this tactic but were nearly powerless to correct a badly enumerated apartment building.

Some housing units contained illegal aliens or people engaged in illegal activities. Would *you* rely on the accuracy of questionnaires filled out at these housing units? Another source of error was language difficulties. While many district offices contained personnel who spoke Japanese, Chinese, or Spanish, the Census Bureau was on shaky ground when trying to elicit information from people whose grasp of English was virtually nonexistent and whose mother tongue was Arabic, Korean, or Urdu.

A further major cause of inaccuracy in many of the large inner cities was the inability to count the homeless and indigent. Enumerators were told they shouldn't take chances and so they tended to avoid high-crime areas. Such high-density haunts of the needy (the inner city) were therefore undercounted. Some loss of representation obviously resulted from this undercount. Will sampling data for future surveys thus be built on a statistical house of cards?

Finally, there were a number of ill-qualified persons who were political appointees running district offices. They were ordered to satisfy the stricture that the census achieve 100-percent enumeration. To accomplish this, they deleted thousands of housing units. It is important to understand that a deleted unit counted as a completion, whereas a "non-response" was treated as something of a statistical failure. Thus, for political reasons, the statistically inaccurate deletion was preferred.

It has been estimated that the effort to obtain data from the approximately 27 percent who failed to respond to the mailed questionnaires cost American taxpayers at least $1.5 billion. Considering the questionable accuracy of this tally that, until the next census in the year 2000, will be used for any number of projections for commercial, governmental, and quasi-government forecasts, we must be wary of any extrapolations or predictions with Census 1990 as the starting point.

Murray Rubenstein is a freelance writer who has written many articles on a variety of subjects.

1. NORC was commissioned to conduct a study regarding the low response rate to the mailed portion of the 1990 census. Its findings have been published and can be obtained through NORC.

Of the 5.3 million who were overlooked, 21 percent live in California, particularly in the black, Hispanic, and other minority neighborhoods. Seeking an adjustment, California sued. To estimate the undercount, the Census Bureau used a postcensus survey (based on a sampling of areas in all 50 states), and concluded that in reality 1.1 million people should be added to California's official count. If the Bush administration had not rejected the adjustment figures—refusing to release the detailed estimates of the undercount—California would have been given an additional seat in Congress beyond the seven the state was due to gain under the official count.[24] The

Bush administration appealed a district court order that had directed the Bureau to release the correct figures to the California Senate. In the meantime, New York, Los Angeles, Chicago, and many other cities, as well as a number of states (New Jersey, Florida, and Texas, among others), also brought suit, asking for a full national census adjustment.

In September 1991, the United States Supreme Court (in a 6–3 ruling) blocked the release of the revised 1990 census data that the California legislature had been seeking for the purpose of redrawing its political districts for the 1992 election.[25] The ruling was seen as a blow not only to California's Democrats but to Democrats in other states as well. There are serious implications for the undercounted areas, affecting state and federal aid, their representation on the state and federal levels, and their political clout in Congress. Since the undercounting occurred in primarily poor areas, Democrats asserted that the Bush administration's decision was politically motivated, intended to block increased representation for these traditionally Democratic areas. I have included the above discussion because I think it is important to understand that the 1990 census was extremely flawed and that samples based on its data are also inherently flawed.

CHAPTER REVIEW

- For a long time, the hearsay rule precluded the admissibility of survey data as evidence. Why?

- On what grounds are survey data now accepted as evidence?

- Once accepted, survey data began to be used to protect trademarks, prevent deceptive advertising, assist the attorney in deciding whether to petition the court for a new trial site, assist in the jury selection process, and as evidence in obscenity and pornography cases.

- The use of opinion polls to assist the attorney in the jury selection process has raised a number of disturbing questions. What do you think about opinion polls being used in that process? What are the arguments for and against such a practice?

- Through the Commission on Obscenity and Pornography, established in 1967 by President Johnson, spent $2 million and two years studying the "puzzle of pornography," its results were rejected by the succeeding Nixon administration.

- Subsequent studies to determine the effects of pornography on persons who consume it have often produced conflicting results. While some individuals claim there is no direct link between exposure to pornography and antisocial behavior, past Harris and Gallup polls have indicated that approximately 80 percent wanted stricter laws to combat the perceived threat from obscenity and pornography.

- The marketplace for data from the study of elite and special groups has grown significantly over the years.

- Pollsters who specialize in economic forecasting ask people about their financial situation and their expectations. In the mid-1970s, Albert Sindlinger created a consumer confidence index. Subscribers pay several thousand dollars annually for access to weekly reports that enable them to develop their investment, expansion, or retrenchment strategies.

- NORC (the National Opinion Research Center), affiliated with the University of Chicago, conducts large-scale comparative community studies of all types, including many that fall into the category of opinion research. More will be said about the NORC sampling frame in Chapter 6.

- The United States Census Bureau has admitted its 1990 census undercounted some 5.3 million people, representing about 2.1 percent of the population. The undercount has serious implications for the cities and states affected and for the survey researchers who use census data to design their sample.

NOTES

1. *Metropolitan Opera Association, Inc. v. Pilot Radio Corporation* 189 Misc. 505 NY Sup. Ct., NY Co. (1947); *Elgin National Watch Company v. Elgin Clock Company* 26 F. 2d 376 D.C. Del. (1928); *Polaroid Corp. v. Polarad Electronics Corp.* 287 F. 2d 492, 495; 128 USPQ 411, 412–413, 2d Circ. (1961). American Motors charged that the Holiday Rambler trademark used for another company's camper infringed upon the Rambler trademark. Holiday Rambler Corporation countersued: *Holiday Rambler Corporation,* Plaintiff-Counterdefendant, *v. American Motors Corporation,* Defendant-Counterclaimant 254 F. Supp. 137; 149 USPQ (BNA) 345 (1966).

2. *Mushroom Makers, Inc. v. R. G. Barry Corp.* 580 F. 2d 44, 47; 199 USPQ 65, 66–67 (1978). This important case is also discussed in *University of Illinois Law Review,* 1988, p. 929, and *Wisconsin Law Review,* 1982, p. 164.

3. *Polaroid Corp. v. Polarad Electronics Corp.* 287 F. 2d 492, 495; 128 USPQ 411, 412–413, 2d Circ. (1961).

4. Eugene P. Sylvester, "Consumer Polls as Evidence in Unfair Trade Cases," *George Washington Law Review* (1951, Vol. 20), pp. 227–228.

5. Norman M. Bradburn and Seymour Sudman, *Polls & Surveys* (San Francisco: Jossey-Bass, 1988), p. 60. What is the justification for the 15-percent criterion? Your guess is as good as mine!

6. *People v. Franklin National Bank of Franklin Square* (1951) 105 N.Y.S. 2d 81, NY Supreme Court, Nassau Co., pp. 90–91; reversed (1953) 281 App. Div. NY 757 (2d Dept.).

7. Lester E. Waterbury, "Opinion Surveys in Civil Litigation," *Public Opinion Quarterly* (Spring 1953), pp. 71–90. Also see Eugene P. Sylvester, "Consumer Polls as Evidence in Unfair Trade Cases," *The George Washington Law Review* (December 1951, Vol. 20), pp. 211–232, and in the same issue, Mark Levin, "Purity as a Basis for Patentability," pp. 232–241.

8. Waterbury, p. 73.

9. Waterbury, p. 73.

10. Irving Crespi, "Surveys as Legal Evidence," *Public Opinion Quarterly* (Spring 1987), p. 85.

11. Sylvester, p. 222.

12. Michael Wheeler, *Lies, Damn Lies, and Statistics* (New York: Liveright, 1976), pp. 230–231.

13. See *The Washington Post* or *The New York Times* coverage of the trial and Edward Tivnan's subsequent *Times* article on "The Jury Selection Process," Nov. 16, 1975, VI, p. 30.

14. Evelyn C. Gerber, letter to the editor, *The New York Times*, May 18, 1974.

15. Bradburn and Sudman, p. 61.

16. Don R. Pember, *Mass Media Law*, 4th ed. (Dubuque, IA: Wm. C. Brown Publishers, 1987), pp. 419–420.

17. Tom Mathews, "Fine Art or Foul?" in *Newsweek*, July 2, 1990, pp. 46–52.

18. David Gates, "The Importance of Being Nasty," *Newsweek*, July 2, 1990, p. 52.

19. Paul B. Sheatsley, *NORC: The First Forty Years* (NORC Report 1981–1982).

20. *NORC Report 1985–86.*

21. See *The New York Times*, July 15, 1990.

22. Letters to the Editor, *The New York Times Sunday Magazine*, Aug. 12, 1990.

23. Robert Reinhold, "Census Office Told to Give California Adjusted Figures," *The New York Times*, Aug. 16, 1991, p. A10.

24. Reinhold.

25. Katherine Bishop, "Court Rejects Release of Revised Census Data," *The New York Times*, Sept. 11, 1991, p. A17.

PART II

Conducting
Your Survey

6

Finding the *n*th Person

Think about—

What is a sampling frame?

What was the significance of A. L. Bowley's Five
Towns Survey?

What is meant by a purposive sample? What are the
characteristics of a good sample?

What is meant by probability theory?

What is significant about the confidence level of a sample's results?

How and why do pollsters use census data?

What are the problems with using such data?

What is meant by the *n*th person or the *n*th house?

Can you explain cluster analysis?

Why use a stratified random sample?

Have you seen Appendix I for a discussion on "beginner statistics,"
including mean, mode, median, and standard deviation?

Which is America's best-selling candy bar? Who is considered the best football quarterback of all time? Do Americans know what is meant by the terms *deficit* and *S&L fiasco*? When the experts talked about the *peace dividend* prior to the Gulf military buildup and the war, did Americans know what was meant by the term? Do Americans know why the KGB–military coup to oust Mikhail Gorbachev was attempted? Do they know why it failed? Do the people in your state support the Clinton health care reform program? Who is the preferred candidate for United States senator from your state in the next election?

While the answer to the first question is easy to find—one just compares national sales figures for the various candy bars—the remaining questions require us to do more research. We must ask the people, but as you realize by now, it is not necessary to ask *all* the people. We can get a reasonably accurate response by asking a sample, some segment of our population. But who will be part of our *sample frame*, that group of people from which we will select those we want to interview? And how do we decide, specifically, who we are going to ask? Where and how do we begin? This chapter is intended to give you an understanding of the complex nature of sampling processes.

UNDERSTANDING THE THEORY

As noted in Chapter 2, the concept of *drawing a sample* originated in the late 1800s. In 1912, A. L. Bowley conducted a pioneer study of working-class households in Reading, England, using random sampling based on the 1911 census.[1] By briefly describing this interesting study we can introduce certain indispensable terminology.

The Reading effort was part of a group survey of five medium-sized towns (which according to the 1911 census had populations of 23,000 to 90,000). The four other towns—Northampton, Warrington, Stanley, and Bolton—had been studied in 1910–1911. In the Reading survey, Bowley sampled 840 of the 18,000 inhabited housing units, which included both upper-class and working-class dwellings.

To ascertain any changes in economic conditions, Bowley repeated the *Five Towns Survey* in 1923–1924, incorporating his Reading experience with random sampling. He now aimed at a sample of 800–1,000 working-class households from each town. In Reading, he obtained his sample frame of 1,200 addresses (which included non-working-class households) by ticking every eighteenth name in the town directory; elsewhere, he used the registry of eligible voters in all households, ticking every eighteenth or twentieth name depending on the town's population.

His next task was to establish definitions and standards for such terms as: *working-class household, kitchen* as distinguished from *scullery* (the former was considered a room because it had a coal range and was usable as a living room), *poverty, gross income* and *net income, shop assistants* (shop assistants were excluded, "except butchers, fishmongers, grocers, greengrocers, and bakers"), *crowding* and *overcrowding*. Such definitions and standards were necessary in order to eliminate nonqualifying households.

In his final report, Bowley analyzed the ways in which bias or other errors might occur:

1. Unsatisfactory definitions and standards create ambiguities and inconsistencies, particularly in marginal cases.
2. Households visited may not be representative of the whole. Theoretically, Bowley's method of random selection should have overcome this problem.
3. The sampling process itself is subject to error that can be statistically estimated. Obviously, if we sampled the entire universe, the error would be zero—*the larger the sample size, the smaller the margin of error.* Thus, as we shall see, the question becomes: Given the time, money, and other assets allocated (including the care with which a sample

frame is constructed), does the error inherent in the study, as formulated, mean that the results will be sufficiently worthwhile to justify undertaking the project?

4. The data collected may be unreliable. Bowley felt, however, that this could be offset by field workers well trained to follow instructions. The small number of personal errors that might be made in one direction, he said, were usually balanced by those that occurred on the other side; and field supervisors were expected to inspect all questionnaires carefully as soon as they were handed in. Those with doubtful or incomplete items were returned for immediate correction in the field. (More will be said on this subject in Chapter 10 when we discuss the reliability of polls.)

Bowley's comparison of the findings for the five towns combined showed:

- a "striking" improvement in the economic conditions of the working class

- the "most pressing social task" confronting Great Britain was to raise the wages of the worst-paid workers

- random sampling based on probability theory could save time and money and yield results with a reasonably high level of confidence (to be explained below)

In 1934, J. Neyman published a paper that initiated another phase in the development of statistical theory associated with probability sampling.[2] Neyman introduced **purposive selection**, which refers to the sampling of a specifically targeted group (for example, conducting a study on the rehabilitation of severely wounded Vietnam War veterans).

Two years later, in contrast to the 10-million-person *Literary Digest* sample, Gallup and Crossley used relatively small samples to correctly predict the outcome of the Roosevelt–Landon election and to prove that quantity does not ensure success. In 1939, in the absence of updated and complete census data, the Works Progress Administration became the first to use a large-scale probability sample in order to estimate the degree of unemployment and the size of the labor force in this country. These successes were followed by hundreds of local, regional, and national surveys and by a growing debate among statisticians and survey practitioners about the role of *randomness* in sample selection.

Random sampling is often referred to as either (a) **restricted** or **stratified random sampling**, or (b) **unrestricted random sampling**. In the former, we divide the universe into different groups (called strata, sub-universes, or sub-groups) and then randomly select every *n*th unit (house, person, organization). In the case of unrestricted random sampling, we might, for example, merely select every *n*th unit from a list representing the totality of our universe. Or, assuming each possible unit of the universe is included, we might randomly select our respondents lottery-style by simply drawing the names, addresses, or phone numbers from the proverbial fishbowl. Better yet, we can program our computer to randomly select every *n*th unit.

As noted earlier, random sampling is based on *probability* theory. The important question here is: What is the probability of selection for each individual? How likely is it that you or anyone else (representative of the universe) will have an equal chance (or any chance) of being included in the sample frame? Our goal is to ensure an acceptable margin of error with a high confidence level in the results obtained when we generalize from the sample to the universe. The selection process must therefore be as bias-free as possible and must contain a sufficient number of individuals. The bias-free problem, as we shall see, has been difficult to resolve because of unanticipated intervening variables.

Until the 1948 polling disaster, *quota sampling*, which emphasized representativeness over randomness, appeared the more cost-effective method of choosing respondents. Once told how many individuals in various categories (based on sex, age, income, ethnicity, and so on) should be interviewed in a particular field location (based on census data), it was left to the field supervisors to ensure that the interviewers followed the guidelines and did not use their own subjective judgment to decide who to interview. In 1948, however, it appears that the interviewers did exercise their own judgment (either because of lack of explicit guidelines or of adequate supervision). This weakness of subjectivity was one of the major reasons for the subsequent reevaluation of sample selection methodology. (More will be said later about the replicability problem of non-probability quota sampling.)

Among the many decisions we must make in planning our study are how large a sample we need and how precise we need to be, particularly when dealing with small sub-groups of our sample. Time and money, as pointed out in reference to the Bowley study, are major factors in choosing our sample design, but we should also recognize that a high degree of precision is more important in some studies than in others.

DETERMINING WHETHER
TO RUN FOR OFFICE

Let's consider the following case study: When Mr. Local Politician first considered a primary campaign for the Democratic nomination to run for the United States Senate, he undertook a poll among registered Democrats to determine how well known he was throughout his state. Since he already knew that his name was not a household word, he merely wanted to ascertain whether he was any less known (among the party activists who are the major participants in most primary elections) than his obscure potential opponents.

Step One: Defining the Units of Analysis   Mr. LP's pollster first defined the *universe* or **target population** (the units of analysis—persons, households, schools, companies, factories, farms, and so one) he wished to study. For LP's purposes, the *ideal* target population would be all registered Democrats in each county of the state—those people who were eligible to vote in a primary. However, after considering the time and money available for the poll, as well as the reality that most eligible voters do not bother to vote in a primary election, LP's pollster was able to define the *survey population*, a modification of the target population. The survey population would concentrate, specifically, on those Democrats who had voted in the previous senatorial primary election that had *not* coincided with a presidential primary election. It is unfortunate, but especially true in nonpresidential campaign years, that primaries usually attract only the most committed activists (or "hacks" as, in a derogatory fashion, they are too often called). These people may be the beneficiaries of patronage jobs or have some other vested interest in the party's success—besides the altruistic aim of helping to choose the best their party has to offer in the November election. Since LP was considering a senatorial run during a nonpresidential election year (an "off year"), his pollster was able to redefine the universe as a much smaller population than would otherwise have been the case. Of course, this definition excludes newly registered voters who might have intended to vote in the next primary, even though they were not party activists. As you can see, the definitional task involves careful consideration.

Step Two: Creating the Sample Design   Here we are concerned with taking a sample from the survey population. At this point, the pollster, having purchased computerized lists of registered voters (from the board of elections in each county in LP's state), could poll every person (unit) who met the definitional requirement of having voted in the last nonpresidential primary. By the way, these lists not only indicate the name, address, and party affiliation of every eligible voter in the particular county; they also indicate whether the person actually voted in the last election and last primary. In fact, depending on how much money you are willing to spend, it is theoretically possible to purchase the record of participation of every eligible voter going back over the past decade,★ if not longer. This is all part of the public record. (Do you see a privacy issue here?)

Not only is polling everyone on the list (taking a complete enumeration) far more time-consuming and costly than doing a sample survey; its results are not necessarily more accurate. Since a sample survey can be completed with greater speed, the results will be more current. In addition, because resources (including personnel) can be concentrated on a smaller number of respondents, these can be interviewed in greater depth. Thus the result will be a higher quality of data.

So now LP's pollster chooses a *sampling frame*. In setting up a sampling frame, we are deciding how we will select the individuals to be interviewed. We must decide on either a *probability* sample (where everyone in the survey population has an equal chance of being included in the sample) or a *non-probability sample*, which will be discussed later in this chapter. In this case, LP's pollster is going to use the simplest form of probability sampling techniques, called **simple random sampling (SRS)**. Before actually using SRS to select the individual respondents, a decision must be made on the size of the sample, which is dependent on a number of factors, including the degree of precision desired.

Step Three: Deciding on Sample Size and the Degree of Precision Needed   There are four quick points to remember. First, don't ask what percentage or fraction of the population you should sample, because population size has virtually no impact on how representative your sample would be. Assuming the same sampling design and procedures are used, a sample size of 1,500 people can be used to describe a state's population of 20 million or the nation's population of somewhere around 230 million with almost the same degree of accuracy. Remember that estimates of sampling errors (variance from one sample to another) are nearly independent of the

---

★I recall the embarrassment of one local candidate at a well-attended forum. His opponent distributed copies of his voting record showing that he had not voted in many elections. His joyful opponent concluded her speech with, "Count for yourself how many times he did not bother to vote in the past few years. It is a 'no-show' record. Is that what you want to represent you, a no-show?" The moral of the story is that you should vote because you never know when *you* might decide to run for office.

original population size from which the sample was drawn. As explained by Bowley, the larger the sample size, the smaller the error variance. However, there is a point of diminishing returns.

Second, the easiest and quickest way to decide sample size is to use the empirical approach, which means you take advantage of the mathematical expertise and experience of others. You can do this by consulting charts based on the work of other researchers conducting similar studies. For example, Gerald Goldhaber asked some well-known pollsters about their thinking on sample size when polling congressional districts and statewide. As you see in Table 6.1, a major concern beyond cost and time is that of precision *when a large sample is stratified*—broken down by variables (sex, age, income, occupation, region, religion, and so on). We should note that many researchers do not support the empirical approach, saying that for certain studies it is inappropriate. In the physical sciences, for example, mathematical calculations will usually be made to determine the sample size used for the collection of scientific data. (However, physical scientists may also have limited resources and may settle for less statistical power.)

The third point is that if you decide not to use the empirical approach and to do your own calculations, you should remember that there is nothing arbitrary about sample size. Choosing the size of a sample is a complicated process, using statistics. In fact, the process itself is the subject of an ongoing debate among researchers and statisticians. Some recommend first deciding how much error they can tolerate in the particular survey and how sure they must be of their results. Put another way, they must decide on the acceptable confidence level of the results (the estimated sampling error). For example, do you think that LP would be satisfied if he were told that it was 95 percent probable (representing the *level of confidence*) that 28 percent (representing the *result*) ± 6 percent (representing the *uncertainty*) of his universe had heard of him? Once LP, under the guidance of his pollster, decides what level of uncertainty he is willing to accept, a calculation (or alternatively a consultation with an appropriate table) will result in a required sample size to achieve that level of certainty. For an extremely simplified example, see Table 6.2. The 95-percent confidence level means that in 95 out of 100 samples of the indicated size, you expect to get the results (estimated error) indicated in the table.

Most pollsters use the 95-percent confidence level. However, there are cases where the greater precision of a 99-percent confidence level is required, just as there are cases where a 90-percent or lower confidence level would be acceptable. In those cases, the appropriate tables would be consulted (assuming avoidance of doing the statistical calculations).

Table 6.1 Polling the Pollsters on Sample Size

POLLSTER	CONGRESSIONAL DISTRICT/ STATEWIDE	EXPLANATION/ COMMENTS
Patrick Caddell Cambridge Survey Research (Washington, DC)	450/1,000	Considers trade-off between costs and needs. Size varies: 450, 700 or 800, or 1,000—depends on sub-groups and sub-regional analysis needs. With 450, it is only possible to make a few demographic analyses ("we'd look at a couple of regions and sex").
Peter Hart Hart Research Assoc. (Washington, DC)	400/1,200	Depends on state, situation, number of media markets in the state. Smaller, homogeneous states (e.g., Utah or Wyoming)—500; California—1,200. To look at sub-groups, "we like to have 150–175 cases in a cross-break."
Robert Teeter Market Opinion Research (Detroit)	400–500/ 1,000	Must compromise between size of error and costs. Sometimes 300 in congressional race. Statewide: considers size/type of race. Small states (e.g., Wyoming, the Dakotas)—500–600; larger, 800–1,000. Uses cross-tabulations with higher error—10 percent: can have cross-tabs of 4 or 5 categories, with cells (sub-groups) of 100 respondents. To examine a particular sub-group with lower error, "we either jack up the overall sample or over-sample that group." To look at trends, "smaller samples are OK."
Richard Wirthlin Decision Making Info. (Washington, DC)	400–600/ 800–1,200	Uses samples "as large as the budget can afford." National studies—1,500; when you approach 2,000, "you get to a point of diminishing returns." Uses cross-tabs "to tell clients their relative strengths and weaknesses."

SOURCE: Gerald M. Goldhaber, "A Pollsters' Sampler," *Public Opinion* (June/July 1984), pp. 47–50, 53.

Table 6.2 Sample Size for 1–7% Tolerated Error at a 95% Confidence Level

SAMPLE SIZE	% OF TOLERATED ERROR
9,604	1
2,401	2
1,067	3
600	4
384	5
267	6
196	7

SOURCE: Adapted from Charles H. Backstrom and Gerald Hursh-César's *Survey Research*, 2nd ed. (New York: Wiley, 1981), p. 75.

Others reject this approach on the basis that the desired precision of a single component of the study (that of sampling error) should not determine sample size. As Floyd J. Fowler, Jr., points out,

> Most survey studies are designed to make a variety of estimates. The needed precision for these estimates is likely to vary from measure to measure.... It is only the exception, rather than the common situation, when a specific acceptable margin for error can be specified in advance.[3]

They argue that the confidence level estimate for the *total sample* is less important than the *separate estimates* necessary to ensure the representativeness of the sample's subgroups. Therefore, you must first identify the small groups within the population you are sampling and then calculate the minimum sample sizes that will yield the confidence levels you can tolerate. This raises the question: How confident must we be in our results, particularly when dealing with the smallest sub-groups in our sample? If we had to be 100 percent certain of our results, we would have to interview everyone in our universe. Since that is not possible, we want to be confident that if our sample varies from the population as a whole, it does so by no more than a few percentage points. The question again is, How large a deviation (how much variability) can we accept? And, again, there are statistical formulas and mathematical calculations (beyond the scope of this text) that are involved in resolving questions of a sample size that must contain small sub-groups of the population. To repeat, when we examine data broken down by sub-groups or sub-strata, we deal with smaller and smaller sample sizes, thereby increasing the margin of error. A researcher engaged in **multivariate analysis** (cross-tabulating and analyzing many variables) will have to choose a sample size large enough to ensure the desired level of precision for small sub-groups.

The fourth point concerning sample size and precision is that low sampling error has not impressed critics of polling because they are fully aware that compared to the other types of unreported errors, sampling error is trivial.

Step Four: Choosing the Individual Respondents LP's pollster made an empirical decision to use a sample size of 400, proportionately divided among the various counties based on the number of registered Democrats per county who voted in the last nonpresidential primary. Using the voter registration lists described above, a total of 400 respondents were randomly selected (taking every *n*th name).

FINDING THE *n*TH HOUSE (OR PERSON)

Before returning to LP's poll, let's discuss the heading above, referring to "the *n*th house." It reminds me of the way in which the disenfranchised are ignored by most public opinion polls and by the census as well. As a result of the economic crunch that has affected many marginal families in the years since the mid-1980s, there has been a tremendous increase in the number of homeless. The old assumption that everyone has an address is no longer valid—if it ever was. Yet it seems that once made homeless, these individuals cease to exist for most pollsters. They argue that without a recognized residence, one cannot register to vote and therefore has no power to affect an election outcome. Despite such thinking, why shouldn't we hear and listen to the opinions of the disenfranchised?

How do we decide which is the *n*th unit—the household (house or apartment) or person—we will interview, face to face, by phone, or by mail? What is the **skip interval** between houses?★ Is it every twenty-fifth house or every thirteenth house? It could be either, or a multitude of other possibilities; but, in fact, it depends on the size of the sampling from which you draw your respondents.

So, returning to LP's poll of 400 registered Democrats who voted in the last nonpresidential primary, let's assume the pollster's list consists of

---

★For Nielsen or Arbitron, the residence is identified and whoever lives in that particular residence unit (house or apartment) will be asked to participate as part of the sample. People without an identifiable residence are of no interest to the rating services.

BOX 6.1   Segments of Tables of Random Numbers

Version A

17 53 77 58 71	71 41 61 50 72	12 41 94 96 26	44 95 27 36 99	02 96 74 30 83
90 26 59 21 19	23 52 23 33 12	96 93 02 18 39	07 02 18 36 07	25 99 32 70 23
41 23 52 55 99	**31** 04 49 69 96	10 47 48 45 88	13 41 43 89 20	97 17 14 49 17
60 20 50 81 69	31 99 73 68 68	35 81 33 03 76	24 30 12 48 60	18 99 10 72 34
91 25 38 05 90	94 58 28 41 36	45 37 59 03 09	90 35 57 29 12	82 62 54 65 60
34 50 57 74 37	98 80 33 00 91	09 77 93 19 82	74 94 80 04 04	45 07 31 66 49
85 22 04 39 43	73 81 53 94 79	33 62 46 86 28	08 31 54 46 31	53 94 13 38 47
09 79 13 77 48	73 82 97 22 21	05 03 27 24 83	72 89 44 05 60	35 80 39 94 88
88 75 80 18 14	22 95 75 42 49	39 32 82 22 49	02 48 07 70 37	16 04 61 67 87
90 96 23 70 00	39 00 03 06 90	55 85 78 38 36	94 37 30 69 32	90 89 00 76 33

SOURCE: This segment of a random-number table was taken from Table XXXIII in Fisher and Yates, *Statistical Tables for Biological, Agricultural and Medical Research,* 6th ed. (London: Longman, 1974).

Version B

53312	73768	59931	55182	43761	59424	79775	17772	41552	45236
16302	64092	76045	28958	21182	30050	96256	85737	86962	27067
96357	98654	01909	58799	87374	53184	87233	55275	59572	56476
38529	89095	89538	15600	33687	86353	61917	63876	52367	79032
45939	05014	06099	76041	57638	55342	41269	96173	94872	35605

SOURCE: The Rand Corporation, *A Million Random Digits with 100,000 Normal Deviates* (Chicago: Free Press, 1955), p. 99.

24,000 units (names). To determine which individuals will actually be interviewed, the pollster creates a **sampling fraction**. In this case 400 (the sample number) is divided by 24,000 (total units in the sample frame): $400/24,000 = 4/240 = 1/60$. That means that LP's sample will consist of 1/60 of all the units on that list.

To ensure the integrity of a random probability sample, we must be as certain as we can be that everyone on the list has the same chance of being chosen to be a respondent. That is why we would *not* start counting from the first name on our list, ticking off every sixtieth name. However, there are a variety of ways to ensure randomness in the choosing of specific respondents. One way to do so would be to begin by using a table of random numbers, commonly found in statistical texts. Box 6.1 presents segments of two of the many versions of such tables.

There is nothing mystical about these tables; indeed, computers can generate thousands of versions. Also, there is no single correct way in which a random table can be used to determine the first respondent. Assume that we worked for LP's pollster and were asked to use version A's full random table (see Box 6.1). Choosing the simplest method, we could casually select a starting number (close your eyes and point). Suppose we randomly selected the number 31 (located in the third row down, the sixth number across). Number 31 on our computerized list would become our first respondent. Putting aside our table, we would then count 60 names, bringing us to the ninety-first name on our list; we would have our second respondent. Counting off another 60 names gives us our third respondent, and so on through the computerized list of 24,000 names to identify our four-hundredth respondent. There are, as we noted above, many other ways to use a random-number table. But LP's pollster has decided to let the computer do the work. It can, of course, be programmed to randomly identify the 400 respondents needed for this poll.

The respondents were interviewed by phone. Although this aspect of polling will be covered in subsequent chapters, I want to point out that in LP's study a very high response rate was possible for the following reasons:

1. LP's pollster was assisted by trained telephone interviewers who persisted in reaching the selected respondents, even when it was necessary to make repeated call-backs.

2. Those who declined to participate, were deceased, or had moved were replaced by other randomly selected subjects.

3. The respondents—all political activists—were encouraged to view their participation in the poll as a way of providing input for their party's nomination process. Even without such an introduction, most were anxious to make their views known.

The result, which might have deterred a less ambitious person, showed that only 28 percent of those sampled had heard of LP. Perhaps he was not discouraged because the other four candidates who were mentioned in the poll were either less known or only slightly better known than LP. Before I tell you what happened to LP, there are three related statistical elements deserving of additional attention. They are:

- the margin of error
- the confidence level
- the size of the sample

The **confidence level** is a measure of the likelihood that we would get the same results if we resampled our universe *n* times. Here, *n* equals an unspecified number of samples, large enough to eliminate the effects of random errors and to ensure confidence in our results. For example, if 100

Table 6.3 Margins of Error for Selected Sample Sizes and Sample Splits

	SPLIT IN THE SAMPLE								
	90%	80%	70%	60%	50%	40%	30%	20%	10%
SAMPLE SIZE									
1,500	2	2	3	3	3	3	3	2	2
1,000	2	3	4	4	4	4	4	3	2
750	3	4	4	4	4	4	4	4	3
600	3	4	4	5	5	5	4	4	3
400	4	5	6	6	6	6	6[1]	5	4
200	5	7	8	8	8	8	8	7	5
100	7	9	10	11	11	11	10	9	7

SOURCE: Adapted from George Gallup, *The Sophisticated Poll Watcher's Guide* (Princeton, NJ: Princeton Opinion Press, 1972), p. 228. A split in the sample close to the following percentages (for example, 90–10, 60–40, and so on) results in the margins of error (±) indicated.

1. Since X's poll of 400 indicated a 28-percent level of name recognition, the statistically calculated margin of error was ±6 percent with a 95-percent confidence level.

samples were drawn from the same sample frame, we should expect the same result 95 percent of the time with a margin of error of ±6 percent. This means that there was a 95-percent confidence level that only 22 to 34 percent of those in the population knew who LP was.

It has been shown statistically (see Table 6.3) that we can anticipate the margins of error in 95 out of 100 similar sample attempts. That is to say, 95 percent of the time we would expect that 28 ± 6 percent of the members from a randomly selected group would have heard of LP. Table 6.3 illustrates the two most important determinants of the margin of error: sample size and the degree of variability in the distribution of responses in a two-category question (such as support/oppose, vote Democrat/Republican). In simple language, the degree of variability refers to the degree to which the split in the sample departs from 50-50.

Let's not get lost in percentages. Let's talk people. From our sample of 400 respondents with an approximately 28-percent recognition factor, we learned that 112 people out of 400 knew of LP (400 people × 0.28 = 112 people). Does this really mean that *every* time we ask 400 people, 112 will say they know him? Obviously not. In fact, if we consider the margin of error of ±6 percent (400 people × 0.06 = 24 people), our uncertainty is 24 people. That means that in a different sample of the same size, perhaps only as few as 112 − 24 = 88 people have heard of him. Our actual interest, however, is in *generalizing* our poll result from the sample to the population from which it was selected, namely people who had voted in the most recent nonpresidential Democratic primary election. Thus we can be 95 percent confident (meaning we can expect approximately the same result to occur 95 out of 100 times) that the true value (in the population as defined for LP's name recognition) is within 6 percent of the observed value in the sample. We know that 28 percent of the sample recognized LP. Again, we are concerned with being able to make an estimate of the percentage of the population who will recognize LP. At the time we are making a *statistical inference* (estimating the percent of the target population who recognize his name), we will consider the margin of error of ±6 percent.

When Mr. Local Politician was told that he was "no less known" than any of the other candidates, he chose to flatter himself and focus on the high end of the 22–34 point spread. He subsequently decided to launch his campaign, investing in television advertising. Although a larger sample would have resulted in greater precision, the smaller sample was adequate for LP's purposes. The problem was not so much with the poll as with LP's interpretation. By the way, LP was blown out of the water by a well-known and better-financed late entry, who went on to become the U.S. senator from his state.

WHY LP'S POLLSTER REJECTED
NON-PROBABILITY SAMPLING

In his *Introduction to Survey Sampling*, Graham Kalton[4] of the University of Michigan discusses three types of non-probability sampling:

1. Convenience, Haphazard, or Accidental Sampling   The units in this sampling frame are selected on a purposive basis, subjectively, depending on whether they are deemed representative of the target group. For example, if LP's pollster went to a number of county political meetings (choosing those that were conveniently located, say within an hour's drive) and polled those in attendance, this sampling frame—while economical— would contain a number of biases that would seriously affect the polling results. First of all, those counties located beyond our pollster's convenience radius may be more or less affluent, populated, politically active, or representative of the state as a whole. Second, those in attendance may not be a representative cross-section of (a) politically active Democrats who reside in other counties, or (b) those who did not attend the particular meetings selected to be polled.

According to critics of the Hite study (examined in Chapter 4), her data were flawed because they contained biases that result from using this type of sampling frame. Similar criticism has been leveled at call-in television polls,* street-corner and mall interviews (and other types of convenience samples), and magazine polls based on pull-out questionnaires. To be clear: The problem is representativeness.

2. Judgment Sample, or Purposive Sampling, or Expert Choice
The selection process is based on the decisions of an expert who deems the units a representative sample. However, a problem arises when other experts do not agree that the judgment sample is, indeed, representative of the universe being studied. If LP's pollster—recognized statewide as a political expert—was constrained by a low budget, the decision might be made to poll only 2 or 3 counties out of the state's 20 counties. In this instance, finances would dictate that expert choice should be used to decide which counties are considered most representative of the entire state. As we will soon see, given the budget to poll half or three-quarters of the counties, statisticians would prefer the use of a stratified probability sample.

3. Quota Sampling   This is the third type of non-probability sampling. If LP's pollster decided to use this type of sampling frame, one concern would be to control selection biases that occur when field interviewers are permitted to exercise subjective judgment in the choice of respondents. Such problems occur, for example, when interviewers wishing to avoid making call-backs simply proceed to interview the next available person. To avoid such biases, controls are used. Specific quotas are assigned to each interviewer in order to ensure the representativeness of the sample, and specific instructions are given regarding nonavailable respondents. Quotas could be based on sex, race, ethnicity, religion, age, and so on, depending on the decisions made by LP in consultation with his pollster. While it is generally faster and costs less to use a quota sample, the cost increases as more controls are imposed in order to minimize the risk of selection bias.

Compared to the probability method of random selections, these three types of non-probability sampling, while more economical, contain a major weakness. For the findings of any poll to be considered reliable, they must be **verifiable;** put another way, it should be possible to replicate the study and its results by using the same methodology over and over again to select

---

*Especially those asking people to call a 900 number. Because such a call can cost between 75¢ and $2 or more, a self-selection bias results.

additional samples. Statistically, no matter how many times a study is repeated using the same methodology, no matter how many samples are selected, there should be very little variance (or difference) in the results. Unlike a probability sample (where each unit has an equal—non-zero—chance of being included and where variability from sample to sample can be measured), there is no way statistically to determine an element's possibility of inclusion in a non-probability sampling. Therefore, there is no way to measure the likelihood of replicability or variability—which means that it is difficult to have confidence in the results of the poll.

EVALUATING THE SAMPLE PROCESS

Perhaps the best way to evaluate a sample is by studying the following three components of the process[5] by which the sample was selected.

The Sample Frame

Although there is no perfect sample frame, it is important to consider how well the sample frame corresponds to the universe the researcher wishes to describe. As we saw at the start, the total list of registered Democrats in LP's state corresponded to the target population he wished to later influence. Once the target population was redefined to focus only on those who had voted in the last nonpresidential primary, it became his sampling frame.

There are three general categories of sampling methods:[6]

1. *One-step list*   Sampling from a list, as in the case of LP.

2. *Self-qualifying respondents*   No list exists, but the people who are sampled are those who go someplace or do something that causes them to be included in the sample. You may recognize certain non-probability elements in the following examples:

   ■ We might sample baseball fans attending a game to determine their opinion on whether Pete Rose should be included in baseball's Hall of Fame.

   ■ Shere Hite created her sample frame from those women who volunteered to complete the questionnaire.

   ■ LP's pollster could have just attended county meetings and asked those encountered about LP and the other potential candidates.

3. *Multistage*   Two or more stages are involved, as in the Arbitron sample frame or in the method identified as pinpoint sampling by George Gallup and later by NORC.

George Gallup briefly mentioned his new **multistage sample design** in the Spring 1951 issue of *Public Opinion Quarterly*. This was the pinpoint or precinct sampling technique that his organization, the American Institute of Public Opinion (AIPO), had used in the congressional and state elections of 1950. Two years later, in the Eisenhower–Stevenson presidential contest, Gallup's precinct sampling method was tested on a nationwide basis for the first time. Commenting later on the success of this method, Gallup wrote that "Post-election studies show that this system came through with an error of only one percent.... The full sweep of the Eisenhower victory was indicated, not only for the country as a whole, but for every major area of the country."[7]

The general characteristics, strengths, and weaknesses of his multistage pinpoint or precinct sample design are as follows:

Primary Sampling Units (PSUs)   These were the existing election districts, but PSUs can be states, counties, cities, and so on. Arbitron refers to its PSUs as parent sample field locations (see Chapter 4). This selection process is also called area sampling. A large area such as an election district can be subdivided and the smaller area can be defined as a block, a neighborhood, or, as in this case, a precinct. The researcher is then able to randomly select the SUs.

Sampling Units   SUs are precincts that are selected at random, taking the following factors into consideration:

- accessibility to resident interviewers
- representativeness in terms of the 1948 election
- distribution within regional and city-size strata (that is, cities with over 50,000 population, cities/towns with under 50,000, and rural communities) based on the population distribution reported in the 1950 census. AIPO selected 112 precincts, distributed within major regions around the United States.

Interviewer Instructions   Within the precincts, interviewers were told to call at every *n*th housing unit and to interview one person in that household. If someone refused to be interviewed, the interviewer noted the sex, approximate age, number of family members, and any other information available. (Such data were useful in discerning a profile of the non-respondent.) In those years, most women did not work outside the home. To eliminate any bias due to the nonavailability of men during the normal workday, interviewing hours on weekdays were limited to 3 P.M.–9 P.M. This increased the likelihood of a proper distribution of respondents by age and sex. The ratios of age and sex were maintained by a rotation plan to which the interviewer adhered.

Much of the subjectivity that had plagued earlier sample designs was therefore eliminated. Explicit instructions were given to the interviewers, who now had no choice in the process of neighborhood selection; nor could they ignore the systematic plan for selecting housing units and the individuals (male/female, young/old) to be interviewed.

Two Enduring Problems   How do you differentiate between those who will vote and those who won't? How do you deal with those who are undecided or who refuse to tell an interviewer their voting choice? Gallup eliminated those respondents who said they did not plan to vote, and in his article, he discussed the concept of a turnout scale based on a series of questions relating to attitudes toward voting and actively participating in the political system. For example, the likelihood of people's voting is greater if they voted in previous general and primary elections, read the newspapers on a regular basis, and display an awareness of the major issues. As for undecideds and refusals, interviewers were told to ask which way they were leaning. Respondents who refused to state their choice were eliminated from the sample. The assumption here was that the non-respondents would divide the same way as those who had given their preference.

Political Representativeness   The random sample (by region and for the country as a whole) ensured representativeness because the sample frame was based on past precinct voting behavior. Because most of the factors that existed on the national level were reproduced in precinct elections, each such election was considered a microcosm of the national election. Hence, Gallup's theory went, interviewer compliance was encouraged through awareness that their survey results could be checked with post-election precinct figures.

Advocates of quota sampling have argued that proper instructions to trained and competent interviewers will eliminate most of the bias that results from subjectivity. They criticize area sampling techniques, arguing that "the exactly computed statistical confidence limits of obtained results are misleading."[8] In particular, they point to the missing data that result when some part of the original sample is discarded because people have refused to be interviewed, were not at home, have moved away, or have died.

NORC, founded in the 1940s, introduced permanent community sampling in the late 1960s. In 1982, NORC and the Survey Research Center (SRC) of the University of Michigan joined forces to create an updated sample frame based on the 1980 decennial census. Between the decennial census years, the national sample frame is modified on a regular basis, using the U.S. Census Bureau's Current Population Surveys (see Appendix III).

All U.S. households in the 50 states and the District of Columbia are included in the universe for this national frame. However, if data are not needed from Alaska and Hawaii, they can be excluded without jeopardizing the integrity of the national frame. Except for the sparsely populated or unpopulated areas of northern Alaska, the national frame provides comprehensive coverage of the United States. The sources of information for the primary database were derived from: (a) county-level records, (b) township-level data, and (c) data on independent cities in places where there are no counties.

The national sample contains two groups of 84 primary sampling units (PSUs); each consists of individual counties or groups of neighboring counties. Normally one group of PSUs is sufficient, but when very large samples are needed, both groups of PSUs are used. Within each PSU, a number of smaller areas are selected. These smaller areas are usually blocks. NORC maintains a comprehensive list of the dwellings on more than 30,000 such blocks.

Clustering, a multistage process, refers to sample units found grouped in the same location. For example, if we wanted to study the attitudes of elderly patients to the care they are being given, we could find them by first randomly selecting hospitals from a list of those serving the elderly. In selecting hospitals, we would consider geographic distribution, socioeconomic levels of the patients being served, hospital specialties, and other variables. Then, within those hospitals, we would randomly select some number of these patients from each ward. The clustering method is economical and works well for studies that target specific groups. (Remember the Claritas clusters?)

Two points to remember: First, from a statistical perspective, any sample can only be representative of the population included in the sample frame; second, researchers usually recognize the trade-offs, weighing comprehensiveness against time and cost.

The Probability of Selection

In Mr. Local Politician's poll, Democrats who registered after the list had been prepared were excluded. Thus new residents and newly eligible young voters were ignored. There is no way of knowing how many of them intended to vote in the next primary. In regard to Shere Hite's study (discussed in Chapter 4), many have argued that women who did not belong to the organizations to which questionnaires were sent had no possibility of inclusion.

Floyd J. Fowler, Jr., explains that while it is not necessary "that a sampling scheme give every member of the sampling frame the same chance of selection, as would be the case if each individual appeared ... on a list," a researcher, as noted above, must be able to statistically determine the *probability of selection* for each respondent chosen. Fowler added:

> However, if it is not possible to know the probability of selection of each selected individual, it is not possible to estimate accurately the relationship between the sample statistics and the population from which it was drawn.[9]

The Characteristics and Efficiency of the Sample

The concern here is with the sample size and procedures used in selecting the specific respondents. An overly inclusive sample can be corrected through the use of *filtering questions*, as we shall see in the next chapter. Also, under-sampling and over-sampling of representative groups must be avoided, or at least recognized and compensated for through weighting the data. As you will recall, representativeness proved to be a major issue in the polling failures of 1936 and 1948.

SOURCES OF SAMPLING DATA

Files, Records, and Lists   If you wanted to do a yuppie survey of graduates from your university, you could frame your sample by using university files or records, perhaps for the period 1970–1980, selecting every *n*th name. Public records (for example, school census, bus routes and pick-up points, building permits, voter registration, personal property and real estate taxes, birth certificates, bureau of motor vehicles, utilities, marriage licenses) can also provide source material depending on what you intend to study. All sorts of lists (by type of business, profession, ethnic group, number of children, home ownership ... you name it) can be purchased. There are many private companies specializing in formulating computerized custom lists. (More than 10 years ago someone in the subscription department of a magazine publisher misspelled my name. I am still receiving a great variety of junk mail with the incorrect spelling. Apparently the list of subscribers was never rechecked, but it has been sold and resold to many different companies.)

Directories   Before CATI (computer-assisted telephone interviewing), telephone directories were a common source of sampling data, even though non-telephone households and those who preferred to have their numbers unlisted were excluded. City directories, which list residences by street address, are also useful, but as is true of all data sources, directories are current only at the moment the information is collected. By the time you're reading it, it's outdated.

Census Data   The United States Census Bureau is a major source of sampling data.* It publishes *Block Statistics*, which provides the number of each housing unit on every block in metropolitan areas. The Standard Metropolitan Statistical Area is the government's designation for a large city and includes the surrounding counties economically tied to it. The Census Bureau produces MEDLIST, a Master Enumeration District List, which identifies areas by location codes. Computer tapes of enumeration districts for all areas are also available, the Census Bureau having deposited them around the country. Among the depositories are certain universities (check yours); planning agencies for states, regions, cities, or towns; and at summary tape processing centers, which are private organizations that permit you to borrow or copy the tape. They will charge, though, if you use their computer service to extract data. The Data Users Service Division of the Census Bureau in Washington, DC, will make certain unpublished materials available, but you will have to pay substantial fees for any specialized or customized analyses.

    In addition to a complete population census every 10 years, the Census Bureau conducts monthly Current Population Surveys (CPS) that focus on economic conditions. Respondents are asked specifically about their employment status and that of other household members, in addition to other demographic questions. The bureau uses the area probability sampling

---

*Robert L. Lineberry reports that the grandfather of the computer was born during the 1890 census when Herman Hollerith invented a machine that tallied punched cards with census data on them. The inventor then founded a company to market his Hollerith Machine. The company, International Business Machines, was the same IBM the world knows today. See *Government in America*, 4th ed. (Boston: Scott, Foresman, 1989), p. 202.

method (similar to Arbitron's procedure) to select about 60,000 dwelling units, of which there is a fall-off of approximately 10 percent due to nonoccupancy. Unlike the decennial census, compliance with the CPS averages around 90–97 percent. A person in each of some 52,000 households, clustered in 449 sample areas, is interviewed. The information obtained in these monthly surveys helps the government formulate national economic policies. Therefore, despite the cost of over $20 million annually, supporters of the CPS justify the expense as worthwhile.

CHAPTER REVIEW

- Among the innovations introduced by Bowley's Five Towns Survey were his sampling technique and his creation of definitions and standards for terms that had often been used arbitrarily.

- Purpose sampling targets a particular group.

- Random sampling is based on the theory of probability and attempts to ensure that each unit in the sample frame has an equal chance of being selected.

- When selecting the sample size, our concerns are time, money, level of confidence, and margin of error.

- To create a sample we must (a) define the target group, (b) create the sample design, (c) decide on sample size and the degree of precision needed, and (d) choose the individual respondents.

- The percentage or fraction of the population we sample has little impact on how representative our sample is. Thus we can use a sample of 1,500 for both state and national polls.

- Using the empirical approach to decide on our actual sample size means that we use the experience of others who conducted studies similar to ours. We can do this by consulting a statistical chart that gives us the information we need.

- There is nothing arbitrary about sample size.

- There is an ongoing debate among researchers regarding decisions pertaining to sample size. Some focus on how much error can be tolerated in the particular survey and how sure they must be of their results. Others focus on the smallest sub-group in the study and argue that the confidence-level estimate for the total sample is less important than the separate estimates necessary to ensure the representativeness of the sample's sub-groups.

- Quota sampling emphasizes representativeness over randomness. Although it is believed to be cheaper than random sampling, bias is introduced as a result of the interviewer's subjectivity in selecting respondents. Supporters of this method advocate training, specific instructions, and other controls to eliminate the subjectivity factor and selection bias. However, there remains a replicability problem when we deal with non-probability quota sampling.

- George Gallup was among the first to use a multistage sample design that consisted of randomly selected primary sampling units (election districts) and sub-areas (precinct sampling units), and included specific interviewer instructions on how to select the individual housing units.

- NORC, founded in the 1940s, introduced permanent community sampling in the late 1960s and continues to update its sample frame on a regular basis. The aim is to make it feasible to conduct large-scale comparative community studies.

- There are three general categories of sampling methods: one-step list, self-qualifying respondents, and multistage sampling. *Clustering* refers to sample units found grouped in the same location.

- Sources of sampling data include files, records, and lists; directories of various types; and census data—all of which raise concerns about how current and comprehensive they are.

- Precision becomes a major concern when a large sample is stratified.

- *Questions*: Does sample size depend on the size of your universe (the population that is the subject of your study—for example, all eligible voters in the United States, men between the ages of 35 and 50, working women in large cities, teens of both sexes)? Do you need a larger sample for San Francisco than for Buffalo, New York? Do you have to eat all the soup to determine whether or not to add more salt? *Answers*: No, no, and no.

NOTES

1. For a summary of Bowley's study see D. Caradog Jones, *Social Surveys* (London: Hutchinson's University Library, 1948), pp. 66–78, or the *Journal of the Royal Statistical Society*, Vol. 76 (1912–1913), pp. 672–701.

2. J. Neyman, "On the Two Different Aspects of the Representative Method: The Method of Stratified Sampling and the Method of Purposive Selection," *Journal of the Royal Statistical Society* (1934), Vol. 97, pp. 558–606.

3. Floyd J. Fowler, Jr., *Survey Research Methods* (Beverly Hills: Sage, 1987), pp. 19–22.

4. Graham Kalton, *Introduction to Survey Sampling*, a Sage University Paper, No. 35 (London: Sage Publications, 1983).

5. Fowler, pp. 19–22.

6. See Fowler, pp. 19–22, and Charles H. Backstrom and Gerald Hursh-César, *Survey Research*, 2nd ed. (New York: Wiley, 1981), Chapter 2, for a detailed discussion.

7. George Gallup, "The Future Direction of Election Polling," *Public Opinion Quarterly* (Summer 1953), pp. 202–207.

8. Norman J. Powell, *Anatomy of Public Opinion* (New York: Prentice-Hall, 1951), p. 54.

9. Fowler.

7

Wording the
Questionnaire

Think about—

What are the different kinds of questions we can ask? What is a
structured question? What is a filter question?

What is a scale and why are scales used in opinion research?

What is the difference between a nominal scale and an ordinal scale?

Have you ever heard of the Thurstone, Likert, and Guttman scales?

What is the value of Gallup's quintamensional approach?

What procedures do we follow to complete a research project?

How do focus groups help in testing questions?

What are connotative questions?

To what do *branching* and *skipping* refer?

Why is question order important?

How are self-administered questionnaires different from other
questionnaires?

Is this list an example of manipulation?

During the fall of 1986, while teaching at a Shanghai university in the People's Republic of China, I lived on campus and biked into the city for most of my shopping needs. All problems or questions (and there were many) were supposed to be taken to the foreign affairs officer (a Communist party functionary) or to our assigned translator (who then went to the same foreign affairs officer). After experimenting with different introductory rituals, I soon discovered the best way to ask for something that really concerned me was to preface the question with, "You are so busy and everyone asks you for things because you are so helpful, but would it be a problem for you to ..." The inevitable response, "No problem, no problem," often meant success.

THE IMPORTANCE OF

KNOWING HOW TO ASK

A friend, who is an assistant district attorney, told me that he always prepares before going to court and he never asks any questions to which he does not already know the answer. Professors do the same thing! In general, knowing how to ask a question is always important and useful, but how much more so when an entire research project depends on it. When Mr. Local Politician wanted to undertake the poll discussed in Chapter 6, he told his pollster he wanted to learn how well known his name was among party activists. His pollster explained that if he actually intended to run for the Democratic senatorial nomination, he would have to address the concerns of the people who usually voted in the primary. This was, the pollster said, a good opportunity to find out what these people think about the direction a political leader should take, and to elicit that information LP should ask the following types of questions:[1]

Fact Questions   These are demographic questions that ask respondents to describe themselves (sex, age, religion, income, socioeconomic status, geographic location) and perhaps their home and family members. While we assume that factual questions will result in factual answers, such is not always the case. Unfortunately, people may lie or shade their answers for any number of reasons. When interviews are conducted on a face-to-face basis, obvious distortions can be detected, but this is more difficult to accomplish in a telephone interview. Demographic information is analyzed based on:

- the presence or absence of certain characteristics (for instance, ethnicity or race)
- degree of possession—high or low (income, education, occupation)

Information Questions   These are designed to find out what the respondents know about a particular subject, their source(s) of information, and how much or how little they understand about the issues involved. Such terms as *selective exposure*, *selective perception*, *selective retention*, and *convergent selectivity* tell us that there is a link between attitude and information, just as there is a link between attitude and behavior. Usually we consciously choose what we wish to be involved with, focus on, and remember. Convergent selectivity is involved in the sense that we often are cognizant of what we choose to learn. If something converges (agrees or does not conflict) with our values and belief system, we pay attention to it. Otherwise, most of us just turn away, often unaware that we have given up an opportunity to learn something new.

Attitude and Opinion Questions   It is debatable if there is a connection between what we know and our attitude. Questions about opinions are designed to extract people's thinking, feelings, and latent opinions about particular subjects. For example: Do you support ...? Are you concerned about ...? How strongly do you feel about ...? Recalling the discussion, in Chapter 1, of Key's thoughts on the characteristics and properties of public opinion, note that opinion and attitude responses are analyzed in terms of:

- presence or absence (Key identified the properties of *salience* and *latency*)
- degree of focus and rationality (or irrationality)
- positivity or negativity (Key spoke of the degree of *consensus*— agreement and support—and *conflict*—disagreement and opposition)
- intensity (Key cited *intensity* as an important property of public opinion)

Behavior Questions   When we ask people to describe their own behavior, we are trying to discover what these individuals might actually do. We are also looking for a pattern of consistency or inconsistency in their behavior. When we probe the individual's self-image, we are searching for more information that will help us to check the statements (claims) being made. Most people describe themselves as they would like to be seen and not necessarily as they are. For example, if as many people read daily newspapers as claim to do so, we would be much better informed than we are. When we analyze responses to questions on behavior, we are concerned with

- Presence or absence of the particular behavior. For example, did the respondent vote in the last election? Has she had a medical checkup in the last six months?
- Frequency of occurrence (how often or how infrequent).
- Extent of performance (how complete or incomplete the action was). For example, does the respondent really exercise a full hour three times a week? Does he really read *The Wall Street Journal* every day?
- The degree of importance (high or low) attributed to the behavior. Is this act really an important part of the respondent's regular routine, or is she only claiming that it is?

QUESTION RELIABILITY, VALIDITY, STRUCTURING, AND SCALING

Reliability and validity are at the heart of question construction. **Question reliability** refers to the consistency of the respondent's answers. We want to provide enough choices (categories) so that respondents will answer the same question in a consistent way over time. Consider the following question: Indicate your highest level of educational achievement: Elementary school [1]; some high school [2]; high school equivalency [3]; high school diploma [4]; some college [5]; associate's degree [6]; bachelor's degree [7]; some graduate school [8]; and so forth. Because of the available choices, an individual is able to find an appropriate answer, and if the same question were asked over a period of time, we could expect his or her answer to be consistent (hence, the reliability test has been met).

Question validity raises the issue of whether the particular question actually and accurately measures what we want to measure. Consider the following: Do you support SDI (Strategic Defense Initiative) backed by former president Ronald Reagan? Here, the respondent is confronted with two stimuli: SDI and Ronald Reagan. If the answer is favorable, is it a response to SDI or to Ronald Reagan? This double-barreled question raises uncertainty as to the validity of the question because we cannot be certain of what we are measuring. Besides the question itself, we must also be concerned about the choice of answers. We must provide enough categories so that individuals who think differently are able to make different responses.

A **closed-ended question** (also called a **structured question**), as opposed to an open-ended question, gives fixed responses from which the respondent will choose. The wording is such that no other responses are possible, and each choice is assigned a rating based on a nominal, ordinal, or interval scale. Leaving the ordinal and interval rating systems aside for now, we will first discuss the **nominal rating scale**. This is a type of measurement scale that is no more than a naming mechanism. The numbers that are assigned to the various responses are merely labels, representing different categories of answers. Nominal scales can be used to label the following types of information: sex, marital status, political preferences (Republican "1", Democrat "2", Other "3"), ethnicity, race, and so on.

Interviewers may circle the appropriate number depending upon the respondent's answer or type it into the computer if the interview is conducted over the telephone. In the case of a self-administered questionnaire, these code numbers are usually omitted and the respondent merely circles or checks the preferred response. Then, during the data-processing stage, the responses are recorded according to the assigned numbers.

The following two examples, from the *Times Mirror News Interest Index* (June 7, 1990)★ illustrate the dichotomous (either/or) and multiple-choice

---

★The survey was conducted under the direction of Princeton Survey Research Associates during the period June 1–4, 1990. The Gallup organization provided interviewing services for this telephone poll of 1,231 adults (18 years of age or older). The report states: "For results based on the *total* sample, one can say with 95% confidence that the error attributable to sampling and other random effects is plus or minus 3 percentage points." (Emphasis added. Review Table 6.2) *Times Mirror Interest Index* (Washington, DC: Times Mirror Center for The People & The Press).

types of structured questions, along with their nominal ratings.

Dichotomous type: Do you know of any savings and loan banks in your area that have been taken over by the federal government because they were in serious financial trouble? (Q. 9)

	(Circle one) [Nominal rating]	
Yes	1	(23%)★
No	2	(76%)
Don't know	3	(1%)

Multiple-choice type: Which of the following groups will pay for the bailout of failed savings and loan banks? (Q. 10)

	(Circle one) [Nominal rating]	
a. Former managers of these banks	1	(3%)
b. Stockholders of the banks	2	(7%)
c. People who had their savings in these banks	3	(5%)
d. Taxpayers like you	4	(79%)
e. None	5	(1%)
f. Don't know	6	(9%)

Notice that the percentages in the second question don't add up to 100 percent. This is because interviewers were told to accept multiple responses.

Because structured questions provide a limited number of options, their results are easier, faster, and cheaper to process. The responses are precoded through the nominal ratings, and field interviewers merely circle or check the option selected. In today's data-reduction process, scanners are then used to read the responses into a computer. Computer-assisted telephone interviewers (CATI) type code numbers into computers as respondents answer structured questions.

The *mode* is the only statistical measure used to determine the *central tendency* of data organized by a nominal scale. By **mode**, I mean the result or answer that appears most frequently. **Central tendency** refers to a *single summary figure* that best characterizes the sample population. If our goal is quantitative (how many hold that opinion) as opposed to qualitative (how

---

★Since this poll was taken, a significantly larger number of banks throughout the country have failed. Thus awareness of troubled banking institutions has increased.

and why respondents think a particular way), this question format, which uses the nominal scale and results in the mode as its indication of central tendency, makes good sense. We can easily make generalizations applicable to the population at large based on the percentage of our sample that answers in a particular way. However, as Shere Hite and other critics have pointed out, constrained or restricted responses lose some of the qualitative (personal or particularistic) feeling of the data being generalized (within the sample and from the sample to the universe). Also on the negative side, Backstrom and Hursh-César explain:

> ... fixing a few response alternatives to complicated issues creates flawed data, since it ... manufactures a "coalition" or summary position that encompasses different if not conflicting views; and [also] forces people to make unnatural choices they wouldn't make in the real world.[2]

When open-ended questions are used, the responses are placed in categories by a trained coder. The difficulty here is to reduce the often large variety of responses into a limited number of categories. The various categories can be assigned a nominal rating for coding purposes. Interestingly, the need to limit the number of categories might undermine the advantages of using open-ended questions. (Review Hite's discussion of this point in Chapter 4, in The Professional Voice 2.) I should mention the following three points about nominal scales:

- The choices are arbitrary. "No" could be identified with a 1 and "Yes" could be identified with a 2.

- The difference between a 1 and a 2 is not quantitative; it is qualitative.

- What is important is that the choices of how the numbers are assigned must be consistent throughout the study.

Another common type of rating scale that ranks the responses is called the **ordinal scale**. This type of rating scale is used to rank the responses along some dimension—from best to worst, highest to lowest (as with economic status or class rank), most prominent to least prominent (which is what LP needed to know)—or to measure how strongly or intensely someone agrees or disagrees with something. The measure of central tendency used with an ordinal scale is the *median*, or midpoint (review Box 4.2). The following example, adapted from a marketing research study for a large travel agency, illustrates this point with regard to a preference ranking. Interviewers used a check mark to indicate the likelihood for each place mentioned; the numbers assigned to each answer column—for example, Definitely Will (1)—are the precoding device of ordinal ranking.

How likely is it that you would plan a vacation trip to the following places in the next two years?

Vacation Spot	Definitely Will (1)	Probably Will (2)	Probably Will Not (3)	Definitely Will Not (4)	Don't Know (5)
New York State					
Florida					
California					
New England					
Midwest					
Southwest					

Interviewers were told to rotate the place names. This means that respondent 2 would first be asked about a trip to Florida and then to the other places, with New York coming last; respondent 3 would be asked about California first and then down the list, ending with Florida; so on for the subsequent respondents. Do you know why this rotation is done?

Another example of an ordinal scale, more common to a self-administered questionnaire than to one read by an interviewer, is the **rank order scale**. This scale is used with a question that asks the respondent to rank items in a specified order, from 1 to some number, based on the respondent's opinion as to which is most likely to succeed, most popular, most honest, and so forth. Take a look at the following example.

Please rank the following professions as to their honesty and ethical standards, using the numbers 1 through 12. The most honest/ethical should be assigned the number 1 and the least honest/ethical ranked number 12.

Profession	Rank (1 = most honest/ethical)
Newspaper reporters	
Druggists/pharmacists	
Bankers	
College teachers	
Business executives	
Clergy	

Local officeholders

State officeholders

Congressmen

Senators

Stockbrokers

Medical doctors

The Gallup organization asked a similar question in a poll taken February 8–11, 1990, except that their list was far more extensive. You may be interested to know that car salesmen ranked last (only 6% rated their honesty and ethics as "very high/high"). They ranked just below advertising practitioners (12%) and insurance salesmen (13%), who were just below stockbrokers (14%).

The following is a third example of a ranking question, using the ordinal (rank order) scale.

Asked to discuss yourself, which of the following would you be most and least likely to mention? Using the numbers 1 through 7, please rank the following to indicate your willingness to discuss the topics below. Use the number 1 for the topic you are most willing to discuss and number 7 for the topic you are least willing to talk about.

Topic   *Rank (1 = most willing to discuss)*

Education

Political affiliation/opinions

Religion

Family

Ambition

Views on abortion

Work-related experiences

One problem with the ordinal scale is that it can be (as in the above cases) extremely subjective, thereby failing the test for validity (Is it measuring what you want it to measure?) and reliability (Will it yield a consistent answer over a period of time?). When it is used to indicate the highest level of educational achievement a respondent received (elementary school [1], some high school [2], high school diploma [3], and so on), it is being used to measure distinct points. It thus passes the validity test because it is measuring exactly what we want it to measure. Also, asked the same question over a period of time, the respondent's answer will be consistent, thereby passing the reliability test. The median will then quickly supply us with a summary figure that characterizes how educated our sample population is. And there is not really a problem when we are dealing with extreme emotions, as when we try to rank a respondent's feelings of strongly disliking or strongly liking a candidate. At those times, it is possible to differentiate between two polar points. However, how can we find the distinct and precise point that differentiates feelings of strongly disliking from disliking, or feelings of neutrality from liking a candidate? As you can see, the problem of subjectivity can be even worse if the interviewer is asked to gauge the intensity of feeling on the part of the respondent, as opposed to the respondent's describing his or her own feelings. Think about the bias this can create in a poll, a type of bias that goes unreported and is therefore unknown to those who read the polling results in the press. This is where scales can play an important role. (I will return to the topic of measuring attitudes and feelings later in this chapter when I deal with the Likert scale, an ordinal scale commonly used in polling.)

Still another type of rating scale used in polling is the **interval scale** of measurement. Here, the assigned numbers indicate different objects that are placed (ranked) in a specific order. The intervals between these objects are equal, and therefore the distances between the numbers have real meaning. In the example that follows, I present a question dealing with the respondent's annual income. Before considering the way in which the question utilizes an interval scale, I call your attention to the fact that asking about someone's annual income crosses into a more personal and sensitive realm for many people. You will note that the question provides an explanation as to why the researcher needs such information and a statement of assurance that the data will be used only in analyses that include other participants in the study. Also, on a self-administered questionnaire, the words "interval rank" would not appear. This question was adapted from a marketing research study undertaken by manufacturers of home entertainment equipment.

Since we are trying to get a better understanding of how decisions to purchase home entertainment equipment relate to income, some idea of your household income is particularly important to us. We will use the information only in combination with information from other participants in the study. Could you please tell me which income category includes your total annual household income before taxes in 1991?

Annual Income in $10,000 intervals	**Interval Rank (Circle One)**
Under $15,000	1
$15,001 to $25,000	2
$25,001 to $35,000	3
$35,001 to $45,000	4
$45,001 to $55,000	5
$55,001 to $65,000	6
$65,001 to $75,000	7
$75,001 to $85,000	8
$85,001 or more	9
Don't know/Not sure/Refused	10

Note that the intervals between the incomes are equal. Generally, this is the most acceptable and statistically correct way to use an interval scale. However, some researchers create different groupings that, for their purposes, seem to make more sense. For instance, in one study the $15,000-to-$25,000 interval was followed by "$25,000 to under $40,000; $40,000 to under $50,000; $50,000 to under $60,000; $60,000 to under $80,000; $80,000 to under $100,000; $100,000 or more." It is more statistically correct to keep the intervals equal, and there is another reason for doing so. The data collected are more precise when the intervals are closer together. It is also interesting to note that while each interval in the table is $10,000, this does not automatically mean that people who earn $30,000 annually are twice as rich as those who earn $15,000. In other words, you cannot make *ratio judgments* based on the interval scale. (Additionally, we should not confuse income with wealth.) The mean, or average, is the measure of central tendency used with the interval scale; it is the summary figure that best characterizes the sample for what is being asked. (There are occasions when the median is the better measure of central tendency for interval- or ratio-level variables—for example, skewed distributions.)

Finally, there is the **ratio scale**, which is primarily used in the physical sciences and only rarely found in public opinion surveys. The ratio scale also uses numbers to identify different objects that are ordered, and the intervals on the ratio scale are of equal value. Ratio scales can be used to measure the following types of variables: time, distance, speed, height, weight, and age. A ratio scale permits us to say, for example, that if I biked 10 miles and you biked 20 miles, you biked twice as much as I did; or if LP received

20,000 votes and the winning candidate in the primary election received 140,000, LP was trounced by a ratio of 7:1. The mean is the appropriate measure of central tendency for ratio-level variables.

MEASURING ATTITUDES

Social psychology, born in the first years of this century, became an invaluable ally of public opinion researchers as it focused attention on the study and measurement of attitudes. In the years that followed, domestic and foreign events and conflicts (the Great Depression, World War II, the onset of the Cold War, the Korean War, McCarthyism,* the civil rights movement, and so on), as well as the normal waning of professional interest in any one subject, influenced social psychologists to study other areas. As a result, there have been three separate periods in which social psychologists' interest in attitude research has peaked and has been of particular value to professional opinion researchers.[3]

Scaling Theory and Group Dynamics: 1920s–1930s

This period's legacy of scaling theory—an attempt to measure gradations of attitude—proved particularly useful to pollsters struggling with the constraints of closed-ended (structured) questions. Researcher L. John Martin notes that until the 1920s attitudinal questions were dichotomous—the answer called for either a yes or a no, for or against.[4] However, in the late 1920s Louis L. Thurstone, an American psychologist, attempted to measure attitude by providing a range of statements and asking people to indicate agreement or disagreement with each of the statements.[5] He was attempting to measure psychological stimuli and to compare them to each other. Thurstone recognized the difficulty of measuring nonphysical stimuli, and the problems inherent when human judgment is factored in.

Writing about the "law of comparative judgments," he explained that for each stimulus there probably exists a "modal discriminal process" on the psychological continuum. He was saying that for every stimulus, it is likely that there exists one response that is most common (the mode),

---

*In the 1950s, Senator Joseph McCarthy of Wisconsin and his right-wing supporters unleashed an attack, now recognized as a communist witch hunt, against liberal and left-wing critics of the government. The senator and his cronies blacklisted writers, producers, entertainment personalities, and scientists. Here's a research project: Take a community sample of those over 50 and ask them if (and what) they remember about the roles played by the following five personalities during the McCarthy era: Presidents Ronald Reagan and Richard Nixon, news commentator Edward R. Murrow, actor Zero Mostel, and nuclear physicist J. Robert Oppenheimer.

occurring more frequently than any other response. As an example, suppose 50 people were asked to rank the prestige of two occupations: medical doctor and schoolteacher. According to Thurstone's analysis, although each person would first exercise his or her own judgment in weighing the relative prestige of a paired comparison, say the occupation of medical doctor (the stimulus) with that of a schoolteacher, there would be a *modal response.* In other words, most people would rank the doctor as the more prestigious occupation of the two. Thurstone reasoned that a prestige continuum (from highest to lowest) could be created. With an expanded list, individual respondents could compare the prestige of various occupations to that of a doctor. Respondents would place an occupation along the prestige continuum, depending upon their individual perceptions of the particular occupation in relation to that of a doctor.

To operationalize the "law of comparative judgments," Thurstone developed three scaling methods: the method of paired comparisons (mentioned above), the method of successive intervals (wherein the items are placed along a continuum), and the method of equal-appearing intervals.[6] The last method is the most complex because it involves several time-consuming and cumbersome steps:

1. A large number of statements (as many as 100), reflecting all shades of opinion on a given subject, must be collected. The statements must be carefully constructed to avoid more than one interpretation; irrelevance to the object under consideration; words such as *always, never, all,* or *none* (because such universals introduce ambiguity); comments that will be agreed to by almost everyone or by almost no one.

2. These statements (covering all possible opinions on the subject) are then examined by a group of judges, individuals instructed to rate the items as favorable or unfavorable toward the subject matter and to sort them into 11 distinct piles, labeled from "A" (those eliciting the most positive feelings) through "F" (those eliciting neutral reactions) to "K" (those eliciting the most negative sentiments).

3. Statistical methods, including using the median for each item, are then employed to discern the degree of consensus on the judges' part toward the various statements and to establish each item's scale value. The aim is (a) to eliminate those statements that are deemed ambiguous because they elicit the greatest disagreement, thereby reducing the size of the piles; and (b) to place each of the remaining items along the continuum from "most unfavorable" to "most favorable," according to its statistically based scale value.

4. The 20 or so items that remain are supposed to clearly represent specific *shades of attitude*, falling into equal-appearing intervals along the scale from favorable to unfavorable. Placed along an attitudinal continuum, the items are supposed to represent the full range of possible attitudes toward the subject.

5. The statements can then be randomly arranged and presented to respondents, who are told to check those statements with which they agree.

6. The scale values of the items checked off by an individual respondent are then averaged, and that average scale value is considered an indication of the person's attitude toward the particular subject of the study.

The extremely complex methodology devised by Thurstone went through various modifications by subsequent researchers.★ His scale, also called a differential scale, falls into the category of **additive scales** used by sophisticated researchers. (A common example of an additive scale is that of a baseball player's RBIs—runs batted in—which consists of the cumulative number of points the player is credited with bringing in for each game played throughout the season.) Scales are used in primarily two ways by opinion researchers: (1) to scale individual answers to attitude items, and (2) to scale the total score a respondent receives for the way in which he or she has answered *all* the items, representing that person's views on the subject. The latter is called "subject-centered."[7]

In 1932, another American psychologist, Rensis Likert, used a modified version of the Thurstone scale. The Likert scale, known as a *summated scale*, is also quite complex, but "no scaling model has more intuitive appeal."[8] The Milton Rosenberg self-esteem scale[9] is an example of the Likert subject-centered procedure. This scale consists of 10 statements. The five positive statements are coded from 5 to 1, with 5 being "almost always true" and 1 being "never true." The coding is reversed for the five negative statements, with 5 being "never true" and 1 being "almost always true." In the case of a negative statement, a response indicating a high level of self-esteem would be "never true," for which the respondent would receive a 5. For each of the 10 statements, the respondent is asked to choose one of the following: almost always true, often true, sometimes true, seldom true, never true. The 10 Rosenberg self-esteem items are:

★In the 1960s, political theorist V. O. Key, for example, used a much-modified version of Thurstone's attitude scale to analyze the *distribution* (how widely a particular opinion is held) and the *direction* of opinion, which includes the degree of *consensus* (agreement and support), *conflict* (disagreement and opposition), or *concentration* (how pervasive the opinion is).

- I feel that I have a number of good qualities.
- I wish I could have more respect for myself.
- I feel I'm a person of worth, at least on an equal plane with others.
- I feel I do not have much to be proud of.
- I take a positive attitude toward myself.
- I certainly feel useless at times.
- All in all, I am inclined to feel that I am a failure.
- I am able to do things as well as most other people.
- At times I think I am no good at all.
- On the whole, I am satisfied with myself.

If you were to take this test, your cumulative score would indicate whether or not you lacked self-worth. A high score on the self-esteem scale indicates a high level of self-worth.

The Likert summated scale involves a weighting scheme and procedures of statistical testing to ensure internal consistency and reliability. These procedures are beyond the scope of this introductory-level text. However, we will look at an example of the way in which many pollsters today use a modified Likert-style scale, which has five or six degrees of possible agreement or support.[10]

An interviewer gives the respondent a card printed with a list of phrases similar to the following:

strongly oppose

moderately oppose

mildly oppose

mildly support

moderately support

strongly support

and then says, "For each of the statements I will read, please choose one of the phrases from the card that best indicates the degree of your support." As the respondent answers, the interviewer records the appropriate preassigned value for each answer. These values are tallied to determine the respondent's overall score, and the scores for groups of respondents can be computed to provide useful information about the respondents' feelings and attitudes.

During the interlude that followed the introduction of the original Likert scaling methodology (from 1935 to 1955), interest moved to the study of group dynamics and processes (decision making, conformity, cohesiveness, conflict resolution, cooperation and competition, power). Remember the morale studies and other wartime research projects? A quick glance at some of the NORC studies during that period (see Chapter 5) will give you a sense of the extrinsic factors (events in the United States and abroad) affecting the interests of social psychologists.

In 1944, sociologist Louis Guttman introduced his method of cumulative scale analysis,[11] the Guttman Scalogram, which was used extensively in army research during World War II and subsequently in psychological testing. Guttman questioned the reliability of the Likert and Thurstone procedures to establish conclusively that a given series of statements belonged on a single (unidimensional) continuum (from most favorable to most unfavorable, for example). Guttman was asking how a researcher could be certain that each statement fitted into a designated place on the scale's continuum, was appropriate, and would yield a consistent response. He argued that evidence of its suitability could be provided by the scale's predictability. Guttman maintained that the respondent's total score should enable the researcher to predict his or her responses to all the component parts. This type of scale can be used with a structured question, yielding a total response score. That score serves to indicate the respondent's attitude in relation to some point on the agree/disagree continuum.

Charles Backstrom and Gerald Hursh-César have used the analogy of a ladder,[12] whereby each acceptable statement (one rung at a time) carries you to the top. Thus if you have accepted all the statements in a group, say a group of five statements (each being worth 1 point), your final score would be 5 points. The score itself predicts that you accepted all the statements (climbed all the rungs). However, if your final score is only 3, it means (the scale predicts) that you rejected statements 4 and 5. In considering the group of six statements below (based on Douglas McGregor's "Theory X/Theory Y"[13]), you will note that while the first is almost universally acceptable, the statements become increasingly difficult to agree with, except for those individuals who believe strongly in stringent supervision in the workplace.

Measuring Your Attitude Toward Motivating People to Work

Interviewer: For each of the following statements, please indicate whether you agree or disagree.

Statement	Point Value (Unseen by Respondent)
1. People like to be treated courteously.	1
2. People need encouragement and assistance.	1
3. Fear of demotion or firing is the primary motivating force that keeps people productive in their work.	1

4. People do not want to think for themselves;
   they expect and depend on direction from above.   1

5. Being naturally lazy, when faced with a choice,
   people will normally prefer to do nothing at all.   1

6. People remain children, merely grown larger, and
   they remain naturally dependent and unthinking.   1

Total possible score = 6

A respondent who believes in close staff supervision will rank higher (have more "favorable" scores) than one who disagrees with any of the statements. The theory is that if the statements truly fit into the continuum, as soon as a respondent finds a disagreeable statement, the rest will surely be disagreeable. Assume that this ordered group of statements had been statistically tested and the results indicated a perfect fit, thereby creating a perfect agree/disagree scale pattern. That perfect pattern (unidimensionality*) would look like Table 7.1 for a group of seven respondents whose individual A/D (agree/disagree) scores fell at different points on the continuum.

If a person agrees with all these statements, this may indicate someone who holds his or her fellow workers or underlings in low esteem. Given the choice, we would probably not wish to work for such a person. However, how would you interpret the results if a large proportion of a polling sample responded in that way? One possible interpretation is that the result signals a reactionary, anti-labor swing. Another interpretation might focus on dissatisfaction with a perceived deterioration in the quality of our work force.

The Guttman cumulative scale is based on the theory that if a respondent answers dichotomously (yes or no, agree or disagree) to a series of questions that deal with *one subject* (one variable), a reading or measurement of the person's attitude can be taken by tallying the points given each answer. The scores can be analyzed, compared, and grouped with those of other respondents. You may recall taking some variation of such tests, in which the same questions seem to appear over and over again, but are worded somewhat differently.

The Thurstone, Likert, and Guttman scales are complex, involving a good deal of statistical expertise; their presentation here is merely an introduction to some interesting methods for eliminating question bias.

---

*Unidimensionality for a sample is determined by the percentage of respondents who fit one of the seven patterns in the table. In practice, we will not get a perfectly unidimensional set of responses, but in some cases we may approximate it.

**TABLE 7.1 A Perfect Continuum Scale Pattern
from "Easiest to Agree" to "Hardest to Agree"**

RESPONDENT NUMBER	STATEMENT NUMBER						AGREEMENT SCORE	RESPONDENT'S RANK*
	(1)	(2)	(3)	(4)	(5)	(6)		
1	A	A	A	A	A	A	6	1
2	A	A	A	A	A	D	5	2
3	A	A	A	A	D	D	4	3
4	A	A	A	D	D	D	3	4
5	A	A	D	D	D	D	2	5
6	A	D	D	D	D	D	1	6
7	D	D	D	D	D	D	0	7

*Rank is based on the degree of agreement.

These scales represent the first effort of social psychologists to measure attitudes. Before turning to the second period of intense interest, I would like you to consider George Gallup's contribution to question design theory.

In 1947, after discussing the problems he hoped to overcome,[14] George Gallup introduced his quintamensional plan of question design. Table 7.2 summarizes his presentation.

Attitude Formation: 1950s–1960s

After their interest in group dynamics waned, social psychologists were drawn back to attitude formation studies. The return to this area of social psychology apparently signaled their deep concern with the impact of group dynamics on the individual, whereas during the late 1960s and 1970s their attention was redirected to the study of social perceptions.

A number of other scales were devised to study the topics of interest in the 1950s and 1960s. I will introduce you to the *Stapel scale* and the *Cantril-Kilpatrick self-anchoring scale*, two of those commonly used by public opinion researchers. However, there is much more to these scales than might be apparent from our brief discussion, and there are many other types of scales that are beyond the scope of this text.

Jan Stapel of the Netherlands Institute of Public Opinion devised the scale shown in Figure 7.1 with 10 boxes—5 white (at the top) and 5 black.[15] By pointing to a box on the Stapel scale, respondents are actually responding to two questions at once: (a) they are indicating positive or negative feelings,

TABLE 7.2 Gallup's Quintamensional Plan of Question Design

PROBLEM	SOLUTION: FIVE TYPES OF QUESTIONS
1. To determine whether the respondent lacks awareness knowledge of the subject.	1. Information/filter type of question. *Example*: "Have you heard/read about the Whitewater case? Which (of the following) is the main reason for the investigation?" Nominal ratings are assigned to the choices offered the respondent.
2. To draw a distinction between those who seriously consider the issue raised and those who make a snap judgment.	2. Open-ended/free-answer type. *Example*: "What do you think about the U.S. military response to the Iraqi invasion of Kuwait? Do you think we should have done something else?" The answers are put into categories that are then assigned nominal ratings.
3. Question wordings may mean different things to different people.	3. Dichotomous/categorical/specific-issue question. *Example*: "Did you support the president's response to Saddam Hussein's invasion of Kuwait? Would you support a special tax of 25¢ per gallon of gasoline if the revenue were to be spent on research for alternative sources of energy?" This implies "Vote yes or no," "Stand up and be counted." Nominal ratings are assigned.
4. Complex issues cannot be reduced to a single dichotomous question. Why the respondent feels a particular way *is* important.	4. Reason-why (category) questions. *Example*: "Why do you feel this way?" Nominal ratings can be assigned to the different categories.
5. How strongly the respondent feels is too often ignored. Is she or he part of the majority or the minority?	5. Intensity (a type of scale) question. *Example*: "How strongly do you feel … very strongly, fairly strongly, or not at all strongly?"

Instructions for the Interviewer

1. The interviewer hands the scale to the respondent and

2. tells the respondent, "Please put your finger on the box that best represents your point of view."

3. The interviewer reads the question and records the box number.

☐ +5   Very strongly agree/
☐ +4   approve
☐ +3
☐ +2
☐ +1
■ −1
■ −2
■ −3
■ −4
■ −5   Very strongly disagree/
        disapprove

FIGURE 7.1 The Stapel Scale

and (b) they are indicating the degree of their feelings at the same time. Gallup reported that when this scale was used in election polling, researchers found the extreme positions (+4, +5, −4, and −5) were "most indicative and most sensitive" to changing circumstances. Since the two positions at each end of the scale are normally combined, the Stapel scale, applied to questionnaires, gives a more defined (more sensitive) reading. This, according to Gallup, more closely approximates the actual election results.

The Cantril-Kilpatrick self-anchoring scale[16] was devised in 1960 and used in a worldwide survey in Nigeria, India, the United States, West Germany, Cuba, Israel, Japan, Poland, Panama, Yugoslavia, the Philippines, Brazil, and the Dominican Republic. In each of these countries, respondents were asked about their hopes and fears and where they felt they stood on the ladder scale (see Figure 7.2). The respondents were told to describe the best type of life they could imagine.

They were told that position number 10 on the ladder represented their greatest dreams, while position number 1 represented their greatest fears. The respondents were asked to indicate where on the ladder they stood today, where they thought they had stood in the past, and where they thought they would stand in the future. The advantage of the self-anchoring scale is that even illiterate people can relate to "climbing the ladder" to reach for their dreams. Apart from problems with literacy, this type of scale is excellent for cross-cultural research.

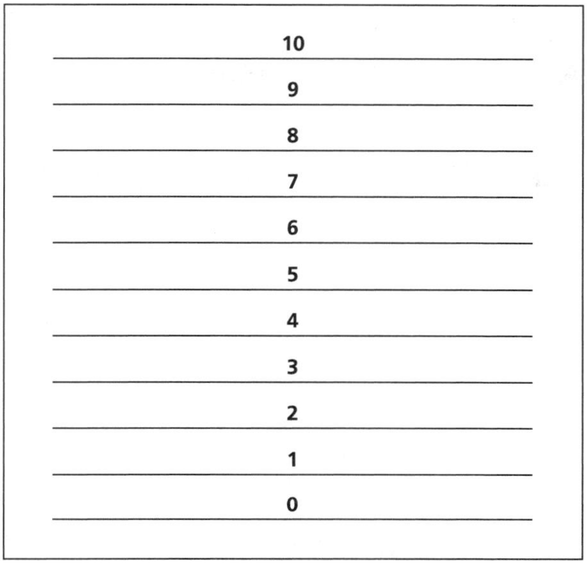

FIGURE 7.2 Cantril-Kirkpatrick Self-Anchoring Scale

Attitude Consistency and Opinion Formation:
1980s and Beyond

In this third peak of interest, some social psychologists returned to the study of attitudes and attitude consistency (social judgment, inference, cognitive responses, and so on), and some social scientists, such as Elisabeth Noelle-Neumann (see Box 7.1), pursued long-held interests in opinion and attitude formation.

During the mid-1980s, interest mounted in the questionnaire as a measuring device. Concerned with the problems of creating a bias-free research tool, the National Center for Health Statistics (NCHS) established a questionnaire research facility called the Questionnaire Design Research Laboratory (QDRL) in October 1985. In doing so, the NCHS acknowledged that the "questionnaire can be the weakest link in the measurement process."[17] (See Box 7.2.) They also acknowledged that while impressive strides have been made in the more scientifically based survey activities (sampling and data processing), in essence, questionnaire design remains an art.[18] In analyzing how to improve the latter, NCHS researchers considered the support provided the former by statisticians and computer scientists. They wondered if cognitive scientists could help survey researchers design more effective and bias-free questionnaires to probe respondents'

BOX 7.1   The Spiral of Silence

In 1947, in the aftermath of World War II, Elisabeth Noelle-Neumann founded the Institut für Demoskopie Allensbach in West Germany. This institute has evolved into a full-service public opinion and market research company that custom-designs surveys for business, government, and universities. While directing the institute, Noelle-Neumann has been a professor of communications research at the University of Mainz, has served as a president of the World Association for Public Opinion Research (WAPOR), and has written extensively on public opinion. She is Germany's leading pollster and a prominent advisor to Chancellor Helmut Kohl.

Perhaps her best-known work among the lay population is *The Spiral of Silence*, which presents a disturbing theory of public opinion formation. Citing Alexis de Tocqueville and others who believed that public opinion is the opinion of the numerical majority, Noelle-Neumann examined the causes and implications of opinion formation by the majority and the phenomenon of flock behavior. Reminiscent of earlier research on crowd behavior (discussed in Chapter 1), her work delves more deeply into the reasons we fear isolation and join the flock or bandwagon:

> There must be something beyond the individual's actual personal relations, an intuitive faculty perhaps, for permanently monitoring a multitude of people....We can see this statistical sense organ as the link that connects the person with the collective.[1]

André Malraux, a French novelist known for his Marxist beliefs, once commented that he never knew what to think about fashions, "the centuries when men must wear beards, the centuries when they must be clean-shaven," and Noelle-Neumann responds:

> [F]ashions are ways of behaving which, when they are new, one *can* exhibit in public without isolating oneself but at a later stage one *must* show in public to avoid isolation....
>
> Fashion's playful character makes it easy for us to overlook its great seriousness, its importance as an integrating social mechanism....
>
> Discontent with fashion's disciplinary power shows itself in many negatively charged expressions: "the whims of fashion," "fad," or "clothes horse," "dandy," "swell." They imply shallowness, superficiality, transience, and a kind of imitation that borders on aping.[2]

Besides fashion that coerces us to consume, there are many other pressures on the imaginary statistical sense organ, clueing us in to what others are thinking. For example, Noelle-Neumann's research confirmed that laws can and do slowly change public opinion. Public speeches, notices, and the media all play a role in changing public opinion, but to what degree is difficult to say. The media's agenda setting may not tell us how to think, but it does provide us with the material to think about.

Consider the question the little boy in the cartoon asked: "Dad, if a tree falls in the forest, and the media aren't there to cover it, has the tree really fallen?"[3]

A crisis or danger to a society exerts extremely strong pressure to conform; especially during that period, "the climate of opinion depends on who talks and who keeps quiet." While Noelle-Neumann's theory was perhaps derived from her early professional years in Nazi Germany,[4] her examples no doubt grew out of her observation of West German politics, particularly during the 1960s and 1970s. However, her spiral-of-silence theory can be universally understood. Simply put, it describes a phenomenon that occurs when we see people expressing themselves openly and defending their views with self-confidence. There is a strong tendency to restrain ourselves if we hold a differing view. As we withdraw and remain silent, others view the vocal supporters as being stronger than they actually are. People are therefore subtly encouraged to express support or to swallow their opposition and remain silent. The spiraling process adds numbers to the supporters, further silencing opponents who fear condemnation and isolation. Winners speak up; losers become increasingly silent.

Although research testing the spiral-of-silence hypothesis has not substantiated Noelle-Neumann's hypothesis, intuitively I still maintain it has merit. Perhaps I am thinking of the crimes of the Romanian and other east European communist leaders and the silence of the people all those years. Or perhaps I am just wondering why during election campaigns, so few of my friends wear political buttons or display political bumper stickers on their cars. During election campaigns, do *you* wear political buttons or display political bumper stickers? Early in the campaign? Late in the campaign? Never? Why?

---

1. Elisabeth Noelle-Neumann, *The Spiral of Silence, Public Opinion—Our Social Skin* (Chicago: University of Chicago Press, 1984), pp. 114–115.
2. Noelle-Neumann, pp. 116–117.
3. Noelle-Neumann, p. 150; cartoon by Robert Mankoff (*Saturday Review*).
4. Noelle-Neumann was an exchange student in the United States from 1937 to 1939, at a time when German exchange students were "selected under the rules of the Nationalist Socialist party Office for Foreign Politics, and the program was an important part of the propaganda apparatus." According to Leo Bogart, "Noelle was picked on the basis of her superb credentials as activist and leader of...Nazi youth and student organizations." Bogart cites "Who Informs America," an article she wrote for *Das Reich* (June 8, 1941), two weeks before the invasion of the Soviet Union. In it, she writes, "Jews write in the newspapers, own them, have virtually monopolized the advertising agencies and can therefore open or shut the gates of advertising income to individual newspapers as they wish. They control the film industry, own the biggest radio stations and all the theaters." In 1990, Noelle-Neumann was the winner of the Helen Dinerman Award (for outstanding contribution to research methodology) of the World Association for Public Opinion Research. For a discussion on Noelle-Neumann's forgotten past, see Leo Bogart, "The Pollster & the Nazis," *Commentary* (August 1991), pp. 47–49.

BOX 7.2   The Measurement Process Reviewed

By now you are familiar with some of the following steps required to complete a survey:

- Decide what you want to measure—the subject of your survey (such as attitudes toward violence on television).
- Design a measurement instrument—questionnaire and interviewer protocol (directions/procedures).

- Draw up the sample plan.
- Contact the respondents/perform the interviews.
- Code results into data.
- Process the data—edit, clean, put into computer-readable format.
- Analyze data.
- Produce reports/disseminate results.

---

attitudes and behavioral descriptions. Cognitive psychology is concerned with the mental systems (such as thinking, memory, understanding, judgment) we use in processing information.

The QDRL began by analyzing the typical questionnaire development procedures used by the NCHS:

1. Define objectives, data needed.
2. Research topics and draft questionnaire.
3. Informally test questions by asking friends and coworkers.
4. Conduct one or two field pretests.
5. Make final revisions and print questionnaire.

When the QDRL examined them, these procedures were found wanting. Primarily, there simply was not enough attention being paid to pretesting questions. A number of changes were then made. For example, *focus interviews* were introduced. The focus interview has had a long history, dating back to the wartime research of Lazarsfeld and Merton discussed in Chapter 2. QDRL focus interviews are unstructured discussions led by a trained moderator. The purpose is to explore the participants' understanding of issues and concepts important to the study. These interviews are held with various demographic sub-groups to observe the variation in knowledge and attitudes. The understanding gained from these exploratory interviews is helpful in drafting questions that are further reviewed and tested. Two of several methods used in this long and involved early phase of questionnaire development are:

1. *Concurrent think-aloud interviews*   Respondents are asked to think aloud as they answer the questions, reporting on whatever comes to

mind. These interviews are audiotaped. The interviewer probes the responses, encouraging the respondents to explore their feelings on the behavior or on the issues presented. For example, when a respondent states that she remembers doing something, a probe would be: How did you remember? What reminded you? What does "usually" mean to you? By using such probes in the testing phase of the questionnaire development process, the researchers are able to refine question wording, adjust question order, and eliminate ambiguity.

2. *Paraphrasing* Respondents are asked to rephrase the questions in their own words. The point here is to determine whether a question is too complex, whether a respondent would miss some important qualifying word or phrase.

Although this is a time-consuming process, this method of repeated testing and probing does help to eliminate potential sources of error and bias that might go undetected in the traditional field test. Thus cognitive scientists at the QDRL have added a new dimension to questionnaire formulation.

By examining the ways in which respondents formulate their answers, that is, their assumptions about question intent and meaning, level of knowledge about the question topic, ability to recall the requested information, ability to retain complex question wording in short term memory, use of "guessing," and use of various estimation strategies, questionnaire designers can gain insights into the cause of response error and develop or revise questions that will minimize the error.[19]

BAD QUESTIONS

Through extensive testing of its questions, the QDRL discovered that some of their questions were bad, for various reasons. Two examples, along with the improvements made in them, are discussed below.

Question 1

During the past year, how often did you usually eat/drink [a list of 56 foods and food groups, including]:

orange juice or grapefruit juice?

other fruit juices or fortified fruit drinks?

beans, such as baked, pinto, kidney beans, or in chili? Do not include green beans.

carrots, or mixed vegetables containing carrots?

french fries or fried potatoes?

chicken or turkey, baked, stewed, or broiled?

ham or lunch meats?

coleslaw, cabbage, or sauerkraut?

The list went on and on and on. The QDRL determined that there were cognitive problems with this question, which required:

- "extremely complex recall and estimation process."[20] Most of the items were combinations that required respondents to think about each item (such as coleslaw, cabbage, or sauerkraut) and then to think about how many times they had eaten it.

- a great deal of patience. It also takes a good deal of concentration and energy to use estimation strategies and not become frustrated by the amount of time necessary to answer accurately.

The cognitive scientists also felt that the wording seemed to demand an exact response and that this was intimidating. Although the National Center for Health Statistics needed the complete data to determine the respondent's eating habits, the researchers were able to ease the burden by breaking down the question and asking separately about each of the foods. They also changed the stem of the question to "During the past year *or so*." This was done to subtly suggest to the respondent that they were seeking data to establish a typical pattern, as opposed to a precise numerical response.

Question 2

If a person stops smoking completely, do you think his/her chances of developing the following conditions will ever be as low as those of a person who has never smoked?

heart disease

cirrhosis

cancer of the lung

cancer of the bladder

emphysema

The QDRL determined that this question was difficult to understand because of the many qualifiers. The respondent would have to grasp seven separate pieces of information before coming to the list of medical problems:

- if a person *stops smoking* completely,
- do you *think*
- his/her *chances of developing*
- the *following conditions*
- will *ever*
- be *as low as* those of
- a person who has *never smoked*

The question was simplified: "Do you believe that if a person stops smoking completely, his/her chances of getting (*fill in one condition*) are reduced?" Thus the question is repeated several times, enabling respondents to concentrate on whether they believe cessation of smoking reduces risk for that particular condition. For those who answered "Yes, cessation of smoking reduces the risk of getting that particular condition," a second question could be asked. The comparative part of the original question then became: "Would this person's chance of getting (*condition*) be as low as that of someone who has never smoked?"

Complexity and intimidating language are just two causes of bad questions. There are others,[21] as outlined below.

The Loaded Question   This is a bad question because it *leads, influences,* or *clues* the respondent to some desired response. It may be an unfair question because it provides poor or bad alternatives, attacks or maligns one side, or damns with faint praise. It may omit names, vary titles, link personalities to programs or programs to institutions. It may use emotive (emotionally charged) words, or stereotypes, or just be embarrassing. Can you identify the problem in each of the following questions and suggest improvements? Is that a loaded question?

Some Really Bad Questions:	*Instead, How About:*
Some people say President Jimmy Carter was incompetent. Do you agree or disagree?	On a scale of 1 to 5, with 1 being extremely competent, how would you rate President Jimmy Carter?
During the Greyhound bus drivers' strike, there was a good deal of violence. Do you support unions when strikers resort to violence?	This is a tough one. After asking, Do you support labor unions?, you might try an open-ended question, such as, Under what, if any, circumstances would you withhold your support?

Some people say Dan Quayle was a poor choice for vice president. Do you agree or disagree?

On a scale of 1 to 5, with 1 being excellent and 5 being poor, how would you rate Dan Quayle as a choice for vice president?

Abortion is killing babies. Do you support abortion?

Which of the following indicates your position on the legalization of abortion? Strongly support, support, neutral, oppose, strongly oppose?

I'm conducting a poll for Councilman Andrew Browne, who is seeking reelection. If the election were held today, would you vote for Mr. Browne or for one of his opponents?

If the council election were held today, for which one of the following candidates would you vote? Ms. Carol Grey, Mr. George White, Mr. Andrew Browne, Ms. Susan Greene.

Do you agree or disagree that Mayor Y's efforts to fight crime in in our city should be supported? Would you support increased taxes for that purpose?

Would you support a tax increase if the money were used to fight crime in our city?

Do you support the star wars technology backed by former President Ronald Reagan?

Are you familiar with SDI (Strategic Defense Initiative)? [If yes, then:] Do you support the SDI program?

How many hours of television do you watch each day?

Which of the following best describes your daily TV viewing habits? Under 1 hour, 1 to under 2 hours, 2 to under 3 hours, 3 to under 4 hours, 4 to under 5 hours, 5 to under 6 hours, over 6 hours.

Have you stopped kicking your dog?

Forget it.

The Easily Misperceived and Misunderstood Question   If a question lies beyond a respondent's frame of reference, there is a good chance that the answer will not be responsive to what is being asked. One census taker reported the following exchange with someone from the Far East, who appeared to have a good grasp of English:

Question: How many adults are in your household?

Answer: There are four adults and three adultresses—seven in all.

Jargon or technical words tend to intimidate those who are unfamiliar with the terminology. Syndicated columnist William Safire refers to the MEGO phenomenon (my eyes glaze over) that occurs whenever a government military expert discusses ICBMs (intercontinental ballistic missiles), nuclear deterrence, delivery systems, and the policy of mutually assured destruction (known as MAD). Unfamiliar combinations of ordinary words may also create confusion because these words have been taken out of their expected context. Then, too, homonyms (similar-sounding words) can cause problems because respondents tend to hear the word they are familiar with and not the one being used. The best questions are those that are written the way people speak. After all, other than the self-administered questionnaire (which usually arrives unsolicited in the mail), questionnaires are read by interviewers to respondents.

The Multipart Question   We create analytical problems when we include two or more parts in a question. With more than one subject to a question, we may not be able to determine which part the respondent intended to answer. In our earlier example on smoking from the NCHS questionnaire, we counted seven separate pieces of information and noted the suggestions of the QRDL.

Questions That Assume Knowledge   It is generally a mistake to assume that the public has specific knowledge about certain esoteric (and not so esoteric) areas. Questions that require specialized knowledge create a number of problems, including the tendency of respondents *not* to admit that they have no idea what the interviewer is asking about. The well-phrased filter question (Have you read/heard about ... ?) can assist but cannot guarantee that the uninformed will be screened out.

The Ambiguous Question   Consider the no-parking sign that read: "No Parking Anytime Except Not on Wednesdays and Fridays." Questions can be ambiguous for many reasons. They can be vague, lacking in precision (What do you think about entrapment?), or they can be incomplete (Do you support the president's actions?). Avoid setting indefinite time periods and using words such as *always, frequently, often,* or *sometimes.* Recall the problem the cognitive scientists had with question 1 (During the past year, how often did you usually eat ... coleslaw?). It is worth repeating that many people, concerned with self-image, will jack up the frequency of good behavior and play down less acceptable behavior:

Question: How frequently do you vote?

Answer: All the time.

Question: How frequently do you drink an alcoholic beverage?

Answer: On special occasions.

A number of studies have shown that abstract words commonly used by the media mean different things to different people. Two examples of early 1980 studies:

- J. F. Fee found that *big government* was interpreted as signifying a welfare state, extensive federal control, and bureaucracy.[22]
- Tom W. Smith found that the word *confidence* was defined in four different ways: trust, capability, attention to the common good, and that which followed the respondent's self-interest.[23]

In fact, researchers have found that certain words trigger specific reactions—positive and negative.

FILTER QUESTIONS AND SKIP INSTRUCTIONS

You will recall that when George Gallup introduced his quintamensional plan of question design, one of the problems he dealt with was the need to identify respondents who either lacked awareness and knowledge of the subject or who did not meet the definition of the target population for one reason or another. His solution was the **filter question** that is placed at the start of the survey, after the interviewer's opening remarks. In the following three examples, the telephone interviewer's instructions appear in small capitals, as is the convention.

(From a survey for a cable TV company)

Do you currently subscribe to cable TV for which you pay a regular monthly fee?

Yes ( ) CONTINUE   No ( ) TERMINATE

(From a survey for a cheese manufacturer)

Do you, or does anyone in your household, work for★ (READ LIST)?
(INDICATE YES OR NO)

an advertising agency	( )	⎫
a marketing research or opinion research company	( )	⎬ (IF ANY OF THESE THREE ARE YES, RECORD ANSWER AND TERMINATE)
a manufacturer, wholesale, or retailer of dairy products	( )	⎭
the airlines	( )	
the government	( )	

★The top three are disqualified for security reasons.

(From a survey of married women 35 and older)

(ASSUMING THE FEMALE HAS MET THE AGE REQUIREMENT . . .)

What is your marital status?

Single	( )	TERMINATE
Divorced	( )	TERMINATE
Widowed	( )	TERMINATE
Married	( )	CONTINUE

Besides eliminating unqualified respondents, a filter question can lead into different sets of specific follow-up questions, a process that is called **branching** and that uses **contingency questions**. A contingency question is only asked of those who answered a preceding question in a particular way; otherwise, the interviewer is told to skip to a particular question. The example below assumes that unqualified respondents have been "terminated."

Question #6: Have you ever taken any courses in political science?
(CIRCLE ONE)

Yes   No   (IF YES, CONTINUE. IF NO, SKIP TO QUESTION #9.)

Question #7: Were these courses taken in

college? ( )   high school? ( )   other? ( )
(IF COLLEGE, CONTINUE. IF NOT, SKIP TO QUESTION #9.)

Question #8: Which college?
(WRITE ANSWER HERE) _____

Question #9: Do you consider yourself a Democrat, a Republican, or an Independent?

Democrat   ( )   Republican   ( )   Independent   ( )

Other   ( )   SPECIFY _____

Don't know ( )   (IF DK, TERMINATE)

Question #10: Are you now registered to vote?

Yes ( )   No ( )   (IF NO, TERMINATE.)

The questionnaire design can became increasingly complex as it incorporates branching and skip instructions. In the case of interviewer-administered questionnaires, careful directions are a must. As we will soon see, when dealing with self-administered questionnaires, it is best to keep the questionnaire as uncomplicated as possible.

THE WORDS AND THE ORDER

Tom Smith studied the connotations of certain words, including *welfare, the poor, the unemployed*, and *food stamps*. He found that the word *welfare* evokes a low level of public support, whereas *help for the poor* fares significantly better: "on average support for more assistance for the poor is 39 percentage points higher than for welfare."[24] He also found that in some respects his results replicated those of Gerald Wright, Jr.,[25] whose 1977 study showed that *welfare* was strongly associated with the respondent's race. However, Smith's study 10 years later found that *welfare* was "no more associated with race" than was *assistance to the poor*. So why the difference in support for spending to help *the poor* as opposed to those on *welfare*? Smith states that his findings suggest an explanation other than racism, namely that the term *welfare* "seems to connote a wasteful program that encourages sloth and sponging." Thus the perception in people's minds is extremely negative: "The negative connotation that 'welfare' carries is apparent from such terms as 'welfare queen' and 'welfare Cadillac.'" In an interesting footnote, Smith indicates that he conducted a "survey of nine dictionaries" and "no dictionary indicated any recognition of any negative connotations associated with the term" *welfare*. The obvious point is that words have denotative and connotative meanings. While the former is found in the dictionary, the latter is found in people's minds. Cognitive psychologists at the QDRL have identified this as a major problem in constructing questions.

In 1989, Kenneth Rasinski, also of NORC, analyzed question-wording experiments in which relatively minor changes were made in a series of

TABLE 7.3 Wording Changes in General Social Surveys

VERSION 1	VERSION 2	VERSION 3
1984, 1985, 1986	*1984, 1985, 1986*	*1984 Only*
Question: Are we spending too much, too little, or about the right amount on …		
space exploration program	space exploration	advancing space exploration
halting the rising crime rate	law enforcement	reducing crime
dealing with drug addiction	drug rehabilitation	reducing drug addiction
the military, arma- ments, and defense	national defense	strengthening national defense
foreign aid	assistance to other countries	helping other countries
welfare	assistance to the poor	caring for the poor
solving the problems of the big cities	assistance to big cities	solving the problems of the big cities

three NORC general social surveys (1984, 1985, and 1986). Wording variations appeared in each of the three years. In 1984, three questionnaires with
wording changes were used; in 1985 and in 1986, two were used. Table 7.3
is a much-shortened version of some of the wording changes.[26] Some of
Rasinski's findings showed that respondents were more willing to support:

- *Halting crime* rather than *law enforcement*   The former appears to
  make people feel safer. It seems to have more positive connotations
  associated with the personal and social benefits of a lowered crime
  rate. Law enforcement, on the other hand, seems to remind respondents of traffic and parking tickets, corruption, and police brutality.

- *Dealing with drug addiction* rather than *drug rehabilitation*   The former
  seems to connote action, while the latter seems status quo-oriented
  at a time when people yearn for an elimination of drugs from our
  society and are frustrated with the lack of progress in the
  government-declared "war against drugs."

- Giving *assistance to the poor* rather than *welfare*   Again, the former
  had less negative connotations.

- *Solving the problems* of big cities rather than *assistance* to big cities
  Here, too, the former connoted action.

These studies illustrate the need for sensitivity to language, particularly when constructing a questionnaire.[27] In addition to the connotative meaning of words, researchers have considered the effects of using *prestige names*. In fact, one rule of survey researchers writing a question is, Do *not* use a prestige name in questions, unless the question is about that person or organization. This is because we want to avoid being unfair when more than one entity (person or institution) is involved. For example, if we want to ask whether the United States should support insurgents in X country who are attempting to overthrow their government, we should not refer to the effort as the president's policy. Doing so may act as a cue and affect the answer given. However, as Eric Smith and Peverill Squire point out, "the findings about the effects of prestige names are somewhat contradictory."[28] They list three points on the subject:

1. Adding a prestige name may *help or hurt* the side associated with the name, depending upon whether the person/institution is respected. One study found that crediting the nonexistent Agricultural Trade Act to President Reagan or to Iowa governor Robert Ray increased support for the act in Iowa. However, attributing the act to Reagan or to Kentucky governor John Y. Brown decreased support in Kentucky.[29]

2. Adding a prestige name to a question of marginal interest to a respondent will not always affect the answer. In 1940 researchers found that adding President Franklin Delano Roosevelt's name to the Lend-Lease bill made no difference—it neither increased nor decreased public support for the bill to militarily aid an endangered Great Britain.

3. When respondents have little or no knowledge on which to base a response, adding a prestige name provides informational cues to influence respondents one way or the other. Smith and Squire note that "the evidence for this is that most published examples of prestige names show that adding a name reduces the proportion of those without opinions."[30] Yet in a 1941 study on whether the United States should do more or less to help Great Britain, opinion changed substantially when the president's name was added, but the Don't Knows (DKs) remained the same. The findings about the effect of prestige names on DKs are contradictory and inconclusive.

In their own research, Smith and Squire document the certainty of what appears obvious:

- Using prestige names adds a partisan component to the questions and political neutrality is lost.

- The partisan component seems to be greatest when respondents know the least, and smallest among those who are knowledgeable.

Still another concern of researchers beyond connotative words and prestige names is the actual order of the names and of the questions. In the case of name order, Albert Cantril tells us that when a question asks the preference of one candidate over another there is "some evidence" that the candidate whose name is mentioned first does better. Cantril suggests that to overcome this type of bias, interviewers can rotate the order of the candidates' names.[31] As to question sequence, some researchers are adamant that it does make a difference in survey results.[32] Peter Hart states that "placement of questions can really determine what the results of asking a question will be," and recommends that the general/open questions precede specific ones.[33]

For example, consider the effect of rearranging the following three questions:

- How would you rate President Clinton's job performance? (Use one of the attitude scales.)

- Do you approve/disapprove of the president's national health care plan?

- Do you approve/disapprove of the president's plan to commit U.S. troops to the U.N.-sponsored peace accord in Bosnia?

When questions are likely to bias each other, the most important one should be placed first. That is why researchers generally place the preference question as early in the interview as possible.[34]

THE SELF-ADMINISTERED QUESTIONNAIRE

The teacher evaluation form you are asked to complete is an example of a self-administered questionnaire. In other instances, this type of questionnaire is used when people have been assembled for the purpose of conducting a survey. The advantages of a self-administered questionnaire distributed to an assembled group are:

- The response rate is generally high or, conversely, the refusal rate is low.

- The respondents are able to read the questions for themselves, thereby diminishing possible interviewer bias. We say *diminishing* rather than *eliminating* because it is conceivable that bias may creep in as the person responsible for distribution and supervision answers questions raised by the respondents.

- Along with explanatory comments, visual aids may be used in group-administered questionnaires.

- The questionnaire can be longer than it would be in a telephone or face-to-face interview.

Yet consider the following disadvantages of the self-administered questionnaire in the same group situation:

- You have no way of knowing if the respondent has completed all the questions until the questionnaire is in your hands (at which point it is too late).

- A shy or self-conscious respondent may not want to raise a troublesome question in front of others.

- The respondent's answers to sensitive questions can be affected by the presence of other individuals, even though assurance of confidentiality is given to the entire group.

As you realize from all the junk mail you and your family probably receive, your name and address appear on multiple computerized lists. Researchers interested in reaching any particular target populations can purchase these lists and use them to send out self-administered questionnaires. In such cases, the overall survey costs are low, but the response rate is also significantly lower than for any other form of interview or questionnaire technique. Why? The answer is simple: A mailed questionnaire is easy to ignore, especially if it looks as though it is going to take a lot of time to complete. A 50-percent response rate for a mailed questionnaire may be adequate,[35] but "one occasionally will see reports of mail surveys in which 5 to 20 percent of the sample responded."[36] Needless to say, this creates a self-selection bias and the resultant sample bears little resemblance to the original sample design. One way to raise the response rate is to include some incentive (beyond a prepaid return envelope). For example, college professors often receive questionnaires from various publishing companies, asking such fascinating questions as "What academic conventions do you regularly attend?" and "When you attend conventions do you visit the publishers' exhibits?" The incentive to fill out the questionnaire in two weeks and to return it ("in the enclosed postage-paid envelope") is usually the choice of a free book—and college professors love free books. The response rate for those surveys is generally considered good (around 60 percent).[37]

Some points to remember here:

- Keep the questionnaire short and uncomplicated (avoid branching-type questions). Remember, the respondent has no one to ask if an explanation is needed.

- Offer some type of incentive to complete and return the questionnaire.

- Enclose a postage-paid return envelope (because without it, even fewer respondents will reply).

- Remember, there is a slow turn-around time.

CHAPTER REVIEW

- You will recall that the first to use a questionnaire was the Scottish landowner Sir John Sinclair (review Box 2.1). During the nineteenth century, straw polls published by newspapers used a short questionnaire of sorts. Such surveys were concerned either with collecting demographic information useful to the state or with predicting intended voting behavior. Attitudinal research was not seriously attempted until the turn of the twentieth century.

- Knowing how to ask a question is important, but it is equally important to know which *type* of question will elicit the information you want.

- There are four types of questions: fact, information, attitude, and behavior. In analyzing the responses to these different types of questions, we look for specific things. Can you give an example for each type of question?

- Such terms as *selective exposure, selective perception, selective retention*, and *convergent selectivity* tell us there is a link between attitude and information, just as there is a link between attitude and behavior. We often consciously choose what we wish to be involved with, focus on, and remember.

- *Question reliability* refers to the consistency of the respondent's answers. If the same question were asked over a period of time, we ought to expect the same response.

- *Question validity* deals with whether the particular question measures what we want to measure.

- Double-barreled questions raise uncertainty as to question validity. The problem is that because such questions contain two elements, we cannot be sure which part of the question the interviewee is responding to.

- Dichotomous and multiple-choice questions are considered structured because responses are provided. What are the advantages and disadvantages of structured questions?

- Open-ended questions provide greater flexibility for respondents, but they are more difficult to process. The problem of subjectivity is often mentioned. Why?

- Nominal, ordinal, interval, and ratio scales are ways of ordering information. Different types of questions call for one or another of these measuring devices. Can you describe the characteristics of each type of measuring scale and identify the type of question that calls for the nominal, ordinal, or interval rating systems?

- *Central tendency* refers to the single summary figure that best characterizes the sample population for the question asked. The goal is to generalize from the sample to the population at large.

- When data are organized by a nominal scale, the mode (the answer that appears most frequently) is the only statistical measure used to determine the central tendency.

- The ordinal scale is used to rank responses along some dimension— from best to worst, highest to lowest, intensity of support or disagreement, and so on. The measure of central tendency used with an ordinal scale is the median or the midpoint. One criticism is that it can be used in an extremely subjective manner.

- The rank order scale, a type of ordinal scale, is used to rank items according to the respondent's preference, from 1 to some number.

- The interval scale enables us to ask about household income, the price of one's home, how much people spend on clothing, food, cars, or other such money matters considered personal by many people. The scale can also be used to gather information about how people spend their time, how long they have been married, and so on.

- It's important to remember that the intervals between the pairs of numbers should be equal. For sample, consider an interval scale of annual income: (1) ... (4) \$35,001–\$45,000; (5) \$45,001–\$55,000;... (10) Don't Know/Not Sure/Refused.

- It's also important not to make the intervals too large. That's because the data collected are more precise when the intervals are closer together.

- The mean is the measure of central tendency used with the interval scale.

- The ratio scale, primarily used in the physical sciences, is rarely found in public opinion surveys. It is useful in that it enables us to make ratio judgments, such as "LP was trounced by a ratio of 7:1." Here too the mean is the appropriate measure of central tendency.

- There were three peaks in the study of attitudes by social psychologists: (1) The 1920s–1930s, during which social psychologists focused mostly on group dynamics and the development of scaling theory; (2) the 1950s–1960s, during which social psychologists renewed their interest in attitude formation studies and the study of social perceptions; (3) the 1980s and since, during which social psychologists have pursued the study of attitude consistency, including social judgment, inference, and cognitive responses.

- When Thurstone (during the first period) wrote about the law of comparative judgments, he was saying that for every stimulus, it is likely there exists a common (modal) response that occurs more frequently than any other response.

- Thurstone developed three scaling methods: paired comparisons, successive intervals, and equal-appearing intervals.

- Social psychologists such as Thurstone, Likert, and Guttman devised attitude scales that were designed to make the questionnaire a more precise and scientific instrument.

- Can you identify the characteristics of differential, summated, and cumulative scales? What are additive scales and why are they best left to the experts to use? What are the advantages of using an attitude scale?

- The Milton Rosenberg self-esteem scale is an example of the Likert subject-centered procedure. The cumulative score is meaningful, conveying information about the respondent, such as degree of self-esteem.

- Sociologist Louis Guttman's Scalogram was used extensively in army research during World War II and subsequently in psychological testing. He argued that a scale's predictability was important in establishing reliability.

- In 1947, George Gallup introduced his quintamensional plan of question design. What were the problems he hoped to overcome?

- The Stapel scale and the Cantril-Kilpatrick self-anchoring scale are simplified versions of attitude scales. To use either of these scales, interviewees merely point to the appropriate box or ladder level to indicate positive or negative feelings in response to particular questions. What are the advantages of scales such as these?

- Although recent studies have challenged Elisabeth Noelle-Neumann's theory of the "spiral of silence," perhaps it is still wise to see it as a warning. Why?

- The National Center for Health Statistics established the Questionnaire Design Laboratory in October 1985 because it had come to view the questionnaire as the weakest link in the measurement process. What are the responsibilities of the QDRL? How does the QDRL use the focus interview?

- What makes a bad question?

- What type of problem do filter questions attempt to resolve?

- Emotive and connotative words can create a bias. Can you explain why?

- Adding prestige names to questions may cause bias.

- Various research efforts have shown that question order is a major concern of survey researchers.

- What are the advantages and disadvantages of branching?

- What are the advantages and disadvantages of self-administered questionnaires?

NOTES

1. See Charles H. Backstrom and Gerald Hursh-César, *Survey Research*, 2nd ed. (New York: Wiley, 1981), pp. 124–128, for an extensive discussion. Also see Jean M. Converse and Stanley Presser, *Survey Questions: Handcrafting the Standardized Questionnaire* (Beverly Hills: Sage, 1986).

2. Backstrom and Hursh-César, p. 132.

3. William J. McGuire, "Attitudes and Attitude Change," *The Handbook of Social Psychology*, Vol. II, 3rd ed., Gardner Lindzey and Elliot Aronson, eds. (New York: Random House, 1985), pp. 233–346.

4. L. John Martin, "The Genealogy of Public Opinion Polling," *Annals, AAPSS*, March 1984, pp. 12–23.

5. L. L. Thurstone and E. J. Chave, *The Measurement of Attitude* (Chicago: University of Chicago Press, 1929).

6. See John P. McIver and Edward G. Carmines, *Unidimensional Scaling* (Beverly Hills: Sage, 1987).

7. W. S. Torgerson, *Theory and Methods of Scaling* (New York: Wiley, 1958).

8. McIver and Carmines, p. 22.

9. Milton Rosenberg, *Society and the Adolescent Self-Image* (Princeton, NJ: Princeton University Press, 1965).

10. Gardner Murphy and Rensis Likert, "A Technique for the Measurement of Attitudes," *Archives of Psychology* (1932), No. 140.

11. Louis A. Guttman, "A Basis for Scaling Qualitative Data," *American Sociological Review* (1944), No. 9, pp. 139–150. Also see Edward A. Suchman and Louis Guttman, "A Solution to the Problem of Question 'Bias,'" *Public Opinion Quarterly* (Fall 1947), pp. 445–455.

12. Backstrom and Hursh-César, p. 138.

13. Douglas McGregor, *The Human Side of Enterprise* (New York: McGraw-Hill, 1960).

14. George Gallup, "The Quintamensional Plan of Question Design," *Public Opinion Quarterly* (Fall 1947), pp. 385–393.

15. George Gallup, *The Sophisticated Poll Watcher's Guide* (Princeton, NJ: Princeton Opinion Press, 1972), pp. 107–109.

16. F. P. Kilpatrick and Hadley Cantril, "Self-Anchoring Scale," *Journal of Individual Psychology* (November 1960); and see Gallup, *Poll Watcher's Guide*, pp. 109–111.

17. Monroe G. Sirken, "Error Effects of Survey Questionnaires on the Public's Assessments of Health Risks," *American Journal of Public Health*, Vol. 76, No. 4, pp. 367–368.

18. See Delbert C. Miller, *Handbook of Research Design and Social Measurement*, 4th ed. (New York: David McKay, 1983).

19. Patricia Royston and Deborah Bercini, *Questionnaire Design Research in a Laboratory Setting*, a paper presented at the American Statistical Association Convention, Survey Methods Section, August 1987 (available through the National Center for Health Statistics).

20. Royston and Bercini, p. 2.

21. See Backstrom and Hursh-César, pp. 140–153, for a detailed discussion with examples.

22. J. F. Fee, "Symbols in Survey Questions: Solving the Problem of Multiple Word Meanings," *Political Methodology* (1981) No. 7, 71–95.

23. Tom W. Smith, "Can We Have Confidence in Confidence? Revisited," D. F. Johnston, ed., *Measurement of Subjective Phenomena* (Washington, DC: U.S. Government Printing Office, 1981).

24. Tom W. Smith, "That Which We Call Welfare by Any Other Name Would Smell Sweeter: An Analysis of the Impact of Question Wording on Response Patterns," *Public Opinion Quarterly* (Spring 1987), pp. 75–83.

25. Gerald Wright, Jr., "Racism and Welfare Policy in America," *Social Science Quarterly* (1977), Vol. 57, pp. 718–730.

26. Kenneth A. Rasinski, "The Effect of Question Wording on Public Support for Government Spending," *Public Opinion Quarterly* (Fall 1989), pp. 388–394.

27. Also see Jean M. Converse and Stanley Presser.

28. Eric R. A. N. Smith and Peverill Squire, "The Effect of Prestige Names in Question Wording," *Public Opinion Quarterly* (Spring 1990), pp. 97–116.

29. Lee Sigelman and Dan Thomas, "Opinion Leadership and the Crystallization of Nonattitudes: Some Experimental Results," *Polity*, Vol. 18, pp. 484–493.

30. Smith and Squire, p. 99.

31. Albert H. Cantril, *The Opinion Connection, Polling, Politics, and the Press* (Washington, DC: Congressional Quarterly, Inc., 1991), pp. 132–133.

32. See, for example, McKee J. McClendon and David J. O'Brien, "Question-Order Effects on the Determinants of Subjective Well-Being," *Public Opinion Quarterly* (Fall 1988), pp. 351–364, and Tom W. Smith, "Conditional Order Effects," *GSS Technical Report*, No. 33 (Chicago: National Opinion Research Center, 1982).

33. Peter D. Hart, "The Art of Asking Questions," *Polling on the Issues*, A. H. Cantril, ed. (Cabin John, MD: Seven Locks Press, 1980), pp. 59–65.

34. Larry Hugick, "The Gallup Polls," *The Public Perspective* (a Roper Center Review of Public Opinion and Polling, Jan./Feb. 1991), pp. 20–21.

35. Earl Babbie, *The Practice of Social Research*, 5th ed. (Belmont, CA: Wadsworth, 1989), p. 242.

36. Floyd J. Fowler, Jr., *Survey Research Methods* (Beverly Hills: Sage, 1987), p. 48.

37. Babbie.

8

The Interviewer

Think about—

What is the role of the interviewer?

What problems confront an interviewer?

What three types of error are interviewer related?

Who applies for the job of interviewer?

How are interviewers trained?

Why standardize interviewers?

How does an interviewer motivate a respondent to reply?

Why is it necessary to supervise, verify,
and validate the work of interviewers?

What is meant by the disposition of a questionnaire,
and what are the steps taken to verify the data obtained?

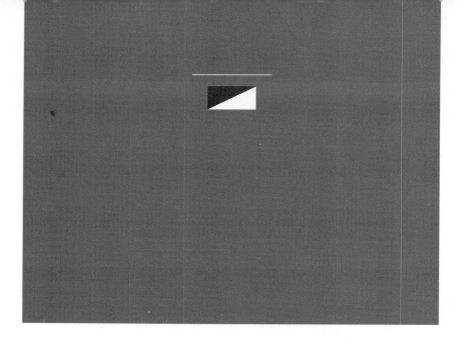

Those of us who grew up in the late 1940s and 1950s recall in-person interviews, usually by a very friendly and personable woman. She was invited into our home and was served coffee while she organized her papers and began to ask questions about our political or marketing preferences. We felt flattered that someone cared enough to actually come to our home to ask about our opinions. The public was generally cooperative in those less cynical days before Vietnam, Watergate, Willie Horton campaign ads, and the savings and loan fiasco. If the target audience was women for purposes of a marketing research study, interviewers rang the doorbell during the day, for most women were housewives on a full-time basis. If the target audience was men, the time to find them at home was either in the evening or on weekends. Interviewers were able to achieve very low non-availability rates by making a few call-backs to those who were not at home the first time around. Refusal rates also tended to be low and their numbers were generally predictable, varying with the subject matter of the study.

Computers were introduced into the field during the 1960s, reducing the costs of undertaking, analyzing, and cross-tabulating findings. Those in social science, business, and government became increasingly interested in collecting data via surveys, and those surveys became more and more complicated. Sophisticated methods were introduced as studies focused on sub-populations (adolescents, ethnic and racial minority groups, Vietnam veterans, people below the poverty level, unwed mothers). New screening and sampling techniques were developed and computer-assisted complex statistical analyses were undertaken. Graduate schools expanded their programs in the field of survey research; professionalism reached new heights (see Appendix II).

However, an interesting social anomaly occurred. As the cost of surveys was reduced and the interest in such research increased, the public became more ambivalent and less cooperative. The nature of our society was changing. The neighborhood mentality that had existed even in the largest cities disappeared. Increased crime, drugs, and other societal problems led to a greater sense of vulnerability and therefore to higher refusal rates when interviewers knocked on our doors. Then, too, more and more women entered the work force, and one-person households became commonplace. Eventually, the pollsters came to realize what the door-to-door Fuller Brush and Avon cosmetics salespeople were among the first to learn: namely, that changing lifestyles and demographic factors were making it difficult to find someone at home or someone willing to take the time necessary for an interview. Telephone interviewing began to replace face-to-face interviews, and the refusal rates began to increase as people resisted the pervasiveness and invasiveness of polling.

RESPONDING TO THE CHALLENGE

In 1973, the National Science Foundation sponsored a workshop that considered the deterioration in survey rates of response. It was decided that sampling statisticians needed to develop statistical and operational (procedural) solutions. In 1977, the National Academy of Sciences considered the problem of both total refusal rates (referred to as the respondent level) and the rate of refusals to specific questions (referred to as the item level). Their findings and recommendations were published in a three-volume report in 1983. Although a number of complex statistical procedures were suggested and developed to offset the bias caused by refusal rates, non-response remained a problem area.

When computer-assisted telephone interviewing (CATI) was introduced back in the 1970s, it expanded the number of sampling design options (see Chapter 13). New telephone sampling methods were developed using computer technology linked to a database for random-digit dialing. By 1986, *92 percent of all households* were reachable by telephone. This correspondence between telephone households and all households is sufficiently close for purposes of most sample surveys undertaken; random-digit dialing even bypasses the unlisted number to reach those who wish to protect their privacy.

However, the fact remains that people can and do simply hang up on interviewers. Thus, non-response rate was again considered in 1987 by a task force created by the American Association of Public Opinion Research (AAPOR). To date, research continues in this area while public opinion researchers are confronted with still other challenges.

THE INTERVIEWER'S ROLE
AND PROBLEMS

Never underestimate the importance of an interviewer. As you probably realize, except in cases where mailed, self-administered questionnaires are used, the successful gathering of data for any public opinion poll or survey depends on the effectiveness of the interviewers. Whether they knock on doors or use the telephone, their role demands integrity, intelligence, patience, flexibility, commitment, self-motivation, assertiveness, enthusiasm, and a variety of skills. An effective interviewer is expected to do the following:

Locate and Gain the Cooperation of the Selected Respondents
This is no small task. Merely reaching the selected respondent can present problems because it depends on that individual's schedule. While the telephone interviewer is required to call back, the in-person interviewer must physically return to the respondent's residence to conduct the interview. On locating the respondent, the interviewer must then enlist the individual's cooperation. A successful interviewer is one with an engaging personality who is capable of projecting confidence that the survey is worthy of the respondent's time, that the respondent will want to participate in it, and that doing so would be a positive contribution.

Later in this chapter we will look at attempts to minimize refusal rates for telephone interviewers, but for now I will mention one interesting attempt to solve the response rate problem. This appears to be an updated version of the old foot-in-the-door approach used by door-to-door salesmen of years past. In a health survey utilizing random-digit dialing (RDD), Robert Groves and Lou Magilavy had one team of interviewers ask only two short questions regarding the respondents' health. These interviewers then told the respondents (in the *experimental group*) that they might be called again as part of a larger survey. The second team of interviewers, phoning the *control group*, did not use this approach, but attempted the long interview on first contact. While there were a number of complications that clouded the results, the following two findings are of interest:

1. There was a greater rate of agreement to the long interview in the experimental group among those respondents who had first agreed to answer the two short questions than there was in the control group.

2. However, a substantial number of people in the experimental group either refused or could not be reached on the first contact. These people produced a very high refusal rate for the long interview, significantly reducing the overall response rate for the experimental group and bringing it to the same level as the control group.[1]

This study, while statistically inconclusive, does illustrate an innovative attempt to deal with the growing problem of high refusal rates.

Motivate the Respondent   The interviewer must convey a sense of the survey's importance and behave in such a manner as to reinforce that belief. If an interviewer rushes through the questionnaire, a sense of unimportance is conveyed. On the other hand, interviewers who read each question with care and who display a patient demeanor signal through verbal and nonverbal cues the inherent significance of the undertaking. It is also necessary for the interviewer to provide assurances of confidentiality and to explain the purpose of the study. Interviewers are expected to behave professionally and in a detached manner, while treating respondents and their answers respectfully.

In the early 1980s, Peter Miller and Charles Cannell used their years of experience studying face-to-face interviewing techniques to conclude that

> careful manipulation of the communication from interviewer to respondent can pay off in improved survey reporting. The general objectives of these manipulations—to better inform survey respondents about the nature of the reporting tasks, and to motivate them to take on the tasks with effort and care—seem to be ones which are relevant to the telephone interview context.[2]

They therefore conducted a study in which they experimented with telephone interviewing procedures and instructions for the interviewer to follow in order to increase respondent motivation. These included:

- *A two-part commitment procedure*   In the first part, the respondent is told of the importance of the research, the need to elicit exact details on every item, and is then asked: "Are you willing to think carefully about each question in order to give accurate information?" If the respondent agrees, in the second part the interviewer gives assurance that all responses will be kept confidential and explains that since the interview is voluntary, "Should we come to any question you do not want to answer, just let me know and we'll move on to the next one."

- *A two-part instruction procedure*   The purpose here is to clarify both the aim of the survey and the way to accomplish the goal. For the former, the interviewer explains why the researchers are asking these questions and what they want to learn. For the latter, the interviewer explains the specific task at hand and how the respondent can best provide accurate information useful to the researchers. For example, when a national market research company conducted a survey among women concerning their reading habits, interviewers were instructed to say at specific points: "Please take your time; sometimes it is difficult to remember such details," or "For the next few questions, you will have to think hard about what you read in the past two years." Interviewers are told specifically when to repeat such instructions during the interview.

- *A feedback procedure*   The researchers had learned from their experience that for a face-to-face interview to be effective, a chaining of behaviors or interaction must occur between the interviewer and the respondent. Feedback (positive and negative) is the instrument by which this chaining takes place. This is necessary to communicate the interviewer's acceptance of the answer's adequacy or lack of acceptance because of the answer's inadequacy. It is also essential to inform and encourage the respondent to make an added effort to provide the relevant information. As we will soon see, *probing*—as a form of feedback—is an important task of the interviewer.

An interesting aspect of this component of the study was that interviewers were required to measure the length of time respondents took to reply to those questions requiring them to remember certain things from the distant past. If a respondent replied in under three seconds, the interviewer was instructed to say, for example: "Sometimes it's hard for people to remember everything. Perhaps if you think about it a little more, you will remember something you missed. Is there anything else that you can recall?" On the other hand, if the respondent appears to have taken the time to think before replying, the interviewer responds with "Thanks very much. This is the type of information the researchers need. It's really important for them to have this information."

Miller and Cannell acknowledged that in the absence of visual cues given during face-to-face interviews to support the commitment, instruction, and feedback procedures, these procedures had only some limited effects when it came to telephone interviews, perhaps because the respondents considered the feedback statements to be insincere. To a layperson, it seems obvious that the telephone interview does not provide the opportunities that exist in a face-to-face situation for visual cues to reinforce verbal feedback. What the researchers were testing was whether, in the absence of such visual cues, more and stronger verbal cues could significantly affect the response quality and results. Their major conclusion was that

> telephone interviewing is not simply the transfer of face-to-face techniques to the telephone. Different communication patterns and respondent motives and the lack of visual cues appear to require considerable developmental research before identifying optimal telephone interviewing techniques.

Despite the acknowledged problems with their study, the Miller-Cannell research makes us aware of the complicated nature of the interview process.

Establish a Good Rapport   This, too, is much more complicated than it would seem. One must appear genial, but not overly friendly. The risk involved in establishing too good a rapport is that the respondent's answers may be influenced by a subconscious desire to please the interviewer. An interviewer must convey objectivity, impartiality, neutrality. It helps if we remember that an opinion cannot be wrong.

Ask Questions in a Standardized Manner   Once the experts trained in the preparation of questionnaires have completed their work, it falls to the interviewers to follow the specific directions they have been given. An interviewer should never deviate from any aspect of the questionnaire design, including the introductory statement of purpose. Each question should be read exactly as it was written and in the exact order in which it appears. There must be no variation in wording, order, emphasis, tone (including any other verbal cues), or expression (including any nonverbal cues). Variation in presentation may affect the answers and bias the results.

Despite the importance of avoiding variation in question reading, interviewers, including the most experienced, make far too many mistakes in this area. Norman Bradburn, Seymour Sudman, and their associates discovered that in a sample of 372 tape-recorded interviews from a national survey,

---

BOX 8.1   A Typology of Probes

Backstrom and Hursh-César have developed a typology of probes that include the following tactics:

- *Verbal encouragement as feedback*   This is the most common. It is a type of positive reinforcement that can create problems if it is not used carefully. Utilizing neutral words, such as "I see," "yes...yes," "uh-huh," "That's interesting," conveys acceptability of the answer and is meant to signal the respondent to continue. The probe symbol might be (*Yes?*) or (*Uh-huh?*).

  In a 1969 study, Marquis and Cannell found that the indiscriminate use of such comments could provide the wrong reinforcement at the wrong time. For example, the researchers found that some interviewers overused positive reinforcement, using such feedback even when a respondent refused to answer a question.

- *Nonverbal encouragement*   This conveys acceptance and encourages the respondent to continue by a smile, nod, or tilt of the head to indicate interest in what is being said.

- *Rereading or repeating part of the question*   Rather than asking, "Anything else?" an interviewer, in the case of an open-ended question such as "What do you think about surrogate motherhood?" might ask, "What else do you think about surrogate motherhood?" The probe symbol here would be (*Else?*).

- *Asking the respondent to rephrase the answer*   The interviewer may say, "I'm not sure I understand what you mean. Could you explain it for me?" This permits the interviewer to continue writing while encouraging the respondent to clarify the previous answer. The respondent may use an ambiguous word, such as *nice*, *several*, *few*, *occasionally*, *weak*, *partially*, or *seldom*, among others. Professional interviewers learn which words are considered to be ambiguous and they are trained to probe

---

reading errors occurred, on average, in one out of every three questions.[3] Such errors included making a false start; reading too fast; incorrectly following a skip pattern; adding, omitting, or substituting words. Although Bradburn and his colleagues found no significant effects from the reading errors, they did find that such errors tended to appear more frequently with the more experienced interviewers. The researchers also felt that the errors added to the "noise" (distractions) that occurs in every survey.

Probe   This is one of the difficult tasks of interviewing. As you have learned, respondents have an opportunity for personal-choice answers

such words. Again, to indicate a probe, the interviewer writes the word inside parentheses as the probe symbol. Some examples are (*Good?*), (*Easy?*), (*Most?*), (*Worse?*), (*Sometimes?*).

- *Echoing the respondent* To encourage the respondent to develop the previous answer further, the interviewer may repeat it while writing it down. For example, we could turn the answer into a question: "So, you say you would support the governor's tax plan?" In this case, (*Support?*) could be the probe symbol.

- *Repeating the question when there is confusion* If a respondent does not understand the question, or says "I don't know," or the interviewer misread the question, the interviewer can respond with "Well, let me repeat the question. Do you support…?" or "I didn't read the question properly. It asks, 'Do you…?'" It is always important to reread the question *exactly* as

it was written and not to paraphrase it. When a repeat probe is used, the interviewer typically uses the probe symbol (*R*) to show that the question was repeated.

- *Seeking greater specificity* When a respondent's answer seems too vague or general, the interviewer should probe further by asking, "Could you tell me a bit more about your thoughts on that?" or "Could you give me an example of what you mean?" or "Specifically, could you explain that for me?" or simply "Why?" The probe symbol used here might be (*More?*) or (*Example?*) or (*Explain?*) or (*Why?*).

- *Pausing or being silent* A short pause can encourage the respondent to continue. However, too long a pause can cause the respondent to become uncomfortable.

SOURCE: Charles H. Backstrom and Gerald Hursh-César, *Survey Research*, 2nd ed. (New York: Wiley, 1981), pp. 268–270.

when they deal with open-ended questions (as opposed to the structured nature of closed-ended questions). As a result, respondents sometimes give an incomplete answer or appear to hesitate for a long time when given an opportunity to express themselves. Under such circumstances, the interviewer must be prepared to ask a **nondirectional follow-up question**. This type of question (or remark) encourages the individual to respond without providing any indication of the interviewer's thinking on the subject. **Probe questions** are usually recorded as **probe symbols**. They are written in a shortened form of one word and enclosed in parentheses, following the respondent's answer (see Box 8.1).

Unlike closed-ended questions, where all the answer choices are provided, when open-ended questions are used, the interviewer has the responsibility of recording precisely what the respondent says. If the respondent does not give a clear, unambiguous, and complete answer, the researchers will have difficulty categorizing the answer. It therefore falls to the interviewer to probe. For example, in a catalog sales survey, the respondent was asked, "What was it that prompted you to make that purchase?" After recording the answer, the interviewer probed, "Anything else?" The exchange was recorded as follows:

Question: What was it that prompted you to make that purchase?

Answer: Our vacuum cleaner broke. (*Else?*) They were on sale.

Record the Answers Accurately   This task is less difficult when closed-ended questions are used. It is then a matter of simply circling or checking off the choice selected by the respondent. However, when open-ended questions are used, the interviewer must write, verbatim, exactly what the respondent says. In the case of CATI, the interviewer types the answers into the computer as the respondent is speaking.

UNDERSTANDING

INTERVIEWER EFFECTS

Researchers have long been concerned with interviewer effects and the role of the interviewer.[4] In September 1949, NORC researcher Herbert Hyman addressed these concerns. After listing a variety of indirect approaches,* Hyman points out that the interview is the most direct approach to finding out someone's opinion.[5] However, he expresses concern with "the isolation, measurement, and control of interviewer effects in opinion research," and notes that

In part, interviewer effects have nothing to do with the interaction that occurs between interviewer and respondent. These effects de-

---

*For example, among his indirect approaches, Hyman includes using data from a content analysis study of the way unmarried women have been portrayed in recent novels as a "clue to attitudes toward the status of women," or using *Nation* magazine subscription data to reach conclusions about radicalism in today's society. He concludes that such examples indicate the unlimited imagination of social scientists to devise indirect approaches.

rive simply from the fact that interviewers are human beings, not machines, and they therefore do not all work identically nor are they infallible in performing difficult tasks.[6]

Certain types of interviewer effects, Hyman states, can be accounted for "by hypothesizing some interaction between interviewer and respondent." To support that analysis, the researcher cited a NORC study conducted in New York City, where Christian respondents were asked whether American Jews had too much influence in the business world. The results showed that among those interviewed by Christians, 50 percent said Jews had too much influence, while among those interviewed by Jews, only 22 percent offered that opinion.[7] Other surveys showed significant differences in results when male and female interviewers were used to interview women respondents★ and when black and white interviewers were used to interview black respondents.[8] Hyman cites a World War II study in which black respondents were asked "whether the army is unfair to Negroes." When interviewed by blacks, 35 percent said yes. However, only 11 percent of the black respondents answered yes when they were interviewed by whites. It therefore appeared that black respondents were less willing to express a negative opinion of their treatment by the army to white interviewers.

In 1954, Hyman and his fellow researchers concluded that southern blacks underreported information about car ownership and education when being interviewed by whites. This race-of-interviewer effect was interpreted as constraining blacks, leading them to represent themselves as passive to their white interviewers.[9] However, in the mid-1970s, S. Hatchett and H. Schuman found that when whites interviewed black respondents, the race-of-interviewer effect was usually restricted to questions pertaining to racial issues, "primarily those dealing with distrust of whites or with other obviously anti-white sentiments."[10] Hatchett and Schuman also found that when the situation is reversed, white respondents will give significantly fewer anti-black answers to black interviewers than they would to white interviewers. For example, on a question dealing with tolerance for racial intermarriage, they found a 46-percent difference between the white respondents' answers to white interviewers and their answers to black interviewers. The researchers cite "general norms of politeness" to a visitor as a logical explanation for this phenomenon. In other words, regardless of one's

---

★One NORC study question asked female respondents whether they agreed with "Prison is too good for sex criminals; they should be publicly whipped or worse." Hyman reports that when interviewed by males, 61 percent said they agreed with the statement, as opposed to a 49-percent agreement rate when female interviewers were used.

personal feelings, it is unlikely that, once having invited someone in, an individual will be discourteous and display hostile feelings to an interviewer of another race. Needless to say, since there are elements here of *response effects*, this complicates analysis of interviewer effects.

Using data from seven election-year surveys (1964, 1976, 1978, 1980, 1982, 1984, and 1986), Barbara Anderson, Brian Silver, and Paul Abramson focused on the effects of the interviewer's race on attitudes related to race.[11] The researchers chose those particular election years because by checking registration and voting records (the process is called **post-election vote–validation studies**), the researchers could determine whether respondents in the survey following the election were truthfully reporting whether they had voted. They were, in effect, studying **response effects**, which refer to the bias (error) in a poll caused by the interviewee's response (reaction) to the interviewer. Their findings included the following points:

- The interviewer's race strongly affected the black respondent's "political attitudes and reported levels of electoral involvement and participation … in presidential election years."
- Black respondents were more likely to express interest and concern about the election outcome, as well as a "strong sense of citizen duty" when interviewed by a black interviewer in a pre-election survey, as opposed to a white interviewer.
- If interviewed by a black interviewer, they were "much more likely" to vote than if the interviewer was white.
- In a post-election survey, non-voting black respondents who were interviewed by black interviewers were more likely to lie and say they had voted than the non-voters interviewed by whites.

The results ran counter to those from earlier studies, indicating that race-matched interviewers were more likely to obtain truthful (more accurate) survey responses. For example, Backstrom and Hursh-César had maintained that

> the more closely interviewers resemble the people they interview, the more likely they are to achieve *rapport*.…
>
> While there are no fixed rules for deciding on how or whether to match interviewers and respondents, we usually try to assign to certain selected neighborhoods interviewers who have the appropriate characteristics.… These signals are *physical appearance* (including language) and *personal mannerisms*.[12]

However, Anderson and her fellow researchers also raise the issue of response effects, explained above. In other words, respondents can change their minds in the time elapsed between pre-election and post-election interviews. As you can see, it is often extremely difficult to differentiate interviewer effects from response effects. And indeed, critics of polls often point to the unpredictability of human behavior as a counterweight to the pollster's professed scientific methodology.

Besides race-of-interviewer effects, researchers have also recognized the potential bias of respondent-perceived interviewer expectations. Put another way, an interviewer who does not convey neutrality and a sense of objectivity, who expresses personal opinions or signals certain expectations through verbal or behavioral cues—even unwittingly—may well bias the respondent's answers.[13] Still another problem that has concerned researchers is that of respondent-perceived **status distance** or dissimilarity of status. J. Allen Williams, Jr., is among those who have studied the effects of status distance between the interviewer and the respondent. In 1964 he reported:

> On the basis of responses from 840 Negroes, race of interviewer was shown to be consistently associated with bias only when status distance between interviewer and respondent is great and when an interview question has high threat potential. Specifically, it was shown that middle-class white interviewers obtained significantly greater percentages of conservative responses from lower-status Negroes than did middle-class Negro interviewers. This occurred only for questions judged as highly threatening. A threatening question in this context is one for which a particular response would be either a behavioral or attitudinal violation of the norms prevailing in a racially segregated social system.[14]

Desiring to minimize interviewer-related bias, Williams continued to study interviewer role performance. In 1968 he published additional findings dealing with status distance and the threat potential of interview questions. It was clear that in order to minimize or dispel respondent fears about possible negative consequences to answers given during the interview, it was necessary for the interviewer to establish a good rapport. Yet, as Williams pointed out, it was equally clear that too good a rapport could bias the results because there was a tendency for the respondent to try to please the interviewer by conforming to some perceived correct answer consistent with the assumed values and expectations of the interviewer.[15]

Interviewer Challenges

No matter how brilliant, experienced, and dedicated the researcher may be, the success or failure of the survey is dependent on how well the interviewers do their job as data collectors. In The Professional Voice 5, Lawrence Cohen shares some of his in-person interviewing experiences, including the problem areas he encountered.

The Professional Voice 5   Slam!

Lawrence J. Cohen

I stared at the fine oak grain. I had seen more wooden doors from a distance of less than an inch than I cared to remember. But it comes with the territory. I guess it takes a certain type of person to do in-person interviewing—someone who can handle rejection; someone who enjoys prying into other people's lives. That's what most people think it's like to be an interviewer.

The truth is that getting a door slammed in your face is a pretty rare occurrence. Once you get past the wall everyone puts up, most people enjoy talking about themselves. In fact, the biggest problem I ever had as an in-person interviewer was getting out of people's homes, not getting in. Maybe it was the fact that a personal interview in the home is now the exception instead of the rule, or that once they get to trust you, people want to talk; but whatever it was, I can't tell you how many times I had to interrupt a respondent's

lengthy monologue and suggest we get back to the questionnaire. Most of my interviews took much longer than the allotted time because of this, but people didn't seem to mind. On the other hand, one of the first questions people ask you after you ring the bell is how long will the interview take. I always told them the truth, but I adjusted the length to reflect only the actual questions and answers.

Getting the respondent to cooperate was a little more difficult. You're not allowed to tell the respondent the details of the questionnaire's topic, as this could lead to a tendency for only those people who are interested in that topic participating, or self-selection bias. But one of the arguments that usually worked for me was to explain that participation in a poll was one of the only ways I knew of where a person's opinion really counted. Even more than in an election, where you have to choose between two candidates who hardly differ on the issues and where neither reflects most of your opinions, in a poll your exact views are recorded on all the issues asked. And because each respondent is randomly selected so that all respondents taken together accurately reflect the entire nation, an individual's answers can carry the weight of around a quarter of a million people. No one single vote has that much influence!

Many people are concerned about privacy, and many of the people I interviewed asked about it. It is always important that you not open your door to any stranger who walks up and knocks. Under the Constitution, a citizen has the right to refuse entry even to police unless they produce a warrant and proper identification. There are some disreputable firms who allege to be doing research; in fact, once they are in your house and a few questions into the questionnaire, they start to sell you something. A legitimate interviewer should have credentials that identify him or her, the organization, and a telephone number that may be called. Some areas require interviewers to register with the local police department. Someone who is doing legitimate research will have all the credentials necessary.

Another issue that concerns respondents is confidentiality. A reputable research organization depends on respondents' complete and honest answers to all of their questions. If they were to release the answers or even the identity of a specific respondent, how could any other respondent trust them? Companies such as Gallup, Roper, Harris, and the others depend on the openness of respondents for their livelihood. They have survived and flourished because the confidentiality they offer to respondents has not been breached. There have even been occasions where the courts subpoenaed the answers of specific respondents, and the companies doing the interviewing refused to release this or any other information. Many believe that the information gathered in an interview is privileged and protected like the conversations between husband and wife, client and lawyer, patient and doctor, or confessor and priest.

With the increasing frequency of telephone interviews and the additional invasion of telemarketing and computerized messages, the idea of in-person, in-the-home interviewing may seem a little out of date. But there is no other way to get the eye-to-eye contact and the other important nonverbal communications associated with in-person interviewing. In-person interviewing also allows for the implementation of a much longer questionnaire than either telephone or mail, so the researcher gets to ask more questions. And because you can use hand cards to explain difficult concepts, show advertisements, or display other visual stimuli, certain measurements may only be accurately gathered with in-person interviews. Whether it is for public opinion, public policy evaluation research, or market research, there will always be a place for the personal approach of in-person interviewing.

Lawrence J. Cohen is now a vice president at Phoenix-Hecht in charge of marketing for all multi-client consumer financial research.

While in-person interviewing is much less common today than it once was, many of the same problems persist with telephone interviewing and some new ones have arisen. Response rates, for example, are generally lower than for in-person interviews.[16] In the case of an in-person interview, a potential respondent generally decides whether to participate in a survey based on initial visual and auditory impressions of the interviewer. Survey content may also be a consideration, but researchers generally have not ranked it as the major determinant. In the case of telephone interviews, all visual cues and impressions have been eliminated. What remains are the auditory stimuli.

Listening to telephone interviewers at work, Lois Oksenberg, Lerita Coleman, and Charles Cannell of the University of Michigan's Survey Research Center were struck by certain unique speech characteristics of those who achieved high response rates. They also noted that most of the refusals occurred in the opening moments of the interview, even before any substantive question was asked. An SRC study showed the following breakdown of refusals:

- one-third occurred in the first few seconds
- one-third occurred during the introduction
- the last third dropped off when asked to list household members, before the first question was asked[17]

Aware of previous and ongoing research efforts to improve response rates by focusing on the content of the interviewer's initial remarks, Oksenberg and her colleagues reviewed the literature on *vocal cues* (see Table 8.1) and decided to focus their research on the voice characteristics of interviewers with high and low response rates. Most of the studies cited used primarily male speakers. Oksenberg and her colleagues believe that the speaker's sex may affect the listener's evaluation of various vocal characteristics, and that somewhat different interpretations of them were offered for male and female speakers. Their study set out to find the answers to the following questions:

Table 8.1 Evaluating Vocal Characteristics

VOCAL CHARACTERISTIC	EVALUATION OF SPEAKER
Intonation (pitch variation)	
Increases in voice pitch	Less competence and less benevolence
Greater variability in pitch	Enhanced persuasiveness
Rate of speech	
Faster speech	Higher ratings of competence, credibility, persuasiveness, intellect, knowledge, and objectivity
Nonhesitant speech	Greater credibility
Hesitant speech (many pauses)	Induces anger, anxiety, conttempt, and boredom
Amplitude (loudness)	
More speech volume	Greater persuasiveness—if volume is linked to a smooth and nonhesitant speaking style

SOURCE: Based on a discussion in Lois Oksenberg, Lerita Coleman, and Charles F. Cannell's "Interviewers' Voice and Refusal Rates in Telephone Surveys," *Public Opinion Quarterly* (Vol. 50), 1986, pp. 99–100.

- Can we reliably judge the vocal qualities of telephone interviewers?
- Is there a correlation between perceptions of desirable and undesirable personal attributes and ratings of vocal qualities?
- Is there a connection between vocal characteristics and rate of refusals?

Using recordings (approximately 30 seconds long) of experienced SRC female interviewers introducing themselves and the survey,* 11 female and 7 male students (ages ranging from 20s to 50s) rated the vocal characteristics of the interviewers. The recorded interviewers included three who had consistently low refusal rates, three with high refusal rates, and one with an intermediate refusal rate. All seven refusal rates were based on the interviewers' work during the preceding seven-month period.

---

*Oksenberg and her colleagues used only recordings of female interviewers for two reasons: (1) The Survey Research Center's staff included a small number of male interviewers, and (2) for various reasons, the researchers had to restrict the scope of their study. The recorded statement was: "Hello, my name is _____. I'm calling from the University of Michigan, in Ann Arbor. Here at the university we are currently working on a study for the Survey Research Center. First of all I need to be sure I've dialed the right number. Is this _____ (telephone number)? Since this telephone number has been generated by a computer, I do not know whether this number is for a business or a home. Which is it?"

Table 8.2 Factors Used to Rate Interviewers

VOICE QUALITY (on a scale of 1–7)	PERSONAL CHARACTERISTICS (on a scale of 1–7)
Average pitch (low to high)	Age (young to old)
Variation in pitch (intonation) (small range to large range)	Disposition (cheerful to uncheerful)
Loudness (soft to loud)	Ability (good to poor at job)
Emphasis of words and phrases ("done appropriately" to "not done appropriately")	Level of interest generated (interesting to boring)
Flow of words (smooth and easy to hesitant)	Self-confidence (self-assured to ill at ease)
Pronunciation (clear and distinct to indistinct or slurred)	Education (educated to uneducated)
Spontaneity (from sounds natural and spontaneous to sounds canned)	Trustworthiness (trustworthy to un-trustworthy)
Rate of speaking (slow to fast)	Enthusiasm (enthusiastic to apathetic); impressive to unimpressive; interested in her task to bored
Accent (yes or no). If yes, rate from pleasant to unpleasant.	Politeness, professionalism, kindness, maturity, pleasantness, appearance
Final question: How pleasant was this voice to listen to? Rate from pleasant to unpleasant on a scale of 1 to 7.	The raters were also asked to identify the interviewer's social class[1] and age[2] and to indicate whether (on a scale of 1 to 7) they would like to be interviewed by that person.

SOURCE: This table is based on the scales discussed in Lois Oksenberg, Lerita Coleman, and Charles F. Cannell, "Interviewers' Voice and Refusal Rates in Telephone Surveys," *Public Opinion Quarterly* (1986), Vol. 50, pp. 97–111.

1. The question read: "What do you think the interviewer's social class is? (Please check) working, lower-middle, middle, upper-middle, upper."

2. The rater was asked to check one of the following age groups: under 20, 20–29, 30–39, 40–49, 50–59, 60–69.

Rating scales were devised to measure vocal characteristics and perceived personal attributes (see Table 8.2) of each interviewer. For the scales used to rate each interviewer's voice quality, the student-raters were asked to "circle the number [1–7] that best describes what you hear." For the scales used to rate each interviewer's personal characteristics, they were again asked to "circle the number [1–7] that best describes your *perception* of the interviewer." (Emphasis added.)

The researchers found a high level of correlation between the vocal characteristics and the perceived personal attributes. Variation in pitch had the highest correlations with interviewer attractiveness, whether measured by general attractiveness or two of its components, positive approach and competence. In addition to a large range of variation in pitch, the following voice attributes were generally associated with the perceived higher social class and general attractiveness of the women interviewers: loudness, fast rate of speaking, good pronunciation, and speaking skills.[18] The most significant finding was that the interviewers rated as having these characteristics turned out to be those with low refusal rates. The researchers were thus able to answer their initial three questions as follows:

- We *can* reliably judge and rate the vocal qualities of telephone interviewers.

- There is a *significant correlation* between perceptions of desirable and undesirable personal attributes and ratings of vocal qualities.

- There *is* a strong relationship between these (rated) characteristics and the rate of refusal.

INTERVIEWER-RELATED BIAS

Because respondents react to voice cues, voice characteristics and voice training should be important considerations in the interviewer-selection process to minimize the type of bias that results from high refusal rates. However, there are other areas with equally great potential to cause errors. For example, how do researchers avoid the bias associated with the unique interpersonal communication skills of the interviewer or with the interviewer's inconsistency in motivating respondents? What are the consequences for the study's accuracy if an interviewer fails to establish an appropriate level of rapport, coming across as either overly friendly or too distant? What can be done about interviewer bias along ideological lines, or interviewer inconsistency in the way they ask the questions or probe? And what of the bias that results from inaccurate reporting? When such causes of bias exist, the credibility of the sample and the study's results are jeopardized.

Aware of such potential pitfalls, researchers have directed a good deal of attention to the recruitment and training of interviewers. As can be seen from Table 8.3, there are a number of different sources for the recruitment of interviewers, and each has its own inherent advantages and disadvantages.

One of the difficulties of finding talented interviewers is that the work is generally intermittent and not particularly well paying for a college-educated person. Although the tasks associated with the interviewing process present much to challenge bright, talented people, not many can afford to pursue this type of work. Potential interviewers are therefore

Table 8.3 Recruiting Interviewers

SOURCE	ADVANTAGES	DISADVANTAGES
Commercial interviewing services that maintain a nationwide pool of paid, trained field staff.	Experienced, paycheck-motivated interviewers available in major cities nationwide.	Quality varies; often lack subject-matter specialization; expensive. Researcher yields control of fieldwork; no way of knowing if the service is combining other studies into a single questionnaire, or if there is a bias against low-income respondents.[1]
Own staff of part-time professionally trained interviewers or novice interviewers to be trained for specific studies.	Direct hiring is less costly, yields increased loyalty, gives researchers control over the selection and retraining, and enables teams of interviewers with subject-matter familiarity. Researcher has greater control.	Using professional interviewers means some retraining must be done. Must avoid the attitude that one survey is just like any other survey.
Volunteer interviewers, including university students.	Commitment level is high; the individual believes the cause is worthwhile, the experience is useful, or there is some other benefit (getting a good grade). Major advantages include low cost and the expectation that they will be supervised—thus they are amenable to training.	Overmotivation may affect interviewing attitude. Training is required to tone down the partisan nature of their enthusiasm. Later, however, their enthusiasm peters out. Besides students, volunteers include housewives, retirees, the unemployed, and those who work at night. Hence, most are not available during weekday evenings or on weekends, when most respondents are home.

1. This occurs when the firm uses samples drawn from its commissioned advertising and marketing studies, which often intentionally ignore low-income areas.

found among those who are between permanent jobs, those who prefer part-time work with flexible hours (usually women with small children), and those who wish to supplement their income with evening and weekend work. The following attributes are requirements for being a good interviewer:

- *Literacy* Since good reading and writing skills are needed, most research organizations require a minimum of a high school diploma, with preference given to those with some college education. When the telephone interviewer is expected to work with a computer, preference is given to those who have some level of computer literacy.

- *Personality and motivation* The ideal interviewer has a friendly, gregarious, yet businesslike demeanor and is a self-starter. The right type of verbal feedback or telephone personality is essential in telephone interviews.

- *Appropriate speech characteristics* Certain unique speech characteristics (pitch, volume, accent, and so on) play a role in achieving high response rates.

- *Maturity and dependability* While age is usually not considered a criterion of the selection process, maturity is. For door-to-door interviewing, obviously a greater degree of physical vigor was necessary than is required for today's telephone interviews. However, intellectual stamina is still a requirement, as is a sense of commitment.

- *Language proficiency* Interviewers may need proficiency in a language other than English. Spanish has become particularly important in many parts of the United States, as have many Asian languages. As a result, large research organizations have a pool of interviewers capable of conducting interviews in various languages.

For an interesting look at the interviewer challenges facing researchers who are conducting surveys outside the United States, see Global View 2, by Manuel Olin.

Global View 2   Carrying Out a Water Consumption Survey in Ghana
Manuel Olin

Prior to planning the rehabilitation and extension of the water supply system for the capital city of Accra and the neighboring harbor city of Tema, a survey had to be made of current water consumption and demand patterns in the district. These data were necessary for determining some of the design parameters and for identifying the demand centers within the city. In addition to demand data, it was also necessary to collect information on household income, mainly because the water system was to be improved with the aid of a World Bank loan; one of the criteria for the granting of such loans was that the project should benefit the poor. The survey was planned for the summer of 1980.

The population of Accra–Tema was estimated at the time of the survey to be between 1.1 and 1.8 million. The last census had been taken approximately 10 years earlier. The true number was not known, and it would have been impossible to determine population size for any section of the city, least of all for the poorest sections: There is strong migration from the country-side to the capital; there is much illegal infiltration from the neigh-boring countries; both birth and infant mortality rates are high, and much of this goes unregistered. The effects of all of these are strongest in the poorest sections of the city.

A random sample of *enumeration areas* (EA) of the city was planned with the assistance of the Central Bureau of Statistics (CBS). They were most helpful, but the data and maps that they were able to provide were outdated and rudimentary. The sample size within each EA was set relative to the population of the last census.

The level of income was very low and telephones were a rarity—certainly among the poor—so a telephone survey was out of the question. Telephones could not even be used to check whether the

interviewers really had visited the address. The complex layout of the city and its streets, as well as the poor level of registration and other types of records, made it impossible to prepare advance lists of addresses to be visited. No up-to-date regis-ter of voters with addresses or other guides could be used to provide the interviewers with lists. In some of the poor districts, which are the most populous, streets were not even identifiable. Huts and shacks leaned against one another in no order. Even in the more established residential sections of the city, street names often did not appear and, where they did, people were rarely familiar with them. It would have been futile to try to locate a house by its address, as houses were un-marked and the addresses were often unknown even to the occu-pants. Normally, an address was lo-cated by its proximity to a well-known or conspicuous structure; for example, "From the big vegetable market, toward the roundabout, turn left at the first corner. You'll see it on the right, under the big tree."

Language was a big problem. At least three local dialects were common in the area of the survey. It could not be known in advance what the language spoken at the household to be interviewed would be. We decided not to translate the questionnaire, for ad-ministrative reasons. It was left in English, to be asked in the language best understood by the household member who replied.

The questionnaire was designed jointly by the researchers and by the engineers and the economists who needed the data, with the help of a socioeconomic research firm. The survey was carried out by an expatriate firm in association with three professors from the faculty of sociology of the largest university in Ghana. The questionnaire was prepared before arrival in Accra, then adjusted after comments from the professors, and finalized after completion of a pretest. The sample was set at 1,800 questionnaires. Most of the questions were precoded multiple choice, while some required a single numerical reply, such as "How much did you pay for water last month?"

The survey was planned to be conducted over a three-week period. This caused considerable consternation among our local partners, as so short a time was unheard of. The number of questionnaires we had planned was thought to be work for at least six months. We, of course, were constrained by budget limitations, the due date of the feasibility study, and the logic of the survey, which would require that the data relate to a fixed point in time so that replies should not be affected by changing prices, the onset of the wet season, and other such factors.

We were told by the professors that students, whom we planned to use as interviewers, would be too occupied with their final exams to answer a call for this type of work. Over their objections as to the futility of trying to hire students at this time, we put up notices on the university bulletin boards. Well over 100 applied (our program had called for only 50 interviewers). They were students mainly from the faculties of sociology and geography. Those selected were familiar with the languages likely to be spoken in Accra. They were advised that they would not be paid unless they filled in at least 10 questionnaires. This was necessary, as there was some fear that many would drop out after filling in only two or three questionnaires. Ghanaians are generally very polite and accommodating. At the training sessions, no student asked a question; it would have been rude to question or challenge, especially where a foreigner and a stranger was involved. It took some effort to obtain the active participation necessary to ensure that all points raised in the training sessions were understood.

However, once the ice had been broken, there was no reticence about asking for higher pay for each questionnaire filled in, even though we were offering a substantially higher rate than that paid by the CBS. We had some compunctions about paying a higher rate, as it could have caused problems for the CBS in the future.

However, as it was clear to us that Ghanaian students would expect an expatriate firm to pay higher rates, we offered such rates on our own. Nevertheless, there was an attempt to stage a strike even before the survey began. There was also objection to the hours that we had set for this work—4:30–7:00 P.M., Saturdays and Sundays, hours when we felt we would find people at home, but would not be intrusive. The students felt that they should carry out the survey during the customary working hours rather than these, which were awkward for them. Ultimately, our hours were accepted.

A problem that we had to anticipate was the natural curiosity of neighbors in what is essentially a village environment in the poor districts. When a stranger comes into the neighborhood, it is customary for everyone to gather round, to see what it is all about. Under such circumstances, the information is not reliable, especially if it pertains to income or to attitudes. When others are listening, the person interviewed is more concerned with the impression made on his or her neighbors than with the facts. Another issue was the suspicion or fear of officials, especially among the illegal immigrants. Any person with a pen in hand, taking down data, was suspect and generally unwelcome. The assurance that all data would be kept confidential was not very convincing. We were not always successful in obtaining privacy for the interviews, but in general, the opening speech that we provided to the interviewers gained people's confidence.

Interviewers were given a formula for selecting homes to be approached so that selection would be random. Because many people live in compounds, it was difficult to know what was another room used by the household you had just interviewed and what was another household. The fact that two households might share a room complicated the issue further. Deciding what was a household was even more difficult, as the separateness of the structure (servants' quarters, for example, or the separate houses of two wives and their children) were not necessarily an indication of separate consuming arrangements. Since our major interest was water, identifying how many people were served by the quantity consumed was important. Interviewers received instructions on how to verify these different points.

Many people bought their water from vendors, by the container. Finding out how much water was used and consumed wasn't straightforward. Virtually any container served the purpose: aluminum cooking pots, earthenware pots, old cans in which powdered milk was sold (a very popular item in Ghana), plastic pails. The sizes and shapes varied, yet the interviewers had to estimate the volume and report how much each could contain. We devoted a session to training them in estimating volume. Ultimately, however, we found that the respondents themselves knew quite well how much water their containers held, and their replies were accepted.

Supervisors were in the field much of the time with the interviewers, checking closely to see that the selection procedures were observed, doing their supervision in real time. This supervision solved problems almost as soon as they surfaced. Transportation problems in Accra forced us to bus the interviewers to their areas and to pick them up, which in itself helped to ensure that they really were out in the field. Interviewers received clear instructions on the time and place they would be dropped off and picked up, and they were pleased to receive computerized accountings of their own progress and to know the progress of the survey as a whole. When we bused the interviewers, the supervisors went out to check up on them, and the supervisors circulated during the survey. The researchers monitored the supervisors. All survey staff, with the exception of two expatriate consultants, were Ghanaian.

Some of the results will be of interest. It was found that 39 per-

cent of our sample normally obtained their water by the pail and that they consumed only 12 percent of the water. They paid up to 20 times the price paid by the better-off population. They spend over 5 percent and up to 25 percent of their income on water, as compared to well under 2 percent for families with house or yard connections, which consumed three to five times as much water. The poor paid both absolutely and relatively more for their water. In addition, households without house or yard connections spent an average of four hours a day fetching their water from their better-off neighbors or from other sources. This work was the responsibility of women and children, who generally carried the containers on their heads.

Major factors in our success were extensive preparatory work, intensive training sessions, real-time supervision, and overall good administrative organization. By the way, we did succeed in completing all fieldwork in three weeks.

Manuel Olin, economist/management consultant, received his M.A. from Tel Aviv University. He consults primarily in Third World countries on development projects, many of which are financed by international funding institutions. His work has taken him all over the world and has taught him how to cope with many different cultures. He makes his home in Israel.

Training to Eliminate Interviewer Bias

Good training can eliminate some of the most blatant causes of interviewer bias. It can instill a professionalism that goes beyond the learning of procedures, requirements, and techniques for a particular study. However, since each survey must be considered unique and engender renewed interest and enthusiasm in the interviewer, follow-up on-the-job training is often necessary to get rid of bad habits and to reinforce desired working values and practices.

Although every research organization has its own system of training interviewers, it is generally agreed that the goal of the training is to ensure—to as great an extent as is possible—a standardized approach to the interviewing process. Because there is also a consensus that interviewer-related bias is nearly impossible to eliminate, some researchers use a computerized synthesized voice that conducts every interview exactly the same way. Although this robotic voice never feels stress, strain, boredom, the need to eat, daydream, visit the lavatory, or just relax for a few minutes, it creates other types of problems, which we will discuss in Chapter 13. In any case, our human interviewers require that we address training goals to their uniquely human characteristics. The following items and attitude goals, usually included in the training, are intended to standardize interviewing procedures as much as possible.

The Need for Consistency   The interviewer-recruits are taught why there is a need for consistency and the way in which inconsistency can bias a respondent and damage the validity of the data. Professionalism, they learn, means conducting the interview according to the specific directions they are given. Individual creativity and interpretation are uncalled for when it comes to reading the questions and recording the responses. Each question must be read precisely as written. Answers must be recorded precisely as given. The desired attitude goal here is to have the interviewer believe in the necessity of following instructions exactly.

An Understanding of Interviewer and Respondent-Related Biases
Interviewers learn how their own personalities can bias a study, and learn ways to prevent their behavior from influencing the respondent. At the same time, they are told that respondents may give inaccurate or false answers and that sometimes a respondent may be inadvertently influenced by the interviewer. The respondent may perceive that certain choices will please the interviewer. This aspect of the interviewer training helps to cre-

ate awareness and sensitivity as to the individual's role in this complex and difficult task. The attitude goal here is for the interviewer to acknowledge the need for neutrality and sensitivity to bias-causing cues.

The Importance of Confidentiality Training reinforces the importance of maintaining confidentiality; the trainees are rehearsed in several standard ways of reassuring respondents that their identities will be held in confidence and that their responses will be used only as part of the entire set of data being collected in the study. Respect for the respondent's privacy is the important attitude goal in this area.

Why and How the Survey Is to Be Conducted The *why* is important because it helps to motivate the interviewer to do the best possible job in collecting the data required. The purpose of the study is explained, and the interviewers are told the societal benefits to be derived from the information they will help gather. The interviewers should come away from the training believing in the importance of the job to be done. The training also enables interviewers to develop a general understanding of the survey research method and to understand the nature of the particular study that is being undertaken. Trainees are taught the important principles of random sampling, as well as why it is imperative that they avoid **judgmental sampling**. Judgmental (as opposed to random) sampling occurs when interviewers decide for themselves who they will interview. With CATI, the judgmental aspect has been greatly limited, since the computer is programmed to select the numbers to be called.

The Pragmatic Aspects When dealing with in-person interviews, the interviewers need to be able to convey familiarity with the subject of the research project. Interviewers learn the characteristics of the population being studied and the areas in which they live. Interviewers are also given lessons in map reading, specific selection procedures, and interviewing procedures. They are taught how to administer the questionnaire, what the various symbols mean, how to deal with the directional information, the importance of legibility, and how to follow the coding system used for dispositional purposes during the monitoring process (discussed shortly).

The coding system conventionally appears on the top or bottom of the questionnaire's first page. Beginning with 0 to indicate that the designated respondent has already been interviewed by another interviewer on the same project, it usually consists of a series of numbers, each assigned to one of the following categories of results or problems:

- Successfully *completed* interview. There is also space to indicate the number of attempts made to conduct the interview.

- The designated respondent *refused* to be interviewed. A space for comments is provided to indicate the reason.

- *No answer* or, in the case of in-person interviews, no one was at home. When in-person interviewers find no one at home, they are usually told to ring a neighbor's doorbell to ascertain when the designated respondent or someone in that household is usually at home.

- The designated respondent is *unavailable*.

- Time of *appointment* for a call-back, which has been set either with the designated respondent directly, with a member of the person's family, or as a result of information obtained from the neighbor.

- *Incapacitated*. The designated respondent is in some way physically unable to be interviewed.

- *Non-English-speaking*. The individual's language is noted so that an interviewer who speaks that language can be assigned.

- *Ineligible* to be included in the sample. The interviewer found that no one in the household met the designated requirements to become a respondent in the study.

- *Miscellaneous* reasons for not conducting the interview are explained in the appropriate comment section.

Besides teaching the interviewer-trainee the necessary skills to do the job, another purpose is to build interviewer confidence, which derives from knowing how to do it well. The recruits are also introduced to their supervisors, who will work with them and who will be responsible for monitoring their activities. The coordination, verification, debriefing, and analytical roles of supervisors are explained, as is the role of the project director. The purpose here is to open lines of communication and to create a sense of team support for an important effort.

MONITORING, VERIFYING, AND VALIDATING

As we saw in the Ghana study, supervision is important and not just to prevent a field interviewer from fabricating data. Especially with inexperienced interviewers, a problem may arise that should be dealt with quickly. Interviewers are given a trouble number to call if a problem occurs, and supervisors are required to monitor the disposition of each questionnaire. They check to see that the questionnaires have been completed and that the responses have been clearly recorded. The monitoring and verification processes serve both as a deterrent to dishonest interviewers and as a corrective measure to ensure the accuracy of the survey.

As supervisors monitor the disposition of the questionnaires, they note the following:

- the time and day of the week the interview was scheduled
- the time needed to conduct the interview
- the number of refusals or incompletes
- the number of call-backs necessary
- the schedule of appointments made to reach respondents who were unavailable at the time of first contact
- the need to schedule another interviewer to keep these appointments because of the original interviewer's unavailability
- the existence of a language problem requiring another interviewer who speaks the respondent's language

Most important, they check to see if there are any troublesome patterns emerging. For example:

- Do particular interviewers show a significantly greater number of refusals compared to other interviewers working in similar locations?
- Are novice interviewers experiencing significantly more refusals than experienced interviewers? This could indicate the need for additional training.
- Is there an ethnic or racial pattern emerging regarding the refusal or incompletion rate?
- Are refusals occurring in particular neighborhoods or sections of the city?
- Is there a significant correlation between time of interview and respondent refusal?
- Are any of the interviewers behind or ahead of schedule? The latter can be used to keep the appointments set by other interviewers or for the purpose of call-backs.

Interviewers are debriefed by their supervisors when they have completed their assignments. The clean-up team then follows through to take care of any incomplete aspects of the work. Supervisors are expected to report any serious problems to the project director. At this point, the work of the interviewer has ended, and the work of the verification team begins. Verification serves as a deterrent and as a corrective measure.

Backstrom and Hursh-César[19] identify four types of verification: sample verification, question verification, question reliability, and question validity (see Chapter 7). In **sample verification**, the key question is whether the designated respondent was interviewed. In preliminary verification, the verifier compares the name, address, and phone number on the questionnaire with a city directory or reverse telephone directory. (In the latter, the subscribers are listed according to their street addresses, rather than by their names.) Once this information has been checked, calls are made to a random sample of the respondents to confirm that they were indeed interviewed. Sometimes postcards are sent to respondents asking a few brief questions, such as how long the interview took, how they were contacted (in person or by phone), and how they would rate the interviewer (from good to poor).

Verification was far more complicated with in-person interviewing because it also involved checking to see if the addresses on the questionnaire were located in the assigned field area, on the blocks assigned, and fitted the pattern or formula of selection the interviewer had been instructed to follow (for example, starting on the northeast corner and selecting every seventh house as the interviewer walks around the assigned block). Whether in-person interviewing or telephone interviewing, if any discrepancies are found in any aspect of an interviewer's work, then all the questionnaires prepared by that interviewer are likely to be verified.

At issue in **question verification** is whether all the questions were asked and all the answers were recorded correctly. There is always concern that interviewers may simply record the correct demographic data and then fill in the rest of the questionnaire themselves. To verify that a questionnaire has not been falsified, the verifier will phone a random selection of respondents, choose a question from the second half of the questionnaire (to ascertain whether the interviewer carried the interview that far), and say something like "It seems our interviewer either missed question number ___ or neglected to record the answer. The question reads...." Here too, if falsification is found, the entire questionnaire will be administered, and the interviewer's entire assignment will have to be checked carefully in all aspects.

In verifying *question reliability* the key question is whether there is a consistency to the respondent's answers. Put another way, would the respondent reply in the same manner if asked the same questions by another interviewer? To test for consistency (sometimes referred to as data trustworthiness), a sample of each interviewer's respondents is reinterviewed by other interviewers, using a shortened version of the questionnaire. Replies are compared with those given to the first questionnaire. Data collected from this secondary process provide insight as to the stability of respondent opinion.

In verifying *question validity*, we are asking whether the particular question actually and accurately measured what we had wanted to measure. We try to validate the data yielded by a question by checking other sources capable of providing the same information. For example, if a question asks about the individual's intention to vote, we can verify whether the person voted simply by looking at the voter records available at the office of the board of elections in each county. Suppose we then learn from this post-election validation process of checking voter registration records that the person did not in fact vote; quite clearly, the question failed to measure that individual's behavior. You will recall that earlier in this chapter I mentioned that Barbara Anderson, Brian Silver, and Paul Abramson used the National Election Study surveys for seven election years to study the effects of the interviewer's race on attitudes related to race. I also mentioned that the researchers had chosen those particular years (1964, 1976, 1978, 1980, 1982, 1984, and 1986) because the data included the Survey Research Center's post-election vote-validation studies. By checking registration and voting records, the researchers were able to determine whether the respondents in the post-election survey had truthfully reported whether they had voted.

This long and involved chapter on the interviewer should have reinforced your awareness of the complexity of the survey process. I also hope it conveys an understanding of some of the weaknesses due to human factors inherent in a process that is often lauded for its scientific methodology. In the next chapter, dealing with respondent bias, we will again encounter problems created by subjective elements.

CHAPTER REVIEW

- In-person interviewers were able to achieve very low non-availability rates by making a few call-backs to those who were not at home the first time around.

- While in-person interviewing was popular during the 1940s and 1950s, societal changes led to greater use of telephone interviewing. What were some of the changes that had an impact on opinion research?

- During the 1960s and 1970s, new screening and sampling techniques were developed, and computer-assisted complex statistical analyses were undertaken.

- In 1977, the National Academy of Sciences considered the problems of total refusal rates (referred to as the respondent level) and of the rate of refusals to specific questions (referred to as the item level). Since then, what types of efforts have been made to resolve the bias problems caused by high refusal and non-response rates?

- By 1986, 92 percent of all households were reachable by telephone, and CATI became increasingly popular. What are the advantages and disadvantages of using a CATI system?

- Discuss the role of the interviewer and the problems inherent in the job.

- What are probes, and why are interviewers told to use them?

- How can an interviewer motivate a respondent to participate and to be conscientious in thinking through each question? What are the techniques professional interviewers use?

- Although feedback is important, what problems may arise as a result of it?

- Discuss the research undertaken to study the effects of the interviewer's race on attitudes related to race.

- Oksenberg and her colleagues focused their research on the voice characteristics of interviewers with high and low response rates. What were some of the results of their study? Why is such research significant?

- What is the connection between interviewer voice characteristics and high or low refusal rates?

- Specifically, what types of bias are interviewer related?

- In the water consumption survey undertaken in Ghana, what types of problems did the researchers confront? Which, if any, of these problems are universal?

- What attitudes and goals form the basis of a typical interviewer training program?

- Why is it necessary to supervise interviewers?

- What is involved in the monitoring process?

- What is the difference between verification and validation?

NOTES

1. Robert M. Groves and Lou J. Magilavy, "Increasing Response Rates to Telephone Surveys: A Door in the Face for Foot-in-the-Door?" Public Opinion Quarterly (1981), Vol. 45, pp. 346–358.

2. Peter V. Miller and Charles F. Cannell, "A Study of Experimental Techniques for Telephone Interviewing," Public Opinion Quarterly (1982), Vol. 46, No. 2; or see their article in Survey Research Methods, A Reader, Eleanor Singer and Stanley Presser, eds. (Chicago: University of Chicago Press, 1989), pp. 304–323.

3. Norman M. Bradburn, Seymour Sudman, and associates, Improving Interview Method and Questionnaire Design (San Francisco: Jossey-Bass, 1979).

4. S. A. Rice, "Contagious Bias in the Interview," American Journal of Sociology (1929), Vol. XXXV, pp. 420–423. Albert B. Udow, "The 'Interviewer-Effect' in Public Opinion and Market Research," Archives of Psychology #277 (New York: Columbia University, 1942). This article also appears in Public Opinion Quarterly (Summer 1944). The National Opinion Research Center's interviewers were the subjects of this study. Selden Menefee's "Recruiting an Opinion Field Staff," Public Opinion Quarterly (Summer 1944), p. 262. This article discusses interviewer qualifications, types preferred, types to avoid, and interviewer training. S. Shapiro and J. Eberhart, "Interviewer Differences in an Intensive Interview Survey," International Journal of Opinion and Attitude Research (1947), Vol. I, No. 2, pp. 1–17.

5. Herbert Hyman, "Problems in the Collection of Opinion-Research Data," American Journal of Sociology (Vol. LV, 1949–1950), pp. 362–370.

6. Hyman, p. 363.

7. Hyman, pp. 365–366.

8. Hyman, but also see S. A. Stouffer, E. A. Suchman, L. C. DeVinney, S. A. Star, and R. M. Williams, Jr., eds., The American Soldier: Adjustment During Army Life (Princeton, NJ: Princeton University Press, 1949), and Daniel Katz, "Do Interviewers Bias Poll Results?" Public Opinion Quarterly (1942), Vol. 6, pp. 248–268.

9. H. H. Hyman, W. J. Cobb, J. J. Feldman, C. W. Hart, and C. H. Stember, Interviewing in Social Research (Chicago: University of Chicago Press, 1954). Also see Howard Schuman and Graham Kalton, The Handbook of Social Psychology, 3rd ed., Vol. 1, Gardner Lindzey and Elliot Aronson, eds. (New York: Random House, 1985), pp. 685–686.

10. S. Hatchett and H. Schuman, "White Respondents and Race-of-Interviewer Effects," Public Opinion Quarterly (1975–1976), Vol. 39, pp. 523–528.

11. Barbara Anderson, Brian D. Silver, and Paul R. Abramson, "The Effects of the Race of the Interviewer on Race-Related Attitudes of Black Respondents in SRC/CPS National Election Studies," Public Opinion Quarterly (Fall 1988), pp. 289–324. Also see Paul R. Abramson, "The Decline of Over-Time Comparability in the National Election Studies," Public Opinion Quarterly (Summer 1990), pp. 177–190.

12. Charles H. Backstrom and Gerald Hursh-César, Survey Research, 2nd ed. (NY: Wiley, 1981), p. 242.

13. See H. L. Smith and H. Hyman, "The Biasing Effect of Interviewer Expectations on Survey Results," Public Opinion Quarterly (1950), Vol. 14, pp. 491–506. Also see D. F. Wyatt and D. T. Campbell, "A Study of Interviewer Bias as Related to Interviewer's Expectations and Own Opinions," International Journal of Opinion and Attitude Research (1950), Vol. 4, pp. 77–83.

14. J. Allen Williams, Jr., "Interviewer-Respondent Interaction: A Study of Bias in the Information Interview," Sociometry (September 1964), Vol. 27, pp. 338–352.

15. J. Allen Williams, Jr., "Interviewer Role Performance: A Further Note on Bias in the Information Interview," Public Opinion Quarterly (Summer 1968), pp. 287–294. Also see Barbara Snell Dohrenwend, John Colombotos, and Bruce P. Dohrenwend, "Social Distance and Interviewer Effects," Public Opinion Quarterly (Fall 1968), pp. 410–422.

16. Lois Oksenberg, Lerita Coleman, and Charles F. Cannell, "Interviewers' Voice and Refusal Rates in Telephone Surveys," Public Opinion Quarterly (1986), Vol. 50, pp. 97–111.

17. Oksenberg et al., p. 98.

18. Oksenberg et al., pp. 107–108.

19. Backstrom and Hursh-César, pp. 297–298.

9

The Respondent

Think about—

What is meant by cognitive structures?

What are the causes or sources of Don't-Know (DK) responses?

Why can't DK responses merely be ignored?

What is meant by ambivalent opinion?

What is the Wilder factor, and if it exists, what does it imply about the future of polling?

What is the significance of the cocooning hypothesis for refusal rates?

Which are you, a cocooner or a connector?

Are older respondents more difficult to interview?

Is there a gender gap when it comes to sensitive questions? Do men or women refuse more frequently to answer sensitive questions?

S oon after the liberation of Holland in May 1945, Jan Stapel and his
associates founded the Netherlands Institute of Public Opinion. Some
of their earliest research efforts focused on respondent-related questions such as:

- Is there a "convivial respondent,"[1] one who is talkative and easygoing?

- Are taller, more slender types more apt to be taciturn and distant?

- Is there a difference in attitude between the "rounded-convivial"
  types and the "angular-reserved" types?

- Can we really correlate personality types and physical characteristics
  with certain opinions?

- Can we correlate refusals with temperament?

- Are introverts more likely to refuse to participate than extroverts?

Are these silly questions? Although I found much of the study amusing,
I believe the following conclusions are of continuing interest:

- Conviviality and rounded physique were highly correlated, as were
  taciturnity and the slim angular physique. Thus there was, the
  researchers said, "some relationship between exterior [physique]
  and deportment [personality]." Although there may have been

"some relationship," I find the word *some* too ambiguous to be meaningful.

■ They also found substantial differences between the replies of extroverts and introverts to questions involving optimistic or pessimistic views of the future. Personality, it was therefore noted, could be an indicator of certain types of opinion.

■ More specifically, it was found that personality types have *little predictive value* when it comes to opinions on political issues, particularly regarding the forecasting of elections.

■ An analysis of refusals in two different nationwide polls showed that "people who refuse to be interviewed do not constitute any one type" as far as temperament is concerned—meaning that among those who refused to participate, both extroverts and introverts were well represented.

KNOWLEDGE STRUCTURES

Since these early studies, research into respondent-related matters has focused on several areas, including cognitive and behavioral dynamics. Response bias was identified during the 1950s by cognitive-perspective researchers working in the field of social psychology. Cognitive psychology is concerned with the mental systems we use in processing information. These mental systems include thinking, memory, understanding, evaluating, and so on. Researchers tried to understand the relations between the *internal cognitive dynamics* and the *external behavioral dynamics*. Summarizing subsequent research trends, Hazel Markus and R. B. Zajonc commented:

> The idea of the human organism as an information processor became popular. The mind came to be viewed by many as a computer-like apparatus that registered the incoming information and then subjected it to a variety of transformations before ordering a response.[2]

Aware that people display selective tendencies regarding what they notice, learn, or remember, emphasis was soon placed on how information input was filtered or screened and processed for various cognitive operations such as inference, attribution, or judgment. Researchers wrote about cognitive structures, now usually called knowledge structures, which were believed to provide the framework necessary for us to organize and interpret our environment (see Box 9.1 on page 272). These internal structures stored specific information used to define not only an object, event, or situation, but the rules delineating any interrelationships among them.

In Chapter 8, I discussed the researchers' enduring concern with interviewer effects. Although my focus now turns to respondent-related problems, it is important to remember that the researcher establishes the frame of reference within which the respondent replies. For example, in Chapter 4 we learned from Shere Hite that

> Many believe that multiple-choice questionnaires represent the height of "scientific objectivity" in that they can be quantified easily and need no "interpretation." However, this is fallacious reasoning since ... all researchers have a point of view, a way of reflecting the cultural milieu in which they were brought up, and these assumptions are subtly filtered into the categories and questions chosen. A strong case can be made that multiple-choice questionnaires (especially those asking about attitudes and emotions) only project onto respondents the researcher's assumptions.[3]

Why do respondents answer the way they do? Do they answer based on what they really believe or on what they think the interviewer wants to hear? For the purpose of surveying public opinion, we are most concerned with whether respondents process the information contained in the questions in a way that results in a response bias. George Franklin Bishop (see *The Professional Voice 6*), who has studied respondent-related problems extensively for a number of years, has concluded that among those who choose to participate, many often respond to questions to which they have given little thought to avoid appearing ignorant.

In 1989, for example, 1,537 respondents participated in a nationwide NORC General Social Survey. In the part of the survey dealing with tolerance of ethnicity, NORC used a ranking scale in which 1 indicated the lowest social standing and 9 the highest. Respondents were asked to rate the social standing of 58 ethnic groups in the United States, including the Wisians, a fictitious group. Tom Smith, director of the General Social Survey, explained: "We were trying to see if people were being too compliant with us, and the good news is that 61% didn't rank the Wisians."[4] However, turning that around, the bad news is that 39 percent determined a mean social standing of 4.12 for the Wisians, compared to the ethnic groups listed in Table 9.1 (selected from the list of 58 that were included in the survey). In explaining the low ranking attributed to the Wisians, Smith said that people probably thought they were foreign-sounding and that if they'd never heard of them, "they couldn't be doing too well."

Table 9.1 Ethnic Groups and Social Standing

ETHNIC GROUP	MEAN SOCIAL STANDING
Native white Americans	7.03
Protestants	6.39
Catholics	6.33
Irish	6.05
Germans	5.78
Southerners	5.77
Italians	5.69
Japanese	5.56
Jews	5.55
People of foreign ancestry	5.38
Chinese	4.76
Poles	4.63
Latin Americans	4.42
American Indians	4.27
Blacks[1]	4.17
Wisians	**4.12**
Mexicans	3.52
Puerto Ricans	3.32

1. Blacks were referred to as Negroes by the NORC survey in 1989 in order to conform to the wording used in its 1964 survey.

The Professional Voice 6   Public Opinion on Fictitious Issues: The Fear of Appearing Ignorant

George Franklin Bishop

Public opinion pollsters have long suspected that a certain number of people interviewed in their surveys will give an opinion on a domestic or foreign affairs issue, such as nuclear disarmament or the federal government's budget deficit, even though they may never have thought much about the subject until they were asked about it by a interviewer. To test this long-held suspicion, my colleagues and I created a question about an issue on which nobody could possibly have formed an opinion prior to any survey: a fictitious 1975 Public

Affairs Act. The wording of the question was as follows:

> Some people say that the 1975 Public Affairs Act should be repealed.
>
> Do you agree or disagree with this idea?

Our interviewers in the Institute for Policy Research at the University of Cincinnati have asked this question a number of times over the years in telephone surveys of the adult population (18 or older) in greater Cincinnati. To conceal the purpose of our investi-

gation, the question about the fictitious Public Affairs Act is always
asked after a number of questions
about various real current issues in
domestic and foreign affairs.
Results from these surveys have
typically shown that anywhere
from 25 percent to 35 percent of
the adult population will give an
opinion on this nonexistent
topic—either agreeing or disagree-
ing with the idea that the Public
Affairs Act should be repealed—
with the rest (65%–75%) volun-
teering that they have never heard
of it or have no opinion on it. Very
similar results have been reported
from national surveys by other researchers who have used nonficti-
tious but equally unfamiliar topics.
So the results are by no means peculiar to Cincinnati.

The more interesting question,
of course, is why some people offer
an opinion on a question about a
nonexistent issue and others do
not. Probably the most important
clue for answering this question is
the difference we have repeatedly
found between blacks and whites,
and between better-educated and
less-educated respondents in the
way they answer such questions.
Time and again we have discovered
that black respondents and less
well-educated respondents in general are significantly more likely to
give an opinion on a fictitious issue
than are white respondents and
those who are generally better educated, most likely because of their

fear of appearing ignorant or stupid
in the eyes (or ears) of our telephone interviewers (most of whom
are white middle-class women)
calling from a university—the very
symbol of the importance of
knowledge and of being well informed about public affairs.

Furthermore, even when we
control for the well-known difference in educational attainment between black and white adults,
black respondents are still significantly more likely than white respondents to give an opinion on
the fictitious Public Affairs Act.
Among those respondents with at
least some college education, for
example, we found that 41.5 percent of blacks gave an opinion on
the Public Affairs Act, as compared
to 22.1 percent of whites. Among
less-educated respondents (those
with a high school education or
less) the corresponding figures for
blacks and whites were 52.2 percent and 30.9 percent, respectively.
The fear of appearing ignorant
may therefore be much more acute
for blacks, especially because they
have been stereotyped as dumb for
so long in our society. Not to have
an opinion on a public affairs issue,
then—however vague it might
seem—would only confirm the
white man's stereotype of blacks,
especially with the phone call
coming from the *white world's* university. Giving an opinion on a fictitious public affairs issue in a
telephone survey thus becomes

another, perhaps more subtle, social indicator of black–white relations in American society today.

George Franklin Bishop is a professor of
political science and a senior research
associate at the Institute for Policy Research at the University of Cincinnati.

THE DON'T-KNOW PHENOMENON

On the other hand, there are those respondents who readily respond with a
"Don't know" (DK). Such responses can be anticipated for specific types
of respondents and questions.[5] Clyde H. Coombs and Lolagene C. Coombs[6]
have discovered a number of reasons why such responses occur, including:

Respondent Uncertainty   For example, in the summer of 1991, the
American Bar Association commissioned Research USA Inc. to conduct a
poll meant to coincide with the two-hundredth anniversary of the ratification of the Bill of Rights.[7] Responding to a multiple-choice question asking them to identify the Bill of Rights, the 507 respondents picked the
following answers:

33%   the first 10 amendments to the Constitution (*the correct answer*)

28%   the preamble to the Constitution

22%   any rights bill passed by Congress

7%   a message of rebellion from the Founding Fathers to the British
monarchy

10%   don't know

While this was a fact question, as opposed to an opinion question, the rather
high DK response of 10 percent indicates uncertainty. We would not have
been able to detect this uncertainty if the DK category had been omitted.
Uncertain respondents would then have been forced to select one of the
other answers, thereby becoming indistinguishable from those who genuinely
did not know, but who thought they did. (Incidentally, here is an example
where I would have hoped for an enormous DK percentage: In a study conducted at the Medical College of Georgia in Augusta, 90 percent of the 6-
year-old respondents correctly linked Old Joe Camel to a cigarette![8])

Lawrence Feick explains that when asked a gray-area type of question,
the respondent shows a tendency to experience uncertainty or ambivalence
and to equivocate. He refers to this source of DK as "item-specific equivocation."[9] However, Feick distinguishes item-specific equivocation from topical equivocation. In the latter case, the respondent may actually have

---

BOX 9.1   Cognitive Structures by Other Names

Various researchers have given a variety of names to these internal devices that evolve from our past experiences and that function as interpretive frameworks. These include:

Theoretician	Defining Terms
J. W. Thibaut and E. E. Jones (1958)	Inferential sets
J. S. Bruner (1951)	Hypotheses
S. Epstein (1973)	Theories
R. P. Abelson (1976)	Scripts
J. H. Lingle and T. M. Ostrom (1981)	Themes
M. Minsky (1975)	Frames
E. H. Rosch (1973); E. E. Smith and D. L. Medin (1981)	Categories
N. Cantor and W. Mischel (1977, 1979)	Prototypes
A. Tesser and C. L. Cowan (1975, 1977)	Attitudes
E. Stotland and L. K. Canon (1972); U. Neisser (1976)	Schemas

While different in some ways,[1] these concepts share certain properties. They have been used to describe internal structures that tend to simplify input when the individual is flooded with information. Thus, the complexity of our environment can be meaningfully reduced and the information can be made manageable through categorization. On the other hand, these structures permit us to process incomplete information. By using memory (accessing categories of information we processed in the past) and analysis, we can put two and two together.

---

1. Although it is beyond the scope of this text to discuss these differences, the reader is referred to Hazel Markus and R. B. Zajonc, "The Cognitive Perspective in Social Psychology," *The Handbook of Social Psychology*, Vol. I, 3rd ed., Gardner Lindzey and Elliot Aronson, eds. (New York: Random House, 1985) for a brief discussion of these differing aspects.

---

thought about the subject but not yet arrived at a conclusion. It therefore does not matter what is asked about that particular topic because the individual has what G. David Faulkenberry and Robert Mason call "ambivalent opinion."[10]

Non-Attitude   This goes beyond uncertainty, ambivalence, and equivocation because it deals with an unknown area. The respondent has *no* opinion whatsoever. Lacking any information on the topic, he or she has never thought about it. As an example, few Americans know anything about the civil strife in Sri Lanka between the Tamils and Sinhalese. As a result, regardless of how the questions were worded, most respondents simply would not know what to say on this subject. Another example, this one from the domestic front, is based on a poll taken in New Jersey two weeks before the November 1990 election: 82 percent of the eligible voters polled in the north Jersey county of Bergen could not identify either the Democratic or Republican nominee for the office of Bergen County Executive, the county's highest officeholder, responsible for administering a county budget of approximately $340,400,000 in 1990.[11] How can one ignore a DK as high as 82 percent? What is being measured here is a non-attitude or non-opinion.

Item Ambiguity   Feick has identified this source of DKs as "error response" because it is "inconsistent with the attitudinal position" of the respondent who actually holds an opinion. In this case, there has been a misunderstanding due to poor instructions, unclear phrasing, distraction, or misplaced emphasis. Then, too, as Ronald Rapoport points out, an attitude holder may be unable or unwilling to express his or her opinion for various reasons, such as a lack of confidence.[12]

Are certain types of people more likely to respond with a DK than others? A number of researchers have found that DK responses are more common among those in the following categories: low income, less educated, non-white, older, women.[13]

Finding an unusually high level of DK responses in his own research in the former Soviet Union (see Global View 3), James Gibson reported that contrary to what researchers such as George Bishop have found in the United States, "it appears that many [former-Soviet respondents] had no opinions about a variety of political issues, and that they faithfully reported their lack of opinions to interviewers."

Global View 3   "Don't-Know" Responses in Soviet Survey Research

James L. Gibson

For those who engage in survey research, the problem of respondents who "don't know" is omnipresent. What does a Don't Know mean? Should such responses be encouraged or discouraged? And how should Don't-Know responses be analyzed? There are no simple answers to these important questions.

Table 1   Views Toward Jews, European USSR, 1990

	DON'T KNOW (%)	AGREE (%)	DISAGREE (%)
When it comes to choosing between people and money, the Jew will choose money.	39.0	**31.6**	29.4
Jews deserve to be punished because they killed Christ.	31.6	**13.3**	55.1
Jews have too much influence over Russian culture.	27.7	**15.8**	56.6
It would be fine with me if a Jew who had a similar family (economic) background to mine joined my close family by marriage.	23.5	53.1	**23.4**
More than any other group in society, it is the Jews who are responsible for the problems the Soviet Union is experiencing today.	21.6	**9.1**	69.3
Jews who wish to emigrate to Israel are a subversive element in society.	14.2	**10.3**	75.6
The government should make every effort to see that the rights of Jews to equal educational opportunity are not violated throughout the USSR.	12.4	81.3	**6.2**
The government should make every effort to see that the rights of Jews to equal employment opportunities are respected throughout the USSR.	11.7	83.0	**5.3**
Jews should be free to decide for themselves whether they want to remain in the USSR or emigrate.	11.4	83.6	**5.0**

Note: The most anti-Semitic responses are shown in bold type. Rows total to 100 percent, except for rounding error; n is approximately 1,500.

Those who were conducting surveys in the former Soviet Union were especially perplexed by the Don't-Know question. As it turns out, Soviet surveys typically reported an unusually high level of Don't-Know responses. For instance, in a 1990 survey of public opinion in the European portion of the USSR, we asked a series of questions about a fairly sensitive topic: attitudes toward Jews. The questions and the percentages of respondents asserting that they don't know are shown in Table 1.

There is a great deal of variation in the percentages of the respondents who don't know whether they agree or disagree with the items. Only 11 percent had no opinion about whether Jews should be free to decide to emigrate from the USSR, while 39 percent didn't know whether Jews would choose money over people. Only 27 percent of the respondents gave an opinion on all nine of the questions, and the average number of Don't-Know responses was 1.9 (standard deviation = 1.9). Fully 10 percent of the respondents gave Don't-Know responses to five or more of the items.

Why didn't the Soviet people know? There are many possible answers to this question, answers that range from poorly constructed questions to reluctance to reveal one's opinion. Let us consider these in more detail.

Were the Soviet people fearful of expressing their opinions to interviewers? The consensus of those then working in the field was that the people were extraordinarily frank, open, and critical of the political system. Certainly the interviewers in our European USSR survey agreed. When asked to rate the openness of the respondents, the interviewers judged 72 percent of the subjects to have given open and honest responses and only 14 percent to have been not very open. This compares with 4 percent who were judged not to be very open in a similar survey in the United States. Moreover, there is little relationship between the perceived openness of the respondents and the frequency of Don't-Know responses to these questions. It is doubtful that the Soviet respondents were trying to disguise their true views by claiming no opinion.

Perhaps question wording has something to do with the problem. One hypothesis is that more ambiguous or more sensitive questions will generate more Don't-Know responses. There is little in Table 1, however, that supports this hypothesis.

There is a hint in Table 1 that Don't-Know responses become more common when the questions concern more difficult issues. Perhaps some Soviets did not know if Jews would choose money over people; perhaps they were quite accurately reporting that they didn't know, possibly because they did not know any Jews. Moreover, since there is a reasonably strong relationship between the respondent's level of education and the proportion of Don't-Know responses, it seems quite plausible that "don't know" actually means *don't know*.

More generally, there is some evidence that Soviet respondents were unusually candid in reporting that they didn't know when they did not have an opinion on the issue. For instance, we asked the respondents to evaluate a variety of social and political groups. We told them to say when they did not know anything about the group. We then put a group to the respondents—Kalakshists—that *did not exist*. Fully 83 percent of the sample properly claimed to have no opinion about the group.

When an American sample was asked an identical question about a fictitious group in a national survey in 1987, only 70 percent reported having no opinion.* Thus there is some evidence that the Soviet people were simply more willing to report having no opinion than they were to fabricate a response for the interviewer.

It is also possible that decades of relatively autocratic rule in the USSR contributed to a citizenry that avoided politics as much as possible. Although there is little evidence today of an unusual level of self-censorship in the CIS (Commonwealth of Independent States, the former USSR), some citizens had no doubt come to view their role in the communist political system as one of disengaged and passive citizens. Whereas in some democratic countries many citizens feel obligated to become informed about a variety of political issues, in authoritarian countries many citizens believe it wisest simply not to know about issues that might be dangerous to know about. Without a sense of obligation to have an opinion, the Soviets were quite willing to report that they didn't know when they actually didn't.

In sum, it appears that many had no opinions about a variety of political issues, and that they faithfully reported their lack of opinions to interviewers. There is no evidence that the respondents were trying to disguise their views by claiming not to have an opinion. Though it is perhaps troublesome for those who would analyze public opinion data to have such large proportions of Don't-Know responses, we can take some comfort in the belief that these citizens feel no compulsion (as they often do in the United States) to make up an opinion on an issue about which they really don't know. More generally, it is more useful for survey researchers to allow respondents the opportunity to express no opinion than to structure the questions so as to encourage the fabrication of opinion.

James L. Gibson is a professor of politcal science at the University of Huston.

*Editor's note: Also see the 1989 NORC study referred to earlier in which 61 percent of the respondents did not rank the "Wisians," a fictitious ethnic group.

DO RESPONDENTS EVER LIE?

Philip Converse attempted to account for certain attitudinal inconsistencies that showed up in a three-wave panel study (meaning the same people were interviewed three times over a period of time).[14] He cited two possibilities:

1. People may fabricate their replies simply because they have not previously considered the subject of the question.

Table 9.2 Pre-Election and Election Results Compared

	DINKINS	GIULIANI	DIFFERENCE
Actual share of vote	50%	48%	2%
The N.Y. Times/WCBS-TV	52	46	6
N.Y. Daily News/Eyewitness News (Nov. 5)	54	40	14*
N.Y. Newsday/Gallup (Oct. 27–31)	49	38	11*

*These percentages are well outside the usually accepted margin of error of ±3–4 percentage points.

SOURCE: Andrew Rosenthal, "Broad Disparities in Votes and Polls Raising Questions," *The New York Times*, Nov. 9, 1989.

2. Inconsistency or instability may be the result of poorly constructed questions that cause measurement error.

Still, to put it bluntly, it does seem that people are lying about their beliefs and intentions more frequently than they did in the past. This is not all that easy to prove, but it is something to consider. It may well sound a warning as to the limitations of polling. Witness, for example, the closeness of the election results in the New York mayoral race of 1989, between David Dinkins, a black candidate, and Rudolph Giuliani, as compared to the pre-election polls (see Table 9.2).

As you can see, some of the polling results are beyond the usual margin of error of ±3–4 percentage points. What happened? Andrew Rosenthal of *The New York Times* asks, "Did voters lie to avoid seeming biased against a black candidate?"[15] Pollsters experienced a similar problem in the 1990 Virginia gubernatorial race between Democrat L. Douglas Wilder, a black candidate, and his Republican opponent, J. Marshall Coleman. Mason-Dixon Opinion Research, Inc., had predicted a Wilder victory with a lead of 10 percentage points. Wilder won by only one-quarter of a percentage point.[16] Again, this is an example of an election return well outside the usually acceptable margin of error. As Michael Oreskes pointed out, "It is well established in social science research that some respondents will shy away from giving 'socially undesirable' answers to poll takers."[17] In Virginia, some white respondents might have felt it undesirable to admit that they were not going to vote for Wilder. Subsequently, this notion of lying to pollsters became known as the Wilder factor.

In the North Carolina senatorial contest that year, most polls predicted an even race between Harvey Gantt, a black candidate, and United States Senator Jesse Helms. Helms won, taking 53 percent to Gantt's 47 percent of the vote. Taking into account the margin of error, most pollsters would continue to stand by their prediction. However, Tony Brown, the black syndicated columnist and television commentator, claims that the polls were faulty because people lie. He states that he predicted before the election that Gantt would lose to Helms, and that he

> ... came to that conclusion not because of any shortcoming on the part of Gantt, but because election after election proves that Whites lie to pollsters when a Black faces-off against a White.
>
> Many Whites will say they are undecided or even that they intend to vote for the Black. But election after election, we find that these are closet-White votes that the White candidate can count on.[18]

Acknowledging that respondents might lie about their support for David Duke in the November 1991 Louisiana gubernatorial runoff election, some pollsters admitted fearing a hidden vote and taking extra precautions in their pre-election surveys to detect, and adjust for, such a vote. Duke, a former Grand Wizard of the Ku Klux Klan and the repudiated Republican nominee, was attacked in Democratic party ads that focused on Duke's neo-Nazi activities. One such ad contained newsreel footage of Nazi Germany, showing Adolf Hitler, with arm outstretched, to shouts of "Sieg Heil" and martial music. The closing caption read: "Vote for Duke. Create a Führer."[19] Running against Duke was the tainted former Democratic governor, Edwin W. Edwards.* In his previous attempts at public office, State Senator Duke had attracted stronger support than some pollsters had predicted, and they were therefore wary about using standard methods in the November runoff. Susan Howell, director of the survey research center at the University of New Orleans, said

> there was still some deception by voters in the pre-election polls.... Whenever one candidate is identified as not socially acceptable, his supporters grow quiet. The more extreme the candidate, the worse the problem.[20]

The deception, Howell said, was primarily due to "middle-class white voters who have a need to be respectable and who travel in circles where it is not O.K. to be for Duke."[21] After making statistical adjustments, Howell's

---

*Edwards' reputation was tarnished because of his excessive gambling and various questionable dealings. Thus, among those who supported returning him to the governor's office only because the alternative was Duke, the election slogan became "Vote for the crook instead of the racist."

polling results a week before the election showed Edwards winning with 55 percent of the vote, and 45 percent going to Duke. After conducting election day exit polling, Warren Mitofsky, executive director of Voter Research and Surveys, rejected the hidden-vote notion:

> There are difficulties in conducting polls, but a hidden vote is not one of them.... People have talked about a hidden vote since George Wallace and the silent majority. Uncertainty on the part of voters can be a problem, but it is nonsense [to say] that people lie to pollsters.

Mitofsky's exit polling through the day showed Edwards leading by approximately a 3 to 2 margin; his closing estimates nearly matched the election results of 61 percent for Edwards and 39 percent for Duke.[22] Mitofsky's results appeared to convince Howell, who said: "If a hidden vote did not cause problems for exit polls in Louisiana, it won't show up anywhere." However, Tony Brown might well remain unconvinced.

It is difficult to prove whether lying, the so-called Wilder factor, is a legitimate explanation to account for these polling problems. Pollsters acknowledge that just as the race or gender of the interviewer can influence results, so too can the race or gender of the candidate. Another explanation involves sampling procedures, filter questions, and the respondent's commitment to vote. Good polls are supposed to filter out non-voters by including appropriate filter questions; they are also supposed to measure a respondent's commitment to vote. If a poll does not properly do that, as much as two-thirds of a random sample may consist of individuals whose voices—registered in the poll—will not be heard on election day. Then too, even if filter questions are included, respondents may feel it is socially undesirable to admit that they do not intend to vote on election day, which brings us back to the Wilder factor of lying.

SAYING NO: RESPONDENT REFUSAL

C. G. Steeh examined the trends in non-response rates from 1952 to 1979 and documented a significant decline in respondent willingness to participate in surveys.[23] These findings, as Howard Schuman and Graham Kalton subsequently pointed out, threaten assumptions that "we are indeed dealing with adequate samples of the general population that is usually our target."[24] During the 1990 election campaigns, pollsters became ever more aware that the normal difficulties of the polling process, including sample selection and questionnaire development, were compounded by a number of factors, including voter resentment. Along with this general anger, there appeared to be an increase in refusal rates.

Michael Berlin, a journalism professor at Boston University, is an adamant critic of polls. His theory on the growth of lying and noncooperation is that "a growing segment of the public regards pollsters as 'them'— the enemy, the establishment, the problem and not the solution." He also believes that many respondents view the poll takers as authority figures. As a result, the respondents may avoid stating their true opinions or giving answers that "stray from conventional wisdom or are not 'politically correct.'" So negative is Berlin's opinion of poll takers that he actually advises: "Say no to poll-takers, on principle. Or, for the adventurous, lie like a bandit. It's the least a politically correct citizen can do.[25]

Referring to the increasing number of people who refuse to be interviewed and also commenting about the growing protest vote seen in the 1990 campaigns, Republican poll taker Fred Steeper said that it was still possible to get a reasonably good sense of voter concerns and disenchantments by asking a *series* of questions, but, because voters are uncertain about what should be done, their answers to the specific question "How would you vote today?" appeared somewhat less reliable.[26] Steeper, who has worked for Robert Teeter (George Bush's 1992 reelection campaign manager) for over 20 years, cited Teeter's emphasis on the importance of "making the questions more relevant and more interesting to the respondent." Teeter reportedly "can read a poll and tell you what's wrong with it, what's wrong with the answers, and what to watch out for."[27] Those abilities, always important, have become all the more so with the proliferation of polls* and the increase in respondent negativism toward them.

Some argue that a screening device, the answering machine, has been a contributing factor to the decrease in response rates because it has made it easier for respondents to avoid the pollster. Peter Tuckel and Barry Feinberg estimated that at the time of their study (May 2 to June 3, 1988), roughly 25 percent of telephone households had answering machines, and the expectation was that answering machine ownership would spiral upward as the purchasing prices for such machines decreased.[28] The Yankee Group determined the demographic profile of answering machine owners as consisting of individuals who are single, college-educated, earning over $50,000 a year. More specifically, as shown in Table 9.3, the Yankee Group found over-represented sub-groups to be owners of such machines.

---

*In an amusing op-ed piece entitled "Let's Have a Polling Frenzy," Russell Baker creates some rules to improve the image of the American news industry. Rule 1: When in doubt, poll. Rule 2: Fit the news coverage to the poll. *The New York Times*, Sept. 7, 1988.

Table 9.3 Telephone Answering Machine Ownership by Population Sub-Group

SUB-GROUP	PERCENT OWNING ANSWERING MACHINES
Home-based entrepreneurs	45.7
Singles	33.3
24–44 years of age	32.6
Men	31.5
Earning over $50,000	49.3
College graduates	40.0
Serviced by the Pacific Telesis Regional Bell Holding Company	41.5

SOURCE: Peter S. Tuckel and Barry M. Feinberg, "The Answering Machine Poses Many Questions for Telephone Survey Researchers," *Public Opinion Quarterly* (1991), Vol. 55, p. 201.

In analyzing whether people with answering machines are less accessible than those without such machines, Tuckel and Feinberg put forth two competing hypotheses:

- *Cocooners*   The cocooners hypothesis refers to individuals who see the world as intrusive and use their answering machines to screen unwanted calls. According to this hypothesis, these respondents are less accessible to pollsters.

- *Connectors*   The connectors hypothesis refers to those who feel a strong need to always be in the loop. They use their answering machines to maximize their accessibility. According to this hypothesis, these respondents turn on their machines only when they are not available. The researchers, in fact, more frequently encountered the use of answering machines on weekends than during weekday evenings (presumably because people were home more on weekday evenings and thus had their machines off).

The complex Tuckel-Feinberg study design began with a sample size of 2,981 and called for up to three telephone attempts to reach the respondent and to complete the interview. Business numbers and nonworking numbers identified after each of the first two calls were excluded before the next call. Thus, the sample size at the end of the second call was 1,982; at the end of the third call, $n = 1,486$. Some of the findings of this interesting study follow.

- A significant proportion of answering machine owners are accessible to pollsters: 55.9 percent of the answering machine households were reached during *two* call attempts, and 19.8 percent of those respondents completed the interviews.

- In measuring the overall likelihood of contacting answering machine households versus other households, the researchers confirmed that answering machines are more common in the urban, more populous communities, where those fitting the demographic profile are more likely to reside. They thus also confirmed the demographic profile of answering machine owners originally described by the Yankee Group.

- As for the difference in completion rates between the answering machine group and the "no answer" and "busy" groups: Once contacted (by the *third* call attempt), approximately 67 percent of the former agreed to participate as compared to about 60 percent for those who had previously either not answered their phones or had a busy phone line. The difference between the two percentages was so minor that it was not statistically significant.

- Since answering machines were most frequently encountered on weekends, scheduling call-backs on weekday evenings appeared to solve that problem.

- The data appear to support the connectors hypothesis more than the cocooners hypothesis.[29]

THE OLDER RESPONDENT

Is it more time-consuming and more difficult to interview older respondents, say over the age of 60? Do they need more assistance, more probing? Are their refusal and DK rates higher? Does the mode of data collection (in-person versus telephone interview) make a difference when dealing with older individuals?

While it has long been accepted that a telephone survey can be conducted for approximately half the cost of a face-to-face survey[30] and that data of comparable quality can be collected from both modes,[31] some researchers have found problems. For example, in their comparison of telephone and personal interviews, R. M. Groves and R. L. Kahn found that missing data (defined as DKs), fewer responses to open-ended questions, and lower response rates were more common with telephone interviewing. Also, in her 1981 study, "Response Styles in Telephone and Household Interviewing," Eleanor Singer found inconsistent evidence as to which mode yields more accurate reporting. A number of studies completed during the late 1970s raised concern over the viability of telephone interviews with elderly respondents in particular. When comparing the results of interviewing older persons by telephone and in person, these studies noted a higher incidence of hearing loss problems, a greater reliance on auditory cues, and a greater need for assistance (including probing).[32]

In an attempt to better evaluate and understand any mode differences when comparing older respondents (60 years of age and older) with younger ones, A. Regula Herzog and Willard Rodgers drew a probability sample of 1,491 households in the metropolitan area of Detroit, over-sampling adults 60 years of age and older (1,016 from 60+ households and 475 from households between the ages of 20 and 59 years)[33] They explained that the over-sampling "yielded estimates with lower standard errors than heretofore possible" and that they were particularly interested in testing the feasibility of using telephone interviews for follow-up surveys. Although this is an extremely complex study, there are a number of aspects worth exploring on the beginner's level.

Their research design included a 90-minute face-to-face interview and a 10-minute telephone follow-up interview conducted about 6 to 8 weeks later. Besides examining the response rate to the reinterview by telephone and any age differences in this rate, their objectives were

> to investigate differences in answers obtained by the two modes
> with respect to response distributions, proportions of missing
> data ... and the amount of interviewer assistance, and, specifically, to
> investigate whether differences between modes on these dimensions
> might be larger among older respondents than among respondents
> of younger ages.[34]

The questionnaire dealt with living conditions; state of mind; concern about health, safety, and crime; difficulties in seeing, hearing, mobility, and memory; trust in government and in people. Some of the questions were dichotomous (yes/no); others used 4- or 5-point scales, and the respondents were asked to rate their responses. Comparing the two ways of collecting data across two age levels, Herzog and Rodgers found:

Response Distributions   Here the statistician sums the answers to each question according to each age group and determines the mean, or average, for each method of data collection. The difference between the two ways of collecting data (represented by Δ) for each group for each question is then statistically determined and the **statistical significance** for each Δ is statistically tested. Finally, the *interaction*, the difference between the Δs, is calculated. Researchers define interaction as age differences in mode differences (here, *mode* refers to the method of data collection) or as age by mode interactions. The purpose of these statistical calculations—undertaken with the help of sophisticated computer programs—is to determine whether there is a statistically significant (statistically meaningful) difference between the way the two age groups (interviewed first in person and then by telephone) answered each question.

Herzog and Rodgers found some differences attributable to specific content matter, such as health-related items, but they did not find significant mode differences. They reported: "[T]hese findings support neither the contention that the mode of interviewing affects survey responses in any substantial way nor the claim that it has a more substantial effect on survey responses by older than by younger respondents."[35]

Missing Data   In this study, missing data were defined solely as Don't-Know answers, as opposed to refusals to answer specific questions. DK answers were given with greater frequency in telephone interviews compared to in-person interviews and sometimes the differences were statistically significant. While the number of DKs for each group increased when the interviews were conducted by telephone, the researchers found a tendency toward a disproportionately large number of DK answers among older respondents. (Herzog and Rodgers report that these findings are consistent with those of other researchers.) Since DK responses are excluded from response distributions, Herzog and Rodgers argue, the quality of the responses of elderly respondents may actually be maintained through greater interviewer assistance (for example, help through repetition or auditory cues).

Interviewer Assistance   There was a tendency for more assistance to be provided in the form of auditory cues in telephone interviews than in those conducted in person. Larger, statistically significant, mode differences were particularly observable in the telephone interviews with older respondents. However, the researchers suggest that this greater reliance on auditory cues during telephone interviews may work to maintain the response quality of the data supplied by elderly respondents. **Response quality** refers to the completeness, appropriateness, relevance, and clarity of the answers. Obviously a DK, providing zero information, is devoid of response quality.

Response Rates   From the 699 respondents chosen to be reinterviewed, 2 had died, 24 had no telephone, and 27 had refused to give their telephone numbers; 14 of the 27 were obtained by using a reverse directory,* and the

---

*While some may not appreciate the research organization's acquiring a telephone number that the individual refused to divulge, one could argue that on receiving the phone call, the individual could still refuse to participate.

Table 9.4 Response Rate by Age

	n	RESPONSE RATE (%)
Over age 59	378	84
20–59	189	92
Overall	567	90

SOURCE: A. Regula Herzog and Willard A. Rodgers, "Interviewing Older Adults: Mode Comparison Using Data from a Face-to-Face Survey and a Telephone Resurvey," *Public Opinion Quarterly* (1988), Vol. 52, p. 90.

other 13 were unlisted numbers. Of the 660 remaining respondents, 567 participated in the telephone reinterview. The somewhat lower response rate found for those over 59 proved to be a statistically significant difference (see Table 9.4).

Overall, response rates, distribution, and quality did not significantly differ. Despite lower response rates, a disproportionately greater number of DK answers, and a disproportionately greater amount of interviewer assistance on the telephone for respondents over age 59, Herzog and Rodgers concluded that telephone interviews—used for follow-up interviews—were suitable as an alternative to the in-person interview, a more expensive mode of data collection.

GENDER AND SENSITIVE QUESTIONS

In 1987, as part of a government-funded general population survey on AIDS, Patricia Murphy and Diane Binson tested the feasibility of asking sensitive questions in a 30-minute telephone survey. The most sensitive questions took about 7 minutes and asked about sexual practices, orientation, and activity, and about the sharing of needles for drug use. These were sandwiched between a 20-minute series of questions dealing with the respondent's knowledge, attitudes, and perceptions concerning AIDS and the final interview segment, covering demographic information, including an item on sexual identity also considered sensitive.[36]

Beginning with an RDD (random-digit dialing) sample size of 7,430 and deducting 1,848 ineligible respondents, 2,586 nonworking, nonresidential telephone numbers, as well as 1,456 refusals, noncontacts, and other eligibles whose interviews were not completed, interviews were completed with a total of 1,540 adults between the ages 18 and 60. In evaluating who says no, Murphy and Binson considered the following characteristics (variables): education, race, ethnicity, age, and sex. While they found no differences in the first four variables between those who had refused to answer specific questions and those who had responded, they did find gender differences: "about 15% of males refused one or more sensitive questions, compared to 9% of females." Interestingly, when the variable of education was introduced, the researchers determined that the item–refusal rate for women who had not graduated from high school resembled the item–refusal rate for men in every education category, and when men and women were classified by racial or ethnic group, black male respondents had the highest item–refusal rate.[37]

The gender gap was also discernible in the refusal results for the first two sensitive questions. Those questions and the male–female refusal rates were:

Have you had sex with anyone in the past 5 years?

Male refusal rate   5.4%

Female refusal rate   3.0%

In the past 5 years, how many different people have you had as a sexual partner?

Male refusal rate   4.5%

Female refusal rate   1.6%

In summarizing their findings, Murphy and Binson admit that they have been bitten by the cognitive psychology bug:

> All of this leaves us with more questions than answers. Is there a gender gap for sensitive questions about sexual and drug use practices? We think there is, but we cannot be sure. We wish we knew more about possible interviewer effects in this survey, and about the interaction of interviewer and respondent characteristics and how this might affect item refusals on sensitive questions.
>
> ... We think the next step should be to look at these sensitive questions, and at respondent-interviewer interactions, in a laboratory setting. We want to know how males and females react to these questions, how they decide what to answer, and whether or not *to* answer.... We also want to talk with respondents after interviews to learn what characteristics of interviewers respondents notice. Do these interviewer characteristics have any effect on responses?

The researchers conclude that when used in a laboratory setting, the "tools of cognitive psychology ... may make it possible to study more aspects of sensitive questions than seems possible in the real world of surveys."[38]

Before closing this chapter, I would like to emphasize that respondents are people, and the act of surveying affects them. While qualitative methods (as we will see in Chapter 11) are apt to give survey researchers greater self-awareness and lead to more self-criticism, the quantitative methods researchers use sometimes gloss over respondent-related considerations. Thus, although it is true that a good deal has been learned since researchers began to focus attention on respondent-related biases, there is still room for improvement.

CHAPTER REVIEW

- Early researchers concluded that some relationship existed between a person's exterior (physique) and deportment (personality).

- People display selective tendencies regarding what they notice, learn, or remember. Information input is filtered and processed for, cognitive operations such as inference, attribution, and judgment.

- Researchers wrote about cognitive structures—internal structures that stored specific information used to define not only an object, event, or situation, but the rules delineating any relationships among them.

- George Franklin Bishop's research has shown that the less educated a respondent is, the more there is a tendency to fear appearing ignorant. What is significant about his research in general and this point in particular?

- In 1989, NORC used a ranking scale and asked respondents to rate the social standing of 58 ethnic groups in the United States, including the Wisians, a fictitious group. (I felt disappointed that 39 percent ranked a fictitious group rather than admit they did not know.)

- Clyde Coombs and Lolagene Coombs discovered that DK responses occur because of respondent uncertainty, non-attitude, and item ambiguity.

- Researcher James Gibson reported that, contrary to what researchers such as George Bishop have found in the United States, many former Soviet respondents faithfully reported their lack of opinions to interviewers.

- Philip Converse, in attempting to account for certain "attitudinal inconsistencies" that showed up in a three-wave panel study, cited two possibilities: (1) people may fabricate their replies simply because they have not previously considered the question's subject; or (2) poorly constructed questions may cause measurement error, thereby creating inconsistent responses.

- *New York Times* reporter Michael Oreskes believes that some respondents "will shy away from giving 'socially undesirable' answers to poll takers." What gave rise to the Wilder factor, the notion that some respondents will lie to pollsters?

- C. G. Steeh examined the trends in non-response rates from 1952 to 1979 and documented a significant decline in respondent willingness to participate in surveys.

- Howard Schuman and Graham Kalton feel that the documented decline in respondent willingness to participate threatens assumptions about the adequacy and representativeness of the samples being used.

- Since the 1990 election campaigns, pollsters have become more aware of voter resentment. This anger may be causing an increase in refusal rates, which compounds the normal difficulties of the polling process.

- Boston University journalism professor Michael Berlin is an adamant critic of polls who believes that many respondents view the poll takers as authority figures and therefore may avoid stating their true opinions or giving answers that are not politically correct.

- Republican poll taker Fred Steeper feels researchers can still get a reasonably good sense of voter concerns and disenchantments by asking a series of questions as opposed to a single specific question.

- Peter Tuckel and Barry Feinberg estimated in 1988 that roughly 25 percent of telephone households had answering machines. The demographic profile of answering machine owners, as determined by the Yankee Group, consisted of individuals who are single, college-educated, earning over $50,000 a year.

- Tuckel and Feinberg put forth the cocooners and the connectors hypotheses. How do these hypotheses differ and what are the implications for future polling efforts?

- A number of studies completed during the late 1970s raised concern over the viability of telephone interviews with elderly respondents. When comparing the results of interviewing older persons by telephone and in person, these studies noted a higher incidence of hearing loss problems, a greater reliance on auditory cues, and a greater need for assistance (including probing).

- What were the goals of the study conducted by Herzog and Rodgers? When they compared two ways of collecting data across two age levels, what did they find regarding response distributions, missing data (DK answers), response quality of elderly respondents, need for interviewer assistance, and response rates? Which of their findings were substantively significant—important enough to remember? Were any of these also statistically significant?

- Patricia Murphy and Diane Binson tested the feasibility of asking sensitive questions. Which variables (characteristics) did they consider in their research? Were there gender differences in respondent refusals to answer sensitive questions dealing with sexual activity and drug use? What happened when the variable of education was introduced?

- Why do Murphy and Binson think "the next step should be to look at these sensitive questions, and at respondent-interviewer interactions, in a laboratory setting"?

NOTES

1. Jan Stapel, "The Convivial Respondent," *Public Opinion Quarterly* (Winter 1947–1948), pp. 524–529.

2. Hazel Markus and R. B. Zajonc, "The Cognitive Perspective in Social Psychology," *The Handbook of Social Psychology*, Vol. I, 3rd ed., Gardner Lindzey and Elliot Aronson, eds. (New York: Random House, 1985), p. 141.

3. See The Professional Voice 2.

4. Tamar Lewin, "Study Points to Increase in Tolerance of Ethnicity," *The New York Times*, Jan. 8, 1992, p. A12.

5. Lawrence F. Feick, "Latent Class Analysis of Survey Questions That Include Don't Know Responses," *Public Opinion Quarterly* (1989), Vol. 53, p. 525.

6. Clyde H. Coombs and Lolagene C. Coombs, "'Don't Know': Item Ambiguity or Respondent Uncertainty?" *Public Opinion Quarterly* (1976), Vol. 40, pp. 497–514.

7. "Poll Finds Only 33% Can Identify Bill of Rights," *The New York Times*, Dec. 15, 1991, p. A33.

8. Jane E. Brody, "Smoking Among Children Is Linked to Cartoon Camel in Advertisements," *The New York Times*, Dec. 11, 1991, p. D22.

9. Feick, p. 527.

10. G. David Faulkenberry and Robert Mason, "Characteristics of Nonopinion and No Opinion Response Groups," *Public Opinion Quarterly* (1978), Vol. 42, pp. 533–543.

11. Paul J. Hendrie, "Bergen's Invisible Election," *The Record*, Oct. 25, 1990, pp. 1, 26.

12. Ronald B. Rapoport, "Sex Differences in Attitude Expression: A Generational Explanation," *Public Opinion Quarterly* (1982), Vol. 46, pp. 86–96; and see his "Like Mother, Like Daughter: Intergenerational Transmission of DK Response Rates," *Public Opinion Quarterly* (1985), Vol. 49, pp. 198–208.

13. Jean M. Converse, "Predicting No Opinion in the Polls," *Public Opinion Quarterly* (1976), Vol. 40, pp. 515–530; Joe D. Francis and Lawrence Busch, "What We Now Know About 'I don't knows,'" *Public Opinion Quarterly* (1975), Vol. 39, pp. 207–218; Rapoport (1982).

14. Philip E. Converse, "The Nature of Belief Systems in Mass Publics," in *Ideology and Discontent*, David E. Apter, ed. (New York: Free Press, 1964), pp. 206–261; and "Attitudes and Non-Attitudes: Continuation of a Dialogue," in *The Quantitative Analysis of Social Problems*, Edward R. Tufte, ed. (Boston: Addison-Wesley, 1970), pp. 168–189.

15. Andrew Rosenthal, "Broad Disparities in Votes and Polls Raising Questions," *The New York Times*, November 9, 1989.

16. Michael Oreskes, "In Year of Volatile Vote, Polls Can Be Dynamite," *The New York Times*, Nov. 2, 1990, pp. A1, 19.

17. Oreskes.

18. Tony Brown, "64% Vote Against U.S. Politics," *The Connection* (Teaneck, NJ), Nov. 17, 1990, p. 10.

19. Roberto Suro, "The 1991 Campaign—On Television: Outsider vs. a Former Governor of Louisiana," *The New York Times*, Nov. 15, 1991, p. A20.

20. Michael R. Kagay, "'Hidden Vote' for Duke Never Materialized," *The New York Times*, Nov. 18, 1991, p. B6.

21. Kagay.

22. Kagay.

23. C. G. Steeh, "Trends in Nonresponse Rates, 1952–1979," *Public Opinion Quarterly* (1981), Vol. 45, pp. 40–57.

24. Howard Schuman and Graham Kalton, "Survey Methods," *The Handbook of Social Psychology*, Vol. 1, 3rd ed., Gardner Lindzey and Elliot Aronson, eds. (New York: Random House, 1985), p. 638.

25. Michael J. Berlin, "Polls Are a Pox on the Body Politic," *The Record*, Dec. 3, 1990, p. B10.

26. Oreskes, p. A19.

27. Adam Clymer, "Washington at Work: A Bush Campaign Chief Who Knows Questions," *The New York Times*, Dec. 8, 1991, p. A34.

28. Peter S. Tuckel and Barry M. Feinberg, "The Answering Machine Poses Many Questions for Telephone Survey Researchers," *Public Opinion Quarterly* (1991), Vol. 55, pp. 200–217. The researchers cite the findings of Walker Research, *Industry Image Study*, 8th ed. (Indianapolis: Walker Research), 1988, that 25 percent of telephone households own an answering machine and those of the Yankee Group, "Telephone Answering Devices: Gaining Consumer Acceptance," *Yankeevision*, August 1988, pp. 13–20, which put the figure at 26 percent. As cited by Tuckel and Feinberg, the Yankee Group found a 15-percent increase in the ownership of answering machines in a period of less than three years.

29. Tuckel and Feinberg, pp. 208–212.

30. See, for example, R. M. Groves and R. L. Kahn, *Surveys by Telephone: A National Comparison with Personal Interviews* (New York: Academic Press, 1979).

31. Groves and Kahn; also see C. F. Cannell, R. M. Groves, L. J. Magilavy, N. A. Mathiowetz, and P. V. Miller, "An Experimental Comparison of Telephone and Personal Health Surveys," *Final Report to the National Center for Health Statistics* (Ann Arbor: Institute for Social Research, 1982).

32. Studies raising questions about using telephone interviewing for elderly respondents include: C. S. Kart, E. S. Metress, and J. F. Metress, *Aging and Health* (Menlo Park, CA: Addison-Wesley, 1978); R. L. Horton and D. J. Duncan, "A New Look at Telephone Interviewing Methodology," *Pacific Sociological Review* (1978), Vol. 21, pp. 259–274; and E. Fleishman and M. Berk, "Survey of Interviewer Attitudes Toward Selected Methodological Issues in the National Medical Care Expenditure Survey," *Health Survey Research Methods: Third Biennial Conference*, DHS Pub. No. (PHS)81-3268 (Chevy Chase, MD: U.S. Department of Health and Human Services, National Center for Health Services Research, 1979).

33. A. Regula Herzog and Willard L. Rodgers, "Interviewing Older Adults: Mode Comparison Using Data from a Face-to-Face Survey and a Telephone Resurvey," *Public Opinion Quarterly* (1988), Vol. 52, p. 87.

34. Herzog and Rodgers.

35. Herzog and Rodgers, p. 91.

36. Patricia A. Murphy and Diane Binson, "Who Says 'No' to Whom: Respondent-Interviewer Interactions in Refusals to Sensitive Questions," a paper presented at the annual meeting of the American Association for Public Opinion Research (Toronto, Ontario, 1988). The Murphy-Binson survey was part of a study, funded by the U.S. Centers for Disease Control through the City of Chicago Department of Health, called "Evaluation Component of City of Chicago's AIDS Risk Reduction/Prevention Program" and was headed by Professor Gary L. Albrecht, Principal Investigator (University of Illinois at Chicago, School of Public Health).

37. Murphy and Binson.

38. Murphy and Binson.

10

Getting and Using
the Results

Think about—

What is meant by data reduction and data cleaning?

What are descriptive statistics? What is the role of inferential statistics?

What is the difference between measures of
central tendency and measures of dispersion?

When is something statistically significant?

What is meant by a null hypothesis? When are
correlations useful, and what is meant by ANOVA?

To choose the best way to analyze survey data,
what questions must you first answer?

What important questions must journalists ask
about poll results before they write their articles?

In general, what are the problems with the
way in which the press reports polling data?

What is mediated public opinion?

What should a thorough survey report tell its readers? What
information should be contained within the report's
abstract? What type of information should be included
in the section dealing with methods and findings?

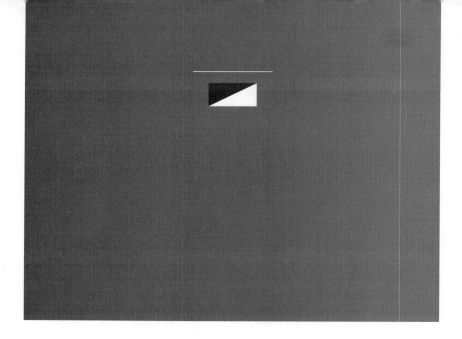

In precomputer days, data compilation—*sorting* (men/women, favor/oppose/no opinion), *counting* (how many in each pile), and *comparing*—was all done manually. Then came various types of punched or perforated data cards. In the 1950s and 1960s, coders wrote code numbers (which had been assigned to each possible answer) on special coding sheets. These code numbers, each representing an assigned *punch position* in a column, were then punched onto IBM cards.

In the 1960s, special computer programs were developed that went beyond the existing software capability of enabling the researcher to enter data directly into a computer. One such program was the **SPSS (Statistical Package for the Social Sciences)**. SPSS gave social scientists their own programs for converting data into meaningful information. Today, the questionnaire itself usually contains the code, as numbers are preassigned to fixed alternative responses, and interviewers circle or blacken the code that matches the response given. Optical scanning devices have made it possible to communicate this coded information to a computer.

THE DATA REDUCTION PROCESS

Although computers have telescoped the data preparation process, there are still five steps to coding or data reduction to prepare survey data for analysis:

1. Creating, Formatting, and Organizing a Data File   Research institutes tend to develop their own styles (conventions) for preparing the information for analysis. Some choose a card-and-column format: Each respondent is assigned a number that will appear on a card, and each question is assigned a **data field**, meaning one or more columns on a data card, which becomes the record of that respondent's answers.

2. Designing a Code   A decision is made as to what number will be assigned to each answer provided for the various fixed-response, structured questions. Answers to open-ended questions (where respondents express their own thoughts) are assigned numbered categories according to the similarity and frequency of response. The categories must be mutually exclusive and exhaustive so that they include all significant data while distinguishing between different thoughts and opinions. There are also codes for "other" responses (those answers that do not fit the established categories) and for missing and inapplicable data, as well as for the DK (Don't-Know) answers.

3. Coding   This refers to the actual process of applying the numbers (codes) to the responses. Coders are carefully trained and detail oriented. If a precoded questionnaire is used, the interviewer accomplishes this function while recording the responses.

4. Data Entry   Here, we transfer (key) the coded numbers onto cards, tapes, or computer disks. This step includes verification, the process whereby a different person enters the data a second time, checking the second entry against the first.

The most advanced systems have eliminated a number of error-prone operations. CATI has made it possible for the computer-assisted telephone interviewer to read the question off the screen and to enter the data directly into the computer as the respondent answers each question. As the answer goes into the computer, the next question appears on the screen. The computer tabulates the input while the interview is continuing. In dealing with open-ended questions, the interviewer usually types the response verbatim into the computer for later coding. However, in the absence of a hard copy, there is no way to verify or correct errors in data entry.

5. Data Cleaning   This is the last step before analysis. Researchers check for inconsistencies. The computer has been invaluable in this area because it can flag any violations of preestablished data rules. For example, when dealing with sums and sizes, the computer will adhere to such basic rules as: (1) the total equals the sum of its parts; (2) the totals for the rows and columns should equal the overall total; or (3) boundary values can be set, so that figures cannot be higher or lower than those numbers. A computer can be instructed to reject those answers that are totally inconsistent with other recorded responses. Thus, as Charles Backstrom and Gerald Hursh-César note, computers can be programmed to detect interviewer cheating, since an "interviewer who enters responses for a nonexistent respondent is not likely to take the time to be internally consistent."[1]

THE SIGNIFICANT ROLE OF STATISTICS

As stated earlier in this text, without a knowledge of statistics, or the capital to hire a statistician, you are not going to get very far in understanding and interpreting the meaning of your data. And to gain even a minimum understanding of the power of statistics, you will have to study the subject. Although this text, directed as it is to the novice, has shied away from statistical calculations, the moment of truth has come. Yes, I am sure you know how to tally columns to determine response patterns—how many respondents fit into the different categories or groups (Democrats, Republicans, Independents; less than high school, high school, or college educated; supporters or opponents of abortion; incomes below $10,000, $10,001–$20,000, $20,001–$30,000, and so on) that you have established; and you probably can find what percentage of the whole sample each of the various categories' totals represents. As for the **measures of central tendency** that tell us how similar or typical responses are—the means, medians, and modes—you probably can calculate those too.

You may know that the term *frequency* refers to how often a particular number (result, score, response) appears. But what about measuring the differences among respondents? Here we are referring to the **measures of dispersion or variation**. There are as many as 20 ways to compute variability. *Range*, the easiest to compute, is the crudest of such measures. It is determined by finding the extremes of a distribution, meaning the lowest and highest scores for a particular item, and then subtracting the lowest from the highest score (for example, the range of scores on a test in which the highest score is 99 and the lowest score is 54 is $99 - 54 = 45$). Two other measures of dispersion are *variance* and *standard deviation*. *Variance* tells us about the distribution of all the scores about the mean. From it, we can see the similarities and differences of a set of scores. The *standard deviation* conveys the same information, but in useful units—for example, in percentage points on an exam. Variance is not measured in those units; it is measured in *squared* units—in our example, it would be measured in percentage points squared. *Standard deviation* (to be explained further in Appendix I) is the *square root of variance*.

Although the mean, percent of total, range, and standard deviation (all called **descriptive statistics**) enable us to identify and describe important characteristics of our data, they are actually the building blocks for **inferential statistics**, which enable us to draw conclusions from the data. If all this seems confusing, it is only the beginning of what you will need to know. The real heavy-duty analysis can be accomplished only with the use of statistical inference, which allows us to generalize from a sample to the population as a whole. At least, that is what pollsters try to do. In polling we are trying to demonstrate that our sample's range of values is characteristic of the population. Put another way, we are trying to show that if the population were polled, its values would *probably* fall within the sample range. We will now look at some of the questions pollsters seek to answer with the help of various statistical techniques.

Correlations

Simple **correlations** indicate a relationship between two variables; multiple correlations involve three or more variables. Some examples of simple correlations are the crime rate and unemployment; the size of a company's sales force and its sales revenue; education and income; age and an increase in DKs. In survey analysis, researchers are rarely satisfied with a search for relationships that ends with a two-way table or correlations between just two variables. Typically, analysts want to understand and try to explain the cumulative impact of several variables on the dependent variable.

When characteristics appear to accompany each other, they are said to be correlated. So as one increases, the other does too, and should one decrease, so will the other. And when characteristics vary in such a way that as one increases, the other decreases, they are said to be **negatively correlated**. An index ranging from +1.0 to −1.0 is used to measure correlations. A +1.0 indicates a perfect correlation; a −1.0 indicates a perfect negative correlation; and the midpoint of the index, 0.0, indicates no correlation whatsoever (or a perfect non-correlation). The various index values—from

+1.0 to −1.0—are called **correlation coefficients**, and they tell us about the magnitude (from weak, 0.1, to strong, 0.9) and about the nature (direction, + or −) of the relationship. From the correlation coefficient we *infer* the true interrelations of how variables go together or are associated in the population (hence the name *inferential statistics*). Statistical tests are then used to determine how significant the correlation coefficients are.

The term *statistically significant* has been used several times in this text. A finding (for instance, a percentage of respondents feeling a certain way) is statistically significant if it provides enough evidence to enable us to reject the *null hypothesis* or to support the *alternate hypothesis*. We begin with a **hypothesis** (often called the alternate hypothesis) such as "Drugs are the number one problem in America." This is in contrast to the default answer, which is called the null hypothesis. In this case, the null hypothesis is "Drugs are *not* the number one problem in America." (Something else— anything else—is.)

Early in the survey process, researchers determine how large the difference must be between the results in favor of the alternate hypothesis and the null hypothesis before the alternate hypothesis can be supported. If the difference is not sufficiently large to overcome chance or sampling error, then the null hypothesis (Drugs are *not* the number one problem in America) is *not* rejected (because the evidence supports it). The burden is on the researcher to demonstrate the *invalidity* of the null hypothesis, thereby rejecting it. In our example, the researchers must demonstrate that drugs *are* the number one problem, so that the null hypothesis can be rejected with confidence.

Usually, researchers report the probability (p) of obtaining a sufficiently deviant value with a statement such as "$p < .05$" or "$p < .01$." This means that the probability is less than 5 percent or 1 percent that the values were obtained neither by chance nor by error. In the Mayseless-Gal survey (Global View 4), which began with the rather large sample size of 5,400, you will read: "All correlations are significant $p < 0.001$ [< = less than]." Because the researchers have such a large sample, the statistical sampling error yields correlations that are likely to be produced by chance *only at the level of 0.001*. (Although sample size is important, it is not the sole determining factor affecting the size of correlation coefficients.) Or, phrased differently, each correlation is 99.9 percent likely to be significant. The level of significance generally has been predetermined, and therefore sample size is mandated in order to achieve that level of precision. In this case, although we don't know what the predetermined level of required precision was, we are being told that there is a probability of less than one-tenth of a percent that the correlations could have occurred by chance. The findings in this case are considered very highly significant because the probability of non-significance of the findings is a mere 0.1 percent.

It is important to note that there is a tendency to equate a high correlation with causality. This is a mistake, because there may be an intervening variable that has not been taken into account. You will recall that in the Herzog-Rodgers study (see Chapter 9) the mode of interview was an important intervening variable when considering the respondent's age and missing data. Multiple correlation, advanced statistics, was necessary in that research project. (For another example, see Global View 4.)

Some points to remember about correlations:

- Sample size affects the statistical significance of the coefficient.
- When a high correlation between two variables is found, don't assume causality (that one thing caused another to happen).
- There are always other variables that have an impact on the relationship of the two correlated variables.
- When a high correlation is found, all you can conclude safely is that a relationship (or linear trend) may exist between the two variables.

How does one interpret correlations? Statisticians have found that it is rare to find values of +1.0 and −1.0 and that it is even rare to find a positive or negative correlation coefficient of .98. These are too large. In fact, anything greater than .90 indicates a very high degree of relationship. We are told by statisticians that this means that *over 81 percent* of the variation in one variable is explained by its relationship with the other. Even .70 to .90 is considered high because *up to 81 percent* of the variation in one is explained by its association with the other. At the other end, a *negligible relationship* is said to exist when the correlation coefficient is less than .20, which means that up to 4 percent of the difference in one variable's measure is explained by its relationship with the other. A low-to-definite correlation is said to exist when the correlation coefficient falls between .20 and .40. This means that up to 16 percent of the variation is explained by the association. Finally, a correlation coefficient of .40 to .70 is said to be moderate to substantial. It tells us that up to 49 percent of the variation in one variable is attributable to its association with the other. As an example of the way the results of a correlational analysis are presented, see Table 2, the six-variable intercorrelational matrix, in Global View 4.

Global View 4   Extrapolating Relationships Among Fear, Hatred, and National Identity from an Attitude Survey

Ofra Mayseless and Reuven Gal

Israel is a country where, due to its security situation, stress is high. The danger to one's life is a rather prominent concern, as is the risk to the existence of the country itself. The Palestinian uprising (*intifada*) in the West Bank and the Gaza Strip has brought these dangers even more into the nation's focus. This article intends to unfold perceptions and attitudes of Israeli high school students regarding these issues and to relate them to other relevant attitudes.

We conducted a national survey of high school students three to five months after the *intifada* broke out in December 1989. The survey included about 5,400 students from 85 Jewish schools across the country, representing all the sectors of Israel's high school population, except the religious independent sector. The questionnaire used in the survey included questions in five domains:

- attitudes toward the country and the military service
- attitudes and intentions regarding one's own military service
- perceptions regarding possible sources affecting these attitudes
- general values

- personal and demographic information

No direct question was asked regarding the *intifada*. However, several of the questions referred to perceived stress and fear from terrorist acts, military service, and danger to one's life. These may refer indirectly to the effects of the *intifada* as well.

This analysis focuses on the two questions presented in Tables 1A and 1B, along with the frequencies of the first answer for each question across various sectors of high school students, including those in the religious and non-religious high schools. Each of these two categories is subdivided into four different types: regular (academically oriented), vocational, kibbutz, and *moshav* (agricultural, noncollective settlements).

As can be seen from the tables, a large majority of Israeli high school students (more than 60%) feel that terrorist acts disturb them very much. The highest disturbance is evidenced by students in religious vocational schools. Similarly, a large proportion of high school students (more than 40%) are very afraid that their acquaintances or friends will be physically hurt while in military service. Here it is the religious

Table 1A Percentage of students endorsing the answer "Very disturbing" to the question "To what extent do terrorist acts in Israel disturb you, hurt you or are perceived as endangering you?"*

NONRELIGIOUS SCHOOLS				
Regular	Vocational	Kibbutz	Moshav	Total
60%	64%	52%	61%	61%

RELIGIOUS SCHOOLS				
Regular	Vocational	Kibbutz	Moshav	Total
65%	72%	58%	64%	68%

Grand Total = 62%[†]

*The full range of choices for this question were: Very disturbing, Disturbing, Not so disturbing, Not disturbing at all.

†The grand total of 62% represents an average weighted by the total number of respondents in each category or group. The same is true of the line totals for each group (that is, nonreligious and religious schools).

Table 1B Percentage of students endorsing the answer "Very afraid" to the question "To what extent are you afraid that your friends or acquaintances will be physically hurt during service in the military?"*

NONRELIGIOUS SCHOOLS				
Regular	Vocational	Kibbutz	Moshav	Total
47%	40%	41%	40%	44%

RELIGIOUS SCHOOLS				
Regular	Vocational	Kibbutz	Moshav	Total
43%	48%	28%	37%	45%

Grand Total = 44%[†]

*The full range of choices to this question were: Very afraid, Afraid, Not so afraid, Not afraid at all.

†As before, the totals represent weighted averages.

kibbutz schools that show the smallest amount of fear.

Having such a high proportion of students who acknowledge fear (at least some of it as a result of the *intifada*) and are strongly disturbed by terrorist acts, we wanted to examine the correlates of these emotions. Specifically, we wanted to see how they correlate with other factors such as nationalism, commitment to the country, political inclinations, and attitudes toward the Arabs (see Table 2). In our analysis we included several scales:

- A scale of *Israeli identity* that includes questions regarding attitudes toward emigration and a general perceived identity as an Israeli.

Table 2 Correlations Among Various Attitude Scales*

		1	2	3	4	5	6
1	Fear of terrorism	1.00	0.07	0.09	0.06	0.06	0.21
2	Israeli identity		1.00	0.27	0.39	0.22	0.09
3	Jewish identity			1.00	0.27	0.42	0.32
4	Nationalism				1.00	0.36	0.25
5	Against giving up territories					1.00	0.52
6	Hatred for Arabs						1.00

$n = 5,400$ All correlations are significant $p < 0.001$ [†]

*This is called an *intercorrelational matrix*. The numbers at the top of the columns refer to the same variables listed down the left-hand side of the table. This matrix measures the interrelationships of six variables. A clue to reading this table: The correlation between a variable and itself is perfect; hence, the diagonal entries are 1.00.

† p refers to the probability. This statement means that the probability is less than a tenth of a percent that these correlations could have occurred by chance.

- A scale of *Jewish identity* that measures the perceived identity as a Jew.

- A *nationalism* scale that includes questions regarding pride and belief in the nation (for instance, belief that Israel will exist forever).

- A question that asks about feelings of *hatred toward Arabs*.

- Questions regarding the occupied territories, pertaining to *left- versus right-wing* inclinations.

Several interesting results emerge from these intercorrelations:

- The different attitudes seem to be positively correlated. Jewish and Israeli identity, nationalism, being politically right wing, and hatred for the Arabs—all correlate positively with a feeling of fear and danger from terrorist acts.

- This feeling of fear and danger is only weakly correlated with attitudes of Israeli, Jewish, or national identity.

- The strongest correlation is with hatred for the Arabs: The stronger the hatred, the stronger the feeling of fear and danger.

- The hatred toward the Arabs was strongly and positively correlated with Jewish and national identity but not with Israeli identity.

The positive (though weak) correlation between feelings of fear and danger and Jewish, Israeli, and national identity is somewhat surprising. We expected, following folk beliefs, that the stronger the fear and anxiety, the stronger the inclination to leave the country or to be on the political left. As an example of such a folk belief, in a national survey performed by the Jaffee Center for Strategic Studies at Tel Aviv University, 45 percent of the respondents believed that the security situation in Israel has the impact of increasing emigration from Israel. In another survey (Landau, 1989), a strong negative correlation was found between the desire to remain in the country and security-related incidents or casualties.

Looking at Table 2, we can see that fear and anxiety do not correlate with the kinds of attitudes we expected. Rather, the contrary is true: The stronger the perceived danger, the stronger the feelings of hate toward the Arabs and the less likelihood of emigrating from Israel. Also, the stronger the perceived danger, the stronger the attitudes of nationalism and feelings of being an Israeli or being a Jew, along with a stronger inclination toward the right wing (in favor of keeping all the occupied territories even if peace is at stake).

Thus the attitudes that are associated with perceived stress are more of the "fight" type than the expected "flight" type. This trend becomes even stronger when we examine sub-populations. Specifically, we expected that heightened fear and anxiety might be correlated differently for left-wing and right-wing students. We

asked the question, "Would you consider returning some of the occupied territories for a peace settlement?" and chose as representing the left wing those students who strongly agreed to do so. As representing the right wing, we chose those students who strongly disagreed. We expected that although for the right wing correlations would be in the positive direction (more stress, more nationalism), for the left wing the correlations would be negative (more stress, less willingness to live in Israel and to feel a part of it).

We performed a two-way ANOVA (analysis of variance) on left versus right wing and low versus high feelings of danger (creating a scale that combined answers on the two questions, measuring perceived disturbance and fear). An in-depth explanation of this statistical procedure is beyond the scope of this text; however, the following findings can be easily understood:

- Students in the right wing do not seem to differ much in their (already) strong nationalistic attitudes as a function of perceived danger.

- It is rather the left-wing students who demonstrate more nationalistic, more Israeli, and more Jewish orientation along with a stronger perceived danger.

In other words, if you are a right-wing supporter, your attitude toward terrorist acts would make no difference regarding your already strong Jewish, Israeli, and national identity. However, if you are a left-wing supporter, the more you fear terrorism and the *intifada*, the stronger your Jewish and Israeli identity. Since this study is a correlational one and there is no basis for either causal direction, this finding can also be put another way: If you are a left-wing supporter, the stronger your identification as a Jew and an Israeli, the stronger your feelings of fear and perceived danger of terrorism.

What do we make of these results? As mentioned before, since this is a survey and the results are correlational, the most we can do is speculate. The following remarks should then be seen as speculations rather than conclusions. There are basically three ways of interpreting the results:

1. We could say that nationalism, being Israeli, and a Jewish identity lead students to perceive danger in terrorist acts and in military service.
2. We could say that fear and a perception of danger leads students to hate the Arabs along with strengthening national feelings as "fight" reactions to the stress. This seems to us a possible explanation, though by no means the only one. The behavior

of the left-wing students is compatible with this explanation.

3. A third possibility is that there is an underlying third factor that is correlated with both feelings of danger and an Israeli or Jewish identity.

In order to test the third possibility, we calculated *cluster analysis* of these data (see Table 3) to identify possible clusters that underlie the reported intercorrelations. We discovered two basic clusters that create the best differentiation among these variables. The result was two sub-groups of subjects—authoritarian and universalistic—that statistically differ from each other. Table 3 shows the differentiation between the two clusters through its presentation of the means for the different attitude scales.

As you can see, three of the attitude scales differentiate clearly between the two clusters. The subjects in Cluster 1 have higher Jewish identity; they are clearly against giving up the occupied territories, and they feel a stronger hatred toward the Arabs. The means for the other three attitude scales are closer.

However, the differences lead us to interpret the first cluster as demonstrating the usual pattern of the authoritarian orientation and the second cluster as presenting the liberal, universalistic, nondog-

Table 3 Cluster Analysis*

Attitudes	CLUSTER 1 N = 3,805 (AUTHORITARIAN)	CLUSTER 2 N = 1,514 (UNIVERSALISTIC)
	Means for Attitude Scales†	
1. Jewish identity	75.4	45.2
2. Against giving up occupied territories	60.0	21.3
3. Hatred toward the Arabs	67.0	36.3
4. Israeli identity	76.7	65.6
5. National identity	84.0	73.7
6. Perceived fear and danger from terrorism and war	80.7	78.0

*Editor's note: Table 3 is presented for the sake of clarity; it is derived from the Mayseless-Gal text. An explanation of the statistical procedure of cluster analysis is beyond the scope of this text.

†The first three pairs of means are sufficiently far apart to justify calling them *differentiating means*, and the next three pairs of means are sufficiently close to justify calling them *similar means*.

matic orientation. Referring to known figures such as T. W. Adorno or M. Rokeach, we find descriptions that match our findings surprisingly well. An authoritarian orientation is usually manifested through hate and fear directed at out-groups (enemies) and strong endorsement of the in-group (for example, high national identity) along with a strong inclination toward religion (Jewish identity) and a tendency to rely on authority and power (political right). The liberal, universalistic orientation is manifested in openness, flexibility, complexity, and tolerance of ambiguity. It is interesting to note that both of these orientations have very high and similar degrees of Israeli identity,

which points to the possibility that there are at least two different ways of feeling Israeli.

What we have been measuring might therefore be two different orientations in Israeli youth. In this case, the reactions to threats or dangers from terrorism or war might be incorporated into an already existing general orientation of authoritarianism or universalism, hence having little direct effect on the youngsters' attitudes.★

Ofra Mayseless and Reuven Gal are with the Israeli Institute for Military Studies.

★Editor's note: I interpret the data to mean that on average—for the group—the "already existing general orientation" may predetermine the youngsters' reactions to new threats or dangers from terrorism or war.

Once two variables are shown to be associated, we can move to prediction. While there are a number of statistical procedures that can be used, the statistical process called **regression analysis** is the one most commonly used by pollsters. The independent **variable** (say, education) is called the predictor; it is used to predict the behavior of the dependent variable (income, for example), called the criterion. When we are using one criterion and one predictor to make a prediction, we speak of *simple* (or *bivariate*) *regression*; when you are using one criterion and more than one predictor, we speak of *multiple regression*.

Comparisons

The Herzog-Rodgers study examined response distributions and compared the results for each question according to mode of interview for each age group. You will recall that the purpose of the statistical calculations was to determine whether there was a meaningful difference between the way the two age groups (interviewed first in person and then by telephone) answered each question. Using the statistical tool of **ANOVA** (analysis of variance), it is possible to compare several groups at the same time or the same group over a period of time. An interesting point about this statistical method (and statistics in general) is that it *cannot prove* there are statistically meaningful differences among groups; it merely provides some evidence that they are not the same.

Trend Analysis

Various statistical techniques (including special forms of ANOVAs) permit us to measure change over a period of time. You may be wondering why you would have to learn statistics to interpret the data you have collected. After all, don't we have computer programs such as SPSS to process the data and present us with easy-to-understand charts and graphs? The answer is both yes and no. Yes, we have computer programs to do all of that automatically, based on a single command. However, certain decisions must be made before the mechanics are turned over to the computer, and only a statistically savvy person can tell the computer which statistical tests are appropriate for which types of data. Also, while the computer program can prepare all kinds of attractive histograms, bar and line graphs, pie diagrams, frequency polygons, and so on, it does not know what the results mean.

There are, therefore, a number of questions that researchers must be able to answer before anything is done with the raw data. In fact, researchers deal with these questions in the early stages of their study design, in anticipation of their subsequent efforts to analyze the data they have collected.[2] Answers to the following questions help researchers decide which are the best statistical tools to use for analyzing data and presenting their findings:

- What is the sample size and how small will the smallest sub-groups be? This is important because it directly relates to statistical tests for significance.

- Do you want to know the degree of association (correlation) between two or more variables? And will you then want to make predictions based on correlations?

- Will you be comparing groups? If so, you will want to use certain statistical tools to determine whether the findings indicate real differences in responses or whether such differences are due to other factors, such as chance occurrence.

- Will this be a longitudinal study, conducted over a period of time? For example, will you be doing a panel study, asking the same group of people the same questions several times over a period of weeks, months, years? Or will you be using the same questionnaire with different samples over a period of time? One example: Some of us recall Ronald Reagan's question in 1980, "Are you better off now than you were four years ago?" Since then, a number of pollsters have incorporated that question into their surveys and asked it of different samples in subsequent election years. By 1992, the findings indicated that most middle- and low-income families were definitely not better off than they had been in the previous decade.

- How will your data be recorded? Will it be recorded as *categorical data* (as numbers and percentages) or as *continuous data* (as scores and averages)? Different statistical techniques are used with different types of data.

- Who is the audience for your findings? Scholars or other professionals with statistical competency, clients interested in testing the market for a new product, a political candidate concerned about strategy for an upcoming election, or the general public? Each of these audiences has different requirements. Sadly, the least demanding may well be the general public. If we look at the way political polls are presented in our local newspapers, we quickly realize how little information we are actually given and how little we are willing to accept.

TO REPORT OR NOT TO REPORT

Reports for the Press

Assuming that your survey topic is of general interest (for example, involving a political poll; a foreign policy issue, such as whether we should aid the countries of eastern Europe or the former Soviet Union; or a matter of public policy, such as a national health plan or our educational system), your findings may be reported in the press. At that point, you are confronted with an interesting problem. Yes, your painstaking effort will receive attention, but you will not have control over what is printed or omitted. Although you will no doubt have much to say, there is usually little space in which to say it. It will fall to the editor, the gatekeeper, to decide which of your findings are the most likely to attract the reader's attention, and those—and only those—will be reported. (Review "The Media, Polling, and Public Opinion" in Chapter 1). For example, a CBS/*New York Times* Poll was taken May 6–8, 1992, immediately after the riots in Los Angeles. In small type, at the bottom of the report's first page, we are told:

> This poll was conducted among a nation-wide random sample of
> 1,253 adults interviewed by telephone May 6–8, 1992. There was a
> special sampling of black respondents, so the total sample includes
> 318 black and 878 white respondents. The error due to sampling
> could be plus or minus three percentage points for results based on
> the entire sample, three points for whites and six points for blacks.
> This release conforms to the Standards of Disclosure of the
> National Council on Public Polls.[3]

The audience for this poll is not told the refusal rate, nor the confidence level of the data collected. Well, we could calculate the refusal rate on our own, and the sample size and margins of error of ±3 and ±6 do give us clues as to the confidence levels. But this is only the beginning of what we are not told about the survey. The 3-page release (issued on May 10, 1992) is attached to 21 pages, containing 63 questions and their results in percentages. There is no demographic information on where these respondents live (state, city), level of education, income, sex, ethnicity, or age. A black–white breakdown is given only for questions 20–63, pertaining to which of the candidates (George Bush, Bill Clinton, or H. Ross Perot) would do the best job of resolving economic and racial problems, the situation in Los Angeles, who or what is to blame, whether the rioting should be seen as an isolated incident or as a warning, and other racially charged issues. However, the responses to the first 19 questions are categorized only by political identification: Republican, Democrat, Independent. This series of *trial heat questions* dealt with how well President Bush was handling the job of the presidency, foreign policy, the economy; whether the respondent's opinion was favorable to Jerry Brown, Pat Buchanan, George Bush, Bill Clinton; how likely it was that the respondent would vote (an amazing 82% of all respondents said they would definitely vote in November 1992); how the respondent would vote if the election were held that day; and other such questions. The three-page summary focused only on questions pertaining to black–white issues, did not provide the exact wording of the questions, and lumped together a number of related questions (taken out of order) under the category heading that seemed the most dramatic, as in Table 10.1.

Are any of these differences in response pattern of statistical significance? There is no discussion of this either in the summary or in the report, nor is there any mention of correlations. But do readers care? Beyond reading off the percentages taken from the summary, the average newspaper reader has no idea of what is meant by one or two standard deviations or most other statistical terms. And it is beyond the scope of the press to explain the nuances implicit in statistically processed and analyzed polling data. The three-page summary does a reasonably good job of presenting the most attention-grabbing data, and the report itself is attached. But unfortunately what often happens is that a reporter—facing a deadline—may not have the time to delve into the report itself to see what ought not to be left behind. While it is true that most journalists are bright, well educated, dedicated, and hard-working, there are some who have not been schooled in the ways of polls.★ They may take a poll at face value and report the more interesting conclusions, without considering how representative of the general population the survey's sample actually was.

Although researchers generally recommend a sample size of at least 1,000 for a survey with national implications, many such polls are taken with only 500 to 700 respondents. Cynthia Crossen noted that this was the case in November 1991 when many national polls were taken about United States Supreme Court Justice Clarence Thomas' confirmation. When the sample was broken down into sub-groups of women, blacks, and so on, the margin of error was as high as 12 percent. Using a sample of 500 adults, about half of them women, the ABC/*Washington Post* Poll found that "more women" (38%) believed Clarence Thomas than believed Anita Hill's

---

★In fact, most prestigious newspapers don't even attempt to have their journalists analyze poll results. Instead, they hire experts in political science and polling to provide the necessary interpretations.

Table 10.1 The Los Angeles Riots: Blame

A LOT OF BLAME*	TOTAL	WHITES	BLACKS
Irresponsible people (Q41)	78%	80%	67%
Frustration with poverty/ discrimination (Q40)	65	65	70
Jury's verdict (Q39)	52	48	76
Reagan/Bush neglect (Q37)	40	36	65
1960s social programs (Q38)	24	22	31

*The question stem for most of the items listed was, "Would you place a lot of the blame or not much of the blame for the riots in Los Angeles on..."

allegations of sexual harassment (28%). However, with such a large margin of error, the opposite could also have been true.[4]

Aware of such problems, the National Council on Public Polls prepared a brochure entitled "Twenty Questions a Journalist Should Ask About Poll Results" (see Box 10.1). We will return to press coverage of polls after we look at how to prepare survey reports for a scholarly community.

Reports for the Scholarly Community

Reports for the scholarly community should contain the following elements:

Abstract   Approximately 150 to 250 words in length, an abstract must convey specific information about the study. The following two examples, despite certain shortcomings, will give you a sense of what an abstract should contain.

[1] This paper examines the role of race in elections where one of the candidates is black. Using the 1982 California gubernatorial election between Tom Bradley and George Deukmejian as a case study, the paper shows that whereas racial attitudes were a significant influence on the voting decisions of whites, Bradley's background did not stimulate an unusual level of racially motivated behavior. The paper argues that the impact of a candidate's race on voting depends on a number of contextual factors, including his prior record and campaign style. The paper also proposes a technique for comparing the results of biracial elections with contests where all the candidates are white as a method for estimating the level of racial voting.[5]

The subject of the study is clearly stated ("the role of race ... where one of the candidates is black"), as is the researchers' main argument ("that the impact of a candidate's race on voting depends on a number of contextual factors"). Although we are not told the sample size and certain other relevant information, we do learn that the study introduces a technique for comparison purposes that would make it possible to estimate levels of racial voting. On reading the report itself, you would learn that this technique involves the use of multivariate analysis to control for such variables as party loyalty, opinions, and nonracial issues. By controlling for those variables, the researchers were able to isolate "the role of racial attitudes" and the statistical effect of such attitudes on electoral decisions.

[2] This paper reports the results of two split-sample experiments designed to examine whether question context can reduce vote overreporting in surveys. The first experiment tests the effects of preceding the turnout item with a question about the location of the polling place. If respondents who overreport do not know where their polling place is, they should be less apt to report incorrectly about turnout after being asked the location of the poll. The second experiment tests the effects of preceding the vote item with a question about lifetime electoral behavior. If inaccuracy is due to respondents' wanting to present themselves in a favorable light, the opportunity to report past or usual good citizenship should reduce the pressure to claim participation in the last election.[6]

As well written as it is, this abstract also has some shortcomings. Compare the two abstracts with the following, which should sound familiar:

A face-to-face survey conducted in 1984 with a sample of 1491 residents of the Detroit metropolitan area (including an oversample of older adults) and a reinterview of a random subset of these respondents by telephone were used to compare the two modes of data collection across two age levels. Except for a tendency toward a disproportionately large number of DK answers and a disproportionately large amount of interviewer assistance on the telephone, respondents 60 years of age and older did not exhibit larger mode differences than did respondents under 60. For both age groups, response distributions were rather similar, suggesting little effect of mode. Likewise, response style differed little by mode, while a higher proportion of missing data (i.e., "I don't know" answers) was given on the telephone. The response rate for the telephone reinterview was 90%, somewhat lower for older than for younger persons. The findings support the feasibility of using the telephone for reinterviewing older adults.[7]

BOX 10.1   Questions Reporters Should Ask

1. What polling firm, political campaign, corporation, research house, or other group conducted the poll?
2. Who paid for the poll and why was it done? Does the motive for undertaking the poll create serious doubts about the validity of the results?
3. How many people were interviewed for the survey?
4. How were those people chosen? Was it a random probability sample, or did the respondents select themselves?
5. From what areas (nation, state, or region) or what groups (blue-collar workers, unemployed, teachers, lawyers, Democratic voters, and so on) were these people chosen?
6. Are the results based on the answers of all the people interviewed or are they based on subgroups? Are there refusals, Don't Knows, or other missing data?
7. Who should have been interviewed and was not? What was the refusal rate? From which demographic groups did these people come?
8. When was the poll conducted, and how long did it take to process the data? Since a poll is a snapshot of a moment, a drawn-out effort to gather the data may affect the poll's accuracy. Those polled later in the survey may have been influenced by some intervening event.
9. Were the interviews conducted in person, by phone, or by mail?
10. Is this a dial-in poll, a mail-in poll, or a subscriber coupon poll?
11. What is the sampling error for the poll results?
12. What other kinds of mistakes can skew poll results?
13. Specifically, what is the exact wording of the questions asked? Are they fair and unbiased?

Consider the amount and type of information contained within this abstract, which fulfills all of the following requirements:

- *Purpose*   To compare two modes of data collection across two age levels.

- *Method*   A face-to-face survey and a reinterview of a random subset.

- *Sample size*   1,491 residents of the Detroit metropolitan area, including an over sample of older adults.

- *Response rate*   90 percent, somewhat lower for older than for younger persons.

14. Does the report given to the press present the exact order in which the questions were asked?
15. What other polls have been done on this topic? Do they say the same thing? If they are different, why are they different?
16. It's two weeks before the election and the poll says it's all over. What now? As you surely realize, unexpected things do happen and people do change their minds late.
17. Was the poll a pseudo-poll, part of a fundraising effort? If so, you can be sure that the respondents, as supporters, are far from objective.
18. So I've asked all the questions and the answers sound fine. Does that mean that this poll is correct? Not exactly. The laws of chance say that because of sampling error, the results of 1 out of 20 polls may be skewed away from the actual views of the public.
19. With all these uncertainties, should the press report poll results? If the poll was conducted by a reputable firm and the public is made aware of the pitfalls, why not? A good poll is still the best way to find out what people are thinking at a particular time.
20. Is this particular poll worth reporting? Think of it as you would any other story. If the source (the polling organization that produced it) is credible and your news judgment tells you the information deserves the public's attention, why not?

Source: Based on Sheldon R. Gawiser and G. Evans Witt's *Twenty Questions a Journalist Should Ask About Poll Results* (New York: National Council on Public Polls, 1992).

- *Findings*   "Except for a tendency toward a disproportionately large number of DK answers and a disproportionately large amount of interviewer assistance on the telephone, respondents 60 years of age and older did not exhibit larger mode differences than did respondents under 60."

- *Conclusion*   "The findings support the feasibility of using the telephone for reinterviewing older adults."

Summary   The summary has more detail than the abstract, but it should not be more than approximately three pages. In addition to identifying the researchers, it distills the report's key components, including the purposes, methods, findings, and conclusions.

Table of Contents   This lists all major sections of the report, along with their page numbers.

List of Charts, Figures, Tables   This lists all illustrative materials.

Glossary   This should explain all abbreviations (for example, RDD, random-digit dialing; CATI, computer-assisted telephone interviewing) and technical or statistical terms (multiple correlation, multifactor analysis, and so on) that are used in the report.

Purposes   As noted in Chapter 5, besides political polling, market research, and opinion research for legal purposes, there are many other uses for opinion and attitude studies. Even in the case of political polling, there are various reasons for a poll to be taken. In the aftermath of the congressional banking scandal in 1992,★ many incumbents commissioned their own polls. They wanted to determine the degree of image damage caused by the news about how many checks they had each bounced. As a result, many decided not to risk defeat by seeking reelection. Also, an unknown candidate may undertake a poll to determine how well known he or she is (remember Mr. Local Politician?).

Methods   This is the factual, descriptive part of the report. It answers several types of questions. First, what *type of survey* was undertaken? Was a self-administered questionnaire sent through the mail or handed to the respondent in person—individually or in groups? Were the data gathered through telephone interviews or through face-to-face interviews? If you used a mail-in questionnaire (or any other method of data collection), what problems did you encounter and which method (if any) do you now believe would have been preferable?

   If you conducted an election poll, what type did you choose? Was it a benchmark survey or a tracking poll? LP, the fellow who wanted to run

---

★The congressional banking scandal (often referred to as the House banking scandal) occurred during the spring of 1992. The press reported that as many as 355 members of Congress had written at least one overdraft during the previous 39-month period. Many of them were guilty of repeated overdrafts totaling tens of thousands of dollars and, in a few cases, hundreds of thousands of dollars. In general, the public was angry that so many of their elected representatives were apparently abusing the public trust. Clifford Krauss, "Bank Overdrafts Split Republicans," *The New York Times*, March 11, 1992, p. A17.

for the U.S. Senate, commissioned a **benchmark survey** designed to tell him how well known he was, as well as the name recognition levels of his competitors. This type of survey generally uses a large sample of up to 4,000 nationally, with 600 to 1,000 in a state. It is conducted very early in the campaign, sometimes up to two years before the actual election. The questionnaire is designed to find out what and how much the respondent knows about the candidate, and the interviewing process can take about 30 minutes. This survey provides a *baseline* from which subsequent progress can be measured. During the summer before the election, a second benchmark survey is conducted. Benchmark surveys (accompanied by additional small polls) are effective tools for monitoring and evaluating how the candidate is doing during the campaign process. Unfortunately, as in the case of LP, when it is done too early, the results can be easily misinterpreted. LP, you will recall, concluded that since he was as well known as any of the other potential candidates, he had a good chance of winning the nomination. However, all of the potential candidates were unknown or little known even to the Democratic-party faithful. In the spring before the election, a new candidate emerged who was familiar to party regulars. This new candidate became the Democratic nominee and won the November election.

As for **tracking polls**, they are conducted on a regular basis—usually a nightly survey—during the last month or so of the campaign, and use small samples of 150 to 300 respondents. Interviews of 5 to 10 minutes focus on how the public views the candidate. The results are then compared with the public's averaged response over the three previous days. (During the last two weeks of the 1992 campaign, CNN/*USA Today* tracking polls indicated a steady erosion of support for Perot and a significant tightening of the race between Clinton and Bush, as the undecideds moved closer to a decision.)

Did you ask a series of **trial heat questions** about the potential candidacy of various individuals in an election in the distant future—the type that ask, "If the 1996 presidential election were held today and former Vice President Dan Quayle headed the Republican ticket, running against incumbent President Bill Clinton, for whom would you vote?" Or was yours an **exit poll**, taken on election day as voters left their voting places? Reporting on election polls is a far less formidable task than social scientists face when they survey to examine an aspect of the human condition.

Next, the methods section explains the *logistics* of the study. Did you have sufficient resources (facilities, supplies, experienced personnel) to accomplish what you had originally intended? When and by whom was the survey conducted? How many interviewers were selected for training? How were they trained, and how many were actually used (and why the drop-off, if any)? Although Manuel Olin's piece (see Global View 2 in Chapter 8) on the water consumption survey in Ghana was merely a summary, we were able to learn a good deal about where and how the study was conducted, how the interviewers were selected and trained, and what problems they encountered.

The methods section then explains what questions were asked by including either a sample of the questions or the entire questionnaire. Also, in this section we learn how the survey was constructed. This deals with validity and reliability by referring to the questionnaire. Who wrote the questions? What was done to ensure validity (that the survey measured what it was supposed to measure)? Were the questions relevant to the information you wanted to collect? Were they worded in a clear, unbiased, precise manner? In the closed-ended questions, were enough categories provided that respondents who felt differently were able to make different responses? Were pilot tests conducted (see The Professional Voice 7)? What was done to ensure reliability (consistency and stability)? If you used the same questionnaire again and the same method of sample selection to choose a different sample, would you get the same results? You may recall from the discussion in Chapter 8 that Backstrom and Hursh-César[8] identified four types of verification: sample verification, question verification, question reliability, and question validity.

The Professional Voice 7   The Survey Researcher as Translator

Alicia S. Schoua-Glusberg

As a survey manager, I design and manage large-scale social science surveys. The studies range from surveys of attitudes toward increasing the number of women in the Air Force, to Soviet emigres' views of life in the former USSR, American youth labor force behavior, or citizens' social and political participation in America. My work is centered on the data collection process, on how to carry it out maximizing the quality of the data and minimizing costs. An anthropologist by training, in my work I use qualitative techniques directed to enhance the quantitative process, particularly in the area of questionnaire design.

Questionnaire design in contract or client-sponsored social survey research places social scientists in the role of translator. They must translate their client's needs and wishes into questions that can be understood and answered by respondents, constructing response categories that represent respondents' possible answers. In that role of translator, survey researchers resemble ethnographers. In ethnographic research, cross-cultural researchers need to understand the meaning that words convey in the culture and context in which native consultants are expressing themselves. They also need to know how to inquire about the native culture in a way that people can understand.

When a questionnaire needs to be administered in a language other than English, one concentrates on ensuring that translation is done appropriately and that the questions make sense in the other culture. In questionnaires administered in English, one must be aware of cultural and language differences that are just as great. The language of scholarly experts often does not coincide with that of "native" experts or respondents.

This is particularly true in surveys of specific groups (for example, seasonal farm workers, divorced parents, young mothers on welfare, armed services personnel) rather than national studies. Such groups are closely related to what ethnographers call cultures, or cultural scenes—groups in which membership entails, among other things, the use of a specific jargon or language.

What qualitative techniques can then be used to translate client needs into appropriate survey questions? Structured *group interviews* in which particular questionnaire topics are discussed are more palatable to survey research than individual ethnographic interviews. This focus group approach—as it is called in market research—takes the respondent as expert rather than, or in addition to, using experts on the topic.

In the context of focus groups, one can use ethnographic interviewing techniques. For instance, survey professionals may face two types of situation when looking for response categories. They may either know the logically possible responses to a question, and simply need to find out how to phrase them so they make sense to respondents. Or they may not have the subject-matter expertise to know the most likely response categories. Either way, eliciting taxonomies in a focus group or in an initial informal open-ended pretest is a good approach to the problem. By asking "What are the other kinds of X?" or "What are the other reasons for this?" one can build a taxonomy of "kinds of" or "reasons for" X, in which the kinds of reasons will be the response categories.

Survey researchers may also face the situation in which they do not know the psychologically and culturally appropriate term for referring to a particular event or phenomenon about which they will inquire; this is especially a problem if there is reason to believe that individual variation will be great. In a survey, rather than imposing an inappropriate term on the respondents, we may ask them to provide the label they wish the interviewer to use from then on. (For example, in a long interview we may wish to refer several times to a job the respondent once held. Early on, we may ask him or her to provide a name to refer to that job later in the interview.)

While the overall design and content of a survey may well be based on the views of a subject-matter expert, questionnaire design profits immensely from consulting expert informants. Survey researchers as translators are most helpful in reconciling the needs and views of those two types of experts.

Alicia S. Schoua-Glusberg is a researcher with the National Opinion Research Center (NORC).

The methods section tells us if the information is relevant to the purpose of the survey (understanding a problem, creating a policy, mapping out a campaign strategy, selling a product, and so on). Assuming it is relevant, the next questions deal with whether it is useful and why. Will it have predictive value? For example, in Global View 4, two Israeli researchers studied the predictability of future reactions to threats or dangers from terrorism or war on the part of Israeli high school students who would soon be called to serve in their army. The researchers concluded that such reactions "might be incorporated in an already existing general orientation of authoritarianism or universalism, hence having little direct effect on the youngsters' attitudes." We can interpret this to mean that with their belief system in place, it is unlikely that the students' attitudes will change.

Next, we learn how the sample was selected and whether it proved adequate. What was the response rate? Were there problems with the follow-up calls?

Survey design is also explained. Most surveys have more than the single objective of describing. Many also seek causal explanation, evaluation, and prediction. Did your survey design enable you to meet your objectives? Did you use a single cross-sectional design that involved a random sample representative of the population at that point? For example:

A cross-section of residents of Meckleburg County (Charlotte, NC) were randomly assigned to view either one of the sexually explicit films and the sexually explicit magazine charged in the criminal case, or a control film. Before and after the viewing, residents judged the materials' appeal to a prurient interest (a shameful, morbid, unhealthy interest in sex) and patent offensiveness (community tolerance for such material).[9]

Or did you conduct an intensive study of natural clusters, such as army units, factories, schools, or hospitals? Did you do a longitudinal study? Or was your study a panel survey? Or was it some sort of combination, as in the following example?

The sources of systematic sample attrition are examined for a community-based panel survey of 1,023 Mexican American and non-Hispanic white female adolescents, 874 (85.4%) of whom were reinterviewed after two years....

This study examines the sources and impact of attrition among a sample of adolescent females surveyed at two points in time.... The data were derived from two sets of interviews conducted with an area probability sample of Los Angeles County Mexican American and non-Hispanic white adolescent females. Time 1 interviews were conducted between January 1984 and May 1985 and time 2 interviews between January 1986 and May 1987....

A three-stage cluster sample frame with an oversample of Mexican Americans was used to select respondents: census tracts, blocks, and household addresses.[10]

Or did you choose cohorts? The following segment from Nicholas Danigelis and Stephen Cutler's study provides an example:

Aging is commonly assumed to be associated with the adoption of increasingly conservative social and political attitudes.... Using three items about law and order [gun control, the courts, and capital punishment], a domain marked by conservative trends, this paper evaluates the aging-conservatism hypothesis with data drawn from 18 national surveys covering the period 1959–1985. Attitude changes in four cohorts [those who were in their 20s and 50s in 1975 and those who were in their 30s and 60s in 1985] are analyzed....

In general, if the aging-conservatism argument is correct, a trend comparison of the attitudes of different birth cohorts should show older cohorts becoming more conservative sooner, and at a faster rate, than younger cohorts....[11]

Discussion of Findings, Analysis, and Conclusions   This section includes the appropriate charts, tables, and figures. What were the results of the survey? What specific hypotheses were tested and were they proven or disproven? For example, in the survey above, Danigelis and Cutler focused on the "notion that aging is associated with a tendency toward the adoption of increasingly conservative attitudes." They wrote: "the aging-conservatism hypothesis would predict that older cohorts lead the conservative wave, showing evidence of earlier change and producing widening cohort differences."[12] In their concluding remarks, they reported that "aging does not appear to be associated with an invariable tendency toward increasingly conservative attitudes, nor does it inevitably result in attitudinal rigidification." The conclusions drawn from your analysis of the findings are interpretive statements that help the reader to understand causes and relationships and why such an understanding is important at this time. These statements are accompanied by predictive statements that explain the implications of the findings for present and future policy making. Finally, prescriptive statements, perhaps recommending the reallocation of resources, are made.

THE MEDIA AND OPINION POLLS

The assumption throughout the hard work of gathering and reporting research findings is that the subject matter is sufficiently important to have made it all worthwhile. Researchers assume that what they have to report will, in some way, affect the way we think about and deal with societal problems. Many also hope that institutional or governmental policy making, based on their findings, will follow. But what about all those political polls that constantly appear in the press? Should they be taken seriously, or are they mere media fluff? Do they convey important information that could make a positive contribution to our society, if only the findings were used correctly?

What do *you* think is the most important problem facing the United States today? That question, in some form or other, has been asked over and over again ever since George Gallup and his contemporaries helped establish public opinion polls back in the 1930s, at a time of great economic crisis for this country. Since then, polling methodology has become increasingly sophisticated, and the media have learned how to present the massive amounts of polling data in attention-grabbing ways. Consider the following three poll-related headlines from the respected *New York Times*:

Poll Shows Price Bush Pays for Tough Economic Times
(January 10, 1992)

In Poll, Voters Are Unhappy With All the Choices (*March 3, 1992*)

Clinton Dogged by Voter Doubt, Poll of U.S. Says (*April 1, 1992*)

Throughout the 1992 presidential campaign, the media competently reported on polls that indicated the American people were distressed by the lack of leadership, the impotence and gridlock of Congress, the perceived predominance of the Japanese in international trade, deterioration in race relations, the high unemployment rate, the cost of health care, the perception that the economy was still declining, and on and on. Yet those substantive issues received little attention from the candidates compared to the time allotted to comments about the "Murphy Brown" television show regarding a career woman's child being born out of wedlock, and the issue of personal and family values.

And, interestingly, although during the first phase of his campaign H. Ross Perot talked about electronic town meetings—making it sound as though our opinions were really important—he rarely discussed the major issues. His "trust me" attitude seemed to belie his stated belief in the acumen of the American people, their ability to understand proposed solutions to troublesome problems, and his professed respect for public opinion. Only when he reentered the campaign, in the fall of 1992, did he begin to provide some details of his proposals. So if all those polls reporting the so-called misery index don't translate into actual proposals for policy changes, followed by action on the part of elected officials, what purpose do they serve? I acknowledge the following purposes for polls, from least important to most important:

1. They make for interesting filler. They help generate news. Even if you ignore the amount of time the electronic media spend, you would be impressed by the amount of space given to newspaper coverage of political polling results. Try your own ministudy: During the last two or three months of the next political campaign, count the columns or pages of your favorite newspaper or magazine that are devoted to reporting, analyzing, and commenting on each poll. Then compare this amount of space to coverage of any domestic or foreign policy issue.

2. They inform and guide the candidate's media handlers (or spin masters) as to what people want to hear and which issues are best avoided. For example, in the 1988 presidential campaign, the results of focus group studies were used by George Bush's handlers. From these data they learned that the American flag and the crime rate evoked deep emotional responses. This led to lots of photo ops when Bush visited a flag factory and to Lee Atwater's infamous Willie

Horton and "revolving door" ads, which proved extremely effective in defeating the Democratic nominee, Massachusetts Governor Michael Dukakis.

3. When a candidate's ratings are high in the polls, it is often easier to raise campaign funds.

4. Polls may, according to sociology professors Kurt Lang and Gladys Engel Lang, "influence the public opinion they purport merely to measure."[13] The Langs discuss direct and indirect ways in which polls may do this:

Direct Effects of Being Interviewed   People tend to view a poll as authoritative. Once asked a question about something, most people tend to become curious. Even if they know nothing about the subject (and may or may not admit it), respondents tend to feel encouraged to learn about it. If they have voiced opinions in the past and experienced a sense of uncertainty when responding to the interviewer, they will, the Langs tell us, reflect further on what they might recognize as an inconsistency. The researchers refer to a catalytic effect on the respondent's voting behavior. In other words, once polled about election issues, not only will the respondent try to find out more about the issues in the questionnaire, but the likelihood of the individual's turning out to vote will increase.[14]

Direct Effects of the Published Findings   While little evidence was found of a *bandwagon effect* when people were generally informed about a topic or candidate, the Langs argue:

> Susceptibility to bandwagon effects is apt to be greater when an issue is just emerging, when it does not touch on firmly held and long-standing beliefs, and when the knowledge on which to base rational judgment is not generally available.

Timing also seems to be an important element when considering the impact and influence of polls. In the first stages of a campaign, people have not yet formulated their opinions; the earlier polls, therefore, appear to have a greater impact than those taken later in the campaign. If there is a bandwagon effect at all, it generally occurs early in the election process. Witness the phenomenon of Texas billionaire H. Ross Perot. Beginning with the New Hampshire presidential primary in February 1992, the American people were able to watch, on a nearly daily basis, the ups and downs of the various candidates, as well as Perot's initial incredible rise. By the end of May, even before the last of the primaries were over, voters were flocking to his camp, although he had not yet articulated his views on the major issues. The bandwagon effect was clearly operating.

The level of frustration with George Bush and Bill Clinton was apparently so high that many people were in what has been called the pink baboon mode—meaning anyone else, even a pink baboon, was preferable to either of the major contenders. Perot himself remarked during an early television appearance (before he pulled out of the race in July, only to reenter on October 1) that the American people were more interested in his principles than in his positions. However, on announcing (re-announcing?) his candidacy, Perot stressed that he would answer only questions relating to the important issues facing America. By that time, most Americans had had it with the draft issue, the extramarital affairs issue, and the family values issue. They wanted to hear about the economy, unemployment, health insurance, and how to kill the deficit.

The Langs also discuss *tactical voting*, when voters use polling results to assess the chance of a candidate's winning the election and to weigh the value of their vote. Thus, as the former senator from Massachusetts Paul Tsongas began to slip more and more in the polls during the 1992 primary season, many Democrats hesitated to waste their votes and began to look more closely at the other candidates from their party.

The same phenomenon was at work in the last days of the 1992 campaign. In late October, the polls reported a steady decline in the support Perot had rebuilt through his participation in the three debates with Clinton and Bush. Although Perot's advertising campaign was initially considered more effective (dealing first with economic issues and then with mushy stories told by friends and family about what a wonderful person he was), he was hurt by his accusations of Republican dirty tricks.* Once again, people began to have second thoughts about Perot and may well have been concerned about wasting their votes. With a number of commentators openly questioning his sanity, and with the allegations against the Republicans unsubstantiated, Perot was once again put on the defensive. The polls soon indicated his loss of support and a tightening of the race between President Bush and Governor Clinton.

Indirect and Cumulative Effects of Published Findings Referring to Elisabeth Noelle-Neumann's spiral-of-silence theory (see Box 7.1), the Langs cite evidence to support the notion that as negative polling data accumulate on a particular candidate or position, "holders of the minority viewpoint are apt to lapse into silence, rather than argue, when confronted

---

*The dirty tricks were supposedly threats to disrupt his daughter's upcoming wedding. Perot's decision to withdraw in July was therefore based primarily on his desire to protect his family.

with an opinion contrary to their own."[15] Once again, education is a key factor when determining the impact of the spiral of silence. The more information the person has, the less likely it is that he or she would be influenced by the cumulative effect of polls.

Two examples of the cumulative impact of polling results are offered. The first involves President Richard Nixon and his unrestrained, steady slide in the polls as more and more information about the Watergate break-in was published. As the hearings on television continued, the polls documented Nixon's decline, and even many of his formerly ardent supporters began to fall silent as the climate of opinion turned against his continuing in office, and he was forced to resign on August 9, 1974.

The second example involves a reverse situation for President Ronald Reagan, the so-called great communicator. Reagan, a former actor, understood the nuances of television and was able to quiet earlier fears of his having a Rambo-like mentality. Called the Teflon president because it seemed that no matter what mistake he had made or what scandal approached the White House, nothing seemed to stick to him, he was, in the view of many millions of Americans, Mr. Nice Guy. The Langs point out that in Reagan's first years in office, the polls confirmed his popularity, strengthened "his presumed mandate and helped him push through a budget, make cuts in domestic programs, and give him a relatively free hand in arms negotiations and foreign policy."

Still another indirect and cumulative effect occurs when polls act as a *corrective* to a collective misperception or ignorance within society. Early studies dealing with public opinion on AIDS showed an enormous intolerance, based on a lack of knowledge. As more people became better informed, their opinions began to change. It remains to be seen whether the cumulative effect of polling results indicating such opinion shifts will act as a corrective, leading to greater understanding, tolerance, and concern on the part of government to fund advanced medical research to discover a cure.

James Fallow, the former chief speechwriter for President Jimmy Carter, commented that the polling data he usually saw when he was part of the Carter administration were "connected with the *salesmanship* of a program, as opposed to the development of its policy." Using the ratification process of the Panama Canal Treaty as an example of how polling data were used as a means to design tactics, Fallow said that the data revealed that most people thought the United States owned the Panama territory, and as many as 70 percent to 90 percent thought it was a bad idea to just give it away. The data also revealed what people thought the impact of the treaty would be. The Carter administration was able to use the polling results to develop effective arguments in support of senatorial ratification.[16] Thus, according to

Fallow, polling data should be used to help political leaders decide *how* to do something, not *what* to do.

Do media + polls + opinion (still) = opinon polls? The implication is that there *was* a time when polls represented the opinions of those sampled by independent researchers, and the media's role was simply to publish the results. However, I would argue that today the media set the communication agenda[17] and therefore play a far greater role than merely publishing the pollsters' data. In 1990, ABC News, CBS News, CNN, and NBC News created Voter Research and Surveys. *The New York Times* and CBS News have also cooperated in polling efforts. Other newspapers and television stations around the country have either taken their own polls or commissioned polling organizations to do so. Either way, the report becomes their property, to dissect any way they wish. As discussed earlier, I believe that while most journalists assigned to write an article based on such reports are competent to do so, there are those who are less experienced and who may not have the background necessary to correctly interpret the data.

Susan King, a former chairperson of the Consumer Product Safety Commission, talked about her experiences conducting trend analyses with the help of polling data. Dealing with government policy making in the regulatory area of product safety, she found polls useful in identifying the issues and problems that bothered people. However, she noted that "polls are not useful to us (at least from my position) in terms of offering much in the way of policy guidance.... What we are to do is quite clear: It's set down in the law."[18] On the negative side, King spoke about the contradictions that can occur within a single poll; she cited as one example a Harris poll of May 1978, when creation of the Consumer Protection Agency was being considered. Consider the following findings from that poll:

- 58 percent of the respondents favored creation of such an agency
- 28 percent opposed it
- 69 percent said creation of such an agency was long overdue
- 65 percent agreed that consumers needed such an agency to fight big business and to protect consumer interests

Sounds good, right? The problem was that 52 percent agreed with the statement "Another bureaucracy would just lead to more red tape and higher taxes, and probably wouldn't help protect the consumer at all." Such a contradiction—wanting consumer protection and fearing the agency needed to fulfill that mission—is illustrative of the problems King found with polls. "I suggest," she added, "that here polls helped shape the debate." Polls and the media can narrow the focus of the public's attention from a general concern (such as fear of excessive government regulation) to a specific area (creation of the Consumer Protection Agency).

Are pollsters measuring the public's views, or are they measuring the media's influence? Nixon supporters would cite the televised Watergate hearings and newspaper articles targeting the administration as an influence on public opinion to reject the Nixon presidency.

Has the poll become a research tool of the media? This is food for thought because polls are now usually front-page news. Or have the media fallen captive to the pollsters? Although we do not know the degree of the media's impact, we do know the media can affect public opinion, and researchers such as the Langs have studied the ways in which polling results themselves can shape opinion. The question is whether we now have a situation in which the polls, which are meant to *measure* public opinion, have become a tool to *influence* public opinion. Is the tail now wagging the dog?

Susan King, speaking of the way polling results may have become a "force that drives rather than reflects public opinion," gave the following as an example:

> An event in the regulatory community—the appearance of Dr. Murray Weidenbaum's study from Washington University in St. Louis on cost-benefit analysis and how much government regulation was costing the American public—was picked up by pollsters. There followed a shift in public opinion, as Harris reflected a few months later. For the first time, the public registered strong opposition to additional government regulation and, for the first time, agreed with the statement that there is too much government regulation of the private sector.[19]

Do the media + polls + opinion = mediated opinion polls? I think the answer is yes. I therefore also think that we should all consider the implications of mediated opinion polls.

CHAPTER REVIEW

- Special computer programs, such as the SPSS (Statistical Package for the Social Sciences), have made it possible to enter data directly into a computer.

- Coded questionnaires use preassigned numbers for fixed alternative responses, and interviewers circle or blacken the code that matches the response given.

- Optical scanning devices have made it possible to communicate hand-coded information to a computer.

- There are five steps to coding or data reduction to prepare survey data for analysis: (1) creating, formatting, and organizing a data file; (2) designing a code; (3) coding (if a precoded questionnaire is used, the interviewer accomplishes this function while recording the responses); (4) data entry (includes verification, the process whereby a different person enters the data a second time, checking the second entry with the first; CATI has made it possible for the computer-assisted telephone interviewer to read the question off the screen and to enter the data directly into the computer as the respondent answers each question); and (5) data cleaning.

- Measures of central tendency—the means, medians, and modes—tell us how similar or typical responses are.

- *Frequency* refers to how often a particular number (result, score, response) appears.

- Measures of dispersion or variation are used to measure the differences among respondents. Range, one of at least 20 ways to compute variability, is the easiest and crudest measure. Two other measures of dispersion are variance and standard deviation.

- The mean, percent of total, range, and standard deviation (all called descriptive statistics) enable us to identify and describe important characteristics of our data. They are the building blocks for inferential statistics, which enables us to draw conclusions from the data.

- When characteristics appear to accompany each other, they are said to be correlated. Statistical tests are used to determine the significance of correlation coefficients.

- A finding is statistically significant if it provides enough evidence to reject the null hypothesis (also known as the default answer). When we reject the null hypothesis, we accept the alternate hypothesis (our original hypothesis), a proposition or statement such as "Drugs are the number one problem in America."

- The burden is on the researcher to provide sufficient evidence to support the alternate hypothesis, thereby rejecting the null hypothesis.

- Once association is established between two or three variables, we can move to prediction. This statistical process is called regression. Bivariate regression refers to the use of two variables (one criterion and one predictor) to make a prediction; when we are using one criterion and more than one predictor, we speak of multiple regression.

- Using the statistical tool of ANOVA (analysis of variance), it is possible to compare several groups at the same time or the same group over a period of time. Neither this statistical method nor any other statistical method can prove there are statistically meaningful differences among groups; it can merely provide evidence that they are not the same.

■ Various statistical techniques (including special forms of ANOVAs) permit us to undertake trend analysis—measuring change over a period of time.

■ Aware of problems with press coverage of polls, the National Council on Public Polls prepared a brochure entitled "Twenty Questions a Journalist Should Ask About Poll Results." What are the major questions a journalist should ask about a poll before writing an article about its findings?

■ Survey reports prepared for a scholarly audience should include an abstract; a summary that distills the report's key components; a table of contents; a list of charts, figures, and tables; a glossary; and discussions dealing with the purposes, methodology, findings, analyses, and conclusions.

■ A benchmark survey, conducted early in the campaign, is designed to find out what and how much the respondent knows about the candidate. It provides a baseline from which subsequent progress can be measured.

■ Tracking polls, which use small samples of 150–300 persons, are usually conducted on a nightly basis during the last month or so of a campaign. The results are compared with the public's averaged response over the three previous days.

■ A series of trial heat questions ask about the potential candidacy of various individuals in an election in the distant future.

■ Can you discuss the issues raised by the idea of mediated opinion polls?

NOTES

1. Charles H. Backstrom and Gerald Hursh-César, *Survey Research*, 2nd ed. (New York: Wiley, 1981), Chapter 6, p. 325; also see Floyd J. Fowler, Jr., *Survey Research Methods* (Beverly Hills: Sage, 1984), Chapter 8, for another good technical book on this subject.

2. Arlene Fink and Jacqueline Kosecoff, *How to Conduct Surveys: A Step-by-Step Guide* (London: Sage, 1989), pp. 75–77.

3. CBS News/*New York Times* May National Poll (New York: CBS News), May 6–8, 1992, p. 1.

4. "Margin of Error—Studies Galore Support Products and Positions, But Are They Reliable?" *The Wall Street Journal*, Nov. 14, 1991, pp. A1, A9.

5. Jack Citrin, Donald Philip Green, and David O. Sears, "White Reactions to Black Candidates: When Does Race Matter?" *Public Opinion Quarterly* (1990), Vol. 54, p. 74.

6. Stanley Presser, "Can Changes in Context Reduce Vote Overreporting in Surveys?" *Public Opinion Quarterly* (1990), Vol. 54, pp. 586–593.

7. A. Regula Herzog and Willard L. Rodgers, "Interviewing Older Adults: Mode Comparison Using Data from a Face-to-Face Survey and a Telephone Resurvey," *Public Opinion Quarterly* (1988), Vol. 52, p. 84.

8. Backstrom and Hursh-César, pp. 297–298.

9. Daniel Linz, Edward Donnerstein, et al., "Estimating Community Standards: The Use of Social Science Evidence in an Obscenity Prosecution," *Public Opinion Quarterly* (1991), Vol. 55, pp. 80–112.

10. Carol S. Aneshensel, Rosina M. Becerra, et al., "Participation of Mexican American Female Adolescents in a Longitudinal Panel Survey," *Public Opinion Quarterly* (1989), Vol. 53, pp. 548–562.

11. Nicholas L. Danigelis and Stephen J. Cutler, "Cohort Trends in Attitudes About Law and Order: Who's Leading the Conservative Wave?" *Public Opinion Quarterly* (1991), Vol. 55, pp. 24–49.

12. Danigelis and Cutler, p. 43.

13. Kurt Lang and Gladys Engel Lang, "The Impact of Polls on Public Opinion," *The Annals of the American Academy* (AAPSS) (March 1984), pp. 129–142.

14. Robert E. Kraut and John B. McConahay, "How Being Interviewed Affects Voting," *Public Opinion Quarterly* (1973), Vol. 37, pp. 398–406.

15. Lang and Lang, p. 139.

16. "The User's Perspective: A Round Table on the Impact of the Polls," *Polling on the Issues*, A. H. Cantril, ed. (Cabin John, MD: Seven Locks Press, 1980), pp. 134–138.

17. Interesting books on this subject include: Robert M. Entman's *Democracy Without Citizens* (New York: Oxford University Press, 1989); Michael Parenti's *Make-Believe Media: The Politics of Entertainment* (New York: St. Martin's Press, 1992); and Kathleen Hall Jamieson and Karlyn Kohrs Campbell's *The Interplay of Influence: News, Advertising, Politics, and the Mass Media* (Belmont, CA: Wadsworth, 1992).

18. Cantril, pp. 138–139.

19. Cantril, p. 140.

PART III

The Ubiquitous Pollsters

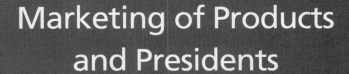

11

Marketing of Products and Presidents

Think about—

What are some of the similarities and differences between pollsters and marketing researchers?

What is the difference between Merton's "focussed interview" and the focus group interview?

What unique contributions do qualitative and quantitative research methods make to marketing?

Why is there a debate over the focus group phenomenon? How have focus groups been used to market candidates?

What is the dark side of focus groups?

What is PRIZM?

What is meant by psychographic market segmentation? How does this technique differ from PRIZM?

What constitutes an ideal test market?

What is the problem with corporate-sponsored studies?

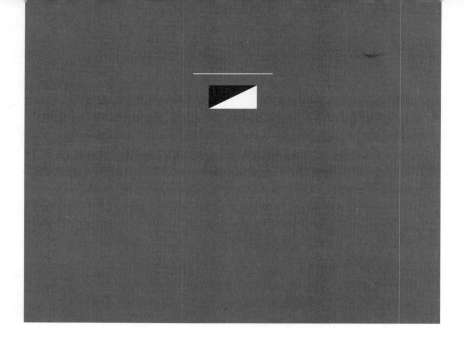

Much of what consumer or marketing researchers do is similar to the work of pollsters. They too use interviews to gather information regarding what various groups think and how they feel about certain issues; they are also concerned with techniques of sampling, questionnaire design, and analysis in order to understand the meaning of the data they collect.[1] However, the issues marketing researchers examine are often quite different from those pollsters examine. Another point of interest is that marketing research yields the information that forms the basis of an advertising campaign.

Also, marketing researchers often rely on qualitative surveys—usually in the form of focus group interviews—to a far greater extent than do independent pollsters. Please take note of the adjective *independent*. This is to differentiate between those who poll for news organizations and those who are hired by candidates. As we will see later in this chapter, political pollsters who have gone to work for candidates are resorting more and more to focus group interviews in order to fashion a saleable image.

THE HISTORY OF FOCUS
GROUP INTERVIEWS

You will recall from Chapter 2 that in November 1941, just weeks before the attack on Pearl Harbor that precipitated our declaration of war, the Office of Facts and Figures★ invited Paul Lazarsfeld, the renowned sociologist at Columbia University and the founding director of the Office of Radio Research, to test audience responses to radio morale programs. Lazarsfeld was joined by Robert Merton and other colleagues—social scientists, mathematicians, statisticians, and philosophers.

On Merton's first trip to the studio with Lazarsfeld, he noted the primitive polygraph-type device that would later became known as the Lazarsfeld-Stanton program analyzer. (This device was the forerunner of techniques used today to record audience reaction to television programs.) Discussing this experience some 46 years later, Merton explained that the dozen or so members of the audience were simply asked to listen to a recorded radio program and to express their negative reactions by pressing the red button or their positive reactions by pressing the green button. Merton was critical of the way in which one of Lazarsfeld's assistants questioned them about their likes and dislikes. He explained that the interviewer

> was not focussing sufficiently on *specifically* indicated reactions, both individual and aggregated. He was inadvertently guiding responses; he was not eliciting spontaneous expressions of earlier responses when segments of the radio program were being played back to the group.[2]

Merton joined the research effort; with the outbreak of war, he found himself interviewing groups of young soldiers in army camps, questioning them about their responses to the morale-building films created by Hollywood (Frank Capra and others) and the army. The researchers found that "Even though Frank Capra thought he was reaching hoi polloi, these kids didn't know what he was talking about."[3] The result was that the messages of subsequent films were simplified and often included cartoon-style figures drawn by Walt Disney Studio artists. By 1943, Merton and the other

---

★The OFF in Washington, DC, was the predecessor of World War II's Office of War Information (OWI), which was, in turn, the predecessor of Voice of America and the United States Information Agency.

researchers for the army were using focused interviews with individuals as well as with groups, and with civilians as well as with soldiers.

Merton points out that, contrary to today's use of qualitative data from focus group interviews, the data at that time were not considered to be "demonstrated findings." Qualitative data collected from these early interviews were not seen as an end product. For Merton and his colleagues, the focused interview was therefore closer to a starting point for their research because it provided an opportunity to test and refine their questions and was a source of "new ideas and new hypotheses."[4] (For an example of such a focused group interview see Nancy Kaplan's description in The Professional Voice 8.)

The Professional Voice 8 Focus Interviews with People Who Are Deaf and Hard-of-Hearing
Nancy Kaplan

In the spring of 1990, The Caption Center asked me to organize focus groups for the study of Deaf and Hard-of-Hearing[1] individuals to help in the development of style guidelines for the captioning of music videos. (Captioning refers to the words and symbols on the TV screen to allow viewers to see what is being spoken.) The initial study was limited to two groups within a specific geographic area. If the data gathered were deemed useful, additional focus group studies from various populations would follow.

As I began to work on this subject, idealism quickly gave way to reality. I realized that most of the guidelines used in focus group research were not going to be possible and that I would have to adapt, discard, or in some cases just create new rules in order to accommodate this specific population. Traditional focus group research calls for the use of relatively homogeneous populations. Criteria such as age, gender, education, and economic background are generally considered.

For this study, it was determined that all participants had to be Deaf and that they had to be able to *sign*, using American Sign Language (ASL) as their primary means of communication. Other considerations, such as timely availability of the participants, created some difficulties. However, with the assistance of the Lexington School for the Deaf in Jackson Heights, Queens, New York, two somewhat different groups were put together.

For the purpose of screening, questionnaires were initially distributed to about 50 potential participants. Of these, approximately 50 percent were returned. In evaluating the returned questionnaires, a number of respondents were automatically eliminated because some were unfamiliar with captioning, others did not use sign language, and many were simply unavailable for the scheduled focus groups. Left with only nine seemingly qualified participants and with an approaching deadline, we determined that as long as a participant was Deaf and communicated in an acceptable form of sign language, he or she would be accepted for our study.

The first focus group, which consisted of 11 high school seniors, all honor students, went well. Unfortunately, unforeseen problems did occur with the second group. This group consisted of 10 men and women in their 20s who were part of VECTOR, an evening program at Lexington. The VECTOR program is an educational, vocational, and social outreach program that attracts individuals whose educational level and vocational skills are generally below average. Some of the participants who showed up as we were about to begin had not completed a questionnaire but asked if they could still participate. Since this group was so small, we permitted them to participate. We did not then realize that two of the new participants could not read.

Katie Tryon, from The Caption Center's Boston office, was selected as our moderator. She was perfectly suited to this role because she was adept at keeping the conversation moving, was tactful when acting as referee or devil's advocate, and as a Deaf woman herself, she was able to communicate in the language of the groups. This helped create a sense of camaraderie and quickly put the participants at ease. Katie was provided with a moderator's guide to ensure that all areas to be researched were covered during the discussions.

At her suggestion, a Koosh ball was used to prevent more than one person at a time from signing. If a participant wanted to communicate, he or she would request the ball; the person with the ball was the one who had the floor. Throwing this brightly colored ball around made it fun for the participants while bringing a sense of order to the proceedings. If too many people had tried to sign at the same time, chaos would have resulted.

Of the many unique features of this focus group study, one element that had an impact on the overall structure was the placement of all people and objects involved. Ordinarily, focus group participants sit around a large table. In this in-stance, the need for two ASL in-terpreters was of primary impor-tance, and their placement was critical. Katie had her own inter-preter, who had to position her-self across from where Katie was seated. The Lexington School provided a second interpreter, who positioned herself near Katie so that she could see and interpret those participants who were sign-ing to the moderator. Since all the participants would be communi-cating in sign language, they had to be able to see each other as well as the video monitor being used for screening the music videos. And there could be no obstruc-tions between any of the partici-pants or between the participants and the monitor.

In addition, everything had to be visible to the video camera being used to tape each session. The videotape later served to ver-ify interpretations. Fortunately, the room we used provided enough space for the participants to form a semicircle in front of the television monitor, and after about 20 min-utes all those involved found their ideal positions.

Lighting was also a critical fac-tor. Although the lights had to be dimmed during the viewing of the videos, it was important that the general lighting be good enough so that the signing was easily seen by all participants, as well as for the video camera being used to docu-ment the proceedings. The ideal room would have had a one-way mirror, enabling Caption Center representatives to view the discus-sion without being obtrusive.[2]

To begin the discussion, Katie introduced herself and explained the purpose of our project. Then the groups were shown three ver-sions of each of four different music videos. Each was first shown without captioning and then a second and third time with two variations of captioning. Some participants had never seen captioning before and some had difficulty following the speed of the captioning. Also, as mentioned earlier, it was only during the dis-cussion that we determined two participants were unable to read. While they did not admit that, their comments were of little use to this particular study.

Despite the difficulties encoun-tered in this unique undertaking, the two initial focus groups pro-vided detailed, qualitative re-sponses to the music video stimuli. While useful tools in the early stages of research, such data should be followed by more rigorous quantitative research. In our initial effort, we used only two groups, hardly enough of a sample on which to base any long-term deci-sions. However, we were able to draw the following generally useful conclusions that have since become part of the policy used when music videos are captioned at The Caption Center:

- The person who uses captioning when watching television wants to know as much as possible—for example, who is speaking at any given time.

- Specific to music videos, the use of captions to inform the viewer about what instruments are playing when there are no lyrics (as opposed to not showing any captioning at all during those instrument-only bridges), as well as the style of music (for example), enhances the viewer's perception and enjoyment of the video.

- Placement of captioning is critical. The location of words is directly related to the location of performers within the frame. Although the intention may be to provide variety and/or to provide the viewer with a sense of the rhythm of the piece, such variation of location can unintentionally mislead the viewer.

Nancy Kaplan is a professor in the communication arts department at Hofstra University.

1. In this essay I have capitalized the words *Deaf, Hearing,* and *Hard-of-Hearing* because I am using these terms to refer to specific groups and the culture with which they identify. In other words, *Deaf* refers to those people who identify with sign-language communities and their values; *deaf* means unable to hear. For further explanation, see James Woodward, *How You Gonna Get to Heaven If You Can't Talk with Jesus: On Depathologizing Deafness* (Silver Spring, MD: T. J. Publishers, Inc., 1982).

2. One unforeseen problem was discovered once we got under way. The Lexington School is located next to LaGuardia Airport, and the noise from low-flying planes, while not disturbing the participants, made it difficult for hearing observers to hear the interpreters. And, of course, this noise was also recorded by the video camera.

As the focused interview moved from the uptown academic world of New York's Columbia University to the midtown business world of Madison Avenue, it became known as the focus group interview. With this shift into marketing came "the quick would-be conversion of new plausible insights into demonstrable gospel truths."[5] Leo Bogart, also critical of today's focus group interview, sees it as a "barbarism" designed to provide the clients of the marketing research agency—unseen behind a one-way mirror—with the feeling that "they are themselves privy to the innermost revelations of the consuming public."[6]

Joshua Libresco, commenting on how the focus group interview can provide "valuable clues for the client in making his message understood," notes that respondents are generally more comfortable talking to each other than to the interviewer. Writing in *Public Opinion*, Libresco tells an amusing story about a focus group discussion concerning women's underwear. It seems that the first thing the female moderator did was to tell the participants—all women—that the discussion would be taped and observed. However, when a model entered the room wearing a brassiere, the participants—forgetting about the observers—began to remove their own blouses in order to compare their brassieres with the model's. The moderator, it seems, was the only one in the room who remembered the one-way mirror and the male observers behind it.[7]

Although Libresco points out that the flexibility provided by group interviewers makes it possible to experiment with different questions, he warns:

> The greatest danger in using group discussions lies in the possibility that their results will be over-interpreted. In fact, some of the advantages of group discussions can be detrimental to careful analysis—the moderator's flexibility can influence the order and character of the discussion from one group to the next.

And, depending on the participants, the particular topic can either provoke extensive comment or fail to stimulate interest. Therefore, the much-touted freewheeling atmosphere of a focus group may, in fact, never materialize.

As to how representative of the population at large the results of a focus group may be, Libresco reminds us that people participate to varying degrees and that group discussions—unless closely monitored by the moderator—can be dominated by those with the strongest personalities. As a result of such drawbacks, "it becomes dangerous to base any important decision solely on the results of several group discussions." The results of focus group interviews should be considered preliminary, with more definitive conclusions necessarily being drawn from quantitative studies, which are, by the way, easier to defend and usually easier to report.[8] On the other hand, in an interview with Laurie Riederman (see The Professional Voice 9), Lewis Gediman, president of The Gediman Research Group, Inc., argues the virtues of qualitative research.

The Professional Voice 9
An Interview with Lewis M. Gediman

Laurie Riederman

LR: Lew, can you please tell us something about your background and about a marketing research project that led to a revised marketing strategy?

LG: I started this company 13 years ago and had been in the business many years before that, starting out as a field interviewer and then working my way up....

One example of a research project that led to a revised marketing strategy is one that many people are familiar with—the cake mix and the egg. Advertising for cake mixes originally stressed convenience. But from focus group research it was learned that when it came to cake baking, women liked to be more role-involved and feel they were preparing more of it on their own. What researchers found was that if you made it necessary for a woman to add a fresh egg, you could address some of those role-involvement concerns without compromising too much of the basic convenience values of the cake mix. So the revised strategy still stressed the convenience factor but let the woman participate more in the cake's preparation.

Sometimes research findings change the strategy in a subtle way. The GE Spacemaker line of appliances that fit under the shelf or cabinet, like toaster ovens, were originally called Space*savers*. That was the strategy, saves you space.

It sounds like a subtle distinction, but in consumer research it turned out to be very important. It's better to *make* space than to *save* space. *Spacesaver* was seen as a kind of negative approach, saying, "God, I've got to save a little of my precious space." *Spacemaker* is much more positive. "Hey, I'm making space! I'm putting this thing under the cabinets. I've made space on the countertop!"

LR: How accurate are the research findings and can they be wrong?

LG: Sure, they can be wrong at times. There is a widespread belief that quantitative findings are more reliable than qualitative findings; that large-scale, structured survey results are more reliable than, say, a few focus groups.

Quantitative research is faster, easier. It has the appearance of precision, because it's all computer-processed. It gives managers a comfortable feeling because it's numerical, therefore it must be true. And I think they very often make too many decisions on sheer number crunching that turn out to be bad decisions because they were based on irrelevant or even misleading numbers.

With qualitative research, you can have an in-depth interview where you let the respondent talk at length about a subject. If it's a focus group, you can really dig deeply into thoughts and feelings, getting interaction going among the respondents. You can explore a subject, uncovering the full range of thoughts and feelings consumers have.

In quantitative research, by definition, "in quantity," you don't have that luxury of actually conversing with people. You are setting up a series of response alternatives, structured questions and scales. You're giving respondents the range of answers, like multiple choice, so they can't qualify their answers or say "I don't like any of these choices." Although

sometimes they can [qualify their answers]—there might be an open-ended question or a "why," enabling them to explain their response—by and large, quantitative research is dependent on very good prior knowledge of the possible range of responses.

However, you don't always know what these responses will be beforehand, so how can you pre-structure response alternatives before you talk to people to find out what's on their minds?

LR: Is this why you specialize in qualitative research?

LG: Well, I don't know which came first, the chicken or the egg. I don't want to knock all quantitative research; we even do some. But when it comes to finding out what consumers really feel and think about a subject, I think qualitative is more useful.

Laurie Riederman is an interviewer who specializes in interviewing corporate executives and professionals. Lewis M. Gediman is the president of The Gediman Research Group, Inc., in Stamford, Connecticut.

MARKETING POLITICAL CANDIDATES

As the focus group interview became part of the marketing research process, it also became a tool of political consultants who understood:

- the dynamic process of image building and the role of the focus group as a source of qualitative data

- the purposes and uses of political polling
- the way in which polling can be a magnifier of successful and unsuccessful image-building attempts
- the ability of polls to provide quantitative data on which to base corrective tactics to build an image when prior attempts have not been successful
- the functions of the media consultant

Thomas Rosser Reeves, Jr., of the Ted Bates advertising agency, was a great believer in the power of television to persuade people to buy products of all sorts. In 1948, he approached New York's Governor Thomas Dewey with the proposal that TV spots could make the difference in what seemed sure to be a close election. Dewey turned him down with a comment that he didn't think it would be a dignified thing for him to do.

However, General Dwight D. Eisenhower recognized the potential of television. By the time he first ran for the presidency in 1952, a transcontinental cable linked nationwide networks, making it possible for a candidate to be seen, simultaneously, on some 19 million television sets around the country. The general hired Reeves, who put together a series of spots called "Eisenhower Answers America." To make these commercials, Reeves spliced footage, filmed at different times, of audience questions and the candidate's answers.[9] One might consider this studio audience as a large focus group raising questions about issues that disturbed them. By today's standards, the resulting spots appear amateurish, staged, and stodgy. Yet they successfully presented the already popular general in a friendly, likable way, minus his glasses—even though his eyesight was extremely poor. By contrast, the campaign spots of the Democratic candidate, Adlai E. Stevenson, the little-known governor of Illinois, made him appear to the average American too intellectual and too aloof. In short, Governor Stevenson had an image problem.

Reeves was one of the foremost advocates of using USP, a unique selling proposition, to market the general. He approached George Gallup and said he was looking for the one issue that most troubled Americans, but Gallup's research yielded three: corruption, rising taxes and inflation, and the Korean War. Reeves transformed these into Korea, corruption, and cost of living (the alliteration created a memorable campaign slogan), the equivalent of a unique selling proposition to sell Eisenhower. He then focused the general's attention on these issues, positioning him as the man of peace, decency, and fiscal responsibility. Although Stevenson's team blasted the Madison Avenue hucksters, the Republicans continued to air their spots. These soon included animation by Disney Studios, accompanied by a lively jingle that concluded "Everybody likes Ike!" By late September, Eisenhower had a 15-point lead, some 4 points higher than the ultimate poll, the November vote.[10]

The fresh, clean images of Eisenhower that flashed across our television sets endure for many. So, too, endures the unsmiling, serious, and nervous-looking image of vice-presidential candidate Richard M. Nixon during his famous "Checkers" speech on September 23, 1952.* James Kearns, Jr., of the *St. Louis Post-Dispatch* reported that Nixon had been carefully coached by TV experts.[11] Whether this was true or not, the speech saved Nixon's candidacy and permitted the Eisenhower-Nixon campaign to go forward to an impressive victory in November and to eight years in the White House. It paid to listen to the image makers.

If 1952 marks the beginning of candidate image making by media professionals, 1960 marks the beginning of extensive publicity for the pollsters themselves. John F. Kennedy hired Louis Harris, and Richard Nixon chose George Gallup's former partner Claude Robinson, head of the Opinion Research Corporation.[12] The year 1960 also marks the beginning of the televised debate as an opportunity for image making by the candidates themselves. Approximately 85 million Americans[13] saw at least one of the four televised debates; public opinion researchers consistently found that viewers of the first debate on September 26, 1960, considered the youthful, tanned, healthy-looking Kennedy the winner. On the other hand, I and many other radio listeners thought Nixon had won.

While the previous day's polling results gave Nixon an insignificant 1-point lead, two weeks after the debate he trailed Kennedy by 3 percentage points—still within the margin of error.[14] Given the usual 3- to 4-point margin of error, the polls were indicative of what would be an extremely close election. Kennedy, hailed as the first television president, won by only 118,550 votes,[15] leaving Richard Nixon to lament his miscalculation of having placed greater importance on what he was going to say than on how he looked. The impact of the televised debate on public opinion was so great and the fear of failure so strong that for 16 years, presidential candidates eschewed the challenge. Not until 1976 would they again agree to appear in such a television format.

---

*Attacked for illegally using campaign funds for personal purposes, Nixon went on television to defend himself and his position on the ticket with Eisenhower. Carefully explaining his personal finances and stating that his wife Pat owned only a modest cloth coat, Nixon admitted that, yes, he had received one gift, which he gave to his young daughters, a puppy called Checkers, which he would not return. On completing his speech, he called upon the American people to indicate by mail or telegram whether they supported his remaining as Eisenhower's running mate. The result was an enormous outpouring of support.

Theodore White explains that public opinion studies fascinated President Lyndon B. Johnson because of their ability to show the contrasts between Republican and Democratic attitudes, measures of voter concern, and approval ratings.[16] In the spring of 1964, the Johnson staff commissioned a confidential poll on the Maryland primary, where 43 percent of the Democratic vote had gone to Alabama's George Wallace. Oliver Quayle & Company provided a 55-page study containing voter profiles and issue measurements. Based on their poll, they reported that Americans were most frustrated and concerned with the seemingly endless Cold War. While the president was doing well on bread-and-butter issues, Democratic strength in the major cities was eroding as a result of a white backlash against black urban violence. However, the polls also told Johnson that this loss of support was "overmatched by a contrary drift of Republicans" to the president.[17]

The Quayle organization was subsequently commissioned to conduct polls on the Indiana and Wisconsin primary results, which confirmed the threat of a Democratic backlash. Yet the Wisconsin study indicated Johnson had surprising support among the traditionally Republican dairy farmers. In June, the Quayle pollsters went to Maine, where the results indicated that Johnson held a commanding lead over Nixon and that approximately half of those who had voted for Nixon in 1960 would consider switching to Johnson as their likely choice. In the end, it was not Richard Nixon who received the Republican nomination to run against the president but Arizona's Senator Barry Goldwater, a man who would also have image problems.

The growing importance of marketing an image became clear during the subsequent Johnson–Goldwater campaign, with the controversial "daisy girl" commercial created for Johnson by Tony Schwartz and the firm of Doyle Dane Bernbach. A little girl was shown picking the petals off a daily while a voice counted down, "10-9-8-7..." and then the world exploded. Although it did not mention Senator Goldwater's name and was shown only once during the campaign, it caused viewers to acknowledge their fear of nuclear war. As subsequent focus group studies have shown, and as Tony Schwartz believes, the best political commercials are not specific, enabling viewers to interpret the message any way they wish.[18]

In addition to the one-time use of the "daisy girl," the Johnson media team put together an extremely effective series of TV spots portraying President Johnson as the only sane choice in the nuclear age. One month before election day, the polls reflected the successful image making of the Johnson team: By a 5-to-1 margin, voters concluded that Senator Goldwater was more likely to start a nuclear war than President Johnson.[19] Barry

Goldwater had been branded a bomb dropper, and not even former President Eisenhower and former General Electric spokesman Ronald Reagan[20] could undo the damage.

Despite Richard Nixon's 1962 promise that the press would not have him to kick around any more, he gradually reemerged in national politics, and this time was ready to listen to a team of effective media advisors. Joe McGinniss, in *The Selling of the President 1968*, details the repackaging and marketing of the former vice president as though he were a soap product:

> That there is a difference between the individual and his image is human nature....
>
>   It is not surprising, then, that politicians and advertising men should have discovered one another. And, once they recognized that the citizen did not so much vote for a candidate as make a psychological purchase of him, not surprising that they began to work together....
>
>   So this was how they went into it. Trying, with one hand, to build the illusion that Richard Nixon, in addition to his attributes of mind and heart, considered, in the words of Patrick J. Buchanan, a speech writer, "communicating with the people ... one of the great joys of seeking the Presidency"; while with the other they shielded him, controlled him, and controlled the atmosphere around him. It was as if they were building not a President but an Astrodome, where the wind would never blow, the temperature never rise or fall, and the ball never bounce erratically on the artificial grass.[21]

Money was no problem, and the Nixon campaign of 1968 would end up costing some $12.6 million.[22]

Ever since then, candidates have increasingly been marketed in the same way in which consumer products are promoted. Pollsters and media consultants such as Richard Wirthlin, Robert Teeter, and others have turned more and more to focus groups to gain qualitative insights regarding the public's opinions on specific issues. Data collected from these interviews have been incorporated in their campaigns to market their candidates. In fact, when Ronald Reagan first met with his media consultants to map his 1980 campaign, he supposedly said something like "I thought you ought to see the package of soap you're going to sell."[23] And it was from such focus groups that George Bush's advisors learned in 1988 that crime and pollution were very much on the minds of the American people. The result was the Willie Horton and "revolving door" ads that addressed the crime issue and the Boston Harbor ad that focused viewer attention on the pollution in the major port of Michael Dukakis' home state. Also, it was from focus groups that the Bush people learned that patriotism was in. The results were the flag pictures and all the patriotic themes of the 1988 campaign.

In the 1992 Bush–Clinton contest, we continued to see the use of focus groups to provide the information media handlers believed was necessary for their image-making efforts. For example, "After focus groups complained about his 'big hair' and said he looked like Elvis, Mr. Clinton began trying to restrain the coiffure that has been compared to the rounded contours of a '53 Buick Roadmaster."[24] It was also from focus groups, according to Bill Clinton's poll taker Stan Greenberg, that they learned about the "Chelsea problem." It seemed the Clintons had protected their daughter Chelsea's privacy so well during the primary season that few focus group participants knew the Clintons had a 12-year-old daughter. As a result, Chelsea became part of the image-making effort and was pushed front and center at the July convention.

However, at times such image-making efforts appeared to have reached ridiculous levels, as when they were directed toward the wives of the candidates. Perhaps you recall the softening of Hillary Clinton through wardrobe changes—from crisp business suits to dresses in soft pastel colors—and the great *Family Circle* cookie bake-off between her and Barbara Bush. As Karen Lehrman noted,

> The Hillary image wasn't working, but it didn't need a total overhaul. A truly independent, career-minded First Lady wouldn't give up any part of her personality or career (unless there were a conflict of interest). And the voters wouldn't mind: A *U.S. News and World Report* poll showed that two out of three respondents approved of Hillary's continuing to practice law if Bill were elected President.[25]

And what about the effort to recast Tipper Gore as a fun person? Once known as the "scourge of scatological rock and roll" because of her crusade for warning labels on records with violent or sexually explicit lyrics, Tipper Gore underwent a noticeable transformation. The image change, reported in detail by the media, included changing her hairstyle "to a pageboy, so that she looks like Hillary Clinton's long-lost twin," a diet "so that she looks as slim as Mrs. Clinton," a revelation that in the 1960s she played drums in high school in the Wildcats, an all-girl rock band,[26] and an unannounced flirtatious call to her husband during his appearance on the Larry King talk show. The latter was apparently meant to show that

Tipper could lighten up, since she knew how to flirt, a quality some may deem useful for a vice president's wife.

And consider the made-for-television images on the evening of July 16, 1992, the third night of the Democratic convention. According to the Nielsen Media Services, some 22 million Americans were watching the multimillion-dollar extravaganza broadcast from New York City's Madison Square Garden: Clinton in blue, daughter Chelsea in white, and Hillary in red, all hugging amidst the glorious glittering tricolor of confetti.

As for the Bush campaign, Republican focus groups conveyed such a positive image of Barbara Bush that she was quickly perceived as one of the president's strongest assets. At the convention, the First Lady was given the unprecedented opportunity to address the delegates. Marilyn Quayle, the vice president's wife, was also given star billing, as a "self-sacrificing 90's supermom." We were being told that Marilyn Quayle had, unlike Hillary Clinton, given up her own career as a lawyer, was "absolutely" committed to her family, shopped in bargain stores, coached soccer, and made Halloween costumes.[27] Some of us were left wondering how any of this was connected to the reality of our problems and to the roles of the chief executive and his second in command.

Thus focus groups played such a prominent role in the 1992 presidential campaign that Elizabeth Kolbert predicted:

> When the history of the 1992 campaign is written, it will be hard
> to find a policy position taken, a television ad broadcast or a strat-
> egy shift executed that has not been approved by a focus group.[28]

Kolbert was troubled by this method of determining public opinion to create more effective propaganda and she commented on the dark side of using focus groups. She pointed out that they have little to do with democracy and that they are based on the assumption that we are fickle in our loyalties and do not understand our own real interests.

I share this negative view of the way in which focus groups are now used to manipulate public perceptions for political purposes. I have seen focus groups electronically rate their positive and negative reactions to a speech by President Reagan. Whenever the participants heard patriotic and optimistic words, they recorded high approval scores. But words dealing with the realities of life—sacrifice, crime, unemployment, deficit, race relations—scored low. The resultant message to the speech writers is to avoid serious, problem-laden subjects and to stick to the superficial. Therefore, I agree with Kolbert that focus groups are grounded in the belief that we are more easily manipulated than enlightened.

CLUSTERING AND
SEGMENTATION THEORY

In Chapter 2, I discussed PRIZM (Potential Rating Index for Zip Markets), Jonathan Robbin's system to match zip codes with census data and consumer surveys and to use computers to sort the 36,000 U.S. zip codes into 40 "lifestyle clusters." His Virginia-based Claritas Corporation has serviced such clients as *Time*, General Motors, and American Express, supplying them with databases detailing buyer behavior, media patterns, political orientation, and lifestyle habits. Since its origin in 1974, PRIZM has been widely imitated. (Review Box 2.3 on the clustering system; also see Global View 5.) However, John Morton of Total Research Corporation argues that *predictive segmentation,* his organization's research method, "provides a quantum-leap improvement over conventional clustering approaches."[29] **Segmentation research**, a branch of which is called **psychographic research**, is a relatively new addition to the field of opinion research.

Global View 5   Psychographics in Russia
Seeking the "Cossacks," the "Kuptsi,"
and other Consumer Clusters

Sir Winston Churchill, Great Britain's World War II prime minister, said he could not predict Russia's actions because it "is a riddle wrapped in a mystery inside an enigma."[1] In the hope of unwrapping that enigma for marketers interested in doing business there, D'Arcy Masius Benton & Bowles (DMB&B), a New York agency with offices in Moscow and St. Petersburg, undertook a study entitled *The Russian Consumer: A New Perspective and a Marketing Approach.*

Stuart Elliott, a *New York Times* reporter, described DMB&B's effort to sort Russians into clusters based on psychological and demographic factors. He commented:

> [T]he study is a blueprint for Western-style segmented, or targeted, marketing, rather than the kind of broad-based, mass marketing one might expect would be more efficacious in a consumer society, like Russia's, in its infancy.[2]

The DMB&B report sorted Russian consumers into five groups, differing from each other in perception, behavior, and interest in Western products. Table 1 gives us a sense of the findings.

Table 1 DMB&B's View of the Russian Consumer

KUPTSI (MERCHANTS)	BUSINESS EXECUTIVES	RUSSIAN SOULS	COSSACKS	STUDENTS
		Percentage of All Men		
30	25	25	10	10
		Percentage of All Women		
45	10	30	10	5
		Major Traits		
Nationalistic, practical, seek value	Western-oriented, ambitious, concerned with status, busy	Fear choices, follow others, passive, but hopeful	Ambitious, independent, nationalistic, seek status	Scraping by, idealistic, passive, practical
		Some Likely Preferences		
		Car		
Volkswagen	Mercedes	Lada	BMW	Citroën 2CV
		Cigarettes		
Chesterfield	Winston	Marlboro	Dunhill	Marlboro
		Liquor		
Stolichnaya	Johnny Walker	Smirnoff	Rémy Martin	Local vodka in Smirnoff bottles

SOURCE: Adapted from Stuart Elliott's "Figuring Out the Russian Consumer," *The New York Times*, April 1, 1992, p. D1.

The group labeled "Kuptsi" (translated loosely as *merchants*) is the largest of the five. They seem, "in an old fashioned sense, [to] prefer Russian products in theory," and dislike *shtampovka*, goods that are indistinguishable, being stamped out and mass-produced. These people admire particularly the well-engineered German and Scandinavian automobiles and stereo equipment.

Although they are extremely nationalistic, the "Cossacks" love Western products as status symbols and tend to leave evidence of such consumption strewn about their apartments. For example, in a Cossack home, one might well find empty Pepsi cans and wrappers from Western candies and high-priced Dunhill cigarette packs sitting on their Western TVs and stereo equipment "as testimony to consumption" of these products.

A third cluster, called "Business Executives," appears to resemble American yuppies. However, although they are aware of Western products, they do not depend on them. They value function as well as image, "and might be as likely to want to drive a Russian Lada automobile as a Western Mercedes-Benz or Honda."

As for Russians, in general, they are "not desperate just to be like the West." Unlike the Hungarians who look to the Austrians as their role models, the Russians just want Russia "to be a nicer Russia."

1. Radio broadcast, October 1, 1939.
2. See *The New York Times*, April 1, 1992, pp. D1, 19.

In discussing the evolution of segmentation theory, Morton explains that although large-scale segmentation (clustering) studies were very popular during the 1970s, the subsequent controversy stemmed from a flaw in the initial concept of clustering. Typically, consumers were isolated into highly differentiated need-based "benefit segments." However, the problem was that their "product usage behavior—for instance, to which brands they were loyal—did not vary much from benefit segment to benefit segment." Likewise, their demographics and media behavior proved to be similar. Morton and his group of researchers wondered why, if these segments were supposedly unique, "did they all act and look the same" when it came to usage behavior. Rephrasing the question, we could ask: Regardless of which of the 40–48 lifestyle clusters—from "Norma Rae–ville"* to "Blue Blood Estates"—we fall into, how come most of us love products like Oreo cookies and Heinz ketchup?

Cecilie Gaziano of Research Solutions argues along similar lines in her essay on segmentation research (see The Professional Voice 10). She points out that a greater degree of variation is observable with sophisticated segmentation research, as opposed to clustering. This is so because the researcher looks for new independent, dependent, and intervening variables, going beyond the most obvious characteristics—age, income, occupation, and such—that had set people off in distinct clusters, even though many of their likes and dislikes were similar.

---

*"Norma Rae–ville" is derived from the name of the Southern labor organizer depicted in the film *Norma Rae*, starring Sally Field. Such clusters are located in lower-middle-class milltowns and industrial suburbs, primarily in the South. See Michael J. Weiss, *The Clustering of America* (New York: Harper & Row, 1989), p. 5.

The Professional Voice 10   Segmentation Research and Theories of Media Audiences

Cecilie Gaziano

Most mass communication research does not go much beyond looking at variations by age, sex, education, and similar demographics. Frequently, researchers will report little or no variation by these characteristics; yet if something is added to these characteristics, *variation does occur.* People of similar educational levels or similar ages vary in their attitudes, and they can be described better by creating further subgroups, based, for instance, on variations in age, education, and attitudes.

Rare in mass communication literature, this kind of analysis is found more frequently in advertising and marketing journals. Suggestions for it come from the notion of *psychographic market segmentation.* Division of audiences into different segments and study of variations in their characteristics can lead to insights into attitudes, knowledge, and behavior of social sub-groups and even into social change. The ultimate result is theory development regarding the composition of society or communities. Statistical techniques are used in segmentation research to develop new independent, dependent, and intervening variables. Although this method relates to the creation of statistical constructs, there is evidence that this works

well enough to approximate reality. Many clients find these constructs useful in developing marketing and advertising campaigns aimed at various social segments—that is, campaigns with different appeals, designed to reach different groups (segments of the population). We will describe three examples of segmentation and relate them to marketing strategies. These examples include typologies of community ties, media dependencies, and newspaper loyalty.

A TYPOLOGY OF COMMUNITY TIES

This is adapted from the typology developed by Keith Stamm and his colleagues. It is useful in looking at markets for newspapers.[1] The way people relate to their communities is also related to their newspaper readership and news interests. Table 1 shows a four-group typology. The percentages refer to their proportions in a given (fictitious) market.

In many markets, "natives" are the best newspaper readers, followed by "settlers" and "relocaters." "Drifters" are usually the least interested in newspapers. Each group has somewhat different needs to be satisfied by newspapers because they are in different stages of connecting

Table 1 Stamm's Typology of Community Ties (Adapted)

LENGTH OF TIME PEOPLE EXPECT TO REMAIN IN THE AREA	LENGTH OF RESIDENCE IN THE AREA	
	5 years or less	*More than 5 years*
5 years or Less	Drifters (23%)	Relocaters (22%)
More than 5 Years	Settlers (13%)	Natives (42%)

Note: "Drifters" have lived in their community for 5 years or less and plan to move within the next 5 years. "Settlers" have lived in their community for 5 years or less, and they expect to remain for longer than 5 years. "Relocaters" are long-term residents who anticipate moving within the next 5 years. "Natives" have resided in the community for more than 5 years and intend to remain for a long time.

to the community. ... Market analysis of these groups might address these questions:

1. What are the demographic characteristics of each group?
2. What proportion of each group reads which available newspapers? What has the best potential for increased readership? To what extent does their readership overlap among the area's dailies?
3. How do the news interests of each group differ? Which news areas represent the greatest potential for readership development?

MEDIA DEPENDENCE SEGMENTS

Another means of segmentation is on the basis of *dependence* on major media. Much of the dependency research compares newspaper and television dependence. Although

newspapers and television are often thought of as antithetical modes of communication, the world does not divide into those who prefer only one or the other. Frequently, these media are complementary. Further, some people do not care much for either medium. *Non-users* of major media may even have similarities to *users*, which need to be understood by those seeking to increase media audiences and those deciding among media as advertising vehicles.

People are highly dependent on mass media as a means of satisfying needs or attaining goals when they are located in social systems in which media have many central information functions. *The larger and more complex the community or society, the greater the dependence on media.* Dependencies are the mechanisms through which outside forces and units can influence attitudes, values, beliefs, knowledge, and behavior. Media use develops from perceptions of utility and availability, in addition to social sanctions and social system constraints.

People and social groups can vary in amount of dependency over time, according to changes in their social and psychological characteristics. *Media dependence* is a concept separate from media use, or exposure, and it tends to change depending upon the content area.... We can divide a sample into four groups: those dependent on both major media, neither of them, mainly newspapers, and mainly television.[2] Imagine you run a local daily newspaper and are concerned about the local television stations' ability to capture advertisers. The research questions here are:

1. How do the four groups vary in demographic and attitudinal characteristics?

2. How do these segments vary in their news consumption behavior? To which media do they attend most?

3. What marketing strategies might be designed for each segment?

Respondents were asked, "If you weren't able to read a daily newspaper for quite some time, which of the following comes the closest to the way you would feel?" This was repeated for "television news."

People who said they would feel lost were considered most dependent. Responses to the two questions were cross-tabulated to obtain four groups (segments), as shown in Table 2.

Newspaper dependents over-represent groups associated with newspaper reading—older people, those with higher education and incomes, married persons, retired people, Republicans, conservatives, and residents of large metropolitan areas.

People dependent on both major media, "dual dependents," share many similarities with the newspaper dependents, except that they tend to be women, less educated, residents of small communities, and political moderates. They include more Democrats and fewer Independents than does the newspaper-dependent group.

Television news dependents have the lowest incomes and education. They are younger and more likely to be Independent than dual dependents are, as well as less likely to identify with any political ideology. They are more likely than average to be black, separated or divorced, urban, Protestant, or born-again Christians.

"Non-dependents" (those dependent neither on newspapers nor on television) differ little from the sample as a whole, except they are disproportionately more likely to include males, people under 35, singles, and those working full time. Non-dependents have a low tendency to identify with any political ideology.

Table 2 Typology of Dependence on TV News and Daily Newspapers

DAILY NEWSPAPER DEPENDENCE	TELEVISION NEWS DEPENDENCE	
	High	*Low*
High	High dependence on both media for news (9%)	High newpaper/low TV news dependence (14%)
Low	High TV news/low news-paper dependence (17%)	Low dependence on either medium for news (59%)

Groups low in political identification are less likely to be interested in news and therefore represent a tougher sell to make them part of the local newspaper's audience. Groups including older people, married people, long-term residents, and church members are more likely to perceive they have a greater stake in their communities and to have a higher interest in public affairs and news.

The local newspaper would not want to concentrate only on older people. Newspapers are concerned about decreasing interest in newspapers among younger people. The non-dependent group is of great concern, too, because of its great size. Many newspapers find themselves hard pressed to attract new readers from segments that have been made up of mediocre newspaper readers in the past.

Respondents were also asked to rate a list of reasons as they applied to them personally when they chose a TV news program to watch or a daily newspaper to read. Overall, people evaluated

these criteria similarly. Having up-to-date news, being an easy way to get the news, helping them feel close to their communities, and providing good conversation topics are the most important reasons. Giving insight into people's lives receives slightly higher emphasis in general for newspapers, and presenting news in an entertaining way is emphasized slightly more for television.

When newspaper and television use scores are compared, newspapers outperform television news programs among all four segments on providing good conversation topics, helping one feel close to a community, and aiding decisions about what to buy. Newspapers do better than television among all groups except the television dependent on voting information and information on day-to-day living. However, newspapers also do well on providing insight into people's lives. Local newspaper marketing departments might want to promote these characteristics widely.

A TYPOLOGY OF NEWSPAPER READERS

Another segmentation strategy is to divide the population into groups based on *relevant behavior* and apparent *likelihood of change* in that behavior. Discriminant analysis "predicts" individuals who are users and non-users of the product or service—or readers and non-readers, in the case of newspapers.[3] This results in a fourfold typology of users: "loyal readers," "potential readers," "marginal readers," and "poor prospects." The groups are analyzed in terms of how they perceive news and newspapers, relate to their communities, use other media and leisure time, interest in various news topics, variation in other attitudes, and demographics.

An optimal marketing strategy is to:

- keep loyal readers happy
- strengthen the franchise among marginal readers
- attract potential readers
- decrease efforts to recruit poor prospects

Applications to different marketing problems would include analyses that address these questions:

1. What is the potential for gains in certain geographic areas and among those in certain occupational categories? What kinds of news products can best at-tract readers among these groups?

2. What is the likely reaction by loyal, marginal, and potential readers to substantial changes contemplated for the news-paper?

3. In strongly competitive markets with substantial overlapping readership, what are the news interests, current readership, and loyalties of marginal and potential readers?

In general, loyal and potential readers are better educated, have higher incomes, and have higher-status occupations than marginal readers and poor prospects. Loyal and potential readers tend to have high interest in most newspaper topics tested. Marginal readers and poor prospects tend to have lower interest in many hard-news topics, instead preferring advertising and soft news. Specific interests vary by market.

CONCLUSIONS

These examples help to show how to combine various characteristics of the people studied to create meaningful sub-groups and look for variations in these groups. Often, variations in media-inde-pendent variables are not highly correlated with variations in audi-ence-dependent variables, but sub-groups within the dependent variables will show variations.[4] Our intention was to show that this type of research can contribute to theories about mass media audiences, as well as to social theories.

Media behavior does not occur in isolation but in concert with many other behaviors, cognitions, attitudes, and values that are integrated into the individual's life as a whole and that are partly influenced by the individual's location in groups and society.

Which segmentation strategy is selected would depend on the company's needs and goals, hypotheses about consumer behavior based on past experience, and the product or service. Strategies can include selecting segments on the basis of consumer needs and interests (for example, media dependence), product loyalty or usage ("loyal" consumers, "potential" consumers, and so on), or relationships to a larger whole, such as the community (for example, a typology of community ties). Segmentation according to product benefits is another possibility. Best results are obtained by an approach that is as customized to the product or service and the company as possible.

Cecilie Gaziano is the president of Research Solutions, Inc. of Minneapolis.

1. Keith Stamm, *Newspaper Use and Community Ties: Toward a Dynamic Theory* (Norwood, NJ: Ablex, 1985); Keith Stamm and Lisa Fortini-Campbell, "The Relationship of Community Ties to Newspaper Subscribing and Use," *Journalism Monographs*, No. 84; Keith Stamm and Robert Weis, "Toward a Dynamic Theory of Newspaper Subscribing," *Journalism Quarterly* (1982), Vol. 59, pp. 382–389.

2. See Cecilie Gaziano, "Media Dependency for News: Some Neglected Groups," *Mass Communication Review* (1990), Vol. 17, No. 3, pp. 2–13, 43.

3. Kristin McGrath, president, MORI Research, Inc., presentation to the International Newspaper Publishers Association, 1985. Data are from projects conducted by MORI Research.

4. An example is Cecilie Gaziano and Kristin McGrath, "Segments of the Public Most Critical of Newspapers' Credibility: A Psychographic Analysis," *Newspaper Research Journal* (1987), Vol. 8, No. 4, pp. 1–17.

Editor's note: This essay has been edited and adapted for presentation in this text.

RELYING ON TYPICAL TOWN, U.S.A.

What do Tulsa, Oklahoma; Midland, Texas; and Wichita, Kansas have in common? These cities, among others in the United States, have been deemed ideal test markets for the products of corporate America. They have been so labeled because demographers have determined that their population mix, age distribution, and so on yield a purchasing pattern that is almost identical to that of the country as a whole.

Table 11.1 The 10 Most Typical Cities

RANK	CITY	POPULATION
1	Tulsa, Oklahoma	367,000
2	Charleston, West Virginia	57,000
3	Midland, Texas	89,000
4	Springfield, Illinois	105,000
5	Lexington-Fayette, Kentucky	225,000
6	Wichita, Kansas	304,000
7	Bloomington, Indiana	52,000
8	Oklahoma City, Oklahoma	445,000
9	Indianapolis, Indiana	731,000
10	Rockford, Illinois	139,000

The idea of finding a typical small town for predictive purposes is not new. You may have seen the old film *Magic Town*, released in 1947. The film starred Jimmy Stewart as a poll taker who traveled to a small Midwest town and declared it the perfect American community because it exactly mirrored the demographic characteristics of the entire United States. However, it was not long before the resultant flood of national attention disrupted the town's quietude and ruined its small-town typicality.

Although today's computer models can predict fairly accurately how consumers will react, most of the big companies prefer to put their new product on a supermarket shelf in a preselected test area to see exactly how well it will fare. Using data from the 1990 census, Donnelley Marketing Information Services conducted a study for *American Demographics*, ranking cities with populations of 50,000 or more, based on "how similar their age and race distribution and housing values are to the national average."[30] Table 11.1 lists the 10 most typical cities out of the 555 ranked by *American Demographics*.

Depending upon the test results, products tested in these markets may never be seen anyplace else. In the late 1980s, John Erwin, a local distributor for Miller Brewing Company, test-marketed three Miller's beers in Austin, Texas; Charleston, South Carolina; Cincinnati, Ohio; Fresno, California; and Lincoln, Nebraska. Although all three tests were considered unsuccessful and the products were withdrawn, Erwin remained confident about the testing process and the cities selected: "They say for every 10 tests, if you can pull one successful product out of that, you've been successful."[31]

So what factors constitute an ideal test market? First of all, demographic representativeness, the same quality that makes for a good polling sample. Second, a low refusal rate, signaling the willingness of people to cooperate with interviewers. Tulsa is a representative market where shoppers are not only "willing guinea pigs," but are also anxious to talk about all sorts of things.[32] Third, economic climate. Austin's success as a test market was based on a combination of the city's economic climate and its demographics. The presence of the University of Texas, the state government, and Bergstrom Air Force Base resulted in a favorable cultural cross-section, a good mix of age groups, and a large number of above-average-income families with above-average educations.[33]

QUESTIONABLE MARKETING STUDIES

As the business of surveying public opinion has grown steadily during the past two decades—expanding far beyond a small number of polling and research companies and universities to include marketing research firms—critics have warned consumers to beware. They say that too many studies "have become vehicles for polishing corporate images, influencing juries, shaping debate on public policy, selling shoe polish and satisfying the media's—and the public's—voracious appetite for information."[34] Cynthia Crossen of *The Wall Street Journal* described some of the questionable marketing studies that have been undertaken by supposedly independent researchers but that in actuality were sponsored by companies interested in the outcome. She includes these examples of manipulative studies:

- Levi Strauss & Co. asked students which clothes would be most popular in 1991. Levi's 501 jeans were preferred by 90 percent of the respondents, *but* Levi's 501 jeans were the only jeans on the list.

- Black Flag's study asked the leading question, "A roach disk . . . poisons a roach slowly. The dying roach returns to the nest and after it dies is eaten by other roaches. In turn these roaches become poisoned and die. How effective do you think this type of product would be in killing roaches?" Are you surprised that 79 percent said "effective"?

- In an attempt to eliminate a major environmental concern of parents who use disposable diapers, the industry hired Gallup to conduct a survey in which the following question was asked: "It is estimated that disposable diapers account for less than 2 percent of the trash in today's landfills. In contrast, beverage containers, third-class mail, and yard waste are estimated to account for about 21 percent of the trash in landfills. Given this, in your opinion, would it be fair to ban disposable diapers?" The predictable answer "no" was given by 84 percent of the respondents.

With regard to the diaper industry study, Crossen points out that at least four studies on diapers have explored consumers' environmental concerns. Two were sponsored by the disposable diaper industry and two by the cloth diaper industry. You guessed correctly: The first two found that soapsuds from washing cloth diapers pollute our rivers and that disposables are more healthful for babies; the second two found cloth diapers better for the environment and the babies. Such diverse results are not uncommon.

Many of us are concerned about the proliferation of questionable marketing studies. I am particularly troubled when corporations undertake survey research not to discern the truth—to the extent that is possible—but rather to create an impression of scientific findings to support some self-serving end.

It is the function of our public officials to sort through the conflicting claims made by corporate and environmental lobbyists. Still, the legislative task has become unduly complicated, time consuming, and expensive. I believe that consideration of these conflicting studies contributes to the already snail-like pace of policy making. I will return to this subject in Chapter 12 when I further consider the effect of polling results on policy making.

CHAPTER REVIEW

- Much of what consumer or marketing researchers do is similar to the work of pollsters, except that marketing researchers rely on qualitative surveys—usually in the form of focus group interviews—to a far greater extent than do independent pollsters.

- In 1941, Paul Lazarsfeld was joined by Robert Merton and other colleagues—social scientists, mathematicians, statisticians, and philosophers—in a governmental effort to test audience responses to radio morale programs. They used a primitive polygraph-type device, the Lazarsfeld-Stanton program analyzer, a precursor to the contemporary perception analyzer, which consists of a dial wired to a computer.

- By 1943, the Army Research Group was using focused interviews as a starting point for their research because they provided an opportunity to test and refine their questions. These interviews were a source of what Merton called "new ideas and new hypotheses."

- As the focused interview evolved into the focus group interview, critics questioned accepting "new plausible insights" as "demonstrable gospel truths."

- While Leo Bogart sees the focus group interview as a "barbarism" designed to provide the clients of the marketing research agency with the feeling that "they are themselves privy to the innermost revelations of the consuming public," Lewis Gediman argues the virtues of qualitative research: "You can explore a subject, uncovering the full range of thoughts and feelings consumers have."

- As the focus group interview became part of the marketing research process, it also became a tool of political consultants.

- Thomas Rosser Reeves, Jr., was an early believer in the power of TV to persuade people to buy products of all sorts, including political candidates. In 1952, Reeves put together a series of spots called "Eisenhower Answers America." These were the forerunners of today's political commercials.

- In *The Selling of the President 1968*, Joe McGinniss details the repackaging and marketing of Richard Nixon as though he were a soap product. Since then, candidates have been increasingly marketed in the same way in which consumer products are promoted, and pollsters and media consultants have turned more and more to focus groups to gain qualitative insights regarding the public's opinions on specific issues.

- In the 1992 Bush–Clinton contest, we continued to see the candidates' media handlers use focus groups for their image-making efforts. Elizabeth Kolbert, troubled by such use to create more effective propaganda, wrote that focus groups have little to do with democracy and are grounded in the belief that we are more easily manipulated than enlightened.

- Since its origin in 1974, Jonathan Robbin's PRIZM has been widely imitated. However, segmentation research, a branch of which is called psychographics, is now touted as a "quantum-leap improvement over conventional clustering approaches."

- Segmentation theorists asked why 40–48 "unique" lifestyle clusters acted and looked the same, using the same or similar products.

- Cecilie Gaziano points out that because the segmentation researcher looks for new variables beyond the most obvious characteristics that had set people off in distinct clusters, a greater degree of variation is observable.

- Gaziano discussed another segmentation strategy: "to divide the population into groups based on relevant behavior and apparent likelihood of change in that behavior."

- Psychographic segmentation research combines various characteristics of the respondents to create meaningful sub-groups. Researchers then look for variations in these groups. No single behavior occurs in isolation.

- Gaziano discusses the customized approach of segmentation research, taking into account the company's needs and goals, hypotheses about consumer behavior based on past experience, and the product or service itself.

- Demographers have labeled certain communities "typical" because their population mix, age distribution, and so on, yield a purchasing pattern that is almost identical to that of the country as a whole. These communities provide a testing ground for new products.

- Critics of public opinion research continue to complain that too many studies are being used to manipulate public perception through their attempts to polish corporate images, influence juries (see Chapter 5), shape the public policy debates, sell everything from shoe polish to presidential candidates, and satisfy our voracious appetite for information and entertainment. Some supposedly independent researchers have conducted biased studies for their corporate clients.

- While conflicting results from similar studies are not uncommon, the danger is that they may paralyze policy making. When lobbyists representing different interest groups and bearing different research findings converge on Washington, our legislators must sort through the conflicting claims.

NOTES

1. Martin Weinberger, "Polls to Sell Products With," *Polling on the Issues*, A. H. Cantril, ed. (Cabin John, MD: Seven Locks Press, 1980), pp. 120–125.

2. Robert K. Merton, "The Focussed Interview and Focus Groups— Continuities and Discontinuities," *Public Opinion Quarterly* (1987), Vol. 51, pp. 550–566.

3. Elizabeth Kolbert, "Test-Marketing a President: How Focus Groups Pervade Campaign Politics," *The New York Times*, Aug. 30, 1992, p. 20.

4. Merton, p. 558.

5. Merton, p. 560.

6. Merton.

7. Joshua D. Libresco, "Focus Groups: Madison Avenue Meets Public Policy" *Public Opinion* (August/September 1983), pp. 51–53.

8. Libresco, p. 52.

9. Edwin Diamond and Stephen Bates, *The Spot—The Rise of Political Advertising on Television* (Cambridge, MA: MIT Press, 1984); see Introduction.

10. Henry F. Graff sees the decline in Eisenhower's lead as reflective, at least to some degree, of the general's lackluster campaign. However, since a 4-point difference falls within the margin of error, Graff's interpretation is arguable. See "Maybe Bush Has Already Won," *The New York Times*, Aug. 27, 1988, Op-Ed page.

11. Diamond and Bates, p. 70.

12. Norman M. Bradburn and Seymour Sudman, *Polls and Surveys— Understanding What They Tell Us* (San Francisco: Jossey-Bass, 1988), p. 30.

13. Michael Emery and Edwin Emery, *The Press and America—An Interpretive History of the Mass Media*, 6th ed. (Englewood Cliffs, NJ: Prentice-Hall, 1988), p. 454.

14. Graff.

15. Emery and Emery.

16. Theodore H. White, *The Making of the President, 1964* (New York: Atheneum, 1965), p. 257.

17. Bradburn and Sudman, p. 44.

18. Tony Schwartz, *The Responsive Chord* (Garden City, NY: Doubleday, 1973). Also see his *Media: The Second God* (New York: Random House, 1981).

19. Diamond and Bates, p. 140.

20. Haynes Johnson, *Sleeping Through History* (New York: Norton, 1991), p. 56, explains that Reagan was GE's spokesman until 1962.

21. Joe McGinniss, *The Selling of the President 1968* (New York: Simon & Schuster, 1969). The quotations are from Chapter 2.

22. Diamond and Bates, p. 172.

23. Bill Moyers, "Leading Questions," a PBS Public Affairs Special on polls and pollsters.

24. Maureen Dowd and Frank Rich, "Garden Diary, There They Go Again: Conjuring Up Camelot," *The New York Times*, July 17, 1992, p. 9.

25. Karen Lehrman, "Beware the Cookie Monster," *The New York Times*, July 18, 1992, p. 23. Also see Joyce Purnick, "Let Hillary Be Hillary," *The New York Times*, July 15, 1992, p. A20.

26. Dowd and Rich; also see *Entertainment Weekly*, July 20, 1992.

27. Alessandra Stanley, "Republicans Present Marilyn Quayle as a Self-Sacrificing 90's Supermom," *The New York Times*, Aug. 18, 1992, p. A7.

28. Kolbert.

29. John Morton, "Predictive Segmentation," in *A Total View*, Vol. 1, No. 45 (Princeton, NJ: Total Research Corporation, 1989).

30. Steven Lohr, "Forget Peoria. It's Now: 'Will it Play in Tulsa?'" *The New York Times*, June 1, 1992, pp. A1, D7.

31. Danni Sabota, "This is only a TEST ...," *Austin Magazine* (February 1988), pp. 32–35.

32. Lohr, p. D7.

33. Sabota, p. 33.

34. Cynthia Crossen, "Margin of Error—Studies Galore Support Products and Positions, But Are They Reliable?" *The Wall Street Journal*, Nov. 14, 1991, pp. A1, 9.

12

Polls, News Making, Policy Making, and Democracy

Think about—

How did polling become a tool of news gathering?

What is precision journalism?

What are the differences between the way polls were once used by candidates and the way in which they are used today?

What were the most influential factors that led to the increased news value of polls?

What is the problem with using campaign volunteers as interviewers to conduct polls on behalf of a candidate?

Why did the polls come under heavy attack during the 1992 presidential campaign? Do you agree with the critics of polling?

What is the supposed rationale for arguing that polls commissioned by candidates are more legitimate than those conducted by press organizations?

How have polls affected the traditional notion of leadership?

Is this a good time to review our discussion in Chapter 10 on mediated public opinion? (Yes, it is.)

Can you define *concurrent majorities, pluralism,* and *hyperpluralism?*

I n your opinion, are the media guilty of shaping our value system, beliefs, and opinions?[1] Are they guilty of the overuse and abuse of polling data as a news-gathering tool? Do polls influence decision making and political behavior? Do they, at least to some extent, set the political agenda? Is there a right way and a wrong way for leaders to use polls in the process of their decision making?

My aim in this chapter is to encourage you to consider the good and the bad of the media's ability to influence our opinions and of the use of polls in our society. I also hope to stimulate debate about the impact of such use.[2]

POLLS AS NEWS

Although the history of the print media's use of polls can be traced to the 1824 presidential campaign,[3] it was not until 1935 that political poll reporting began to resemble the way it appears today. At that time, the Gallup and Fortune polls began their syndication; during the 1930s, mass-circulation magazines occasionally conducted polls and published the results as part of their reports on specific subjects. Soon a number of states undertook surveys supported by sponsoring newspapers, whose readers benefited from the data's publication. In 1944, the *Minneapolis Tribune* started the Minnesota Poll, and not long after, the *Des Moines Register and Tribune* launched the Iowa Poll. Through the 1940s, as we have seen, academic researchers in various universities around the country undertook attitudinal and behavioral surveys, which began to attract media attention. As the print media incorporated the survey findings of Crossley, Roper, Yankelovich, Gallup, Harris, and other pollsters, the public became familiar with their names.

In the post–World War II years, novice politicians such as Jacob K. Javits, later a much-respected U.S. senator from New York, discovered the value of polling during their election campaigns and the ease with which newspapers agreed to publish findings provided free of charge (see Box 12.1).

By the 1950s, the Gallup Poll's syndicated columns were printed in more than 200 newspapers and were a primary source of polling data for the public. As the advent of computers aided the increase in social research, professional journalists soon realized that they were ill equipped to handle the avalanche of incoming data. Bill Kovach of *The New York Times* commented that although journalists had formerly treated polls in an unsophisticated manner,

> the polling tool has been so completely factored into our decision-making process, especially in political reporting, that I have difficulty remembering how we worked before we had this tool.[4]

Kovach's comment is consistent with that made by a director of polling for *The Washington Post*: "We've bred a group of political writers who can't write a story without a poll."[5]

Until the 1960s, the press mostly used the pollsters' services, but after that things began to change.

> Slowly, a new public information and feedback system was being instituted, gradually supplementing or supplanting the individual and collective indicators of popular sentiments and the legislative actions that had previously been accepted as valid manifestations of public opinion.[6]

In 1967, following a series of urban race riots, the Detroit *Free Press* sponsored a study that yielded many of the data used by the Kerner Commission to create a profile of the urban rioter. The survey was the idea of Philip Meyer, then a reporter for Knight (now Knight-Ridder) newspapers. Meyer believed that news research—or **precision journalism**, as he called it—should include both the quantitative element common in social research methodology and traditional qualitative news reporting. The

---

BOX 12.1   How Jacob Javits Used a Poll the First Time He Ran for Office

In July 1946, Jacob K. Javits, an aspiring congressman, asked Elmo Roper to find out how well his views squared with those of the voters in his New York City, upper West Side congressional district. As a first-time public office seeker, the future senator was anxious to appraise his qualifications for a seat in Congress. To prepare for the election, the previous February Javits had begun to set forth his views on national and international issues in the New York *Herald Tribune*.

Javits felt that by undertaking a public opinion poll he was embarking on a new course. He wrote:

> I left the beaten path of traditional politics and entered upon a new avenue to winning the approval and support of the people who cast the votes on election day. I was initiating a novel

twist in political campaigning by focussing on issues instead of on personalities and by airing my views instead of concealing them under a thick blanket of pious generalities.[1]

Working with the Elmo Roper organization, the candidate put together a questionnaire with questions that fell into three categories:

- those that had already been answered on the basis of a nationwide sample, so that the results of his district could be compared with national averages
- those that dealt with major issues (wage and price controls, housing, labor, atomic energy, veterans' affairs, U.S.–Soviet relations), so that the district results could be compared with his own views
- those that dealt with issues that would come before Congress but

---

Detroit Urban League provided funding, and the University of Michigan's Institute of Social Research provided technical assistance.

The results surprised many. For example, Meyer and his team found that, contrary to what most people believed, education and income were not predictors of whether someone would participate in a riot. In other words, not all of those who had engaged in violence, vandalism, arson, and theft were unemployed, unemployable, underprivileged, hopelessly frustrated people. In fact, a good many of the looters, as was the case in the April 1992 riots in Los Angeles, were people who had jobs and who, under ordinary circumstances, would not have broken the law. They were merely opportunists seeking to capitalize on the tragic chaos of the moment.

Following the Detroit study, Meyer conducted other surveys in California, Florida, Ohio, and elsewhere for the Knight chain. By 1973, when his

that were not necessarily relevant to a metropolitan area such as his district (for example, on the subject of farm prices and subsidies)

In addition, there were demographic questions and filter questions to screen out those not eligible to vote (those who were underage, not registered, nonresidents, and noncitizens).

Javits released the survey results to the public, and on October 11, 1946, the New York *Herald Tribune* editorialized:

This represents a considerable advance over the old torchlight processions, the street corner tub-thumping and rabble-rousing which used to constitute the major weapons in a political campaign.

Javits saw the opinion poll as a "substantial and accurate starting point for fixing attention on and creating interest in particular issues that relate to the district as well as for measuring existing opinion." In explaining the use and value of the polling data, Javits wrote that the findings had crystallized voters' opinions, enabled them to compare his known views with theirs, and set the campaign agenda by laying the foundation for political debate between him and his opponents.

Question: How does this use of polling data differ from the way in which such data are used today?

1. Jacob K. Javits, "How I Used a Poll in Campaigning for Congress," *Public Opinion Quarterly* (Summer 1947), p. 223. Javits later served as a U.S. senator from New York for 24 years.

book, *Precision Journalism*, was published, Meyer's work had not only gained the respect of many journalists, but had also attracted the attention of journalism educators, leading to the founding of a branch of news research now called precision journalism.

As political candidates and special interest groups increasingly turned to pollsters to learn where they stood with the public and to help map their strategies, reporters, "confronted with the choice of relying on suspect sources or their own intuition to interpret complex situations, came to see precision journalism as a credible alternative."[7] Thus, the press began to find polling data increasingly useful to supplement their coverage. Since the candidates and the special interest groups paid for the surveys and were particularly anxious to disseminate any positive polling results, the print media benefited from what was, essentially, a freebie.

However, with growing competition from TV news—especially at election time—the press began to support and to integrate polling as part of their news operations. Thus by the 1970s newspapers had gone from "buying access to syndicated polling data or sponsoring special polls," or waiting for "handouts," to becoming major actors in the development of surveying public opinion.[8] Thomas Patterson undertook a content analysis study of the media's increased use of polling data.[9] He found that whereas in 1940 some 10 poll reports might have represented a newspaper's quota for an entire presidential campaign, the *Los Angeles Times*, for example, published a similar number of poll-related articles during the *last week* of the 1976 presidential campaign. And a study by David Paletz found that *The New York Times* published a total of 380 polling reports—nearly 1 every 3 days—during the nonpresidential election years 1973, 1975, and 1977.[10] When Paletz examined television network use of polling data during the 1973–1977 period, he found a much more moderate use; sometimes weeks could pass without the mention of a poll. This finding was consistent with the results of Gladys Lang and Kurt Lang's study, which found that during the year before Nixon's resignation (on August 9, 1974) the networks reported on only approximately 25 percent of the Gallup Poll press releases related to the Watergate affair.[11]

The need for cost sharing led to cooperative efforts and to the creation of joint polling ventures by various network television stations and newspapers, such as the CBS News/*New York Times* Poll and the ABC News/*Washington Post* Poll. Sometimes, in smaller markets a local TV or radio station would join with one or more newspapers to share the costs involved in a community poll or in a state- or local-level political poll. Also, the switch from face-to-face interviewing to telephone interviewing "broke down a number of barriers to the spread of news polling."[12] The newspapers' existing telephone banks in the classified advertising or circulation departments were used to keep polling costs down. Wide-area and national surveys became increasingly feasible with the introduction of WATS (Wide-Area Telecommunications Service) lines and random-digit dialing. Most important, whereas in the 1930s the turnaround time for a poll was weeks or even months, in the 1980s it shrank to hours because of new technologies such as CATI. Among the most influential factors that led to the increased news value of polls, Charles Turner and Elizabeth Martin have identified the following:

- increased literacy and numeracy
- near-universal access to the telephone

- increased power and decreased costs of automated information processing.[13]

The proliferation of polls by 1980 led columnist Nicholas Von Hoffman to comment on their pseudo-event quality, which he found objectionable. He criticized in-house polls and those commissioned by news organizations, saying that in such cases the press is creating its own news and "flacking it as though it were an event they were reporting on over which they had no control, like an earthquake or traffic accident."[14]

A major criticism leveled at pollsters and the so-called soothsaying journalists who interpret polling results is that "Polltalk is ... often self-fulfilling."[15] *Pack journalism*, a derogatory term used to describe a group of journalists covering a particular candidate or event, is also blamed for a cycle of self-fulfilling prophecy, described by critics as follows:

- A negative assessment of the candidate's performance is offered by a respected political analyst.

- Other reporters for both the print and electronic media (the pack) pick up the story, exploring it further.

- Extensive press coverage attracts the public attention, thereby influencing public opinion.

- Polling results soon indicate a shift in support away from that candidate.

- The polling results are then used as evidence of the poor performance cited in earlier news releases.

- Renewed media focus on the candidate's deteriorated position once again affects the public's perception, which is once again measured by the next poll. And so the cycle continues, with the candidate falling into political oblivion.

For example, there are those who say that the soothsaying journalists, polltalk, pack journalism, and the self-fulfilling prophecy cycle are what did in President Gerald Ford (see Box 12.2).

There are those in the academic community (see The Professional Voice 11) who ask whether polls really measure public opinion. Susan Herbst presents three thought-provoking arguments that raise fears that, as a result of today's emphasis on polling, we may witness the demise of the reciprocal public debate, the give and take of public argument that characterized political expression in the past.

BOX 12.2   Self-Fulfilling Prophecy

Gerald R. Ford did not come to the presidency with any public mandate. He was selected by President Richard M. Nixon to replace Vice President Spiro Agnew, who had been forced to resign. (Agnew had been dogged by corruption charges in his home state of Maryland.) When Nixon resigned, it was left to Ford to clean up the mess, restore trust in and respect for the office of the presidency, and generally heal the wounds inflicted on the body politic by the attempted cover-up of the Watergate affair.

Initially, President Ford's ratings in the polls climbed quickly from just under a 40-percent approval rating to 71 percent. He was perceived as a man of integrity, decency, and honesty, inspiring the public's confidence. To be sure, at first he seemed to be a respite from the previous chaotic years. The press, in the view of its critics, seemed anxious to make amends for their excesses during the Nixon era.

Ford was shown jogging, swimming, smiling, coming to the White House carrying a portfolio of good-luck letters written by young children from around the country.

However, two months into his presidency, he pardoned Nixon "for any crimes he might have committed while in office." The media were saturated both with the news itself and with political analyses and commentaries, most of which predicted dire consequences to Ford's image as "Mr. Clean." "A deal was made!" was practically shouted from the rooftops. As a result of the pardon (or was it as a result of the coverage of the pardon?), his rating tumbled 20 percentage points,[1] and for the rest of his presidency, Ford never got above a 50-percent approval rating.[2]

Despite the damage done by the pardon, he attempted to build a consensus to gain congressional support for his first initiative, which was to Whip Inflation Now. Although

---

The Professional Voice 11
Do Polls Really Measure Public Opinion?

Susan Herbst

In contemporary American political discourse, journalists, policymakers, and citizens tend to assume that polls measure public opinion. This assumption is so deeply ingrained in political culture that we often think of polls as synonymous with public opinion.

Although the notion that polls reflect public opinion seems reasonable, not all scholars believe that survey research truly captures the texture of public sentiment. In fact, several respected social scientists have dismissed polls as irrelevant to the study of public opinion:

Ford tried to rally the public to support his WIN campaign, he had a difficult time of it. On October 9, 1974, *The New York Times* criticized his speeches as "weak...and generally disappointing," and other newspapers were even less kind. The television networks turned him down when he requested time to address the American people, saying the equivalent of "There's no news here." According to Ford's press secretary Ron Nessen, the president was "virtually forced" to command the airwaves.[3] Ford tried to bypass the media by making a great number of personal appearances including visits to retail chains and numerous speeches to numerous groups, but the grass-roots support for his program never materialized. A Harris survey in early May 1975 showed a slight increase in his approval rating from 42 percent to 46 percent. Yet, when we consider the margin of error of ±3 to 4 percentage points, the poll did not indicate a significant change in Ford's standing. The WIN buttons went unworn, became a joke with the late-night comics, and his inability to arouse public enthusiasm and support was mirrored by continued unimpressive poll ratings on the evening news.

Ford's next project—swine flu immunization—also provided TV comics with more bad jokes and did nothing to enhance his approval ratings. In March 1976, on the basis of a dozen or so cases of swine influenza reported at an army camp in New Jersey, Ford went public with his fear of a flu epidemic. He even spoke of a flu pandemic. He quickly requested that Congress appropriate $135 million for an immunization program and again took his case to the American people. Six months later, a Gallup Poll reported that 93 percent of the public knew about and supported the program.[4] Then a number of deaths were reported among some elderly persons who had

Continued

They argue that polls are blunt, unrefined instruments that either mismeasure true public opinion or bypass it completely.

There are many important theoretical and methodological criticisms of public opinion polls. I will discuss three arguments often advanced by critics:

1. Not all people have informed opinions on all topics.

2. Public opinion is expressed by groups, not individuals.

3. Polls measure *private* opinion, not public opinion.

NOT ALL PEOPLE HAVE INFORMED OPINIONS

One problem with classical democratic theories is that they assume all citizens care about politics and have opinions on most issues.

BOX 12.2   Continued

received the vaccine, and people began to panic. With the administration claiming the deaths were unrelated and coincidental, the president and his family took to national television to show an anxious nation that they were not afraid to be vaccinated. And so we watched the First Family being vaccinated and the panic subsiding. However, most of us declined to be vaccinated, deciding to take our chances with the evanescent flu.

By November—with no further flu cases reported anywhere and with increasing awareness of the negative publicity about the vaccine itself—the polls showed a steady decline in the number of people who intended to be vaccinated. Americans soon learned that over 500 people had developed nerve paralysis and 32 had died from the vaccine (out of the 48 million vacci-

nated).[5] There were no other reports of swine flu, either in the United States or elsewhere in the world.[6]

And, by then, having seen the photos portraying a clumsy man banging his head or falling down, having heard about the gaffe during the debate with Jimmy Carter that Poland was not then under the domination of the Soviet Union, and having read or heard the WIN and swine flu jokes, the electorate had voted Ford out of office. As a lame duck president, he could no longer even hope to counter what some felt had been another media assault.

Poor Gerry, many of us thought, never had a chance. Media critics blamed the press for its portrayal of an inept and incompetent man who, as Lyndon Johnson is supposed to have said, "played football too long without his helmet."[7] In this instance, one could argue that pub-

---

Public opinion pollsters also make this assumption. Yet social scientists, who have studied political attitudes and behavior over the past few decades, have found that this assumption is a false one. As a matter of fact, there is widespread apathy and ignorance among the American citizenry: Many people cannot name their own representatives to Congress or identity the party these members belong to. Critics of polls believe that most polling data are flawed because people will state an opinion to a

pollster without having given much thought to the issue at hand. Academic survey researchers have been trying to find ways to determine the intensity of a stated opinion, but are far from a solution to this problem.

PUBLIC OPINION IS EXPRESSED BY GROUPS

The idea that public opinion is determined by aggregating many individual opinions is a relatively

lic opinion polls were clearly a reflection of what people read, saw, and heard through media coverage. The self-fulfilling prophecy cycle seemed to be at work during Ford's time in the Oval Office.

In any event, early in the Ford presidency the message to Congress was clear: Here was a president without clout. Nixon's resignation had elevated the former long-term congressman to the most powerful position in the country. Can the media really take a respected veteran politician and former athlete and turn him into a bumbling boob who can't walk and chew gum at the same time?

1. Thomas E. Patterson, *The American Democracy* (New York: McGraw-Hill, 1990), p. 196.

2. Robert L. Lineberry, George C. Edwards III, and Martin P. Wattenberg, *Government in America*, 5th ed. (New York: HarperCollins, 1991), p. 490.
3. Ron Nessen, *It Sure Looks Different From the Inside* (Chicago: Playboy Press, 1978), p. 75.
4. George Gallup, *The Gallup Poll: Public Opinion 1972-1977* (Wilmington: Scholarly Resources, Inc., 1978), p. 855.
5. *The American Journal of Epidemiology* (Number 110), pp. 105–123, reported that eight times the normal rate of vaccinees developed nerve paralysis, known as the Guillain-Barre Syndrome.
6. See Barton Bernstein, "The Swine Flu Vaccination Campaign of 1976: Politics, Science and the Public," *Congress & The Presidency* (Vol. 10, No. 1, 1983), pp. 95–103, for a broader discussion on the conduct of the swine flu campaign and its implications.
7. Brock Brower, "Under Ford's Helmet," *The New York Times Sunday Magazine*, Sept. 15, 1974.

new one. Up until the development of the straw poll in the nineteenth century, public opinion was thought to be a societal consensus about an issue or issues. Jean-Jacques Rousseau, who wrote extensively about public opinion in the years before the French Revolution, argued that public opinion is represented by the general will of a society.

Many critics of polls think that national sample surveys, which tabulate the opinions of strangers around the nation, are not tapping into the more stable values and attitudes held by groups or entire communities. Herbert Blumer and other sociologists have argued that polls fail to tell us how institutions, social networks, and other aspects of the social structure affect public opinion development and change.

Structured questionnaires, these critics argue, do not help us understand the most important forces in public opinion processes. Students of public opinion should study the relationships among interest groups, policymakers, and concerned members of the public in order to understand how and why a particular issue develops. Why take a poll on an issue when the opinions of interest groups or a legislator's own opinion actually determine outcomes in that policy area?

POLLS MEASURE PRIVATE OPINION

Many critics of public opinion have pointed out that the opinions expressed in polls are private in nature. Pollsters and survey researchers always remind their respondents that answers to poll questions will be kept strictly confidential. In fact, if you ever participate in a legitimate poll, no one can ever attribute your opinion to you since you are assigned a respondent number. Any opinions you express in your conversation

with the interviewer are private ones, not public ones.

This idea that public opinion is actually private opinion presents a serious problem with polls and has great implications for contemporary political debate. Polls are now seen as one of the most influential sources of public opinion, yet the expression process is an anonymous one. A person need not stand up in public to articulate an opinion so that others know how he or she feels. The potential results of privatization are grave: Many fear that the ongoing, reciprocal public debate, which characterized public expression in earlier periods, may disappear as the result of polling.

Susan Herbst is a professor of communication studies at Northwestern University.

Those directly connected to either the print or the electronic press have also criticized the media's increased use of poll reports. *Boston Globe* editor Tom Winship commented, "I hate the God-damned things.... They snoop, they over emphasize. They sway votes, and they dry up campaign funds."[16] Edwin Diamond, media critic for *New York* magazine, has pointed out that:

> In theory, publishing poll results isn't supposed to influence voters' subsequent behavior. Specifically, polling specialists argue against any bandwagon effect, the movement of undecided voters toward the candidate consistently leading in the polls. In practice, so many elements go into the decision to vote—or stay home—that no one knows the cause-effect relationship.... Hal Bruno, ABC News's political director, acknowledges that "more research" into polling effects is needed—the standard response. Ocean dumpers usually call for additional studies, too.[17]

The reference to ocean dumpers is followed by a reference to polling as a kind of campaign pollution, which is followed by the point that nothing "will slow the rush to quantify; when a technology exists, it's used." Speaking about the 1988 presidential race between George Bush and Michael Dukakis, Diamond concludes:

> No one really needs a poll, or a critic to know that the Bush campaign has become an instant classic, a textbook case of media management. Thus a safe prediction: If you liked '88, you'll love '92.

How right he was. You will recall the discussion in the previous chapter of the extensive use of focus groups by both President Bush and Governor Clinton. It was indeed a very poll-conscious and therefore a very image-conscious campaign, as well as a very confusing one. What started out as a two-man race became a three-man race, with Ross Perot initially running surprisingly well in the polls as a result of much voter dissatisfaction with both major candidates. Then, by May, Perot began to slip in the polls as doubts about him increased.

During the July Democratic convention in New York City, Clinton named Al Gore as his choice for vice president, giving the Democrats an impressive boost in the polls. Perot, slipping further in the polls, graciously withdrew, saying he did not want to be a spoiler. Once again, it was a two-man race. Yet in mid-September, with his name on all 50 state ballots and with his platform more or less spelled out in his book,[18] Perot began to signal that he might jump back into the race—if his 50 state coordinators brought word that was what the Perot supporters wanted. On October 1, Perot was again declaring himself a candidate. A *New York Times*/CBS News Poll taken October 2–4 reported that 72 percent of the respondents felt Perot should not have reentered the campaign and 75 percent of them agreed that "Perot cannot be trusted to deal with the problems a President has to deal with."[19]

Through September and October, it seemed there was a new poll almost every day. And Rush Limbaugh, conservative talk show host, complained on his ABC radio program that there were so many polls with different results that he had lost interest in them. However, he differentiated between candidate-sponsored polls and polls conducted by news organizations. While he saw the former as serious attempts to find out what people were thinking about a candidate, the latter, he said, were suspect because those polls were merely undertaken to make news, to give the press something to talk about. Limbaugh was merely echoing an old and common criticism, one long acknowledged by Albert Gollin and Nicholas Von Hoffman. While Limbaugh and other critics of opinion polling appear to be blaming the messenger (the press), there are many others who blame the message—the poll itself—for its impact on various types of decision making.

USING THE POLLS TO SET A
WINNING POLITICAL AGENDA

When John F. Kennedy ran for the presidency, his father paid a half-million dollars to a pro-Republican Massachusetts newspaper editor to endorse the young senator, thereby directly attempting to influence public opinion. JFK was a bit more subtle. He hired pollster Louis Harris to help "shape his daily decisions."[20] Harris did this by tracking public opinion for the senator during his 1960 campaign against Vice President Richard Nixon. While the polling reports led to a winning strategy, they also helped open the debate about the way politicians use their money and their media handlers to manipulate the press and to set the political agenda.

During the Kennedy administration, Russell Baker published his first "Observer" column for *The New York Times* (July 16, 1962), spoofing an all-purpose presidential press conference and attesting to the enduring criticism of the press and the influence of polls. Baker wrote:

> Q. Would you comment on the Gallup Poll report that most Americans think we reporters are not asking you significant, penetrating questions in these conferences?
>
> A. No institution makes a more valuable contribution to democracy than these press conferences.... I know some people think it very unfair that we cannot ... get the Congress moving again or get Secretary [of State] Rusk into better physical condition, but life is unfair, and it is not always easy.... So I am hopeful that we can make a determination to keep these meetings as useful and as fruitful as they have been in the past, even though, as Dr. Gallup says, it is not an easy matter.[21]

Twenty-six years later, a still-critical Russell Baker lamented:

> How depressing, how dreary, how stupefyingly dull, how preposterously uninteresting we are all able to become, thanks to the omnipresent omniscience of our omnipollsters reducing each of us to a dehumanized omnisample of hemi-demi-semi-humanity.[22]

Polls may appear to be omnipresent and omniscient, but M. Margaret Conway has warned against basing campaign decisions on surveys that have used volunteer interviewers. As an example, she cites a 1978 U.S. Senate campaign in which the incumbent senator used volunteer interviewers as a cost-saving device for a survey conducted late in the campaign. She states that slight deviations in question wording could have produced significantly different response patterns, and some insufficiently supervised volunteers may have tired of their task and falsified some of the interviews.

Advertising decisions for the last weeks of the campaign were based on this faulty survey. Contrary to the actual situation, the incumbent was assumed to be an easy winner in a particular part of the state. Instead of buying additional media space and time, a mistaken decision was made to cut back on advertising there. This enabled the campaign to focus on other areas of the state where, based on the polling data, the challenger was deemed to be stronger. However, according to Conway, a different pattern of media buys might have ensured election victory. Although she acknowledges that volunteers are usually highly motivated, she emphasizes the need for extensive training and supervision. In this case, had professional interviewers been used, the survey would have cost approximately $3,500 more.[23] The moral of Conway's story: Only a poll–illiterate candidate would not recognize the value of paying for the services of a professional pollster who works only with well-trained and closely supervised interviewers.

Many people have begun to question the use of polling results to set strategy and to determine the candidate's political agenda. They have begun to see polls as manipulative and even damaging to the democratic process. Although John F. Kennedy used Louis Harris' surveys to map a winning strategy in 1960, it was not until 1972 for the Democrats and 1976 for the Republicans that the pollsters' influence grew dramatically. By 1980, Richard Wirthlin, advising Ronald Reagan, and Patrick Caddell, assisting President Jimmy Carter, were attending every major campaign meeting and helping to decide how, where, and how much money should be spent on which messages to reach which constituencies.[24] Caddell once observed, "A pollster is both an objective surveyor and a campaign consultant. We try to make the differences understood between survey data and our own instincts."[25] Once little more than behind-the-scenes technicians, a few pollsters have emerged as latter-day oracles (see Box 12.3) with impressive campaign clout.

In 1990, satirist and syndicated columnist Art Buchwald wrote, "At what stage of a recession may a president declare an economic downturn?" His answer was, "When all the economic indicators are falling and his popularity is dropping in the polls."[26] And in July 1992, Peter Passell, discussing President Bush's plunge in the polls, commented that "20-point-plus debits in the opinion polls have a way of focusing politicians' minds."[27]

Thinking about what some have called poll-driven, politically motivated election-year decisions[28] and what Dee Dee Myers, a Clinton campaign spokeswoman, dubbed "pure pork barrel politics,"[29] we noted that during the last days of August and early September, the Bush-Quayle team announced the following:

BOX 12.3   Our Latter-Day Oracles?

We have polls.
We have the Gallup Poll, the Roper
  Poll and the Harris Poll.
We have the ABC News/*Washington
  Post* Poll.
We have the *New York Times*/CBS
  News Poll.
We have the NBC/*Wall Street
  Journal* Poll.
Yes, my friends,
without these polls
and thousands like them
our politics would be only half as
  boring....
Did we forget to mention the
  Time/Yankelovich poll?
The famous Field poll,
so articulate about the California
  psyche?
Without these polls,
we would never know
what cattle feel like.
And don't forget the tracking polls.
And the exit polls.
And the entrance polls.
The lobby polls, the parlor polls
  [and]
the master bedroom polls....
The polls enrich us
with awareness
of our essential cipherhood....[1]

According to Mark R. Levy, a former manager of election analysis for

NBC News and a consultant to the
Carter-Mondale campaign in 1980,
the following people have the most
impressive track record, nationwide,
in all phases of recent presidential
politics. On the Republican side, he
names Richard Wirthlin and his
Decision/Making/Information,
Robert Teeter[2] of Market Opinion
Research, and V. Lance Tarrance and
Associates. On the Democratic side,
he lists Patrick Caddell of Cambridge
Survey Research, Peter D. Hart
Research Associates, and William R.
Hamilton and staff.

Referring to them as "gurus of
survey research," Levy says they are
now "key decision makers in every
aspect of presidential campaigns...
from deciding whether a politician
will run at all to interpreting the
winner's election mandate."[3]

---

1. I have quoted Russell Baker's column
and adapted it for this text. Russell Baker,
"Observer: Nearing Rope's End," *The New
York Times,* Nov. 9, 1988, Op-Ed page.
2. In 1992, Teeter was the campaign
manager for the Bush-Quayle reelection
effort.
3. Mark R. Levy, "Polling and the
Presidential Election," *The Annals of the
American Academy* (AAPSS) (March 1984),
pp. 85–96.

■ to employees at the General Dynamics tank facility in Warren,
  Michigan—support for a Pentagon program to spend $250 million to
  begin the multibillion-dollar upgrading of the army's M-1 tanks.
  (Defense Secretary Dick Cheney and his aides had previously argued
  that, with the demise of the Soviet Union and the end of the Cold
  War, the upgrade was no longer necessary; the Bush administration
  had previously refused to spend the money Congress had appropri-
  ated for the upgrade.)

- to the people in South Florida in the wake of Hurricane Andrew's devastation—a pledge to rebuild Homestead Air Force Base (previously a candidate for closing) at a cost of $500 million.

- to defense industry employees in Missouri, Connecticut, and California—support for a $9 billion deal with Saudi Arabia, consisting of $5 billion for the sale of 72 F-15s and $4 billion in contracts for parts and maintenance. While raising concerns among Israel's supporters about fueling the arms race in the Middle East, the proposed deal could save some 40,000 jobs in 45 states, including Missouri, Connecticut, and California.[30]

- to General Dynamics Corporation employees in Fort Worth, Texas—approval of the controversial sale of up to 150 F-16 fighters to Taiwan, thereby saving thousands of jobs not only in Texas (a must-win in the November election) but also in military plants in California, Connecticut, and Indiana.

- to rural South Dakota and West Texas farmers—a promise to subsidize American wheat sales abroad to the tune of $1 billion, although the president had previously supported free trade and had demanded that other countries end their subsidies for farm exports.

Taking into account all of the above decisions, we could conclude that it was a sign of the political trouble President Bush was in that he adjusted policy to help himself.

New York Times political reporter R. W. Apple, Jr., wrote on September 16, 1992, that in Colorado, generally considered Republican territory, *The Denver Post* Poll, with only six weeks left until election day, showed Governor Clinton with an 8-point lead over President Bush.* With an unemployment rate of 6.2 percent (somewhat below the national average of 7.7 percent), the major issue in Colorado was still the economy. However, concern for the environment, according to Governor Roy Romer, a popular moderate Democrat, also ranked high as an important issue. When Bush, concerned about the erosion of support due to economic issues, promised to block renewal of the Endangered Species Act unless it took jobs into account, the gap between the president and Clinton widened.

---

* *The Denver Post* Poll was taken between August 21 and September 1. It sampled 618 respondents and had a margin of sampling error of ±4 points. Clinton was leading 45 percent to 37 percent. However, the refusal rate was 7 percent, and 11 percent said they were undecided. Both Democratic and Republican leaders thought that the refusals and undecideds were probably Perot supporters who were having difficulty making up their minds. Clinton's apparent lead of 8 percent is meaningless because of the margin of error. See R. W. Apple, Jr., "Anti-Bush Sentiment Could Break Colorado's Tradition of Loyalty to G.O.P.," *The New York Times*, Sept. 21, 1992, p. A14.

On September 20, the Clinton campaign broadcast its first general election commercial attacking President Bush on the state of the economy. This was *the* topic shown by polls to be "foremost on the minds of voters."[31] And on September 21, despite the President's promised largess and nearly constant reminders about the Clinton draft issue, an ABC News/*Washington Post* Poll reported that, in a survey of 637 likely voters, Bill Clinton's lead had risen to 21 points (58% to 37% for President Bush).[32]

Finally, on September 29, White House Chief of Staff James A. Baker (who had returned to the White House from the State Department to take charge of the president's flagging reelection effort) convinced the president to drop his support for a recommendation by Dan Quayle's Council on Competitiveness. (The recommendation would have permitted businesses "to treat millions of tons of dangerous chemical wastes the same as household garbage and dispose of the material in ordinary landfills."[33]) With Baker's guidance, Bush also reversed his stand on the Endangered Species Act, dropping his opposition to renewal. Seen as an election-year flip-flop, the decisions did appear to be direct responses to increasing public concern about the environment. Were these other examples of the polls setting the political agenda?

THE LEADERSHIP DEBATE

If polls are influential enough to determine campaign tactics and effective enough to set the political agenda, what is their impact after the election? Do polls serve or hinder democracy? Such questions are constantly being considered by political scientists and pollsters. Among the first to raise such questions was John C. Ranney, who believed that polls were making

> a constructive technical contribution by reflecting sensitively and
> flexibly the currents of public feeling, by making this information
> available to political leaders in a way which is neither rigid nor
> mandatory, and by testing the claims of special interests to represent
> the desires of the people as a whole.[34]

Ranney said that no other agency performed these services and that they should not be underestimated. However, in answering the question of whether polls serve democracy, Ranney, writing in 1946, cited the most frequent objection: "polls destroy political courage and leadership."[35]

The impact of polls on the policy environment has been of continuous concern. As noted in Chapter 10, James Fallows, President Jimmy Carter's former chief speech writer, spoke of Carter's use of polling data for purposes of salesmanship, as opposed to the development of policy. Carter used polling data to learn *how* to do what he and his administration had already decided to do for other reasons. When Carter faced a ratification battle in the Senate for the Panama Canal Treaty, he studied the polling data and learned that most respondents believed the United States owned the Panama territory. Knowing why they objected to the treaty helped him develop arguments that enhanced the prospects of selling it.

In line with what had troubled Ranney so many years earlier, Fallows also spoke of the danger of using polling data to decide *what* to do instead of merely *how* to do it. Because polling is merely a snapshot of a moment, it focuses on short-run opinion and the immediate effect, rather than on a consideration of the long-term impact, of a particular policy.

On the subject of how democratic societies resolve their problems, Alexis de Tocqueville observed that they have a tendency to follow their feelings rather than their calculations, and that carefully thought-out, long-matured plans are too often forsaken to gratify momentary passions.[36] As an example of presidential political courage and leadership, as opposed to a president being led by public opinion, Tocqueville discusses the way George Washington handled his conflict with the House of Representatives over the question of American neutrality in the war between England and France. The extremely strong public support for a declaration of war against England was echoed by Congress, and Washington was left to voice his opposition through intense argument and inflexibility, and by testing his immense popularity to the limit. His view barely prevailed. Tocqueville stated: "The majority pronounced against the policy; now the whole nation approves it."

Joseph Goldberg has studied the link between public opinion polls and policy views and decisions in Congress. Particularly in regard to foreign affairs, Goldberg argues against presidential reliance on polls and on the advice of those who adhere too closely to constituent opinion. He states:

> [T]he opinions of the public are often responses without serious reflection. Polls themselves ... offer aggregate numbers without reasoned argument. A question might receive overwhelming agreement, but without reasons why such responses are given, the conclusions are of little value to thoughtful Congressmen. When the question concerns a technical matter, respondents may offer symbolic responses at best.[37]

While Franklin D. Roosevelt has been praised for his use of opinion polls to support presidential leadership,[38] Ronald Reagan has been criticized for using polls to manipulate public attitudes through his administration's management of the presidential agenda. For example, Morton Kondracke cited Reagan's luck, flexibility, and ability to manipulate public attitudes as the three factors that contributed to making his ratings at the end of his second year in office better than would have been expected given the state of the economy in early 1983.[39]

Speaking about the influence of opinion polls in the modern presidency, Richard Beal and Ronald Hinckley noted that

> Roosevelt had Cantril, Kennedy had Harris, Johnson had [Oliver] Quayle, Ford had Teeter, Carter had Caddell, Reagan has Wirthlin, while Nixon used most of them…. From 20 January 1981 until 1 July 1983, Wirthlin met with President Reagan more than 25 times to discuss politics and polls. During this interval he delivered memoranda on the results of more than 40 presidential studies to the White House.[40]

Beal and Hinckley group the reasons for the primacy of polls during the Reagan administration into three categories:

1. improvements in polling methodology and technology along with the growing importance of information in society
2. the growing acceptance of public opinion in democracy, and the need for modern presidents to demonstrate their responsiveness to the citizenry and to establish the general will as opposed to private interests
3. as a counterweight to conflicting staff opinions and advice; as a source of strategic information; and as a way to track presidential popularity and its tendency to decline during a president's term in office

There is no question that public opinion affects the mood in the White House. As Lyndon Johnson sat in the Oval Office in the early months of 1968, looked at his plummeting ratings in opinion polls, and listened to the anti–Vietnam War demonstrators across the street shouting, "Hey, hey, LBJ! How many kids did you kill today?" he knew his reelection chances were nil. In March 1968, he announced that he would not seek reelection. And when leading Republicans looked at Richard Nixon's plummeting ratings in opinion polls, and listened on July 31, 1974, to the members of the bipartisan House Judiciary Committee recommending his impeachment because of his role in the Watergate cover-up, they knew that their own credibility and that of the entire Republican party was at stake. After a visit from a group of his party's leaders, Nixon resigned the presidency on August 9, 1974.

His successor, as we have seen (Box 12.2), briefly enjoyed a 71-percent approval rating. With his announcement of a full pardon for Nixon, President Ford lost it. Addressing the role of leadership and its relationship to polls after he left office, Ford said:

> I do not think a president should run the country on the basis of the polls. The public in so many cases does not have a full comprehension of a problem. A president ought to listen to the people, but he cannot make hard decisions just by reading the polls once a week.... [W]hat a president ought to do is make the hard decisions and then go out and educate the people on why a decision that was necessarily unpopular was made.[41]

President Jimmy Carter, like Gerald Ford, would also learn—after his brief success in gaining the ratification of the Panama Canal Treaty—that a president who cannot maintain public support for his programs is soon history. Isn't that what democracy is all about?

PLURALISM VERSUS HYPERPLURALISM

The theory of classical pluralism (a system that permits a wide array of interest groups and opinions) is based on the need to preserve political stability, protect minority rights, and avoid the political extremes of a totalitarian government and the anarchy of a mass society. Until not that long ago, it was fashionable to praise our pluralist system as one in which diverse interest groups were free to voice their opinions and lobby for their share of the economic pie. According to James Madison, one of the first supporters of pluralist theory,

> Complaints are everywhere heard from our most considerate and virtuous citizens ... that the public good is disregarded in the conflicts of rival parties, and that measures are too often decided, not according to the rules of justice and the rights of the minor party, but by the *superior force of an interested and overbearing majority.*[42] [Emphasis added.]

Madison believed that factions (interest groups), despite their tendency to cause mischief, could counter the negative power of government by exercising a form of veto. Thus the father of the Constitution wrote that with

> a greater variety of parties and interests ... you make it less probable that a majority of the whole will have a common motive to invade the rights of other citizens; or if such a common motive exists, it

will be more difficult for all who feel it to discover their own strength and to act in unison with each other.[43]

For his part, Alexis de Tocqueville also feared the rise of despotism and lamented a tendency for *majority opinion* to have too strong a hold on individual Americans. Fortunately, Americans were, he said, a "nation of joiners," and the groups they joined acted as a counterweight to the rise of an all-powerful state.[44] Dissenting opinion therefore played an important role in perpetuating the democratic status quo.

Tocqueville's nineteenth-century contemporary, John C. Calhoun, took an extreme pluralist position in the national debate over slavery. Arguing for states' rights and as a justification for the continuation of slavery, Calhoun advocated a system of "concurrent majorities" and spoke about "taking the sense of the community." He freely acknowledged regional and sectional interests within the community as a whole. Calhoun explained the necessity and importance of permitting minority veto power on national policy, and he said that for representative government to survive, the interests of dissenting minorities had to be safeguarded.[45] (However, one could argue that the Civil War repudiated Calhoun's argument.)

At the core of pluralist theory are several requirements: competent and ethical elites to lead, an active electorate voluntarily associated with groups to speak out and fight for their interests, a decentralized government that permits public input and access on the grass-roots level, and government awareness, understanding, and involvement in matters of public concern. There is an underlying assumption that, for the sake of maintaining the system, the economic and political elites will be responsive not only to the voice of the majority but also to the veto power of the minority. If a pluralist system achieved all of these virtues, it would be almost impossible to criticize. And, if our system fit a pure pluralist model, it would be difficult to fault.

What works in theory obviously does not always work in practice, and critics of our system call it *hyperpluralism*. This term refers to a perverted form of pluralism characterized by a big, ineffective, fragmented government, a large number of powerful single-issue groups that are usually reluctant to compromise, and an apathetic citizenry that often fails to vote. Theodore Lowi, a much-respected Cornell University political science professor, is perhaps the most articulate critic of what he calls interest group liberalism, another name for hyperpluralism. According to Lowi, the activities of a multiplicity of large, well-funded, politically powerful interest groups has led to a paralysis of government. Lowi explains that when each and every group functions as a voice for its own single interest—clamoring to influence policy making in that particular narrow area—and when government attempts to placate every group, the resultant policies are muddled and often contradictory.

In particular, this phenomenon is most clearly at work during political campaigns. Candidates travel around the country and make promises, promises, and more promises. Their positions become less and less defined, resulting in a blurred image. For example, Bill Clinton expended a good deal of effort courting business groups. His summer campaign stop on Wall Street was designed to symbolize his pro-business stance. And one month before the November election he endorsed the Bush-sponsored North American Free-Trade Agreement (NAFTA) with Canada and Mexico, the result of more than a year of negotiations. Clinton was faced with today's version of the concurrent majorities: the conflicting interests of business, which supported the agreement, and labor, which opposed it. Not wanting to alienate either bloc of voters, he endorsed the agreement "with reservations," promising to "move aggressively to address the serious omissions from the agreement."[46] By endorsing the agreement "with reservations," the candidate was trying to placate both business and labor.

You will recall the discussion of the Republican strategy to court blacks (see Box 1.4) in an attempt to siphon off 20 percent of their vote from the Democrats. At the time, the Republicans assumed that President Bush would be able to retain the so-called Reagan Democrats and that 20 percent of the black vote would help solidify Bush's reelection chances. They could not then have anticipated the prolonged economic downturn, the increase in racial tension, the bolting of the Reagan Democrats, the family values controversy, and some of the other issues important to the country's concurrent majorities.

And this is where polling comes under criticism. Critics say that the candidate who best knows how to listen to the concurrent majorities and how to use polling data will not necessarily make the best elected official. There are those who agree with Professor Lowi that many of the problems we face today have come about because our leaders have listened too closely to the special interest groups. They also say that polls give voice to today's concurrent majorities—to our diverse sectional, economic, and cultural elements—and that the data enable candidates to tailor their messages to specific groups. This allows them to calculate which groups need attention (promises) and which can be ignored either because it is considered impossible to win their support or because their animosity toward the other candidate is so great that they could not possibly vote for him or her. It may be enough to add "with reservations" (a form of policy camouflage) when announcing your support for something the polls have told you a group opposes. Can you figure out what, if anything, this has to do with representative democracy or with leadership?

FINAL WORDS

Do we need to feel self-conscious about being such a polling society? Is there really something wrong with our press constantly reporting and interpreting polling data or with our candidates studying why, how, and what we say and then adjusting their rhetoric to conform to what we, the public, want? In theory, this *is* what democracy is about—a free press reporting what a free people wish their leaders to do. Yet in practice something goes wrong—perhaps because our politicians have only told us what we want to hear and have not always intended to follow through. (Remember the Bush statement: "Read my lips; no new taxes.")

What went wrong? Why did our democratic system limp, wounded, into the 1990s? While searching for a rational explanation, some of us got lost in our leaders' clever rhetoric, which was built of words forged in focus groups. Thus it seemed easier to blame the media—and the pollsters too—for mucking up things. That, of course, is easier than examining the real causes of what went wrong: Too many of our political leaders had abused their power and betrayed the trust of the American people. And too many of us lost sight of what was best for the country as a whole. As fictional character Murphy Brown said in her famous rebuttal to real-life character Dan Quayle, "There's enough blame to go around."

CHAPTER REVIEW

- In the post–World War II period, Jacob Javits used opinion polls as a starting point for creating interest in particular issues as well as for measuring existing opinion.

- Until the 1960s, the press mostly used the pollsters' services, but gradually a new public information and feedback system evolved. This replaced what had previously been accepted as valid manifestations of public opinion.

- In 1967, Philip Meyer undertook a study that created a profile of the urban rioter. Meyer's team found that education and income were not predictors of whether someone would participate in a riot. In fact, a good many of the looters were people who had jobs and who, under ordinary circumstances, would not have broken the law.

- Meyer believed that news research, or precision journalism, should include both the quantitative element common in social research methodology and traditional qualitative news reporting.

- During the 1970s, the press increasingly used polling reports to supplement their coverage. Candidates and the special interest groups paid for the surveys and disseminated the data free of charge.

- Competition from TV news led newspapers to undertake their own polling efforts.

- The need for cost sharing resulted in cooperative efforts and in the creation of joint polling ventures by various network television stations and newspapers.

- The switch from face-to-face interviewing to telephone interviewing helped the spread of news polling, as the newspapers' existing telephone banks in the classified advertising or circulation departments were used to keep polling costs down.

- Whereas in the 1930s the turnaround time for a poll was weeks or even months, in the 1980s it shrank to hours because of new technologies such as CATI. Charles Turner and Elizabeth Martin have identified other influential factors that led to the increased news value of polls: increased literacy and numeracy, near-universal access to the telephone, and increased power and decreased costs of automated information processing.

- Columnist Nicholas Von Hoffman has criticized the press for creating its own news through the use of in-house and commissioned polls.

- Pack journalism can be blamed for a negative self-fulfilling prophecy cycle. Polling results may be used as evidence of a candidate's poor performance, which renews media focus on the candidate's deteriorated position, leading to further polls and further coverage, and so on down to political oblivion. Some say that the soothsaying journalists, "polltalk," pack journalism, and the self-fulfilling prophecy cycle did in President Gerald Ford.

- Susan Herbst presents three thought-provoking arguments and asks whether polls really measure public opinion. There are fears that we may witness the demise of the "reciprocal public debate," the give and take of public argument that characterized political expression in the past.

- What, according to M. Margaret Conway, are the problems that have resulted from candidates' using volunteer interviewers?

- Just as the media have used polls to force something onto the policy agenda, presidents have used them as the basis for creating consensus and momentum to move Congress on a particular issue, to be responsive to the general will.

- How does the classical theory of pluralism differ from pluralism in practice? Hyperpluralism, or interest group liberalism, according to Theodore Lowi, has led to systemic paralysis. Why?

- How and under what circumstances is elite behavior influenced by polling results? Is our government hearing, listening, and responding to the concurrent majorities—the major sectional, economic, and cultural elements in the United States?

NOTES

1. Michael Parenti, *Make-Believe Media: The Politics of Entertainment* (New York: St. Martin's Press, 1992).

2. See Kurt Lang and Gladys Engel Lang, "The Impact of Polls on Public Opinion," *The Annals of the American Academy* (AAPSS) (March 1984), pp. 129–142.

3. James W. Tankard, Jr., "Public Opinion Polling by Newspapers in the Presidential Election Campaign of 1824," *Journalism Quarterly* (Summer 1972), pp. 361–365.

4. Bill Kovach, "A User's View of the Polls," *Public Opinion Quarterly* (Winter 1980), pp. 567–571.

5. Barbara Matusow, "Are the Polls Out of Control?" *Washington Journalism Review* (October 1988), pp. 16–19.

6. Albert E. Gollin, "Polling and the News Media," *Public Opinion Quarterly* (Winter 1987, Part 2), p. S87.

7. Arnold H. Ismach, "Polling as a News-Gathering Tool," *The Annals of the Academy* (AAPSS) (March 1984), p. 109.

8. Gollin, p. S88.

9. Thomas E. Patterson, *The Mass Media Election: How Americans Choose Their President* (New York: Praeger, 1980).

10. David Paletz, "Polls in the Media: Content, Credibility and Consequences," *Public Opinion Quarterly* (Winter 1980), pp. 495–513.

11. Gladys Lang and Kurt Lang, *The Battle for Public Opinion* (New York: Columbia University Press, 1983).

12. Gollin, p. S88.

13. Charles F. Turner and Elizabeth Martin, eds., *Surveying Subjective Phenomena* (2 vols.) (New York: Russell Sage Foundation, 1984).

14. Nicholas Von Hoffman, "Public Opinion Polls: Newspapers Making Their Own News," *Public Opinion Quarterly* (Winter 1980), pp. 572–573.

15. Dan Nimmo and James E. Combs, *Mediated Political Realities*, 2nd ed. (New York: Longman, 1990), p. 177.

16. As cited in Ismach, p. 116.

17. Edwin Diamond, "Media/Too Much, Too Soon," *New York* magazine, Nov. 21, 1988, p. 28.

18. Ross Perot, *United We Stand: A Plan for the 21st Century* (New York: Hyperion, 1992).

19. See poll results and accompanying article by Robin Toner, "80% of Texan's Ex-Supporters Mistrust Him—Bush Still Lags in Crucial Ratings," *The New York Times*, Oct. 6, 1992, pp. A1, 14.

20. Bill Kovach, "Too Much Opinion, at the Expense of Fact," *The New York Times*, Sept. 13, 1989, p. A31.

21. Russell Baker, "Observer," *The New York Times*, republished on July 16, 1992, p. B2.

22. Russell Baker, "Observer, Nearing Rope's End," *The New York Times*, Nov. 9, 1988, Op-Ed page.

23. M. Margaret Conway, "The Use of Polls in Congressional, State, and Local Elections," *The Annals of the American Academy* (AAPSS) (March 1984), pp. 97–105.

24. Mark R. Levy, "Polling and the Presidential Election," *The Annals of the American Academy* (AAPSS) (March 1984), pp. 85–96.

25. Cited in Levy; also see William J. Lanouette, "When a Presidential Candidate Moves, a Pollster May Be Pulling the Strings," *National Journal*, Dec. 15, 1979, p. 2092.

26. Art Buchwald, "Presidential Downturn," *Los Angeles Times*, Dec. 6, 1990.

27. Peter Passell, "Economic Scene: Will George Bush Read Their Lips," *The New York Times*, July 23, 1992, p. D2.

28. Michael R. Gordon, "In Election Year, Politics Greases Arms Decisions," *The New York Times*, Sept. 3, 1992, p. A20.

29. Michael Wines, "$8 Billion Directed to Wheat Farmers and Arms Workers: Votes Courted By Bush," *The New York Times*, Sept. 3. 1992, p. A1.

30. "The President's Promises," *The New York Times*, Sept. 12, 1992, p. 6.

31. Richard L. Berke, "The Ad Campaign—Clinton: Criticizing the President," *The New York Times*, Sept. 21, 1992, p. A14.

32. See "Clinton Takes 21-Point Lead Over President in a New Poll," *The New York Times*, Sept. 22, 1992, p. A24. The poll's margin of error was ±5 percentage points.

33. Keith Schneider, "Campaign Concerns Prompt White House to Drop Waste Plan," *The New York Times*, Sept. 30, 1992, pp. A1, A18.

34. John C. Ranney, "Do the Polls Serve Democracy?" *Public Opinion Quarterly* (Fall 1946), p. 360.

35. Ranney, p. 351.

36. Alexis de Tocqueville, *Democracy in America*, Vol. 2 (Garden City, NY: Doubleday-Anchor Books, 1969), pp. 228-229.

37. Joseph E. Goldberg, "Congress: The Deliberative Body in the National Security Process," *Grand Strategy and the Decisionmaking Process*, James C. Gaston, ed., (Washington, DC: National Defense University Press, 1992), p. 272.

38. Seymour Sudman, "The Presidents and the Polls," *Public Opinion Quarterly* (Fall 1982), p. 302.

39. Morton Kondracke, "White House Watch: Another Year Older," *New Republic* (year-end issue, 1982), p. 11. Also see the Langs' "The Impact of Polls on Public Opinion," [see note 2], p. 141.

40. Richard S. Beal and Ronald H. Hinckley, "Presidential Decision Making and Opinion Polls," *The Annals of the American Academy* (AAPSS) (March 1984), p. 74.

41. Gerald R. Ford, "Imperiled, Not Imperial," *Time*, Nov. 10, 1980, p. 31.

42. James Madison, Federalist Paper No. 10. See Clinton Rossiter, ed., *The Federalist Papers* (New York: American Library, 1961), p. 77.

43. Madison, p. 83.

44. Tocqueville, pp. 690–702.

45. For a discussion on concurrent majorities see John C. Calhoun's *Disquisition on Government* (Indianapolis: Bobbs-Merrill, 1953).

46. Gwen Ifill, "With Reservations, Clinton Endorses Free-Trade Pact," *The New York Times*, Oct. 5, 1992, pp. A1, A16.

13

New Technologies, New Concerns

Think about—

Can you identify the following technologies: CAPI, Ci2, Ci3, LANs, NIC, ESCAPE/600, DBM?

What's wrong with sugging, frugging, VIP, and COP?

Why do the new technologies and new applications of research methodology raise concerns about invasion of privacy?

You've been asked to participate in a poll and have been assured of confidentiality and anonymity. On completion of the interview, you are asked if you'd be willing to speak with a reporter or if you'd mind being identified with the opinions you have expressed. Any problems here?

Who should set the standards, the government or the researchers?

Has the public's attitude toward polling soured? If so, why?

What do the experts say about improving the public's opinion of public opinion polls?

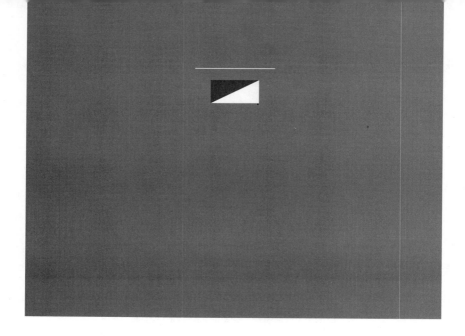

I know you have heard about CATI and RDD, but what about CAPI, the Ci2 or Ci3 systems, LANs, NIC, ESCAPE/600, DBM, QT, sugging or frugging, VIP, and COP? All these strange-looking terms are relatively recent additions to the world of polling. Some of them deal with technology; the rest deal with issues relating to the proliferation of pseudo-polls. In this final chapter we will consider the impact of both technology and pseudo-polls on the field of survey research, as well as some new concerns that trouble the pollsters and the public.

Having previously considered the impact of the media in general on public opinion and the impact of polls on journalism, later in this chapter I will turn the issue around and consider the impact of journalism on the reputation of polls. Finally, I will discuss the need to improve the public's opinion of public opinion polling.

THE NEXT GENERATION

Computer Interviewers

Computer-assisted personal interviewing (CAPI), around since the 1970s, is today's version of the face-to-face interview. Here, the interviewer carries a computer terminal to the respondent's location (such as a shopping mall, trade show, or convention) and connects the terminal to a central computer via telephone lines. As each question is downloaded from the computer, the interviewer reads it to the respondent and then types, or keys, the response into the terminal. The keyed-in response is then sent back (via telephone lines) to the central computer. Until recently CAPI interviews have usually been interviewer-administered (as opposed to self-administered) to avoid technical glitches. However, as we will see, new software has made it possible to replace interviewers with computers.

The *Sawtooth News* is a newsletter published by Sawtooth Software of Ketchum, Indiana. While lauding their computer programs for survey researchers, they also include interesting case studies and tidbits of information about new developments in personal computers and PC-based interviewing. In their Winter/Spring 1991 issue, Stu Cox of Kentucky Fried Chicken described his company's ongoing Research Guidance Test (RGT). The company's RGT group conducts taste tests, interviewing 120 respondents twice each month to determine consumers' perceptions and preferences. Deciding to automate their RGT, they converted their program to computer interviewing. This meant that respondents would sit in front of a computer, read the directions, and then type their responses to the questions that appeared on the computer screen, in effect interviewing themselves. Needless to say, by eliminating the interviewer they not only eliminated interviewer bias, but made the research process more cost effective.

The RGT group faced some unique problems in deciding how best to automate a testing process that involved food taste tests, analysis at the time of testing, and the immediate recording of respondent perceptions and preferences. The first thing they did was to develop a detailed program to evaluate their software needs. They subsequently decided on Sawtooth's Ci2 (an update of the first Sawtooth computer interviewing system). Ci2 is used for stand-alone PCs; the respondent responds to questions that appear on the computer screen. Ci2 therefore differs from Ci2 CATI (computer-assisted telephone interviewing), which is used by telephone interviewers whose PCs are connected in a local area network (LAN).

The Ci2 software could handle 100 to 1,000 questions (including single response, multiple response, numeric, open-ended, and constant sum) and, at the time, ran on IBM PCs or compatibles. (More powerful software updates subsequently made it possible to run the program on Macintosh computers.)

When it came to selecting the hardware (the computers themselves), they began by "drafting a graphical flow scenario that showed how respondents would move through [the] facility during automated RGT studies."[1] The flowchart created a greater awareness of the logistical problems and brought to their attention such issues as space, availability of electrical outlets, lighting, and hardware portability. The researchers were concerned that computer glare might make it difficult for the respondents to read the instructions and the questions; they were also concerned that a large desktop system could cast shadows on nearby test products. According to Stu Cox, they listed 20 attributes necessary to evaluate their hardware needs, including: processor type/speed; memory; video display type/resolution; dimensions and weight; keyboard type/size; utility software; and price, warranty, and service.

IBM and IBM-compatible hardware vendors then demonstrated their computers using Sawtooth's demo Ci2 questionnaire and respondents in the RGT facility. The researchers considered four different types of computers:

- *Desktops*   These computers offer the best display quality because they can have 13- to 14-inch color displays. However, they require AC power and a great deal of space at each interviewing station, and if there is a need to move them to a different test site or to other interviewing stations, disassembling or shipping them can be a problem.

- *Laptops*   These portables generally weigh 7–20 pounds and can be plugged in or run on batteries. Although the heaviest are often dubbed "luggable," all offer good display quality. However, only monochrome is available at a reasonable price.

- *Notebooks*   These weigh only 5–8 pounds, can also run on batteries, and offer the same video display quality as laptops. They are considered the ultimate in portability.

- *Clipboards*   These can run on either AC power or batteries. They are the newest lightweight portable computers and are also called electronic clipboards or pad computers. What makes them particularly interesting is that many of these computers can recognize printed handwriting and can display questionnaires or forms as they would appear on paper. Instead of an actual keyboard, these hardware systems have an attached "pen," used to write on the display or to make entries from a video keyboard.

Testing the hardware with Sawtooth's software in the RGT facility enabled the researchers to also get the respondents' reactions to computer-interviewing technology before any final decisions were made. Researchers used their regular taste test interviewing procedure and then asked the respondents if they would participate in a special survey on computers. Using a 5-point scale, 78–79 percent of the respondents said they liked the computer interviewing experience very much. The second interesting finding was that the reaction to computer interviewing was independent of age, sex, and race.

A notebook system won the day. Kentucky Fried Chicken's RGT group decided on some slight modifications: To enhance readability, they used colored key labels on the keyboards, and to protect the keyboard from spills and messy fingers, they added a protective skin.

Cox reports that since the conversion to computer interviewing technology, cost-effective benefits have been realized in the following areas:

- It now takes about one hour to prepare questionnaires, as opposed to the three to five hours it once took.

- Since the questionnaires appear on the computer screens, there is no need to photocopy them for use by the respondents. Not only does this again save staff time, it saves an enormous quantity of paper.

- The average time per interview has been cut by 50 percent.

- Since the foods to be taste-tested must be carefully prepared and served consistent with rigid guidelines, the time saved by computer interviewing also helped the researchers better plan the logistics of having the food products ready when the respondent-taster is ready.

- Within 30 minutes of a study's completion, data are now ready for analysis, and the analysis itself is completed by the next day.

- In addition to the elimination of interviewers, computer interviewing technology also eliminates the need for staff to check the completed questionnaires for missed questions, errors, or inconsistencies. The computer program automatically does all of that.

The real value of the Sawtooth stand-alone program is that it can be used to conduct interviews in shopping malls, "without the cost of hiring an interviewer," and that

Interactive interviews can be used by museums to interview visitors, by retailers to build customer profiles, or by ad agencies to test ad responses. *Research shows that people are more honest with a computer than with a human interviewer.*

... Collecting data is the easiest thing about Ci2. You can create as many copies of "field disks" as you need. Field disks run the questionnaire from any computer with one floppy disk drive... [and] you can transfer Ci2 data files to a format compatible with survey tabulation and statistical analysis programs with the CONVERT program.[2] [Emphasis added.]

The idea that people are more honest with a computer than with a human interviewer was supported by Sara Kiesler, a professor of social psychology at Carnegie Mellon University. Kiesler, who studies business organizations, said that respondents are more reluctant to "reveal negative information or any information about themselves" to human interviewers.[3] Professor Kiesler and Lee S. Sproull compared findings about respondents in an electronic (computer) survey with those involving respondents in a paper survey (prepared with a high-quality laser printer).[4] They found that the respondents who used the computer

- completed more items and completed them with fewer mistakes

- gave longer answers to open-ended questions

- talked more about themselves

- less frequently chose agree responses and the middle responses in 7-point Likert scales (see Chapter 7)

- admitted to more socially undesirable behavior and reported more personal traits and feelings

In 1992 Sawtooth released its Ci3 program, the new version of its Ci2 software. Ci3 can handle more complex questions and sequences of questions. For example, if you specify a list of items and the question you want to ask, the computer will repeat the question for each item specified. In addition, depending on the memory capability of the computer, the Ci3 program can handle well over 1,000 variables. Its new user interface (mode of interacting with the user) provides pull-down menus, dialog boxes, and on-line help.

The Behavioral Risk Factor Surveillance Program of the Centers for Disease Control (CDC) selected the Ci3 CATI system for its ongoing studies conducted by individual states. These studies track smoking, diet, exercise, and other behaviors related to chronic diseases. Each month, the participating states and territories survey 100–330 of their residents, selected through RDD (random-digit dialing). They use a CDC questionnaire with a standard battery of questions and provide CDC with the data for analysis.

Although in the near future this may be the way it's all done, there are limits to what computers can do. Critics have pointed to the following negatives:[5]

- Machines cannot initiate social chitchat to engage reluctant respondents.

- While a "help" capability can be programmed to assist the respondent in understanding the instructions, the computer cannot explain questions that may not have been properly understood.

- Computers cannot prompt a respondent, recognize a superficial or ambiguous answer, or ask a respondent to elaborate when an answer is unclear.

- A computer cannot ask a follow-up question in response to a comment that is particularly provocative.

- The computer cannot solicit a long response from poor or slow typists. In most cases they will merely answer in a perfunctory manner.

- Some people perceive a telephone call from a computerized, synthesized voice as an annoyance or as an invasion of privacy and simply hang up.

LANs and Predictive Dialing

Local area networks (LANs) now permit PCs to share information. To connect PCs to the network, each PC must have a **network interface card (NIC)** installed, and each network must have a PC that acts as a *file server.* A file server is a mass storage device, the contents of which (for example, questionnaires and data files) are accessible to all of the PCs on the network. An NIC is a high-speed communication device capable of transmitting and receiving data over a network. The actual *topology* (layout or pattern) of the network determines the type of NIC to be used. Network topology is determined by the physical location, the number of interviewing stations, the distance between the PCs, the desired speed of interaction, and cost factors. There are several network configurations (linear, ring, and so on), each with its own advantages and disadvantages.

Improving on preview, power, and anticipatory dialing (see Box 13.1), telemarketers have developed predictive dialing. This is still another way to lower costs by replacing manual dialing with an automated dialing system and by—in assembly-line fashion—timing the dialing so that the system keeps the LAN interviewers moving from a completed call to a waiting call.

Theodore Reed, president of the Data Group, Inc., explains that this new technology requires an initial investment of about $5,000 to $8,000 per interviewing station; although this is expensive for most survey researchers, the system is becoming increasingly appealing. It can dial a telephone number, detect an answer, and immediately switch the call to a human interviewer who is part of the LAN. Reed reported that one predictive dialing system recognizes the human voice in 20 milliseconds and the call is instantly switched to an interviewer "so quickly that the interviewer hears virtually the entire 'Hello' and can begin the conversation without an awkward

---

BOX 13.1   Automated Dialing

There were three modes of automated dialing commonly used in telemarketing before predictive dialing:

Preview Dialing
This is similar to the way in which we press a button on our home phone to initiate the dialing of a preprogrammed number. In this case, the interviewer, using an on-line sample, can signal the computer to initiate dialing. While this is faster and more accurate than manual dialing, the interviewer must still wait for someone to answer the telephone.

Power Dialing
This is used primarily in telemarketing, and it is commonly used for computerized/synthesized voice interviewing. Power dialing eliminates nonworking numbers and is also faster than manual dialing. A preset rate determines when the call will be initiated. The assumption is that the potential respondent will be reached just as the interviewer becomes available. However, the system will automatically hang up if the interviewer is not ready to accept the call. Unfortunately, this practice results in many nuisance calls, a major disadvantage.

Anticipatory Dialing
Akin to power dialing, this mode has the same advantages and disadvantages, except that it slightly reduces the rate of nuisance calls. With anticipatory dialing it is possible to adjust the dialing rate in response to the length of the interviewer's talk time (interview length). Still, once the dialing time is set, there is little flexibility.

---

pause."[6] If the system reaches a busy signal, it redials, and it can detect a telephone company message and a ringing phone. Reed added:

> What makes a predictive dialing "predictive" is that it statistically predicts how fast it must dial to keep all interviewers occupied. If its pace results in too many nuisance calls, the system slows down; if the interviewers are idle, it speeds up. Overall, it eliminates the frustration interviewers experience with repeated dialing while ensuring that they are kept productive.

While telemarketers have praised predictive dialing, perhaps we should pause to question whether we want a mechanical system ensuring that we are kept productive.

The Synthesized Voice

Another computer-related innovation is the tele-research tool ES-CAPE/600. The acronym ESCAPE stands for the *E*lectronic *S*ynthesized *C*omputerized *A*utomatic *P*olling *E*quipment, which is connected to telephone lines. This is a type of LAN without live interviewers. The package includes an IBM computer to process questions and answers to telephone surveys, instantly breaking down the data into meaningful statistics that can be printed out. More specifically, the equipment enables the researcher to program a computer to do the following:

- call preselected telephone numbers or random-digit dial
- record a digitized voice (male or female) that will speak to whoever answers the call
- instruct the listener (through the synthesized—recorded—voice) to respond by dialing/pressing numbers on the phone (for example, "press 1 for male, 2 for female")
- begin the questioning, pause three seconds for each response, and proceed to the next question
- branch, depending on the respondent's answer, to an alternate set of questions. (For example, a respondent can answer either 1 for yes, or 2 for no to the question, "Are you between the ages of 18 and 25?" A yes answer will automatically lead to one set of questions, while a no answer will lead to an alternate branch.)
- thank the respondent at the end of the interview and break the connection, sending the data to the computer while it continues calling until the desired number of calls have been completed
- recall busy or no-answer numbers a predetermined number of times until the call is completed or the cutoff point is reached
- process the data and present computer printouts of the results in a bar chart, matrix, or column format, with numbers and/or percentages

The ESCAPE/600 system can be operated unattended for a programmed time period so that it shuts itself off during designated times of the day or night. It also records the telephone number of each respondent. Follow-up contacts for more in-depth interviewing are therefore possible should a respondent answer yes to the question "May we call you back and talk with you in more detail?" Another intriguing aspect is the equipment's

**Table 13.1 Respondent Comparison
for ESCAPE/600 and Live Interviewers**

	NUMBER CONTACTED	NUMBER OF COMPLETIONS		TOTAL NUMBER OF COMPLETIONS	RESPONSE RATE
		English	*Spanish*		
ESCAPE/600	1,397	204	3	207	15%
Live interviewers	1,063	427	123	550	52%

SOURCE: Mitchell E. Shapiro (University of Miami, School of Communication), "A Comparison of Respondents to ESCAPE/600 vs. Live Interviewers," an unpublished paper based on a study (conducted May 12–May 15, 1986), commissioned by M. A. Kempner, Inc., Pompano Beach, Florida.

ability to faithfully reproduce anyone's voice. (I understand that President Reagan's voice was recorded and used successfully for fundraising purposes in certain districts in Florida.)

Mitchell E. Shapiro of the University of Miami conducted two concurrent surveys using randomly generated telephone numbers of residents of Dade County, Florida. The purpose of the surveys was to compare the results of two Dade County samples using the same questionnaire for each, but using different interviewing techniques. One set of respondents was called by an ESCAPE/600 synthesized female voice, while the other set was interviewed by four female interviewers who had been professionally trained.

One of several interesting aspects of this survey was the language problem. The live interviewers were bilingual (English and Spanish), and the ESCAPE/600 system was programmed to administer the questionnaire in either language. A problem arose, however, in that the introduction was in English, followed by the first question, also in English, asking the respondent which language was preferred. It is thought that on hearing an English introduction, Spanish speakers probably hung up without waiting to hear the first question. To some extent, this helps to explain the disparity in response rate, which can be seen in Table 13.1.

Because of the low number of Spanish-speaking respondents in the ESCAPE sample, the researchers decided to compare the following:

1. English-speaking respondents from both surveys: 204 from the ESCAPE sample and 427 from the live-interviewer sample.
2. The results from the ESCAPE sample ($n = 207$) and the entire live-interviewer sample ($n = 550$).

Table 13.2 Comparison of English-Speaking Respondents by Age

	PERCENT OF SAMPLE		
AGE OF RESPONDENTS	*ESCAPE*	*Live (English)*	*Live (Total)*
Under 17	29%	8%	7%
18–34	37	47	42
35–49	19	22	22
50 and over	14	23	29

SOURCE: Mitchell E. Shapiro (University of Miami, School of Communication), "A Comparison of Respondents to ESCAPE/600 vs. Live Interviewers," an unpublished paper based on a study (conducted May 12–May 15, 1986), commissioned by M. A. Kempner, Inc., Pompano Beach, Florida.

The questionnaire consisted of five demographic questions (asking the sex, age, race/ethnic origin, income, and education of the respondent) and several questions dealing with attitudes toward the Dade County police. Shapiro reported that on the first comparison, when the English-speaking respondents were compared, there were no significant differences on four demographic variables: race, sex, income, and education. There was, however, a significant difference on the age variable when the English-speaking respondents were compared. As can be seen in Table 13.2, it was found that the ESCAPE sample was younger than the live-interviewer sample. Older respondents appear to be more receptive to a live interviewer than to an automated, synthesized voice.

On the second comparison, the ESCAPE and total live interviewer samples were compared and no significant differences were found on three of the demographic variables: sex, income, and education. A significant difference was found on the remaining two variables: age and ethnic origin. However, as Professor Shapiro states, the differences on the ethnic origin variable should be discounted because of the language problem explained above.

Using the ESCAPE technology, 31 percent (334) more people were contacted than were reached by the live interviewers during the same time period. The system has proven most popular for short political opinion polls. It is used by a number of newspapers and radio and television stations around the country. Some researchers think the system is efficient and cost effective for many types of surveys.

Although the technology is impressive, perhaps we ought to pause to consider the social implications. Mechanized dialers randomly select our phone number; a synthesized voice introduces itself and begins to ask questions to which we respond by dialing or pressing specific numbers. We may be giving rough estimates of our income, relaying that we own or rent our home, describing how large our family is, and providing other such information, which is transmitted electronically to a computer. This depersonalization of the polling process raises questions about access and invasion of privacy. Is there a difference if you are called by a human interviewer? What do you think?

Disk-by-Mail Surveys

POPULUS, Inc., a marketing research and consulting firm, has been one of the pioneers in disk-by-mail (DBM) surveys. DBMs may be the most cost-effective way to administer complex questionnaires to *targeted* but geographically dispersed audiences. Lesley Bahner of POPULUS has discussed a number of concerns and complications connected with the need to protect their own system from a computer virus caused by a returned disk that had been "infected."[7] Explaining how POPULUS has tried to protect itself from respondents who get curious about the data and programs on the questionnaire disks and who try to manipulate files (as computer hackers are known to do), Bahner said:

> We put a level of security between important Ci2 files and the respondent by using DOS [Disk Operating System] batch files [containing procedures] to create our own "shell" for giving information to the respondent. [The shell creates a working environment that shelters the operating system from the respondent.] It checks to make sure the questionnaire has been completed and it provides on-screen instructions for returning the questionnaire.... We hide or make "read only" the program and data files so that respondents cannot erase or manipulate them—either accidentally or on purpose. We don't make respondents suspicious by hiding all our files; however, we do only enough to protect ourselves.

POPULUS tries hard to have their materials reflect a professional and legitimate look. They use first-class postage to send their disk surveys and first-class, prepaid return mailers. Under special circumstances, when getting a respondent's attention is especially important, they enclose a preprinted and prepaid airbill for overnight delivery.

As noted, DMB surveys are used only for specifically targeted groups, as are surveys by electronic mail, sent to on-line computer users. On completing the electronic survey, the respondent merely types a command to send the file to the designated "address."

QT's Power

Some time ago, I attended a conference at which Quick Tally Systems (QT) demonstrated its portable audience response system. The large ballroom of the hotel was filled with a convenience (non-scientifically selected) sample of 286 attendees, sitting at long narrow tables placed in dozens of rows. At each of our places we found a small handset with a 12-button keypad for responses from 1 to 10 and "Yes" and "No." In addition, the handset had an 11-point slider (0–10) to register degrees of approval, agreement, and so on, as well as a liquid crystal display (LCD), enabling us to read our own responses easily. At the front of the room there was a large viewing screen on which the questions, instructions, and instantaneous tallies of our responses appeared. It was incredible.

We were first asked demographic questions (age, sex, income, highest degree, professional affiliation—university, marketing or research firm, and so on—political affiliation, race). The question would appear on the screen; then seconds later the instructions … and the words "press now." No sooner had we registered our responses than the data appeared on the screen in the form of cross-tabulations, multivariate correlations and analyses, colorful graphs, tables, and pie charts. QT could break the data out into 18 different sub-groups. We were also shown political commercials and asked to use the 11-point slider to continuously register our approval (by moving the slide toward 10) or our disapproval (by moving it in the other direction, toward 0). As we watched the commercials and registered our reactions, we were able to see the cumulative data superimposed on the lower portion of the screen. We were shown the tallies instantaneously (and given an opportunity to look at the way the variables interacted) as part of the professional demonstration, but in a normal research situation the respondents would not necessarily see the result (or impact) of the cumulative recorded data.

Among the interesting revelations was that QT, driven by a small laptop computer, is able to collect data every second, and that a complete system of 25 handsets (for small-group research projects) can fit into a medium-sized suitcase. However, perhaps most interesting—and potentially disturbing—was the realization that the wiring of the individual handsets enabled operators to identify and create profiles of the individual respondents.

Since then, the general public has become acquainted with QT-type technology. During the 1992 presidential debates, groups were assembled, supplied with handsets, and asked to record their reactions. Ted Koppel's "Nightline" viewers were thus able to see colorful graphic displays of the respondents' approval or disapproval for the various candidates' answers.

REGULATING SURVEY ABUSE

Self-Regulation to Stop Unsavory Practices

Along with the new technologies have come new forms of abuse of the survey process. **Sugging**, selling under the guise of research, has attracted a good deal of attention in Great Britain, where there is an effort to take suggers to court. The British cite their data privacy laws, and American researchers, seeking a similar ban, say that "there is an element of fraud among those who engage in sugging."[8]

Frugging, fundraising under the guise of research, has also attracted the wrath of survey researchers. The American Association of Public Opinion Research (AAPOR) has criticized a number of senators and congressmen and various special-interest groups, such as the Union of Concerned Scientists, the Moral Majority, and the National Rifle Association, for this practice.

Besides the unseemly practices of sugging and frugging, AAPOR has also condemned *political canvassing* under the guise of surveying. Although AAPOR has no problem with traditional political canvassing, in which the person being canvassed is aware of the call's purpose (to identify and mobilize political supporters), the organization has protested the use of "identified lists for political, marketing, and other nonresearch purposes without a respondent's explicit, informed consent." It has therefore cited two sections of its code relevant to these practices:

§II D 1 — We shall strive to avoid the use of practices or methods that may harm, humiliate, or seriously mislead survey respondents.

§II D 2 — Unless the respondent waives confidentiality for specified uses, we shall hold as privileged and confidential all information that might identify a respondent with his or her responses. We shall also not disclose or use the names of respondents for nonresearch purposes unless the respondents grant us permission to do so.[9]

The Executive Council of AAPOR cited the following two cases involving abuses of its research standards:

The Choice Attitude Survey   In a study designed to identify and record abortion attitudes of voters in Minnesota, Nancy Brataas Associates, Inc., and Planned Parenthood of Minnesota used telephone directory information and volunteer interviewers who read the following script:

Hello ... Is this _____ ? (Pause for confirmation of name.)

My name is _____ and I'm a volunteer working for the Choice Attitude Survey. We are calling you—as a Minnesota voter—to survey your attitude about keeping abortion legal. I have a couple of questions that will take less than a minute of your time.

A few questions on abortion followed, and the responses were linked with the names. The result was a database for subsequent mailings. When AAPOR complained that the mailing lists were created without the respondents' knowledge or consent, Planned Parenthood of Minnesota responded that "the generation of a database was not the only purpose of the project—the results [of the survey] were tabulated and widely disseminated." Following discussions between the AAPOR Executive Council and representatives of Planned Parenthood of Minnesota, the latter promised to honor AAPOR standards in future surveys, and AAPOR admonished (rather than censured) Planned Parenthood of Minnesota "for having misled respondents and having violated their confidentiality."

VIP and COP   The National Right to Life Committee (NRLC) has for some years undertaken two related canvassing efforts—the Voter Identification Program (VIP) and the Citizen Opinion Poll (COP)—which have been criticized by AAPOR for the same reason the organization criticized the Choice Attitude Survey. Both VIP and COP used telephone directory information and were designed to identify and record abortion attitudes and political party preferences of voters. This is a nationwide effort, as the NRLC and its affiliates maintain records at the local, congressional district, and state levels. The VIP script follows:

Hello, may I speak with _____ ?

I am a volunteer with the (National Right to Life Committee/ Name of State Organization). We are conducting a national survey of registered voters and would greatly appreciate your help. May I ask you a few short questions that will take only about 60 seconds?

This introduction is followed by six questions—four deal with respondent attitude toward abortion, one asks the number of other registered voters in the household who agree with the respondent's position on abortion, and the remaining question asks the respondent to identify his or her political party affiliation. Here, too, the information has been linked with the person's name, producing canvassing or mailing lists without the respondent's knowledge or consent.

When AAPOR complained to the NRLC, they did not respond. As a result, AAPOR's Executive Council recommended public censure of the NRLC for "misleading respondents and violating their confidentiality."

Mervin Field, the chairman of Field Research Corporation, cites another disturbing practice that may not at first appear unethical. Respondents, after being interviewed, are asked whether they would agree to speak with a reporter and to have their comments identified. If they agree, a reporter calls to discuss their opinions. This is touchy for several reasons. First, although the respondent was initially assured of confidentiality and anonymity as is expected, the next step—introducing a reporter into the polling situation—raises privacy concerns. Another reason this is a disturbing practice involves psychological vulnerability. Because interviewers endeavor to establish a rapport with their respondents through their opening remarks, assurances of confidentiality and anonymity, and general tone, Field believes that respondents are "psychologically vulnerable to 'giving away' their privacy by agreeing to a follow-up interview." In addition, he states that

> there is the palpable risk of creating doubt about our assertions of confidentiality, particularly among respondents who refuse the follow-up....
>
> If respondents are identified with their stated views, in the context of a public opinion report presented by the media, other members of the public would sense that, were they to participate in such a poll, they and their comments would also be identified."[10]

He therefore predicts that if public identification of respondents is permitted to increase, refusal rates will also increase, thereby undermining professional survey operations.

Reacting to the various unsavory practices described above, in March 1990 AAPOR joined the Research Industry Coalition (RIC) of professional and trade associations in the fields of marketing and opinion research. The AAPOR Council voted to support the RIC statement condemning the following unethical practices under the guise of research:[11]

- "Offering products or services for sale, or using participant contacts as a means of generating sales leads" (sugging)
- "Requiring... or soliciting monetary contributions from members of the public as part of a research process" (frugging)
- "Revealing the identity of individual respondents to a survey or of participants in a research process without their permission"

Self-Regulation to Protect Anonymity

Field Research Corporation (FRC) has long been concerned with protecting a respondent's anonymity and with maintaining confidentiality. These concerns have intensified over the years as FRC became increasingly involved in *litigation studies* (this topic was introduced in Chapter 5). Although FRC did its first litigation survey in 1956, it was only in 1968 that a court ordered FRC to reveal respondent names. Hired to survey the need for a change of venue in the Juan Corona serial murder case, FRC's interviewers gave their customary assurances of anonymity to their respondents. The judge subpoenaed the questionnaires, promising to examine them *in camera* (in his chamber, privately). Although he had promised not to turn the questionnaires over to the prosecution, he later reversed himself and allowed the prosecution to examine the questionnaires and to summon some survey respondents as witnesses. This action violated FRC's explicit assurances to its respondents of confidentiality and anonymity.

In an effort to prevent a repetition of such violation of respondent anonymity, FRC drew up an expanded consultation agreement, which potential lawyer clients must sign before any survey work is undertaken. The agreement includes the following statements:

> Under no circumstances can the names or addresses of interviewees drawn for a sample be made available to counsel, opposing counsel, or to the court....
>
> To make this policy operational, FRC maintains as a standard practice the procedure of removing and destroying respondent names upon completion of interview verification.[12]

The agreement also spells out the procedure in cases where the names have been supplied by clients wishing to survey a special population. In those instances, FRC will still act to protect the anonymity of the respondents, by not identifying the answers with individual interviewees.

In short, FRC simply will not permit a repeat of the experience they had in the 1968 Corona case. As a result, FRC has successfully ensured respondent anonymity in over 100 subsequent litigation-related surveys.

In anticipation of a subpoena, FRC and other opinion researchers advocate destroying respondents' names and addresses once the data have been collected and verified. This is the simplest and most practical way of ensuring that respondent anonymity will be protected. Mervin Field explains that it is also solidly based on the theory that the result of a public opinion survey constitutes an objective description of the aggregation of private opinions on public issues; thus, specific identities are irrelevant. In the final analysis, it is the summary descriptions—derived from careful consideration of the statistical data—that are important.

Impact Assessment conducted a survey on behalf of certain Alaskan municipalities relating to the 1989 Exxon oil spill. When Exxon (the defendant) and certain plaintiff attorneys petitioned the court to do so, the court required Impact Assessment to supply revealing information relating to their respondents' identities. The court order reinvigorated an ongoing debate relating to prelitigation surveys and to legal maneuvers that have increasingly threatened the integrity of survey research.

Harry W. O'Neill, vice chairman of the Roper Organization, warned against keeping respondent-identifiable material in the files, which might be subpoenaed during the pretrial discovery process. Prior to the trial itself, the attorneys for both sides search for material to support or rebut evidence that could be produced during the trial. The attorneys may request documents from public opinion researchers believed to be helpful to their case. O'Neill recommends discarding anything that can be used to identify respondents.[13]

On the other hand, Burns W. Roper does not agree with his vice chairman's "admittedly air-tight solution to the problem of protecting respondent anonymity." He feels that destroying the names and addresses of respondents creates a credibility problem for the research organization once the researchers are called to court. The court, Roper explains, does have a legitimate right to determine that the survey was conducted, that the respondents were interviewed, and that they answered freely and without coercion. Roper is concerned both with the need to protect respondents and with the need to satisfy the legitimate interests of the court regarding the integrity of the survey itself.

While refusing to turn over the identifying material, Roper offers to do either of the following two things:

1. Go back to survey respondents (some or all), tell them that the survey on which we interviewed them was now in a court case and ask them if they would be willing to have us turn their names over to the court, with the understanding that if they were called by the court: (a) they would only be asked to answer questions about the circumstances of their interview (and not the validity of the survey design) and (b) their time and expenses would be compensated.

2. Develop a short, mutually agreed-upon (by plaintiff, defendant, and court) re-interview questionnaire. The questionnaire would be designed to ascertain whether the person had been inter-

viewed before, whether s/he had felt coerced in any way, and to determine certain basic things about his/her demographic characteristics, brand usage, etc. that would serve to validate the previous survey responses.[14]

Roper warns, however, that the researchers "must be wary ... of repeating opinion questions on which a respondent's views could well have changed since the time of the original interview." The reinterview would be administered by new interviewers in the presence of a court-appointed witness or notary public, who would then attest to the validity and integrity of the reinterview.

After saying that his approach protects the respondent, ensures the maximum effectiveness of the survey, and is responsive to the legitimate interests of the court, Roper states:

> Moreover, the first time I go to jail for refusal to divulge respondent names will also be the last time, for that will be the last legal evidence survey I ever conduct.
>
> Harry says to cheer up, however, for he will come to see me on visiting days!

What would you do in similar circumstances? Which approach— O'Neill's or Roper's—do you agree with?

The Malpractice Suit

AAPOR reports that legal action against market researchers is nothing new. During the 1950s congressional hearings were held to investigate the system of television audience ratings, and in 1975, Time Inc. and *Esquire* sued W. R. Simmons & Associates Research, which had provided magazine audience estimates. Time Inc. sued when Simmons' comparative estimates of magazine readership for *Time* and *Newsweek* proved to be "remarkably" inaccurate. *Esquire* sued because Simmons did not include it in the survey, seeming to imply that it was "insignificant in the magazine industry."[15] And in 1987 the television networks and ad agencies were locked in a dispute over viewership estimates. Audience measurement systems differed, one from another, by as much as 10 percent. When you consider that each rating point equals approximately 1 million viewers and that advertising rates are determined by the rating points, you can begin to understand the importance of accuracy in measurement.

This overview is merely a lead-in to a brief discussion on methodological malpractice suits. In 1987, Beecham Inc. filed a $24 million liability suit against Yankelovich, Skelly and White/Clancy Shulman (then under different management), claiming that "Yankelovich was guilty of negligence, negligent misrepresentation, professional malpractice and breach of contract."[16] Yankelovich had conducted a marketing research study for Beecham and recommended that "with an $18 million introductory year media budget, Beecham's new cold-water wash product, Delicare, would achieve market shares of 45 to 52 percent, thus capturing leadership from Woolite." When Delicare's market share did not reach even 25 percent, Beecham sued. In the meantime, Yankelovich's new management team conducted another study, which yielded more modest predictions.

G. Ray Funkhouser of the University of Pennsylvania feels that there is often a gap between promise and result—between "the need to sell the project to the client and the ability of research methodologies to provide valid and reliable data." However, when a client stakes a large amount of money on the results of a survey, and when the promised result fails to materialize, the client's disappointment can lead to litigation. Funkhouser says that the danger comes from two sources: from over-promising and from over-believing.

Self-Regulation Versus Freedom of Information

In 1985, the New York State Freedom of Information Law and the public's right to know came into conflict with AAPOR's Code of Professional Ethics. This code, as you recall, promises confidentiality and anonymity. The conflict grew out of a survey of pharmacies by New York City's Department of Consumer Affairs. The survey, which asked the respondent-pharmacists about drug prices and delivery services, promised confidentiality (in accordance with the AAPOR code and to encourage cooperation). However, when the survey's findings were made public, *The New York Times* filed a request under the Freedom of Information Law for the names of the participating pharmacies. Responding to the request, the Department of Consumer Affairs supplied the requested information, and the *Times* published an article identifying some of them. A subsequent complaint filed with the AAPOR Standards Committee led to a review of the apparent breach of respondent confidentiality. In the end, censure was not deemed necessary because extenuating circumstances were acknowledged, including the requirements of the New York State Freedom of Information Law and a promise by the Department of Consumer Affairs that future survey participants would be informed of the possibility that, under the state's Freedom of Information law, the agency might be compelled to release respondent-identifying information.

Setting Standards and
Avoiding Government Regulation

Back in 1947, Stuart C. Dodd created a set of standards for judging a poll-ster, the polling group, and the quality of its poll. He listed a number of factors to consider when evaluating a research organization,[17] which I find to be still relevant:

Agency Credence Standards   These should be based on how well it fulfills its responsibility to report who executed the survey, who controlled the policies and purposes, to whom the results were reported, and who paid for the survey. The integrity of the agency should be considered. This is determined by its willingness to be inspected, whether it is nonpartisan (preferable) or bipartisan or monopartisan (which can lead to questions of integrity), and whether there have been plausible charges of falsification. Its impartiality is important and can be undermined by partisan connections. Does the agency undertake validity studies, correlating its survey results against criteria such as elections, censuses, government statistics, and larger samples? And how accurate—the best test of validity—have its predictions been? How long has the agency been in business, and what is the probabil-ity of continuance for at least another year so that validity data can be ob-tained? (Dodd pointed out that if an agency is at least 10 years old, there is a "probability above 95 per cent" that it will continue for another year.) In addition, the agency "should be able to present endorsements by public leaders and social scientists of high integrity and variety of political views," and "should publish a manifesto promising honest and reliable fact finding and reporting."

Questionnaire Standards   Here one looks at the scope of the agency's questionnaires. Do they ask only opinion-type questions? Are they de-signed to gather useful information and record observations regarding be-havior? Are they usually pretested either on experts or on a small sample of the eventual sample? Are the criteria of exactness, clarity, thoroughness, and fairness observed? Do the questionnaires measure intensity of opinion? Is there an absence of phrasing bias?

Sampling Standards   Is the universe from which their samples are drawn specified (and reasonably explained) in exact detail? Are their sam-ples randomly selected, are their sizes adequate, and are they representa-tive? For the sake of nonexperts, sample size should be stated in absolute numbers. Dodd stated that "sampling errors must be published in full," and it is desirable that errors in sampling be published in a technical journal.

Interviewing Standards   According to Dodd, the best agencies will standardize their interviewing techniques so that 99 percent of their interviews will be "overt, oral, single, identified ... unhurried, undistracted, and short." Does the agency supply a general instruction manual to its interviewers and does it provide effective training and supervision? The interviewers themselves should be carefully selected according to definite standards relating to maturity, education, languages spoken, general intelligence, personality, competency (includes honesty, rapport, carefulness, quality of record keeping, and productivity), experience, references, and residence. Seeking to avoid interviewer bias, Dodd suggested that compatibility of interviewers with respondents or "social distance" should be considered.

Reporting Standards   All surveys, according to Dodd, should routinely be made available to the widest possible audience both through popular reporting and through professional publications. Along with the numerical findings, reports should include the verbatim quotation of the questions discussed, as well as the universe and size and nature of the sample. An important point dealing with both objectivity and public interest is that the agency should ensure a "rigorous separation of civic and commercial surveys."

Obviously, discussion of setting standards did not end with Stuart Dodd's suggestions. AAPOR, founded in 1947, eventually adopted a code of standards that included many of Dodd's suggestions; from time to time, the organization reviews its code, modifying it whenever the members deem it necessary. A major concern, however, stems from the possibility of government attempts to regulate the polling industry. Veteran researchers Norman M. Bradburn and Seymour Sudman cite the restrictions imposed on pollsters in several European countries during the final weeks of election campaigns. In addition to noting that California, Maryland, and Washington, as well as a number of other states, have attempted to impose similar restrictions, they state that some communities "have banned or attempted to ban face-to-face interviewing, and there is some discussion about restricting telephone interviewing as well."[18] As a result of such legislative activities, in 1985 AAPOR formed a Committee on the Regulation of Survey Research to oppose regulation of *legitimate* polls. AAPOR's members differentiate between authentic efforts and pseudo-polls, such as those discussed earlier.

Where do you come down on this issue? Should we fear government regulation of the polling industry? Is self-regulation by pollsters (along with fear of malpractice suits) adequate to ensure high standards for polling procedures and data reporting to the public? Who should set the standards? And, considering the computerization of the collected data and the creation of huge databases, need we fear an invasion of our privacy? Bradburn and Sudman point out that invasion-of-privacy concerns are even stronger in Europe than in the United States, where our government officials can access an enormous amount of information about each and every one of us by using our Social Security numbers. Think about all the times you have been asked to include yours on one form or another. Also, think about those devilishly bright computer hackers capable of breaking into some of the most secure on-line computer networks.

However, just to reassure you, there *is* a difference between an administrative (government-originated and -controlled) database and most surveys conducted by research institutes and pollsters. Usually, most surveys deal with our attitudes or behavior regarding issues that come and go. The opinions we express today can easily become irrelevant tomorrow or, for sure, a week or a month later. Also, when it comes to a privately conducted survey, we can always choose to answer the questions any way we like. In fact, some researchers and political commentators are questioning the truthfulness (and hence the accuracy) of certain polling results. We can also simply refuse to participate (see the Professional Voice 12).

The Professional Voice 12
The Non-Responder Conspiracy
David A. Farbman

As varied and frequent as our attempts are to learn what people think, there is one major category of our great society that has not been tracked through polling: namely, those who are approached by pollsters and flatly refuse to respond. By definition, the opinions of those who refuse to be polled must remain unrevealed. Yet is this really a problem?

Most likely, these individuals—non-responders, we will call them—are quite normal, just a bit more private than the average. Such is the case of an acquaintance of mine, a person who claims she is determined to eliminate from her life all annoying elements of society, including, in her case, a nagging pollster. However, because she is a resident of New Hampshire—

where every fourth year, during primary season, the number of polls taken actually appears to exceed the number of residents—her determination to avoid pollsters is severely tested. Out of curiosity I wanted to learn how she deals with this likely possibility of being polled. I thought I should begin innocently. "Considering you live in New Hampshire," I asked, "have you ever been polled?" Looking at me suspiciously, she responded that she had indeed been approached twice by pollsters, once at her door and once on the telephone. She continued by stating, in no uncertain terms, that she had won the battle for the privacy of her opinion because she had promptly closed the door and slammed the receiver down before a sentence could be uttered by either of the two pollsters.

It is true that her actions border on rudeness, but, more important, this piece of information can be useful in trying to contemplate more deeply the nature of the non-responders. Certainly, they demonstrate a strong need to be left alone. What remains then is the inevitable paradox of trying to document the motives of those who refuse to cooperate in sharing their motives. Guesswork remains our only tool.

On that note, let us suppose for a moment that refusal to respond to polls is not an isolated personality quirk of an otherwise mainstream individual. Rather, it may be a frightening indicator of all beliefs such a person may have. Is it not possible then that these opinions—of which we have no formal record—are radically different from everyone else's (that is, those who have been polled and those who are willing to be polled)? Is it not possible to imagine that these introverted individuals, who look upon pollsters as the enemy, see all government, indeed all people, as the enemy? Perhaps they are merely anarchists. Or, put more precisely, perhaps they are misanthropic anarchists—living in the seclusion of their mountain retreats, or typical small towns, U.S.A., or in their multistoried apartment buildings in our largest cities, or perhaps even hidden away in the libraries of our best universities and research centers pursuing some esoteric end. There they sit, laughing maliciously to themselves as they observe everyone else's thoughts being transformed neatly into polling statistics that they consider the destroyers of individuality. Perhaps these misanthropes can even identify one another and meet in secret, vowing to shield their ideas from the public they despise; maybe they covertly plan to rid the world of all others, especially the pollsters. "No matter how persistent pollsters are," their pledge of allegiance would state, "never ever let them discover that our opinion of the issues is that there shouldn't be any—issues or opinions."

As misanthropic anarchists, still a rare anarchistic subspecies, they dream of the day when the world will be devoid of society as we know it. They seek a new world, free from the overpopulated, over-polluted mass civilization to which we are accustomed. By overthrowing the world's governments, they will remake the earth. It will be a place where contact with anyone else will not be expected, much less needed. Best of all, the only use for polls will be to hold up the telephone wires; yet since they themselves would be a hateful reminder of the pathetic connection with lesser humans, even these will have to be eliminated.

Have I, a youthful researcher, gotten carried away? Is there really a non-responder population waiting in the wings to destroy civilization as we know it? The next time your friendly neighborhood news organization cites a poll with a suspicious-looking group of non-responders, consider the possibility that this figure may represent all the masterminds bent on destruction, lurking behind all those slammed doors and hung-up phones, waiting, waiting. Consider further that the larger this no-response percentage becomes, the greater the chances our world as we know it will disappear. Indeed, the very poll that indicates the growing number of non-responders may be the last one ever seen. While some of you who are also fed up with polls may not think of this as a particularly bad result, imagine that the end of polls really means the emergence of a dark world where you yourself are the enemy. Who could be sure? How could we ever know, if they do not respond?

David A. Farbman is a Ph.D. candidate at Brown University.

IMPROVING OPINION
OF OPINION POLLS

Do you think there is a need to improve the public's opinion of public opinion polling? Apparently many do question the value of polls, because the researchers themselves speak of the need to establish the social significance of their work. For example, J. Ronald Milavsky, NBC's vice president of news and social research and a past president of AAPOR, has expressed concern for the public's respect.[19] In this regard, he made the following points:

- On the obvious need for respondents: Milavsky cited the inverse relationship between the refusal rate and the prospective respondents' respect for the research being undertaken. The less respect the respondents have for the subject matter of the study for which they are being solicited, the more likely they are to refuse to be interviewed.

- On the need for encouraging the public to want information about public opinion research: The media will increase their coverage of surveys if there is significant public interest in them. The greater the coverage, the better informed the public will be, not only about the particular studies but also about the value of the research effort itself. This would lead to a decline in the refusal rate.

- On the need to inform our legislators to ward off crippling regulation of legitimate research efforts: The better our lawmakers understand the nature of legitimate surveys, the more likely they will be to target only those who engage in pseudo-research efforts by drafting legislation that "shoots at junk phone calls."

- On the role of survey research in a democracy: In a democracy, public opinion is expected to play a role; as a matter of self-interest, it is important that decision makers, whether public or private, consider the survey data an essential part of the decision-making process.

Milavsky also discussed three "critical contact points" and their opportunities to shape a more positive public view of polling:

The Interviewer-Respondent Exchange   Since the first contact respondents have with a survey is through interviewers, it is imperative that they be well trained and, especially, able to attract the respondent's attention within the first 20–30 seconds. Milavsky warns against cost cutting, which could result in a deterioration of interviewer staffing and training, and advocates fair compensation, thorough training, and conscientious supervision.

Newspaper Coverage   Focusing on the print media, rather than on television, Milavsky pays particular attention to those polls that are designed and conducted by the news organizations themselves. He argues that despite precision journalism, "the way journalists report poll data does not take full advantage of the opportunities presented." He also states that although a story often includes a good deal of dense data content, it "does not always yield high information value," and that "poll reporting as journalism is and probably will remain different from poll reporting as survey research." Milvasky continues:

One aims at providing opinion as news, the other views opinion as elucidating a more general social process.[20]

Often I found no apparent logic or narrative thread in the stories. The lead paragraph was generally the most important news-worthy finding. Only rarely was the stage set by explaining why the study was done.... Because there is little narrative logic, the obliga-tory sentence reporting sampling error can be placed almost any-where in the article.[21]

Another problem cited by Milavsky has to do with the way results of polls commissioned for partisan purposes are interpreted and passed along to the press. The "canned" misplaced emphasis can be misleading if a re-porter does not make an effort to compare the actual data with the inter-pretation presented in the press release. Thus, among the reasons people have increasingly undervalued polling, Milavsky cites (1) news stories of media-collected data that usually lack analysis and interpretation, and (2) one-sided stories that are based on the biased interpretation of data col-lected by partisan or special-interest groups.

What can be done to improve the public image of polls reported in the press? The recommendation here is to study how people actually perceive polling results, how well they understand the findings, and how well they understand various aspects of polling, such as margin of error. The results of such studies should be given to reporters and editors so that they can apply the lessons learned and so that their stories about polls will be more interesting and meaningful to the reader.

Polls and Policymakers   I discussed this "contact point" in Chapter 12. It deals with the politicians' use and abuse of polls. Specifically, I cited a number of examples of how polls (and focus groups) were used throughout the 1992 presidential campaign to manipulate the public's perception of everything about the candidates and their wives. Here, my focus is on the public's perception of the way politicians primarily use polls to gain and maintain political power. Some of us find that use troublesome.

We would prefer that policymakers use polls to find out what we know and think about important issues and the solutions they are proposing. Armed with the information on what we need to know to support their positions, our leaders can—as President Carter did in the case of the Panama Canal Treaty—explain more fully the policy they believe is best for our country.

The use of polls for the purpose of governance—as part of the policy-making process—can help define leadership, can contribute to the democratic process, and can enhance the public's perception of opinion polls. Milavsky, therefore, recommends research efforts to document such uses of polling data. He believes that the publication of such studies would lead to a more positive attitude toward public opinion polling and hence to lower refusal rates.

However, during the 1992 presidential campaign, there were so many polls that critics became ever more vocal. It wasn't just that we were constantly bombarded with a great number of polls. Rather, it was that their results sometimes varied by as much as several percentage points beyond the usual margin of error. And without all of this, our own indecision might not have been so painfully obvious (see The Professional Voice 13).

The Professional Voice 13
1992: Were There Too Many Polls?
Paula Stern

As the 1992 election became history, it was clear that the public's attitude toward polls had changed. The role of the poll—to clarify and to determine the public's attitude toward particular issues—seemed to be undermined by the number of polls and their inconsistencies, and by the candidates' ability to manipulate and use the results for their own purposes.

With computerized polling technology yielding almost instantaneous results, awareness of the polling process grew while its perceived importance diminished in the closing days of the 1992 presidential campaign. Throughout the summer months and into October, everyone watched nightly as Clinton moved up and then down in the polls. Toward the end of October, the daily fluctuations

yielded a perception that the gap was closing. It even seemed that Bush might yet succeed in his quest for reelection. As the American people listened attentively, it seemed as if the polls would tell them what they were thinking and would even announce the winner, without the voters' ever having to bother to cast their vote. Magically, on November 3, the polls would announce the next president.

However, the proliferation of polls began to wear thin as contradictory and confusing results were made public. A surprisingly positive result of the polls' lack of consistency was that voters began to question what, if anything, the polls really meant. In the last days of the campaign, ABC anchorman Peter Jennings reminded listeners of the time factor that limited a poll's usefulness. The poll, he insisted, reported how America had felt *yesterday* and thus had relatively little impact on how America was feeling at that moment, or how it would feel tomorrow.

Even though the polls were right in the end, for many they lost their credibility because of the constant fluctuations that reflected our own indecision. Perhaps it was the fact that on any given day there were as many as 10 percentage points separating polls that dealt with the same issue (for example, Clinton's lead over Bush), which reminded the voters that ultimately *they* elect a candidate and not the polls. With so many polls telling us what we were thinking, many finally decided to vote according to *their* beliefs.

Given polling results once a week, instead of daily, perhaps our indecision might not have been so painfully obvious. Weekly polls would have picked up the trend toward a Clinton victory, while sparing us the day-to-day con-

frontation of our indecision and lack of commitment. Our apparent unhappiness with our choices, and our inability to commit, led Jay Leno to quip, "If God had wanted us to vote, he would have given us a candidate." We tended to blame the pollsters because we felt dogged by our dissatisfaction with the candidates, distracted by the nightly polling reports, and further frustrated with our inability to decipher a trend. Even some of the so-called experts were stumped, and only in the final hours did we begin to hear predictions of the electoral-college landslide that resulted in Clinton's victory.

Thus, while the lingering memory may be that the nightly polls confused us, we are hopeful that one result of the 1992 polling season would be that Americans learned there is no such thing as a guaranteed outcome, or a wasted vote—poll or no poll.

Paula Stern is a political commentator and freelance writer.

THE UBIQUITOUS RESEARCHERS
AND CLOSING WORDS

Because pollsters have become ubiquitous particularly during political campaigns, it is important to understand that there is much more to survey research than political opinion polling. Researchers provide us with an extraordinary amount of information to help call attention to the many different types of problems in our society. Consider the following research studies:

The bipartisan National Commission on Children (NCC) commissioned two research organizations to conduct surveys on the state of family life in the United States. The National Opinion Research Center conducted a face-to-face survey of 1,400 adults, and the Princeton Survey Research Association conducted a phone survey of 1,700 parents and 900 children ages 10–17. The results, published in November 1991, presented a worrisome and gloomy picture of the respondents' views about life outside their own homes, but a more positive view of what was happening in their own family lives. Parents generally indicated fear for the safety of their children outside their homes; among members of the black and Hispanic communities, the level of fear was higher. The level of anxiety among parents was high with regard to how hard they were working, how little time they had for their families, the cost of living, street crime, AIDS, and so on.

Senator John D. Rockefeller, Democrat of West Virginia and NCC chairman, said that in his view we were in for a "long war on the subject" of the status of the American family.[22] The NCC recommended $52 billion to $56 billion in programs to aid families. Predicting what would happen in the 1992 presidential campaign, Rockefeller said that while we would hear a lot about family values from those running for office (because it was a popular topic), it remained to be seen who would take a stand. "Are they willing to put up," Rockefeller asked, "or is it just rhetoric?" What do you think?

Another important study was commissioned by the National Mental Health Association (NMHA). Peter D. Hart Research Associates, Inc. (widely known for its political surveys) was hired to conduct a telephone survey of 1,022 adults on the subject of depression. The study found that about 50 percent of the respondents said they or their family members had, at one time or another, suffered from depression; and, interestingly, some 43 percent admitted that they viewed depression as a "personal weakness." The survey found that while 53 percent of those polled would be willing to tell friends if depression struck someone in their family, 30 percent would not want friends to know. When asked to select up to three sources of help, 45 percent chose a "medical or family doctor"; 60 percent suggested one of the following: a psychiatrist, psychologist, "shrink," therapist, counselor, mental health clinic, or psychiatric hospital; 20 percent suggested a member of the clergy; 14 percent suggested a relative (spouse, parent, family member) or a friend. Elisabeth Rukeyser, chairperson of the NMHA, commenting on the Hart findings, said that most Americans "need to know that depression can be treated effectively in 80 percent of the cases."[23]

In another study, the Older Women's League (OWL), a Washington-based women's rights group, used data from the Census Bureau, the Labor

Department, the Health Insurance Association of America, and other sources to compile a report on the health insurance problems faced by women in their mid-40s and older. OWL reported:

> Women are likely to have low-paying jobs, work part-time and for small businesses, all of which contribute to lack of health insurance coverage.... Care-giving responsibilities impede women's participation in the work force, making women vulnerable to losing health insurance.... Women constitute 52 percent of the age group between 40 and 64, but pay 62 percent of the out-of-pocket cost for physician services.

Felicity Barringer, writing about OWL's findings in *The New York Times*, pointed to the insurance gap between women and men in the same age group. She wrote that "in the age bracket between 45 and 64, before women qualify for Medicare, only 55 percent of working women have health insurance provided by their own employers, as compared with 72 percent of men in the same age group."[24]

These surveys—concerning the state of the American family, mental health, and the health insurance problems of older women—are only three examples of the enormous number of important research efforts being undertaken outside the world of political opinion, marketing, and litigation studies. All such surveys make useful information available to us. What we choose to do with it is up to us. We can be passive consumers of the data or we can choose to act. We can become part of the attentive public that tries to bring about necessary changes in our society by making our political leaders aware of the fact that we *are* aware and that we hold them responsible—both for their action and their inaction. I hope you will choose awareness and involvement.

CHAPTER REVIEW

- Discuss the advantages and disadvantages of each of the following technologies: CAPI, Ci2, Ci3, LANs, NIC, ESCAPE/600, DBM.
- Why have these technologies raised invasion-of-privacy fears?
- What cost-effective benefits have been realized by those who converted to computer interviewing technology?
- Why were the participants in the QT demonstration both impressed and somewhat frightened by this technology?
- The proliferation of pseudo-polls has raised a number of concerns among public opinion researchers. What are some of these concerns?

- While researchers praise LANs and predictive dialing, what might be some of the concerns raised by potential respondents? How do you think the interviewers feel about robotic dialing setting the pace for them?

- What are the issues raised by the Choice Attitude, VIP, and COP surveys?

- If you were a researcher and a court demanded respondent-identifiable information from you, what would you do? Which approach— O'Neill's or Roper's—do you agree with? Why?

- On what basis can one undertake a malpractice suit against a researcher? What can researchers do to protect themselves from such a lawsuit?

- What criteria can be used to evaluate surveying organizations?

- What can be done to improve the public's perception of public opinion polls? Why is this necessary?

- If polled, will you choose to be a respondent? Why?

- Finally, will you choose to be part of the attentive public?

NOTES

1. Stu Cox, "Selecting Computer Interviewing Hardware at Kentucky Fried Chicken," *Sawtooth News* (Ketchum, IN: Sawtooth Software, Winter/ Spring 1991), Vol. 7, No. 1, p. 3.

2. Diane Crispell, "Microcomputing: Interview with Ci2," *American Demographics* (1987), available in reprint from Sawtooth Software.

3. Selwyn Feinstein, "Computers Replacing Interviewers for Personnel and Marketing Tasks," *The Wall Street Journal* (1986), available in reprint from Sawtooth Software.

4. Sara Kiesler and Lee S. Sproull, "Response Effects in the Electronic Survey," *Public Opinion Quarterly* (1986), Vol. 50, p. 406.

5. Feinstein.

6. For a discussion of Theodore L. Reed's paper, "Predictive Dialers: Applications for Research on Low Incidence Products," presented at the American Marketing Association's Sales and Marketing Technology Conference in June 1990, see "More on Predictive Dialing," *Sawtooth News* (Fall 1990), Vol. 3, No. 2, pp. 1, 6.

7. Lesley Bahner, "Improving Control in Disk-by-Mail Surveys," *Sawtooth News* (Winter/Spring 1991), Vol. 7, No. 1, p. 6.

8. John Gilfeather, "Sugging and Frugging," *AAPOR News* (Fall 1987), Vol. 15, No. 1, p. 4.

9. The AAPOR Executive Council, "Survey Research or Political Canvassing?" *AAPOR News* (Spring 1991), pp. 3 and 6; and see Tom W. Smith's "Be Vigilant," p. 3

10. Mervin Field, "Speaking Out: Another Threat to Respondent Access," *AAPOR News* (Fall 1987), Vol. 15, No. 1, p. 4.

11. "AAPOR Opposes Unacceptable Practices," *AAPOR News* (Fall 1990), Vol. 18, No. 1, p. 7.

12. Mervin Field, "Anticipating the Subpoena," *AAPOR News* (Spring 1992), Vol. 19, No. 3, p. 5.

13. Harry W. O'Neill, "They Can't Subpoena What You Ain't Got," *AAPOR News* (Winter 1992), p. 4.

14. Burns W. Roper, "But Will They Give the Poll Its Due?" *AAPOR News* (Winter 1992), p. 5. See Roper's article in the *American Bar Association Journal* (January 1965), Vol. 51, p. 44, where he first proposed this approach.

15. G. Ray Funkhouser, "Speaking Out: Methodological Malpractice Suits," *AAPOR News* (Winter 1988), Vol. 15, No. 2, p. 5.

16. Funkhouser.

17. Stuart C. Dodd, "Standards for Surveying Agencies," *Public Opinion Quarterly* (Spring 1947), pp. 115–130.

18. Norman M. Bradburn and Seymour Sudman, *Polls and Surveys*, (San Francisco: Jossey-Bass, 1988), p. 194.

19. J. Ronald Milavsky, "Presidential Address: Improving the Public's Opinion of Public Opinion," *Public Opinion Quarterly* (1987), Vol. 51, pp. 436–437.

20. Milavsky, p. 442.

21. Milavsky, p. 440.

22. "2 U.S. Surveys Find Anxiety About the State of Family Life," *The New York Times*, Nov. 22, 1991.

23. "Many View Depression as Weakness," *The New York Times*, Dec. 11, 1991.

24. Felicity Barringer, "Study Says Older Women Face Insurance Gap," *The New York Times*, May 7, 1992, p. A19.

Appendix I

Introducing Basic Descriptive Statistics

ERIC PAUL RUBENSTEIN

The purpose of this appendix is to introduce the novice to descriptive statistics. Some of our examples will be drawn from typical student experiences in addition to the field of polling.

You enter Prof. D. Stat's class after a midterm only to be met with a blackboard full of the following descriptive statistics concerning the class's performance on the exam:

N exams = 20   (20 students took the exam)

Mean score = 75.45

Median score = 76

Mode score = 94   (the score that appeared most frequently)

Std. Dev. $(n - 1)$ = 16.31 $(n = N)$

Prof. Stat explains that the grades for this exam are 96, 95, 94, 94, 92, 89, 86, 82, 80, 78, **76** (which is the median score, to be explained shortly), 73, 70, 69, 67, 65, 59, 57, 46, and 41. These 20 scores represent our data set; they also represent your hard-earned grades. To find the mean, also known as the average, all we do is add up all of these numbers and divide by the total number of grades that go into this sum.

Eric Paul Rubenstein is an astrophysicist at Yale University.

So for these scores, we have the sum equal to 1,509. We write this as:

Σ grades = grade 1 + grade 2 + ... + grade 19 + grade 20 = 1,509

where the Greek letter Σ means *sum of* and is pronounced "sigma," and where "..." means all of the scores in between are added up as well.

The mean, identified by the symbol $\overline{X}$ (pronounced "X-bar") is simply calculated now by dividing this sum by the number of scores that went into it (20). Therefore, the mean is:

$$\overline{X} = \frac{1509}{20} = 75.45$$

This can be written as:

$$\overline{X} = \frac{\Sigma \text{ scores}}{N} = 75.45$$

Note that no one actually has to receive that particular score for 75.45 to be the mean. This number, the mean, tells us one and only one thing about these scores. We now know the *center of the distribution* of grades, but nothing about how they are distributed about that average value. To gain insight into the more detailed *distribution about this mean*, we need more information—a new statistic. The most common expression used to impart a greater understanding of how clustered or spread out the scores are is the *standard deviation*. To determine the standard deviation for a data set, it is necessary to first calculate the mean. Once this is done, the standard deviation can be calculated *very simply* as follows:

Standard deviation = σ_{n-1}

$$= \frac{\sqrt{\Sigma(\text{scores} - \text{mean})^2}}{N-1} = \frac{\sqrt{\Sigma(\text{scores} - X)^2}}{N-1}$$

The Greek lowercase letter σ (pronounced "sigma") is used to denote the standard deviation. In our example we have obtained 20 independent measurements. These are called degrees of freedom in descriptive statistics parlance. We can extract from this data set *at most 20 independent* pieces of information about the data and their distribution, one for each independently measured data point. With regard to data, each datum is independent of all others *if* it is measured separately and the result of that measurement does *not* depend on *any* other measurements. This is a very important point. If one data point is affected by any other data point (say by one student copying another's test verbatim), the points are linked. Any effort to draw a conclusion from such data is tainted. In the case of survey research, if an inexperienced interviewer were to tell a respondent what the typical answer to a particular question was before eliciting a response, the respondent's answer might well be affected.

With regard to independence of descriptive statistics, a similar point can be made. Since the standard deviation of a data set about a mean is *not* independent of what the mean is, the standard deviation is based not on N data points for the total degrees of freedom, but rather on N data points *minus* the one value that had been derived from the sample ($N-1$). Each statistic we calculate from the data set uses up one degree of freedom in the sense that one fewer quantity can be calculated subsequently. Because we have used up one of these degrees of freedom in calculating the mean, the "$N-1$" (rather than "N") is necessary.

$$\sigma_{n-1} = \frac{1}{N-1} \ [(96 - 75.45)^2 + (95 - 75.45)^2 +$$

$$\ldots + (46 - 75.45)^2 + (41 - 75.45)^2] = \mathbf{16.31}$$

Standard deviation is most easily understood in a relative sense. That is, if the scores on the midterm were tightly clustered about the mean such that the standard deviation was 5, the grades would be much more tightly grouped than the actual grades above. Conversely, if the standard deviation were instead 30, the grades would have been more spread out than in our case. The degree to which scores are clustered about the mean is of interest in many contexts.

For example, in the case of polling, the standard deviation of some defining property of a sample group, say income, is a good determinant of whether the group is homogeneous or heterogeneous. Among the demographic questions asked in a poll, there is usually one dealing with income. Assume for the moment that one of the substrata polled was the "Hard Scrabble" cluster, identified as America's poorest rural communities. In such a poll, if the standard deviation of the respondents' income is $20,000, we immediately see that the sample of "poor people" is severely contaminated. Such a large standard deviation in this case means that either:

1. There are a significant number of people making in excess of $20,000 above the approximately $13,000 per annum that the average "Hard Scrabble" cluster member makes.
2. There are a few *very* wealthy individuals tainting the sample.

It is important to note that with only statistics on central tendency (mean, median, and mode) and standard deviation, it is *not* possible to differentiate between these two cases. Since the process of reducing and then analyzing data inexorably eliminates the details present in the raw data, one way of differentiating between these two possibilities is to look at the raw data itself. Always remember that data reduction is just that. However, generalizations about a population as a whole (and after all, this is the goal of survey research) can rarely be drawn from raw data, necessitating the evils of analysis.

Let's return to our exam scores. You will note that in addition to the mean, the median (76) and the mode (94) scores were given. Often the median is used as a stronger indicator of the center of a distribution than the mean. This is because a mean can be pulled way off (above or below) what would appear to be a reasonable middling value by just a few wildly discrepant data points—or exam scores. In the case of our exams this did not occur. The median and mean track the middle of this distribution equally well.

However, when dealing with scores that are more spread apart or income levels that are extremely different, the median is more representative. The median value is simply the middle value of whatever variable is being examined. The only caveat to this is that when there is an even number of data, the median is defined as the lower of the two middle values.

This appendix serves as only a very brief introduction to the rich field of statistics and statistical analysis. Certainly anyone who hopes to pursue a career in survey research *must* become proficient in using these and many other tools of quantitative analysis.

Appendix II

Survey Research as a Profession

SO CAN I EARN A GOOD LIVING AT IT?

The answer is yes, and you can have fun too! Surveying public opinion is one of the most dynamic, vibrant, and exciting fields to enter. It attracts imaginative and talented people with varied interests, providing them with opportunities to grow and develop. The American Association of Public Opinion Researchers (AAPOR), based in Princeton, New Jersey, includes in its membership both commercial and academic researchers. Each May, AAPOR's annual conference provides the setting for members to discuss not only the state of their professional world but the greater world in which they work. Discussions cover a wide range of subjects, including various aspects of survey methodology and opinion research studies on anything and everything: political advertising; nationwide studies on teenagers, women, and sex; racial tension; the changes in eastern Europe; Middle East tensions; the psychology of influence; AIDS; media content; media influence in election campaigns; and on and on. When there is no panel in session, you can always find a very sociable group arguing, discussing, exchanging ideas.

AAPOR publishes *Careers in Survey Research*, an informative pamphlet that can give you some idea of the field. The following is a sample of what opportunities exist for those interested in this growing profession. It is not meant to be exhaustive, but merely to provide a sense of the possibilities.

The entry level requires a minimum of a bachelor's degree and at least the intention to pursue graduate studies if you ever want to move up the ladder. Most companies include in their benefits a tuition reimbursement program to help you obtain a master's degree or a doctorate. Undergraduate courses that are helpful include those that familiarize you with computers and give you a sense of marketing research, statistics, psychology, sociology, and political science. It will be taken for granted that you have excellent written and oral communication skills and are discreet and reliable. Companies rarely are specific when it comes to salaries. Usually they say, "Salary commensurate with experience and ability." So here is a short list:

Research Technician   An entry-level position for a careful, detail-oriented person. The RT's responsibilities include data entry, clerical work, checking and editing questionnaires, and other research support functions.

Research Assistant   Also an entry-level position, requiring no experience. Usually a degree in marketing/business and exposure to the research process through coursework and/or class projects are pluses. Similar to the RT, the RA helps staff members with activities related to proposal requests and day-to-day project management, including budgeting, background research, field management, code development, data processing plans, analyses, and written reports.

Research Assistant/Data Analyst   This position includes responsibility for a range of tasks associated with survey sampling, management of data collection, and use of computer files to check logical relationships between data items. Analytical and interpretive abilities are essential in this position.

Senior Research Assistant/Research Associate   With one to three years of market or survey research experience, one can work with senior staff in planning a project, collecting and analyzing data, and reporting results to clients. Knowledge of SPSS (Statistical Package for the Social Sciences) is desirable but not always required because firms are often willing to provide training in this area.

Research Associate/Research Director   With three to five years of market research experience, having acquired the skills of questionnaire development, quantitative analysis, writing of research proposals and reports, and with the ability to manage projects independently and direct junior staff activity, this level offers the responsibility to manage multiple projects.

Market Research Analyst   With a minimum of three to five years of market research experience and strong mathematical skills, the MRA can analyze data and summarize reports.

Magazine Research Manager   With three to five years of experience involving all phases of primary research from questionnaire design to finished report, the magazine research manager will be responsible for contact with sales staff, advertisers, and clients.

Senior Marketing Research Analyst   Requires a minimum of two years of experience in management of survey research projects and in the application of statistical techniques to marketing problems. Responsibilities include working on projects involving advanced statistical methods and the ability to integrate complex analyses, make marketing recommendations, and interact with clients.

Account Executive/Senior Project Manager   Requires five years of experience in the area of design research and analysis, along with the ability to develop new business, maintain successful client relationships, and oversee a project team.

Director of Field Interviewing   With five years of survey research experience and demonstrated knowledge of area probability sampling and personal interviewing, familiarity with computers, and the ability to supervise in-house staff and interviewers, a DFI will oversee a department that is responsible for all non-telephone interviewing, recruitment, and supervision of in-home interviewers, liaison with group and shopping mall facilities, and mail survey send-out and check-in.

Statistician   Develops large-scale sampling frames and complex survey designs. Requirements include statistical background/advanced degree(s), a thorough knowledge of the survey research field, strong computer and communications skills, and relevant work experience. Duties include proposal and report writing and attendance at client meetings.

Quantitative Research Director   An East Coast survey research firm advertised this opening in their government research division. They wanted someone to manage a complex survey of household energy consumption and other technically oriented survey research projects. The position required an advanced degree in statistics or social science, computer skills, and three years of experience in the design and implementation of automated systems for survey research sampling and analysis. Responsibilities included management and training of junior-level staff and communication with clients.

Somewhere along the way, many in the field decide to open their own research companies. Here's the background of a young woman who did:

Bachelor of Arts degree in psychology and communication arts; Master of Management degree in marketing and quantitative methods; entry-level position leading to research analyst; then 10 years of experience working on hundreds of consumer and business-to-business *qualitative* (focus group interviews or one-on-one in-depth interviews) and *quantitative* (personal interviewing at a central location or off-site, telephone interviewing, mail surveys) marketing research studies. She was responsible for designing, implementing, and analyzing research projects such as marketing planning studies, image studies, sales prediction studies, concept tests, advertising evaluations, performance tests, pricing studies, taste tests, packaging studies, attitude and usage studies, distribution studies, and tracking studies. Her clients included consumer goods companies, business products manufacturers, telecommunications firms, retailers, direct-mail marketers, professional associations, and advertising agencies.

Occasionally, one sees an opportunity to break into a new field, such as that provided by ARBOR, Inc. Located in Pennsylvania, ARBOR is a full-service market research firm with over 200 employees. Their clients specialize in packaged goods, leisure services, restaurants, pharmaceuticals, broadcasting, and other fields. Although they are a marketing research firm, they advertised openings for project directors at the B.A., M.A., and Ph.D. levels without requiring knowledge of marketing or opinion research. Rather, they offered an intensive training program covering all phases of market research. However, they did insist on a grade point average of 3.0 or above, with strong verbal and math abilities.

The Gallup Organization, with main offices in Princeton, New Jersey, and with affiliates around the world, is one of the oldest (founded in 1935) and largest full-service survey research firms. Gallup is best known for its political opinion polling, but it also engages in extensive consumer research. Utilizing bilingual interviewers, the organization has 600 telephone interviewing stations, 400 with RDD–CATI (random-digit dialing–computer-assisted telephone interviewing). Gallup specializes in research on public policy, corporate image, financial services, packaged goods, health and medical products, with nightly tracking of advertising and purchasing behaviors.

In 1989, UAI Technology signed an agreement with the Gallup Organization to conduct and market syndicated financial services research under the name Phoenix-Hecht/Gallup (also located in Princeton). Lawrence J. Cohen (see The Professional Voice 5), who was a senior project director and consultant for numerous Gallup financial studies, became a vice president at Phoenix-Hecht/Gallup, in charge of marketing for all multi-client consumer financial research. His career path is interesting: B.A. in arts and sciences from Syracuse University (1974) and an M.B.A. from Rutgers

University in 1990. In between, he worked for Gallup, Louis Harris, Roper, and Mathematica Policy Research, Inc. His experience includes research project management, presentation, writing, personal interviewing, and customer service.

Louis Harris and Associates, Inc., based in New York City, conducts survey research in 65 countries. Its specialties are public policy and governmental services, as well as telecommunications, health care, consumer marketing, financial services, and work for the automotive industry. It, too, uses the CATI system. The Louis Harris Data Center, located in Chapel Hill, North Carolina, maintains archives of public opinion polls from Louis Harris and Associates, Carolina Poll, *USA Today*, and other state and national polls. They do trend analysis, cross-tabulations, and frequencies (*frequency distribution* refers to how often a particular response is given), and they also supply data tapes.

The Roper Organization is also based in New York City and provides the *Syndicated Roper Reports*, national surveys with face-to-face interviews, 10 times a year. It designs custom, national, regional, and local studies of general and specific publics.

The Roper Center for Public Opinion Research, located at the University of Connecticut, houses data in computer-readable form from over 8,000 major studies conducted in the United States and in 70 other countries, along with printed reports on thousands of others. Among those who deposit their data at the center are: Gallup, Roper, Yankelovich, Clancy Shulman, NORC, the Opinion Research Corporation, the CBS News/*New York Times* Poll, the ABC News/*Washington Post* Poll, the NBC News/*Wall Street Journal* Poll, the *Los Angeles Times* Poll, Canadian Gallup, Gallup's British affiliate Social Surveys Ltd., and Brulé Ville Associés in France. It is possible to access the center's data from a personal computer, through POLL, an on-line information retrieval system.

Yankelovich, Skelly & White/Clancy Shulman in Westport, Connecticut, has branch offices in Boston, Newport Beach, London, and Toronto. The company provides surveys in marketing and corporate communications, evaluations of marketing and advertising strategies, along with product quality and customer service measurement. Yankelovich is also recognized as a leader in public opinion research and for its worldwide consulting service.

Much smaller in size of operation but also much respected for its work is the Eagleton Poll. Eagleton is part of the Center for Public Interest Polling at Rutgers University in New Brunswick, New Jersey. The Center conducts quarterly statewide public interest surveys, *The Star-Ledger*/Eagleton Poll, and public–policy oriented contract research primarily for government.

Besides Rutgers, a number of other universities are affiliated with research centers and offer excellent graduate programs. Check out the graduate program at your own university and ask your professors for their opinions. The following is merely a sample of the many fine schools that offer appropriate programs:

A Sample of University Survey Research Centers

University of California, at Berkeley and Los Angeles

Indiana University, Bloomington

University of Southern Maine, Portland

University of Maryland, College Park

University of Michigan, Ann Arbor

Ohio State University, Columbus

University of South Carolina, Columbia

Washington State University, Pullman

University of Wisconsin, Madison

For a more complete list, see AAPOR's *Agencies & Organizations*, its little "Blue Book," and "Academic Research Organizations in the United States and Canada" in *Survey Research* (1987), published by the Survey Research Laboratory of the University of Illinois.

We can take a quick look at four of those on our sample list:

The Institute for Policy Research, University of Cincinnati. The institute is a full-service organization that handles all aspects of survey, evaluation, and policy research. It conducts national, regional, and local telephone surveys; mail and personal surveys of selected audiences; and the semi-annual Greater Cincinnati Survey, as well as the quarterly Ohio Poll. The latter two are cost-shared, omnibus surveys of social and political concerns. One example of an institute project was the Fine Arts Fund Tax Levy Survey, completed in 1987. The study of 686 registered voters in Hamilton County, Ohio, was designed to ascertain whether voters would support a property tax levy for fine arts institutions, their reasons for support or opposition, demographics of supporters and opponents, and the impact of public funding on private donations to the fine arts. RDD–CATI interviews were conducted, with a response rate of 74 percent.

The Minnesota Center for Survey Research, University of Minnesota. The center handles mail and telephone surveys in the Twin Cities, Minnesota, and the upper Midwest, focusing on public policy issues and the specific needs of academic researchers. Their omnibus surveys have included topics such as the environment, shopping locations, entrepreneurship, tax policy, and telephone regulations. An example of one of their projects was the Federal Tax Survey (1988), funded by the National Science Foundation. Its aim was to determine the degree and nature of noncompliance with filing federal income tax returns. Approximately 1,200 Minnesota households that had filed their tax returns were interviewed by phone and were asked their views about where they received tax information and instructions, the Internal Revenue Service, and IRS penalties for tax delinquency.

National Opinion Research Center (NORC), a Social Science Research Center, University of Chicago. NORC, founded in 1941 by Harry H. Field, is a nonprofit organization that provides consultation and/or services on all phases of surveys: planning, design, sampling, data collection, data reduction analysis, and reporting. The center maintains a nationwide field staff and specializes in face-to-face interviewing.

The Public Opinion Laboratory (POL) at Northern Illinois University also offers a full CATI capability and can handle national, state, and local community sampling. The POL has experience in cross-sectional and longitudinal sampling. Longitudinal studies are carried out over a significant period of time. An example would be a panel study that follows a group of people, such as adolescents, for a number of years. Cross-sectional research, on the other hand, compares people of different ages or groups during the same period of time. The laboratory prepares survey designs and analyses for scholarly and commercial clients.

I hope this discussion has given you some understanding of the challenges to be found in survey research, an exciting profession.

Appendix III

NORC's Permanent Community Sample

Since 1941, when a small group, including the distinguished Harry H. Field, founded NORC (National Opinion Research Center, now affiliated with the University of Chicago), it has expanded to include a staff of several hundred researchers and assistants working in the following specialized sections:

- *The Survey Group* includes the field staff and is responsible for the design (sample and questionnaire), execution (data collection and presentation), and management of all NORC surveys.

- *The Research Group* includes the Economics Research Center, the Methodology Research Center, the Chapin Hall Center for Children, and the Center for the Study of Politics and Society.

  Chapin Hall's work includes monitoring and updating data on the condition of Illinois children, research on foster care, and so on. Their *State of the Child* reports have presented some disturbing findings.

- The Center for Computing and Information Systems develops and tests new automated systems to support NORC's survey activities.

In 1968, NORC established a data collection apparatus to obtain information from a large number of cities. The aim was to make it possible to conduct large-scale comparative community studies. At the time, the permanent community sample (PCS) consisted of 200 cities with a 50,000+ population, stratified according to population size, and organized in each city as follows:

1. A social scientist, associated with a local college/university, was employed by NORC on a part-time basis and trained in NORC methodology to collect and process information, statistics, and documents about community decisions and policy-making elites.

2. A NORC-trained interviewer, also employed part-time, assisted in collecting statistics, interviewing community elites, gathering newspaper files, and collaborating with the social scientist in each research project.

3. The social scientist and interviewer enlisted 5 to 10 local elites to serve as a panel of advisors/judges, a source of community information. The panelists were to be asked for their opinions about variables that were uneconomical to measure.

4. This structure was to be made available to social scientists interested in comparative research on American cities.

5. These data, supplemented by election statistics and data from U.S. censuses of population, government, and manufacturing, and data available from other organizations, would be entered into a data bank and made accessible for further analysis.

Glossary

additive scales Used in survey research to scale the total score a respondent receives for the way in which he or she has answered all the items. A baseball player's RBIs (runs batted in) is an example of an additive scale.

ANOVA Abbreviation for analysis of variance, a statistical procedure that makes it possible to compare several groups at the same time or the same group over a period of time. While it cannot prove that there are statistically meaningful differences among groups, it can provide some evidence that they are not the same.

Areas of Dominant Influence (ADIs) Also identified as primary sampling units (PSUs), ADIs had to have at least one commercial, nonsatellite home station. Arbitron divided the United States into 210 ADIs, market areas ranked according to the number of television households. These ranged from New York, with over 7 million TV households, to Pembina, North Dakota, with under 7,000.

benchmark survey Conducted early in a campaign (up to two years before the actual election), it generally uses a large sample of up to 4,000 nationally, with 600–1,000 in a state. It is designed to determine the degree of name recognition a candidate possesses in relation to competitors, and it provides a baseline from which subsequent progress can be measured.

branching Depending on the way a respondent answers a particular question, the interviewer may follow up with (branch to) a specific set of questions. Also see *contingency question*.

central tendency A single summary figure (mean, mode, median) that characterizes the sample population and that enables us to generalize from the percentage of the sample that responds in a particular way to the population at large.

closed-ended question   See *structured question*.

clustering   A multistage process that involves sample units found grouped (clustered) in the same location. The clustering method is economical and works well for studies that target specific groups.

confidence level   A statistical measure of the likelihood that we would get the same results if we resampled our universe enough times to eliminate the effects of chance errors and to ensure confidence in our results.

contingency question   One that is asked of those who answer a preceding question in a particular way; otherwise, the interviewer either follows the normal question order or skips to a predesignated question. The process is called *branching*.

convenience sample   A non-scientific (non-random), non-representative sample; one based on the availability and willingness of people interested in participating.

correlation   Simple correlations indicate a relationship between two variables; multiple correlations involve three or more variables.

correlation coefficients   Various index values (ranging from +1.0 to −1.0) used to tell us the magnitude (from weak, 0.1, to strong, 0.9) and the nature (direction, + or −) of the relationship. From the correlation coefficient, we infer the true interrelations by which variables are associated in the population.

critical reader   One who can analyze, evaluate, and critique the material she or he has read.

data field   Refers to the column(s) assigned to each question. Each respondent is assigned a number that will appear on a data card used to record all of that person's answers. Each question is assigned a data field, meaning column(s) on the data card, which becomes the record of each respondent's answers.

demographic variables   Generally include sex, age, income, education, geographic distribution, and so on.

descriptive statistics   Enable us to identify and describe important characteristics of our data. They include the mean, median, mode, percent of total, range, and standard deviation (see Appendix I), and they are the building blocks for inferential statistics, which enable us to draw conclusions from the data.

dominant social paradigm (DSP) The dominant belief structure. Within this country, it has been based on free-market and old Yankee values.

Don't Know (DK)   Researchers have discovered that there are a number of reasons why respondents answer a question "don't know," and it's not just that they really do not know about what is being asked. They may respond in that manner when they are uncertain, ambivalent, or undecided on their opinion, or have an opinion but don't want to express it. Whatever the reason respondents use the DK category, there is concern among researchers about what it is they are measuring in that category.

elites Used in a political sense to refer to those in positions of power and influence, such as elected and appointed political figures, business and corporate leaders, those who represent powerful interest groups, and those within the moneyed class whose wealth has been used in pursuit of their goals.

enumerators Individuals sent out to list all housing units in selected field locations. Those sent by the Census Bureau are also called enumerators.

exit poll Based on a random sample of voting places, this type of poll is taken on election day as voters leave after casting their ballots. Such polls, often the target of criticism, enable the media to make early predictions.

filter questions Questions used to screen respondents to ensure a representative sample. For example, in a poll to determine the candidate most likely to win the election, the aim would be to exclude those not qualified (registered) to vote.

frugging Fundraising under the guise of research. It is considered unethical and harmful to the research profession.

hearsay Testimony derived from something the witness heard others say. When evidence depends on the credibility and competency of someone other than the witness, it is generally inadmissible because the testimony could not be subjected to cross-examination.

hypothesis Often called the alternate hypothesis, this is the basis of our research. For the example hypothesis "Drugs are the number one problem in America," the null (or default) hypothesis is "Drugs are not the number one problem in America."

inaccessibility Circumstances that can hinder poll-taking efforts.

inferential statistics Enable us to infer something from the data. These statistical procedures allow us to draw conclusions, to generalize from a sample to the population as a whole.

infrared scanning system Nielsen engineers developed this scanning device to determine if a human presence is in the room with the turned-on television set. This system sweeps the area in seven seconds and can detect and record heat generated by the presence of people. The computer programming of this scanning device can distinguish between humans and other heat sources such as pets, appliances, and lamps.

interval scale Type of ranking scale used to determine and code a respondent's income range: (1) under $15,000; (2) $15,001 to $25,000; (3) $25,001 to $35,000; (4) $35,001 to $45,000; and so on. Note that the intervals between the incomes are equal.

judgmental sampling As opposed to random sampling. Occurs when interviewers decide for themselves who they will interview. This was a major problem with quota sampling. Interviewer training emphasizes the necessity of the interviewer's following the established respondent-selection guidelines to ensure a random sample.

local area networks (LAN) Permit groups of PCs to share information. Each PC within the group (area) must have a network interface card (NIC) and each network must have a PC that acts as a file server, a storage device that enables all the PCs in the group to access the stored information.

limited- (minimal-) effects theory Holds that the media are not powerful or influential enough to have a direct effect on the audience. In contrast to the magic bullet or hypodermic needle theory, this theory sees an indirect influence of the media operating through opinion leaders.

mean The average.

median As distinguished from the average, or mean, the median refers to the mid-point in the data, the point at which one finds an equal number of data points above as below.

measures of central tendency See *central tendency*.

measures of dispersion or variation Enable us to understand the distribution of the data and see the similarities and differences among the sample's subgroups. There are many different ways to compute variability. Those mentioned in this text are range, variance, and standard deviation.

mode The result or answer that appears most frequently. For example, the mode for the answers to a question on the respondent's income would be the income range that is most often checked off.

multistage sample design As with the Arbitron sampling frame, the process of selecting the respondents passes through several stages.

multivariate analysis Cross-tabulating and analyzing three or more variables (for example, age, sex, education, income, ethnicity, and so on). When two variables are involved, researchers usually refer to bivariate analysis.

negatively correlated Characteristics (variables) are said to be negatively correlated if as one increases, the other decreases and vice versa.

network interface card (NIC) See *local area networks (LANs)*.

new environmental paradigm (NEP) The major concern is the environment and its preservation, despite economic considerations.

nominal rating scale Used to measure answers that provide information such as sex, marital status, ethnicity, race, political party preference, and so on. This scale provides a naming mechanism in the form of numbers assigned to the various responses. The numbers are merely labels, representing different categories of answers.

non-directional follow-up question Encourages the individual to respond without providing any indication of the interviewer's thinking on the subject. Also see *probe questions* and *probe symbols*.

opinions Thoughts, beliefs, attitudes, and ideas.

ordinal scale Ranks responses along some dimension—for example, from best to worst, highest to lowest, most prominent to least prominent, intensity of agreement or disagreement, and so on.

People Meter A sophisticated microprocessor used by Nielsen to measure the television viewing behavior of its national sample of households.

percentage points The number of points between what was predicted and the actual result.

plurality error The difference between the estimated tally and the actual vote tally.

post-election vote-validation studies Used to confirm that the respondent voted. Your voting record is open to the public. Thus, researchers are able to access it to determine whether—after you said you intended to vote—you actually voted. If you did not vote, one could conclude that your stated intention to vote may have been a less than truthful response to the interviewer.

precision journalism Meyer's term to describe news reporting that should include quantitative as well as qualitative news research. Thus, Meyer advocated that journalists learn about opinion research so that they would be prepared to analyze and evaluate polls.

primary sampling units (PSUs) Arbitron refers to its PSUs as parent sample field locations. The primary sampling process is often called area sampling, and it can include an election district, which can be subdivided into sampling units (SUs, such as a precinct, ward, neighborhood, or block).

probe questions Used when respondents give an incomplete answer or appear to hesitate for a long time when given an opportunity to express themselves.

probe symbols Abbreviations for probe questions. The interviewer records the probe by writing only one word, enclosed in parentheses—for example, (Else?), (Why?), (Explain?), (Yes?), and so on.

psychographic research A branch of segmentation research that divides the population into different kinds of segments (meaningful sub-groups) according to non-traditional variables, taking into account behavior, attitudes, values, knowledge, and so on. Examples of unusual variables that have been considered are media dependence, length of residence/community ties, product loyalty, and so on. See *segmentation research*.

purposive selection Refers to the sampling of a specifically targeted group (for example, conducting a study of persons suffering from AIDS).

question reliability Refers to the consistency of the respondent's answers. A question is reliable when, over a period of time, it elicits the same answer from a respondent.

question validity Refers to whether a particular question accurately measures what we want to measure. In the case of a double-barreled question, there is uncertainty as to the question's validity because we cannot be sure of what we are measuring. The choices of answers offered are also important.

question verification To verify that a questionnaire has not been falsified and that all the answers were recorded correctly, the verifier will phone a random selection of respondents, choose a question from the second half of the questionnaire (to ascertain that the interviewer carried the interview that far), and re-ask the question.

quota sampling A sampling process designed to ensure proportional representation of the groups making up the sample. See *demographic variables*.

random sampling   See *simple random sampling (SRS)*.

rank order scale   Asks the respondent to rank items from 1 to some number, based on the respondent's opinion as to which is most/least honest, popular, important, and so on.

ratio scale   Primarily used in the physical sciences to measure and compare (through a ratio) such variables as time, distance, speed, height, weight, and so on. Sometimes used in survey analysis, it enables us to conclude, for example, that one candidate trounced the other by 7:1.

refusal rate   Refers to the number of turndowns, the number of selected respondents who refuse to be interviewed.

regression analysis   Having shown that certain variables are associated, we can use one of a number of statistical procedures to make predictions. Regression is one of the most common statistical procedures used by pollsters to predict the behavior of a dependent variable (say, income), called the criterion, based on an independent variable (education, for example), called the predictor. *Bivariate regression* refers to the use of two variables —one criterion and one predictor—and multiple regression refers to the use of one criterion and more than one predictor. See *variables*.

representative sample   A sample is representative of the universe from which it is drawn when everyone in that population has an equal chance of being selected.

response effects   Refers to the bias (error) in a poll caused by the interviewee's response (reaction) to the interviewer. For example, voter-validation studies have shown that black respondents interviewed by black interviewers react (respond) differently than when interviewed by white interviewers.

response quality   Refers to the completeness, appropriateness, relevance, and clarity of the answers. A DK, providing zero information, is devoid of response quality.

restricted (stratified) random sampling   The universe is first divided into different groups (called strata, sub-universes, sub-groups) and then, through a process of random selection, every *n*th unit (house, person, organization, and so on) is chosen.

sample verification   The verification team checks to see that only designated respondents were interviewed. Calls are made or postcards are sent to a random selection of respondents for confirmation of the interviews.

sampling fraction   Used to determine the skip interval (and the individuals who will actually be interviewed). For example, if the sample number (say 400) is divided by the total units in the sample frame (say 24,000), we get 400/24,000 = 1/60, so the sample consists of 1/60 of all listed units. As a result, every sixtieth name on the list becomes a respondent (a part of the sample).

sampling frame   In creating this, we are deciding how we will select the individuals to be interviewed (the respondents or interviewees). The sampling frame contains all the households (names, units, and so on) from which the actual sample will be drawn.

segmentation research   The followup to lifestyle cluster studies undertaken in the 1970s by Claritas Corporation and others. Later theorists criticized attempts to divide the population into discrete clusters. Product-usage behavior, they argued, did not necessarily vary from group to group. Thus segmentation theorists advocated going beyond an examination of age, sex, education, and similar demographics, arguing that variation would be discernible if researchers looked for new independent, dependent, and intervening variables. See *psychographic research*.

self-selecting bias   Bias (error) occurs when certain types (sub-groups) or individuals overwhelmingly decide to participate (or not to participate) in a survey. The polling results are thus skewed (biased).

simple random sampling (SRS)   A process that ensures that all units (individuals, houses, and so on) in the population to be sampled (the survey's universe) have an equal chance (an equal probability) of being included in the sample.

skip interval   Refers to the count-off between respondents. Whether you interview every twenty-fifth name or every fifty-fifth (or some other number) depends on the size of the sample you have decided on and the sample frame from which you draw your respondents.

spin doctors   The political pollsters and media consultants hired by politicians to shape their public image.

SPSS   Statistical Package for the Social Sciences. It provides social scientists with software (computer programs) to convert data into meaningful information and enables them to illustrate data through different types of charts (line, bar, pie, 3-D, and so on).

statistically significant   A finding is statistically significant if it provides enough evidence to enable us to reject the null hypothesis—the default answer. Early in the survey process, researchers determine how large a difference there must be between the results in favor of the alternate hypothesis and the null hypothesis before the alternate hypothesis can be supported. The difference must be sufficiently large to overcome chance or sampling error. See *hypothesis*.

status distance   Refers to the perceived difference in social status between the interviewer and the respondent.

strata   Sub-groups making up the sample, determined by demographic variables such as age, sex, education, income, and so on.

stratified samples   Consist of sub-groups of the given population. These sub-groups are generally based on census data.

structured question   Also called closed-ended; gives fixed responses from which the respondent will choose. These can be either dichotomous or multi-choice.

sugging   Selling under the guise of research. This is considered an unethical practice and is damaging to the research profession.

trial heat questions These ask about the potential candidacy of various individuals in an election in the distant future "If the presidential election scheduled for _____ were held today between X and Y, for whom would you vote?"

tracking polls Conducted on a regular basis to follow the ups and downs of a political campaign. Usually, they are conducted during the last month or so and use small samples of 150–300 respondents. Short interviews focus on the public's view of the candidates, and the results are compared with the public's averaged response over the three previous days.

universe Includes everyone in the population to be studied.

unrestricted random sampling Also called simple random sampling, this occurs when we randomly choose our respondents from a list (of names or addresses), selecting every nth unit (person, house, business, and so on) by some predetermined, randomly selected number, so that everyone on the list has a non-zero probability (an equal chance) of being selected.

variables Population characteristics such as age, education, income, ethnicity, and so on. Certain variables are associated with others and can affect their behavior. There are independent and dependent variables. An independent variable (say, education) is called the predictor, which can be used to predict the behavior of the dependent variable (income, for example), called the criterion. Thus it is generally possible to use level of attained education (an independent variable) to predict income. See *regression analysis*.

verifiable A study is verifiable if it and its results can be replicated by using the same methodology repeatedly to select additional samples. There should be little variance in the results no matter how many new samples are selected and polled.

weight/weighting Statistical terms referring to the relative merit of an item in a statistical compilation. Within a given sample, sub-groups vary in size in proportion to their size within the population as a whole. The smaller the sub-group, the larger the margin of error. When a statistical adjustment (correction) is made, the data obtained from sub-groups can be said to have been normalized. That is, the data will be counted in accordance with its relative weight in proportion to that of larger groups. This means that a value from a small sub-group, with its higher error potential, would count less. Thus the statistical correction enables the researcher, in the final analysis, to use data of varying quality without the results being unduly skewed by the somewhat questionable data sets.

Index

Abramson, Paul, 242, 261
abstract. *See* report
additive scales. *See* scales
Agar, Herbert, 81
Albig, William, 81
Almond, Gabriel A., 39–40, 47, 48
American Association of Public Opinion Research
    (AAPOR), 100, 204, 406–408, 411–415, 417,
    A5, A10
Anderson, Barbara, 242, 261
ANOVA (analysis of variance), 303, 306
Arbitron, 119–123
Army Research Branch, 69–72. *See also* Hovland,
    Carl I.; Lazarsfeld, Paul; Merton, Robert R.;
    Office of Radio Research
attitudes. *See* measuring attitudes
Atwater, Lee, 321. *See also* Horton, Willie
automatic dialing, 398

Backstrom, Charles H., 172, 195, 228–229, 238–239,
    260, 296, 316
bandwagon effect, 322, 376
Beal, Richard, 384
Belden, Joe, 87, 106
benchmark survey, 315
Berelson, Bernard, 36–39, 48
Berlin, Michael, 280
Bernoulli, Jacques, 57
bias in polling, 64–68, 72–79, 89, 95–99, 103–105,
    116–119, 165–167, 172, 178, 133–136,
    242–243, 249–251, 256–258, 271–273, 276–279
Billygate, 34–35
Binson, Diane, 285–286
Bischoping, Katherine, 104
Bishop, George Franklin, 268–271
Bogart, Leo, 211, 339
Booth, Charles, 60
Bowley, Arthur L., 62, 80, 81, 165–166, 167
Bradburn, Norman M., 83, 237–238
Bradley, Bill, 78
branching, 219–220
Brown, Tony, 278–279
Bryce, Lord James, 22–23, 46
Buchanan, Patrick J., 309, 310, 346
Bureau of Applied Social Research (BASR), 70–72
Bush, George
    and Clarence Thomas, 31
    Clinton campaign, 65, 308–309, 320–21, 347–348,
        379–382, 387, 421
    Dukakis campaign, 28, 32–34, 346–347, 377
    Iran-Contra, 29
    the 20-percent solution, 30

Caddell, Patrick, 171, 379, 380, 384
Cahalan, Don, 68, 82
Cannell, Charles F. , 235–237, 246, 248
Cantril, Albert H., 223
Cantril, Hadley, 68

Cantril-Kilpatrick self-anchoring scale, 206, 208–209
CAPI (computer-assisted personal interviewing),
    394–399
Capra, Frank, 70, 335
Carter, Jimmy, 34–36, 100, 324, 380, 382–285, 419
CATI (computer-assisted telephone interviews), 194,
    233, 240, 257, 295, 314, 370, 394, A10, A11
census, U.S., 55–56, 154–158
central tendency, 194–195, 296
Claritas cluster type. *See* cluster analysis/clustering
    system
classical pluralism, 385–386
Clinton, Bill, and the Bush campaign, 65, 308–309,
    321–323, 347–348, 377, 381–382, 387, 421
Clinton, Hillary, 347–348
cluster analysis/clustering system, 61–62, 189, 305,
    319, 349, 351
cognitive psychology, 267, 286
cognitive structures, 272
Cohen, Lawrence J., 242–246, A8–A9
Coleman, Lerita, 246, 248
Committee on Analysis of Pre-Election Polls and
    Forecasts (1948), 74–78, 83
Commission on Obscenity and Pornography,
    147–148
computer content analysis, 32–34
computers and polling, 32–34, 61–62, 111–120, 129,
    168, 174–175, 184, 194, 230–233, 240, 257,
    285, 294–295, 306, 367, 394–405
Comte, Auguste, 20–22, 46
confidence level, 170, 172, 175–177
content analysis, 34, 36, 370
contingency questions, 219–220
Converse, Philip, 276
Conway, M. Margaret, 378–379
Coombs, Clyde H. and Lolagene, 271
correlations, 297–299, 302–304
Crossley, Archibald M., 66–68, 75, 80, 367
cumulative scales, *See* scales
Cutler, Stephen, 319, 320
Czechoslovakia, 89–92

Daniels, Lee A., 10
Danigelis, Nicholas, 319, 320
data cleaning, 296
data file/field, 295
data reduction process, 295–296
data sources, 183–185
DBMs (disk-by-mail surveys), 404
Demophobia, 20–22
Dewey, Thomas, 343
    and the 1948 election polls, 72–79
Digest poll, 63–68, 166
Dodd, Stuart C., 87–88, 413–415
dominant social paradigm (DSP), 24, 26
don't know (DK) phenomenon, 14, 220, 271–279
    among older respondents, 282–285, 297, 313

Dukakis, Michael, and the Bush campaign, 28, 32–34, 322, 377

Eisenhower, Dwight D., 342–343, 344, 346
elite, 14, 149–150
Elrick and Lavidge, 111–112
Emery, Michael, 35
Entman, 14–15, 34–36, 47, 48
ESCAPE/600 (electronic synthesized computerized automatic polling equipment), 401–404

Fallow, James, 324–325, 382–383
Fan, David P., 32–34, 46–47
Farbman, David P., 415–417
Faulkenberry, G. David, 272
feedback, See probe questions
Feick, Lawrence, 271–272
Feinberg, Barry M., 280–281
Feinstein, Dianne, 25–26, 78
Field, Harry H., A9
Field, Mervin/Field Research Corporation (FRC), 408–410
filter question, 76–77, 183, 218–220
Florio, James, 10, 78
focus (focussed) group/interview, 317, 335–342, 348, 419
Ford, Gerald, 371–375, 384–385
Frankovic, Kathleen, 25
frugging (fundraising under the guise of research), 406

Gal, Reuven, 298–305
Gallup, George/The Gallup Organization, 66–68, 74–75, 78–79, 80, 81, 149, 176, 193, 218, 343–344, 366–367, 375, 378, A8
  Gallup Institutes, 92–93
Gallup Moscow, 100–103
Gallup Quintamensional Plan of Question Design, 207–208
Gallup Study on America's Youth, 150–151
Gaudet, Hazel, 36–39
Gaziano, Cecilie, 351–357
Gediman Research Group, Inc., 340–342
gender gap, 25–26
Gerth, H. H., 81
Gfk Group (German research company), 101–102
Gibson, James L., 273–276
Gitlin, Todd, 36, 48
Goldwater, Barry, 345
Gore, Tipper, 347–348
Groves, Robert M., 234, 282
Guttman, Louis, 204–205

Harris, Louis/Louis Harris and Associates, Inc., 148, 344, 367, 377–379, 422, A9
Hart, Peter, 171, 380
Hatchett, S., 241
hearsay versus legal evidence, 142–144
Hennessy, Bernard, 13
Herbst, Susan, 11, 371–376
Herzog, A. Regula, 283–285, 299, 306

Hinckley, Ronald, 384
Hite, Shere and the Hite Reports, 111, 126–136, 179, 268
Horton, Willie, 28–29, 321, 346
Hovland, Carl I., 70, 82
Howell, Susan, 278
Hursh-César, Gerald, 172, 195, 228–229, 238–239, 260, 296, 316
Hyman, Herbert, 240–241
hyperpluralism, 385–386
hypothesis, alternate/null, 298

interval scales, See rating scales
interviewer
  effects, 240–243, 248–251
  monitoring/supervision, 255, 258–260
  recruitment/training, 250–251, 256–257

Jensen, Richard, 81
Johnson, Lyndon Baines, 147, 345, 384
Jones, D. Caradog, 81
jury selection, 145–147

Kahn, R. L., 282
Kalton, Graham, 177, 279
Kaplan, Nancy, 336–339
Kennedy, John F., 344, 377, 384
Kennedy-Nixon debates, 344
Key, V. O., 23–24, 27–29, 39, 45, 46, 48, 59
Kiesler, Sara, 397–398
King, Susan, 325–326
Kornhauser, 82

Lang, Gladys Engel and Kurt, 15, 47, 132, 322–323, 370
LANs (local area networks), 399–401
Lazarsfeld, Paul, 36–39, 69, 335
LeBon, Gustave, 20–22
Levenstein, Adolf, 62
Lewin, Tamar, 10
Libresco, Joshua, 340
Likert, Rensis, 202–203
Lippmann, Walter, 12, 16–17, 47
Literary Digest polls, 63–67, 166
Lowi, Theodore, 11, 386–387

Madison, James, 385–386
Magilavy, Lou, 234
malpractice suit, 411–412
marketing political candidates, 342–348
marketing research companies, 102, 111–126, 395–404, 408, 411–412
marketing studies, 334, 357–360, 411–412
Markus, Hazel, 267, 272
margin of error, 175–176, 277, 309, 381. See also bias in polling
Marsh, Catherine, 7–10, 47
Marshall, Leon Soutierre, 20
Martin, Elizabeth, 370–371
Martin, L. John, 57–58
Mason, Robert, 272
Mayseless, Ofra, 298–305

McCarthy, Joseph, 51
McCarthy, Philip J., 82
McGinniss, Joe, 346
McGregor, Douglas, 204
measuring attitudes, 200–213
Merton, Robert K., 69, 82, 335–336
Metromail sampling frame, 120
Meyer, Philip, 367–369
Milavsky, J. Ronald, 417–420
Milbrath, Lester W., 48
Miller, Peter, 235–237
Mills, C. Wright, 81
Mitofsky, Warren J., 100, 107, 279
Montesquieu, Charles-Louis de, 19
Moore, Michael, 40–41
multivariate analysis, 172–173, 298–305, 311
Murphy, Patricia, 285–286

National Center for Health Statistics (NCHS)/
    Questionnaire Design Research Laboratory
    (QDRL), 207, 210–215
National Opinion Research Center (NORC), 53,
    151–154, 221–222, 240–241, 268, A9, A11,
    A13–A14
New environmental paradigm (NEP), 26–27
Neyman, J. and purposive selection, 166
Nicaragua, election polling (1990), 103–105
Nielsen, 101, 112–119, 123–125, 348
Nixon, Richard, 148, 342, 344–346, 370, 378,
    384–385
Noelle-Neumann, Elisabeth, 210–211, 323
nominal scales. See rating scales

Office of Radio Research, 69–70
Oksenberg, Lois, 246–247, 248
Olin, Manuel, 251–255, 316
O'Neill, Harry W., 410–411
opinion, public (defined), 8, 11–14
ordinal scales. See rating scales

pack journalism, 371–375
Parenti, Michael, 41–42, 48, 110
people meter, 112–113
People's Choice studies, 36–39, 46
percentage points, 59
Pergamon AGB, 123–125
Perot, H. Ross, 308, 321–323, 377
pluralism, 385–386
plurality error, 56. See also bias in polling
polls,
    and the courts, 140–149
    earliest, 52
    and economic forecasting, 150
    effects of, 10, 14–16, 36–39, 320–326, 382–385,
        387–388, 417–420
    exit and street, 56, 100, 315
    first international, 94–99
    measuring private opinion, 376–377
    as news, 364–379
    primacy of, 384
    purposes of, 321

tracking, 315
standards. See regulation
straw, 53–55, 63–68
Powell, Norman J., 83
precision journalism, 367–369, 418
predictive dialing, 399–400
PRIZM. See clustering system
probability sampling, 76
probe questions/symbols, 236–239
psychographic research. See segmentation theory
Public opinion
    agreement on, 16
    characteristics of, 23–24
    definition, 8, 11–14;
    history of, 17–23
    influences on, 36–44, 383
    properties of, 27–29, 32

QT (Quick Tally) Systems, 405
Quayle, Dan, 41, 315, 382
Quayle, Oliver & Company, 345, 384
question(s)
    order, 99, 220
    probe, 238–240
    reliability and validity, 192–193, 197, 259
    trial hear, 315
    types of, 191–193
    verification, 260
    wording, 97–98, 220–222, 317
questionnaire, self-administered, 127–130, 133–134,
    193, 223–235
Questionnaire Design Research Laboratory (QDRL).
    See National Center for Health Statistics
quota sampling, 76–68, 167, 178

rank order scales. See rating scales
Ranney, John C., 382–383
Rasinski, Kenneth, 221–222
rating scales, 195–200, 248
rating services. See Arbitron and Nielsen
ratio scales. See rating scales
Reagan, Ronald, 29, 34–35, 61–62, 193, 307, 324,
    346, 348, 379, 383–384
Reeves, Jr., Thomas Rosser, 343
refusal rate, 99, 233, 246–247, 267, 279–282, 284,
    286, 358, 417
regression analysis, 306
regulation, 406–415
report, writing of, 310–316
Research Industry Coalition (RIC), 408
respondent, the older, 282–285
response distribution, 283
    effects, 242
    quality, 284
    rates, 284
Riederman, Laurie, 341–342
Robbins, Jonathan, 61–62
Robinson, Claude E., 64–65, 81, 344
Rodgers, Willard, 283–285, 299, 306
Roosevelt-Landon poll. See Digest poll

Roper, Burns W., 410–411
Roper, Elmo/Roper Organization, 66–68, 73–75, 79, 99, 367, 368, 410–411, A9
Rosenberg, Milton, 202–203
Rubenstein, Eric P., A1–A4
Rubenstein, Murray, 154–157

Safire, Bill, 13
sample size, 169, 175
    and degree of precision, 169–171
sample verification, 260
sampling
    and Arbitron, 119–123
    convenience, 177
    fraction, 174
    frame, 120, 169; 179–180
    and Hite's Reports, 128–129, 131–134
    multistage, 180
    and Nielsen, 112–116
    and probability theory, 57, 167, 174
    purposive, 178
    and quotas. See quota sampling
    simple random, 169
    sources, 183–185
Sawtooth Software, 395–398
scales
    additive, 202
    cumulative, 202
    rating, 193–200
    and scaling theory, 200–209.
    self-esteem, 202–203
    summated, 202
ScanAmerica. See Arbitron
Schmalz, Jeffrey, 48
Schoua-Glusberg, Alicia S., 316–318
Schuman, Howard, 104, 241, 279
segmentation theory, 349–359
self-fulfilling prophecy, 371–375
Shapiro, Mitchell E., 402–403
Sherrill, Kenneth S., 34, 48
Silver, Brian, 261
Sinclair, John, 57
Singer, Eleanor, 132–136, 282
skip interval, 173
Smith, Eric, 222
Smith, Tom, 53, 81, 220, 268
soothsaying journalists, 371–375
special groups, 149–151
spin doctors, 53, 321
Squire, Peverill, 67–68, 82, 222
Stanton, Frank, 69
Stapel, Jan, 88, 206, 208, 266
Statistical Package for the Social Sciences (SPSS), 294, 306
statistical significance, 283, 297–298
statistics, 57–58, 296, 297, A1–A4
Steeper, Fred, 280
Stempel III, Guido H., 48
Stephan, Frederick F., 82
Stern, Paula, 420–421

Stevenson, Adlai E., 343
stratified samples, 96, 122, 167
straw polls. See polls
Sudman, Seymour, 83, 237
sugging (selling under the guise of research), 406
summated scales. See scales
survey design, 318–319
Survey Research Center (SRC), 246–247, 261
surveys and polls
    distinctions, 9–10
    history of, 50–51

Tarde, Gabriel, 20–22, 28, 39, 47
technologies, new, 394–405
Teeter, Robert, 171, 280, 346, 380, 384
test markets, 357–359
Thurstone, Louis L., 200–202
Time/Roper International Poll (1948), 94–99
Tocqueville, Alexis de, 383, 386
trademark cases, 140–142
trend analysis, 306–307
trial heat questions, 315
Trotter, Wilfred, 20, 23
Trudeau, G. B., 44, 48
Truman, Harry S., and the 1948 election polls, 72–79, 167
Tuckel, Peter, 280–281
Turner, Charles, 370–371
two-step flow, 37–39

universe, 94, 96

validation, 258–259
variance. See ANOVA
venue change, 145–147
verification, 260–261
vocal characteristics, 247
voter research and surveys, 26, 31
vote-validation studies, 242
voting trends, 45

Watergate, 324, 370. See also Nixon, Richard
Weber, Max, 60, 62, 80, 127
Weiss, Ann E., 81
Weiss, Michael J., 61–62
Westley, Bruce H., 48
Wheeler, Michael, 75
White, Theodore, 345
Whitman, Christine Todd, 10, 78
Wilhoit, G. Cleveland, 34, 48
Williams, Jr., J. Allen, 243
Wilson, Francis Graham, 47
Wirthlin, Richard, 171, 346, 379, 380, 384
World Association of Public Opinion Research (WAPOR), 89
World War II surveys, 69–70, 86–90, 151, 335–336;
Wright, Jr., Gerald, 220

Yankelovich, Skelly and White/Clancy Shulman, 149, 367, 412, A9

Zajonc, R. B., 267, 272